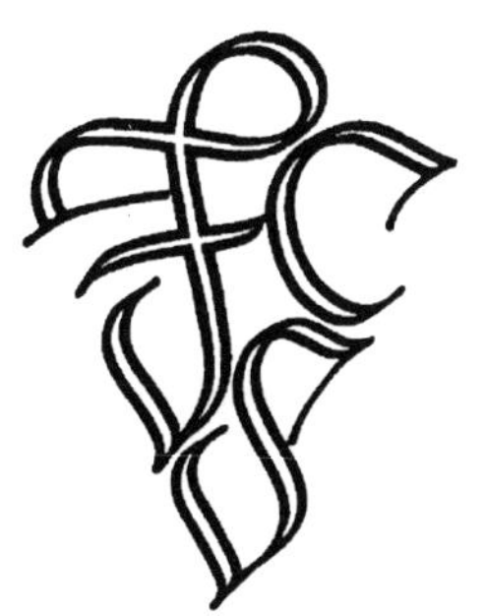

Advisory Board

Fifteenth-Century Studies

Volume 24

Edited by
William C. McDonald

CAMDEN HOUSE

ISSN: 0164–0933
ISBN: 1–57113–266–x

First published 1998
by Camden House,
Drawer 2025, Columbia, SC 29202–2025 USA

Camden House is an imprint of Boydell & Brewer Inc.
PO Box 41026, Rochester, NY 14604–4126 USA
and of Boydell & Brewer Limited
PO Box 9, Woodbridge, Suffolk IP12 3DF, UK

This publication is printed on acid-free paper.
Printed in the United States of America

Fifteenth-Century Studies appears annually.
Please send orders to Boydell & Brewer at the above addresses.

For editorial correspondence and manuscript submissions, write to:
William C. McDonald
Germanic Languages and Literatures, 108 Cocke Hall
University of Virginia
Charlottesville, VA 22903 USA
Articles and book reviews submitted for publication may be edited to conform to
FCS style. Self-addressed envelopes with return postage must accompany
all manuscripts submitted.

Submit books for review to:
Everett U. Crosby
History Department
Randall Hall 220
University of Virginia
Charlottesville, VA 22903 USA

Information on membership in the Fifteenth-Century Society,
which entitles the member to a copy of *Fifteenth-Century Studies,*
is available from Prof. Edelgard E. DuBruck, Marygrove College,
Detroit, MI 48221 USA

CONTENTS

Essays

Reviews

The Current State of Research on Late-Medieval Drama: 1995-96. Survey, Bibliography, and Reviews.

Edelgard E. DuBruck

This article is a regular feature of Fifteenth-Century Studies. *Our intent was to catalogue, survey, and assess scholarship on the staging and textual configuration of dramatic presentations in the Middle Ages. Like all such dated material this assessment remains incomplete. We will therefore include 1996 again in the next listing [vol. 25]. Our readers are encouraged to bring new items to our attention, including their own work.*

The medieval theater has been the subject of four general studies: by Kröll, Muir, Ortolani, and Ogden. Katrin Kröll and Hugo Steger edited a collection on *Mein ganzer Körper ist Gesicht: Groteske Darstellungen in der europäischen Kunst und Literatur des Mittelalters,* in other words, on the grotesque, which has rich implications for the stage. The iconography of human bodies in contortion, in exaggeration of some parts (torso, face) at the cost of others, may be used in a disruptive, inversional mode. Going beyond Wolfgang Kayser and Mikhail Bachtin, the studies treated drama very little, unfortunately. Lynette R. Muir's excellent *The Biblical Drama of Medieval Europe* is discussed in a (subsequent) review. Special mention is made here of the medieval section of Benito Ortolani's *International Bibliography of Theatre: 1992-93*. Dunbar H. Ogden studied set pieces and special effects in liturgical drama and found that the more different the scenes were from the liturgy, the more imaginative (theatrically) they were. The second part of his article lists special effects, as, e.g., curtained pavilions and flying devices (Annunciation, Ascension, and Pentecost) — a dove in Padua (fourteenth century), an angel lowered by way of an aperture in the church roof (Parma, fifteenth century), and Christ ascending by a rope (Moosburg, fourteenth century). A number of general treatments were also devoted to the medieval English stage. Richard Beadle edited *The Cambridge Companion to Medieval English Theatre*. While some reviewers found a lack in attention to liturgical ceremonies and plays, Meg Twycross's contribution on the theatricality of English drama is excellent. There are good articles on the York Cycle (Beadle), the Chester Cycle (Mills), the Towneley plays (Meredith), N-Town (Fletcher), and the non-cycle plays of East Anglia (Coldewey). Cornish drama and the round stage were treated by Murdoch. David Smith et al. edited *The Theatrical City* which we hope to review in the next issue. Another collection was brought out by John A. Alford, *From Page to Performance*, and Sydney Higgins wrote on *Medieval Theatre in the Round*. C. E. McGee reported on a performance at a Dorset inn, while Howard B. Norland contributed a monograph on early Tudor drama

(1485-1558). Pamela Sheingorn compared medieval drama studies and the new art history. An interesting article on politics, topical meaning, and English theater audiences came from Paul W. White, and Patricia Badir analyzed un-civil rites and playing sites (Kingston-upon-Hull).

English mystery and passion plays were again the subject of much ongoing research. Studies devoted to character figures were contributed by Corbett (God), Dixon, Kinservik, and Witt (Mary), Gusick (Lazarus), Riggio (Abraham), Stevens (Herod), and Diller (the four daughters of God). The latter investigated the debate of Justice, Mercy, Peace, and Truth, which had also a key role in French mystery plays, with its biblical source, Psalm 84, 11-12. While the redemption was the work of Mercy, Justice insisted on Christ's death. Barbara I. Gusick observed that the Towneley Lazarus seemed ungrateful to Christ, preached a *Memento mori*, and would have to die a second time. He urged awareness of physical deterioration in spiritual bitterness. Matthew J. Kinservik's article showed that the struggle over Mary's body brought about the theological and dramatic resolution in the N-Town Assumption: the devil abused his power in considering Mary sinful, but, in fact, she did not lose importance after Christ's death, and her bodily integrity was needed for his work of salvation. David Bevington studied visual contrasts in N-Town passion plays, while Victor Scherb related liturgy and community.

Five contributions were devoted to York plays. Philip Butterworth wrote on the York Crucifixion, Pamela M. King on urban piety and the case of Nicholas Blackburn, mercer: the pageants were a tremendous enterprise, and distinctions must be made between author, producer, performer, and audience; the mercers paid for the Doomsday pageant, belonging, as they did, to the urban "feudal" class. Zina Petersen reported an unwholesome rebellion of York's cordwainers (shoemakers) at the Corpus Christi rite in 1482 (because they had to march with the weavers!), and Charles B. Moore described a stained-glass record of York drama. Elza C. Tiner proved that the trial sequence in the York plays swarmed with legal errors (in a manuscript dated 1475), even though the author must have been familiar with English courts of law and their procedures. Christ was blamed here for six delicts (and not for fifteen, as in Arnoul Gréban).

Further studies concerned gender conflict and identity in Innocents' plays (Theresa Coletti), anachronism (James J. Paxson), and modern revivals of the Chester plays (David Mills). Staging was considered by Butterworth (comings and goings; and Hugh Platte's collapsible wagon), and by Thomas Pettitt: the (medieval) stocking of Kent in *King Lear*. Robert Weimann and Richard K. Emmerson turned to the morality stage: the latter proposed a semiotic approach to the *Castle of Perseverance*, and Weimann studied divided authority. John D. Cox pinpointed devils and vices in English non-cycle plays. "'Sinnekins' and the Vice: Prolegomena" was the title of an article by Peter Happé and Wim Hüsken (Netherlands).

Cornish drama was the theme of two articles by Gloria Betcher: 1) When the First Doctor (in the *Passio Domini*) compared the two-fold nature of Christ to a mermaid, one has to remember that mermaids were indeed thought to be half diabolic and half symbolic of Christ (half women — half fish). 2) Betcher also reassessed date (between 1395 and 1419) and provenance (near Bodmin in Central Cornwall) of the Cornish *Ordinalia*.

Late-medieval French drama research saw the excellent edition of *Jean Molinet (?). Le Mystère de Judith et Holofernés* by Graham A. Runnalls (reviewed subsequently), as well as his article on compilation in the *Mistere du Viel Testament* (le *Mystère de Daniel et Susanne*). Paula Giuliani translated *Arnoul Gréban. The Mystery of the Passion. The Third Day* which we hope to review soon. The *Passion Isabeau (1398)* was the subject of another study by Edelgard E. DuBruck (miniatures), while Leslie A. Callahan investigated the stage of Fouquet's *Torture of Saint Apollonia*. Olga A. Dull found that Mother Folly the Wise, in Erasmian ambivalence, embodied sin and vice, but also highest wisdom; in Gringore, who catered to the royal court, Folly was Mother Church or the Pope. A paradoxial portrayal was thus a rhetorical as well as an epistemological phenomenon. We are delighted to announce (and to review) an interesting addition to profane theater, namely, the *Comedia sine nomine* by an anonymous fifteenth-c. author, now translated into French by Monique Goullet.

In German drama, Hansjürgen Linke reflected upon the *Erfurter Moralität* (18,000 verses). Its first part brought virtues and vices, while the other three sections were a dramatization of biblical parables (ten virgins, prodigal son, and *dives* and Lazarus), intricately interwoven with the following extra-biblical eschatological themes: 1) the quarrel of the daughters of God, Misericordia vs. Justitia; 2) *judicium particulare* (for *dives*); 3) *judicium generale* (Last Judgement). Linke saw the figures as interrelated, e.g., the ten virgins and the prodigal (i.e., five foolish virgins); the prodigal and Lazarus, etc. The moral (biblical) lesson was that any repentant sinner can be saved. This article is truly remarkable for its logic and structure.

Johan Nowé examined the *Ahlsfelder Passionsspiel* and its symbolism carefully planned by the arrangement of the stage, the treatment of figures, and the logical order in its more than 8,000 lines — probably for a presentation in 1501. Even the number of scenes (33) was symbolic. Joseph on the margin of the *Mérode Altarpiece* was the subject of Joseph Vasvari's research — with implications for staging. Even though Ernst Schubert's monograph, *Fahrendes Volk im Mittelalter*, analyzed many professions in addition to performers, we have reviewed it further on.

We hope to examine eventually Terry Gunnell's *Origins of Drama in Scandinavia*, but for now, mention must be made of two other monographs and an article on Scandinavian theater: Leif Sondergaard's

Paris' Domfra antikt motiv til middelalderligt fastelavensspil (Denmark), and Bengt Stolt's *Medieval Theater and Ecclesiastical Art on the Island of Gotland*. The latter scholar pointed out that until the mid-fourteenth century when the Hanse took over, the commercial activities on Gotland created an economic background suitable for artistic life. S. seemed especially interested in crossing the borderline between theater and the visual arts. Theater was here defined as religious drama, but since he brought no written sources on the Gotland stage and just concluded from areas close to this Swedish island, his text was not really convincing. Nils H. Petersen has discovered a fragment of a *Visitatio Sepulchri* in Stockholm, one of more than 17,000 medieval liturgical pieces, as yet uncatalogued, in Swedish archives. The two independent parchment leaves (thirteenth century) were sewn together, used as bindings for Renaissance accounts, and stemmed from the Southern provinces of Sweden or medieval Denmark.

To our knowledge, one article was contributed on the Italian stage, treating liturgical drama in late-medieval Venice: Nils H. Petersen pointed out that in emphasis on the symbolic role of the Doge and his dependency on Christ the *Quem Quaeritis* ceremony took place in San Marco on Easter Day, as far back as the thirteenth century. A collection of studies was furthermore edited by Annamaria Cascetta and Roberta Carpani on dramaturgy and spectacle at Milano during its Spanish period. Pamela M. King wrote on Corpus Christi in Valencia, and Charlotte Stern just published a monograph on *The Medieval Theater in Castile*. As always, we regret the lack of information on Eastern Europe.

BIBLIOGRAPHY

Alford, John A., ed. *From Page to Performance: Essays in Early English Drama*. East Lansing: Michigan State University Press, 1995.

Badir, Patricia. "Un-Civil Rites and Playing Sites: Some Early Modern Entertainment Records from Kingston-upon-Hull," *REED Newsletter*, 20 (1995), 1-11.

Beadle, Richard, ed. *The Cambridge Companion to Medieval English Theatre*. Cambridge: University Press, 1994.

Betcher, Gloria. "A Reassessment of the Date and Provenance of the Cornish *Ordinalia*," *Comparative Drama*, 29 (1995-6), 454-65.

—"A Tempting Theory: What Early Cornish Mermaid Images Reveal about the First Doctor's Analogy in *Passio Domini*," *EDAMR*, 18 (1996), 65-76.

Bevington, David. "Visual Contrasts in the N-Town Passion Plays," *Mediaevalia*, 18 (1995), 407-26.

Burton, Janet. "New Light on the 'Summergame'," *Notes & Queries*, 240 (1995), 428-29.

Butterworth, Philip. "Comings and Goings: Medieval Staging Conventions," *EDAMR*, 18 (1995), 25-34.

—"Hugh Platte's Collapsible Wagon," *Medieval English Theatre*, 15 (1993), 126-36.

—"The York *Crucifixion*: Actor/Audience Relationship," *Medieval English Theatre*, 14 (1992), 67-76.

Callahan, Leslie Abend. "The Torture of Saint Apollonia: Deconstructing Fouquet's Martyrdom Stage," *Studies in Iconography*, 16 (1994), 119-38.

Cascetta, Annamaria, and Roberta Carpani, eds. *La Scena della Gloria: Drammaturgia e Spettacolo a Milano en Età Spagnola*. Rome: Vita e Pensiero, 1995.

Clopper, Lawrence M. "Communitas: the Play of Saints in Late Medieval and Tudor England," *Mediaevalia*, 18 (1995), 81-109.

Coletti, Theresa. "'Ther be but women': Gender Conflict and Gender Identity in the Middle English Innocents Plays," *Mediaevalia*, 18 (1995), 245-61.

Corbett, Anthony G. "God: One Intention of the York Old Testament Plays from *The Fall of the Angels* to the *Expulsion*," *Medieval English Theatre*, 14 (1992), 102-19.

Cox, John D. "Devils and Vices in English Non-Cycle Plays: Sacrament and Social Body," *Comparative Drama*, 30 (1996), 188-219.

Diller, Hans-Jürgen. "From Synthesis to Compromise: the Four Daughters of God in Early English Drama," *EDAMR*, 18 (1996), 88-103.

Dixon, Mimi Still. "'Thys body of Mary': 'Femynyte' and 'Inward Mythe' in the Digby *Mary Magdalene*," *Mediaevalia*, 18 (1995), 221-44.

DuBruck, Edelgard E. "Image — Text — Drama: the Iconography of the *Passion Isabeau (1398)*," *Studies in Honor of Hans-Erich Keller*, ed. Rupert T. Pickens. Kalamazoo: Medieval Institute Publications, 1993. 287-307.

Dull, Olga Anna. "Rhetorical Paradoxes of the French Late Middle Ages: Mother Folly the Wise," *Fifteenth-Century Studies,* 22 (1996), 68-84.

Emmerson, Richard K. "The Morality Character as Sign: A Semiotic Approach to the *Castle of Perseverance*," *Mediaevalia*, 18 (1995), 191-220.

Goullet, Monique, tr. *Anonyme. La Comédie sans nom. XVe siècle*. Grenoble: Jerome Millon, 1996.

Giuliano, Paula, tr. *Arnoul Gréban. The Mystery of the Passion. The Third Day*. Binghamton: Medieval and Renaissance Texts and Studies, 1996.

Gunnell, Terry. *The Origins of Drama in Scandinavia*. Woodbridge, Suffolk: Boydell & Brewer, 1995.

Gusick, Barbara I. "Time and Unredemption: Perceptions of Christ's Work in the Towneley *Lazarus*," *Fifteenth-Century Studies*, 22 (1996), 19-41.

Happé, Peter, and Wim Hüsken, "'Sinnekins' and the Vice: Prolegomena," *Comparative Drama*, 29 (1995), 248-69.

Higgins, Sydney. *Medieval Theatre in the Round*. Università degli Studi di Camerino, 1994.

King, Pamela M. "Corpus Christi, Valencia," *Medieval English Theatre*, 15 (1993), 103-10.

—"York Plays, Urban Piety and the Case of Nicholas Blackburn, Mercer," *Archiv*, 232 (1995), 37-50.

Kinservik, Matthew J. "The Struggle over Mary's Body: Theological and Dramatic Resolution in the N-Town Assumption Play," *Journal of English and Germanic Philology*, 95 (1996), 190-203.

Kröll, Katrin, and Hugo Steger, eds. *Mein ganzer Körper ist Gesicht: Groteske Darstellungen in der europäischen Kunst und Literatur des Mittelalters*. Freiburg i. Br.: Rombach, 1994.

Linke, Hans-Jürgen. "Figurengestaltung in der *Erfurter Moralität*. Geistliche Dramatik als Lebensorientierung," *Zeitschrift für deutsches Altertum und deutsche Literatur*, 124 (1995), 129-42.

Manley, Lawrence. "Of Sites and Rites," in: *The Theatrical City*, eds. David Smith, Richard Strier, and David Bevington. Cambridge: University Press, 1995. 35-54.

McGee, C. E. "A Performance at a Dorset Inn," *REED Newsletter*, 20 (1995), 13-15.

Mills, David. "The 1951 and 1952 Revivals of the Chester Plays" and "'Reviving the Chester Plays': A Postscript," *Medieval English Theatre*, 15 (1993), 124-36.

Moore, Charles B. "A Stained Glass Record of York Drama," *Studies in Iconography*, 14 (1995), 152-87.

Muir, Lynette R. *The Biblical Drama of Medieval Europe*. Cambridge: University Press, 1995.

Norland, Howard B. *Drama in Early Tudor Britain 1485-1558*. Lincoln: University of Nebraska Press, 1995.

Nowé, Johan. "Die Regie als gestaltende und symbolstiftende Instanz des *Ahlsfelder Passionsspiels*," *Germanisch-Romanische Monatsschrift*, 45 (1995), 3-23.

Ogden, Dunbar H. "Set Pieces and Special Effects in the Liturgical Drama — I," *EDAMR*, 18 (1996), 76-88.

Ortolani, Benito, ed. *International Bibliography of Theatre: 1992-93*. Theater Research Data Centre, 1995.

Paxson, James J. "The Structure of Anachronism and the Middle English Mystery Plays," *Mediaevalia*, 18 (1995), 321-40.

Petersen, Nils Holger. "Il Doge and the Liturgical Drama in Late Medieval Venice," *EDAMR*, 18 (1995), 8-24.

—"A Newly Discovered Fragment of a *Visitatio Sepulchri* in Stockholm," *Comparative Drama*, 30 (1996), 32-40.

Petersen, Zina. "'As Tuching the Beyring of Their Torchez': The Unwholesome Rebellion of York's Cordwainers at the Rite of Corpus Christi," *Fifteenth-Century Studies*, 22 (1996), 96-108.

Pettitt, Thomas. "Renaissance Poets and Medieval Play Goers: the Stocking of Kent in *King Lear*," *EDAMR*, 18 (1995), 39-41.

Riggio, Milla C. "The Terrible Mourning of Abraham," *Mediaevalia*, 18 (1995), 283-319.

Runnalls, Graham A. "La Compilation du 'Mistere du Viel Testament': *Le Mystère de Daniel et Susanne*," *Bibliothèque d'Humanisme et Renaissance*, 57 (1995), 345-80.

—ed. *Jean Molinet (?). Le Mystère de Judith et Holofernés. Une édition critique de l'une des parties du Mistere du Viel Testament*. Genève: Droz, 1995.

Scherb, Victor I. "Liturgy and Community in N-Town Passion Play I," *Comparative Drama*, 29 (1995-6), 478-92.

Schubert, Ernst. *Fahrendes Volk im Mittelalter*. Bielefeld: Verlag für Regionalgeschichte, 1995.

Sheingorn, Pamela. "Medieval Drama Studies and the New Art History," *Mediaevalia*, 18 (1995), 143-62.

Smith, David, et al., eds. *The Theatrical City*. Cambridge: University Press, 1995.

Sondergaard, Leif. *Paris' Domfra antikt motiv til middelalderligt fastelavnsspil*. Odense: Odense Universitet Center for Folkesproglige Middelalderstudier, 1995.

Stern, Charlotte. *The Medieval Theater in Castile*. Binghamton: Medieval & Renaissance Texts and Studies, 1996.

Stevens, Martin. "Herod as Carnival King in the Medieval Biblical Drama," *Mediaevalia*, 18 (1995), 43-66.

Stolt, Bengt. *Medeltida teater och gotländsk kyrkokonst (Medieval Theater and Ecclesiastical Art on the Island of Gotland)*. Visby: Odins Forlag, 1993.

Tiner, Elza C. "English Law in the York Trial Plays," *EDAMR*, 18 (1996), 103-12.

Vasvari, Joseph. "Joseph on the Margin: the *Mérode Altarpiece* and Medieval Spectacle," *Mediaevalia*, 18 (1995), 168-89.

Weimann, Robert. "'Moralize two meanings' in One Play: Divided Authority on the Morality Stage," *Mediaevalia*, 18 (1995), 427-50.

White, Paul Whitfield. "Politics, Topical Meaning, and English Theater Audiences 1475-1575," *Research Opportunities in Renaissance Drama*, 34 (1995), 41-54.

Witt, Elizabeth A. *Contrary Marys in Medieval English and French Drama*. New York: Peter Lang, 1995.

REVIEWS

Goullet, Monique, tr. *Anonyme. La Comédie sans nom. XVe siècle*. Grenoble: Jerome Millon, 1996, 221.

The *Comédie sine nomine* is, to our knowledge, the only Latin drama of the fifteenth century. It is found in a single manuscript at the Bibliothèque Nationale, Paris (lat. 8163), and was edited first by Émile Roy in the *Revue Bourguignonne de l'Enseignement Supérieur*, IX (1901). The complete title of his contribution is: "Étude sur le théâtre français du XIVe et du XVe siècle. *La Comédie sans titre*, publiée pour la première fois d'après le manuscrit 8163 de la Bibliothèque Nationale."

In her introduction, Goullet marks the value of Roy's edition, which she translates here into French; it gave the sources of the theme and its similarities to certain folk tales, above all Grimm's story of the girl whose hands were cut off. Furthermore, Roy listed the Latin writers who inspired the anonymous author, showing the latter's admirable erudition. In his prologue, the dramatist described the function of his work: to blame vice and praise virtue, as the ancients did, at "our time," when this is necessary again (23). He did not give a name to the comedy but hoped that this will be done if it is successful, mingling pagan and Christian elements.

Emolphe, king of the Carilles (an imaginary people), sees his wife on her deathbed who entreats him to remarry, but a woman just like her, beautiful and intelligent. After her death and an unsuccessful search, he falls deeply in love with their daughter who indeed meets the requirements. Appalled of this incestuous intention, Hermionide wishes to commit suicide, but her nurse devises a plan in order to gain a respite, and she flees with the girl to Phocide (Greece) whose king, Orestes, falls in love and marries her. Hermionide gives birth to a son in her husband's absence, and a messenger (Epiphanius) falsifies the news upon instigation of Orestes's evil mother, Olicomestre, to read: Hermionide has a black son. Following another misrepresentation requiring the death of mother and baby, the latter is placed into a tarred Moses basket carrying gold and jewels, and set afloat. Found by a friend who contacts Orestes, the child is then with his father, who is soon reunited with his wife and kills Olicomestre as revenge. In the meantime, Emolphe has died, and Hermionide becomes queen of the Carilles, a happy ending indeed.

We have not been able to check the translation against the original; however, this French version is smooth and probably betrays the stylistic qualities of the Latin text which, in spite of its early humanist intention, still sounds medieval (or baroque?) by its chaotic intrigue. A profane miracle play, it has been compared by Roy to the thirty-ninth *Miracle de Notre Dame par personnages*, in addition to the folk-tale mentioned above, and, as Goullet explains, it is a literary variant of three other texts: *La Manékine*, a poem of 8,590 octosyllabic verses by Philippe de Rémi (Ph. De Beaumanoir), 1230-40; *La Belle Hélène de Constantinople*, an anonymous poem of 14,000 alexandrins (thirteenth century, fifteenth-c. prose version by Jean Wauquelin); and *Le Roman du Conte d'Anjou* by Jean Maillart, 8,156 octosyllabic verses (fourteenth century). The anonymous author's originality was, in addition to writing in Latin, to have adapted to the stage a non-theatrical tale. There are many changes of scene which span far distances, and the seven acts comprise one year at least; narrative passages have been avoided in this play of apprenticeship and initiation, which uses false letters, and also dreams, apparitions, and sudden recognitions.

The language of this patchwork of themes and allusions shows erudition as well as negligence, mannerism and clumsiness, archaisms and neologisms, Latin grammar and modern syntax. Yet, gratuitous erudition and pastiche are avoided. We have no evidence of theatrical performance; the play may have been meant for recital only, G. concludes. Because of its originality, this mysterious manuscript constitutes a welcome addition to what is known about the medieval stage. Incidentally, it was not mentioned in Ernst R. Curtius's *European Literature and the Latin Middle Ages* (Princeton: Bollingen, 1953; seventh printing 1990).

Muir, Lynette R. *The Biblical Drama of Medieval Europe*. Cambridge: University Press, 1995, xxiii; 320.

This new magisterial work on religious drama of the Middle Ages is a detailed survey and analysis of over 500 plays from the tenth to the sixteenth century. Translations are given for quotations from non-English theater; perhaps the Latin renderings into English could have been omitted. The scarcity of secondary sources — because they may not "encourage and facilitate ... critical investigation" (xiii) — is nevertheless regrettable, for it blocks out valuable dimensions of research. For example: how can we appreciate the Ascension in a cloud (143) without having at our fingertips Francesc Massip's article on "The Cloud: A Medieval Aerial Device, Its Origins and Its Use in Spain Today" (*EDAMR*, 16 [1994], 65-77)? Or, speaking of *Le Garçon et l'aveugle* (255) without mention of Jean Dufournet's bilingual edition and dossier of this *jeu* (Paris: Champion, 1989)?

In the first part of the monograph, Muir presents the biblical theater from the viewpoint of organizers, performers, and audience: the theatrical community. She describes liturgical plays and traces the birth of vernacular lay drama to the twelfth and thirteenth centuries, created to meet the spiritual needs of an increased population who did not understand the Latin used in church services. M. gives full credit to the influence of two thirteenth-c. works, the *Legenda aurea*, and especially the *Meditationes Vitae Christi* which provided and encouraged the addition of emotionally sensitive material to the Bible stories, in the spirit of St. Bernard and the Franciscans.

Civic involvement and initiative later grew in centers of commerce, and processions and plays were created for obligatory feast days, above all for the new Corpus Christi event. Temporarily diminished during the Hundred Years War, theater suffered a set-back on the continent, but it reflourished afterwards in numerous passion plays in France, Germany, Italy, the Low Countries, in post-*reconquista* Spain and Catalonia, and then in the Catholic countries of Eastern Europe: Poland, Bohemia, and Hungary (in Russia not until the late seventeenth century). M.'s historical treatment of biblical drama resembles that of Young, Chambers, Accarie (i.e., the first part of his *Le Théâtre sacré de la fin du moyen âge: étude sur le sens moral de la 'Passion' de Jean Michel* [Geneva: Droz, 1979]) and of others; however, and this approach is invaluable, the development is spatial, including many European countries.

The second part views the theatrical text, i.e., the use of the Bible in Corpus Christi and passion plays: creation and fall (necessitating salvation), the covenant and the kingdom, prophets and precursors of redemption, birth, childhood, and public life of Jesus, passion and resurrection, and pentecost to judgement. M. compares the execution of scenic detail as it occurs in various plays on the same subject, and her skillful method shall be shown here by one example:

> Almost all plays include the healing of Malchus's ear (John 18: 10-11 is the only version which gives the name). In Eger 164, Malchus declares, "Jesus is a magician but I've got my ear back"; in Künzelsau 133 Jesus tells him: "Stop yelling, I'll heal it"; whereas in Castellani's Passion, Jesus promises Malchus he will heal his ear miraculously: "I intend to show how humane I am towards these hostile and cruel people" (I, 312). (131)

To demonstrate the "loving" addition of scenes from contemporary life to the Bible stories, let me quote M.'s note 38 to Adam's and Eve's postlapsarian existence:

> There had been a few such realistic touches already, like Eve's spinning or Adam lamenting because the corn he had planted was filled with weeds (Anglo-Norman *Adam* 56; Breton *Creation*, X, 453). After the Expulsion two plays include a scene of Adam building (or finding ready) a house into which they retire, to emerge first with infants and then with grown sons (Mons 13; Breton *Creation*, X 210); in the latter Adam laments the lack of the necessary tools needed for life on earth (X 443). A few texts include Adam instructing his sons in the need to sacrifice to God and in the meaning of tithing (Cornish *Creation* 91; Troyes 94; Gréban 22). In *Ordinalia* 33 it is God himself who instructs Adam. (207)

In New Testament scenes, the attention to the Gospel of John is noticeable and in some plays a mingling of pagan and Christian themes has occurred (102).

A few details have received short shrift, unfortunately. Thus, Lazarus's report from hell in some narrative and verse passions, as mentioned on page 119, should have been connected with vision literature and iconography. Generally, art and its interplay with literature has been somewhat neglected in M.'s book. The "Pains of Hell" in Towneley and Rouergue (121) would have profited from this juxtaposition as well. Also, it should have been shown that such descriptions served to alert Christians to pray for the dead and for themselves, and to buy masses to be read — after purgatory had been "invented" in the twelfth century.

Why was the death of Christ necessary for salvation? M. cites Aquinas's three reasons: it fulfilled the prophecies, it reconciled Justice and Mercy of God, and it showed God's love for man (124). The dream of Pilate's wife was inspired by the devil in most plays (134), because the demons feared that, if Christ died, He would surely "harrow" hell and free its captive inhabitants. After the miracles at Christ's death (136), the conversion of St. Denis occurred, because the latter took the eclipse as a sign that the Christian God was more powerful than the heathen deities. (These few remarks are added here to answer questions a reader of M.'s book might have, not to criticize it.) Each part of the work is followed by eight illustrations of relevant scenes from twentieth-c. productions.

The conclusion takes the author's inquiry to 1700. Religious plays were banned in Paris in 1548, but they continued to flourish in countries which remained Catholic. Both Calvinists and Protestants allowed eventually plays on biblical subjects, above all Latin and Greek school and university drama. Although it has seen many changes, the *Oberammergau Passion* is still played at ten-year intervals, and the twentieth century has revived quite a few medieval religious productions.

Muir's notes cover eighty-nine pages. We should like to draw attention to the following points. Page 204, note 16, *oysseuse*: here, a reference to Jean Batany's article in *Guillaume de Lorris. Études sur le Roman de la Rose*, ed. Jean Dufournet, would be welcome (Paris: Champion, 1984, 7-36). Page 211, note 62: for the scene of the masons building the Tower of Babel (*Viel Testament*, I, 259), see E. DuBruck, "The Emergence of the Common Man in Fifteenth-Century Europe," *Fifteenth-Century Studies*, 1 (1978), 83-109. Page 238, note 33: the Longinus episode demands mentioning the work of Carla Dauven-van Knippenberg ... *einer von den Soldaten öffnete seine Seite... Eine Untersuchung der Longinuslegende im deutschsprachigen geistlichen Spiel des Mittelalters* (Amsterdam: Rodopi, 1990). Page 241, note 57: on *Courtois d'Arras*, Dufournet's bilingual edition is now available (Paris: GF Flammarion, 1995). Pages 249-50, note 31: the reproaches addressed to Jesus in Gréban's mystery are, in fact, fifteen, which I enumerated in "The Late-Medieval Theater of Salvation in Continental Europe" (*Fifteenth-Century Studies*, 23 [1997], 171-83: 173).

A bibliographical index of plays follows (17 pages), performance records and references (3 pages), and a good index (20 pages, double columns).

* E. K. Chambers, *The Mediaeval Stage*, 2 vols. (London: Oxford University Press, 1903); Karl Young, *The Drama of the Mediaeval Church*, 2 vols. (Oxford: Clarendon Press, 1933).

Runnalls, Graham A., ed. Jean Molinet (?). *Le Mystère de Judith et Holofernés. Une édition critique de l'une des parties du 'Mistere du Viel Testament.'* Genève: Droz, 1995, 275.

While the entire *Mistere du Viel Testament* (fifteenth century) in the critical edition by Baron James de Rothschild and Émile Picot (SATF, 6 vols. Paris: Firmin Didot, 1878-91) should be re-edited because of faults in transcription and a neglect of the *mise-en-scène*, language, and versification, it is at this point advisable to re-edit smaller units of its 49,486 verses. Runnalls has chosen for edition *Le Mystère de Judith et Holofernés* (vv. 41,856-44,325 of the Rothschild edition), which, in spite of its considerable art in structure and theatricality has been left practically unstudied or misunderstood by specialists of medieval theater. At the same time, the British scholar attributes the anonymous work to the *grand rhétoriqueur* Jean Molinet, and his reasons for so doing are fairly plausible, while absolute proof is still missing.

In his introduction, R. gives a detailed résumé of this somewhat unusual mystery play (a tragi-comedy, even a comical melodrama) based on the Book Judith of the Vulgate Old Testament. In his desire to be recognized as one of their gods, Nabugodonosor wants to conquer some Western nations (cities) not yet under his control: Bethulia, Mesopotamia, and Esdrelon. He calls his chiefs of staff, specifically Holofernés whose cowardly and rivaling character is reflected in the words of two boasting soldiers, Turelututu and Grande Vuyde. Esdrelon capitulates, refusing all resistance — and the two soldiers are very disappointed not to be able to plunder and loot. Mesopotamia first remains opposed, while its leaders regret the loss of their peaceful life, but yield later; Bethulia and its Jewish high priests, ready to capitulate after a siege, begin to shock Judith who — like a Joan of Arc — plans to destroy the Assyrians all by herself, but in another manner. Donning her best garb, she proceeds to seduce Holofernés who, in his turn, hopes to impress her in courtly fashion. She promises to lie with him, provided that she receive safe conduct back to Bethulia. Left alone with him, she decapitates him with his own sword and departs hastily under the obscenities of the Assyrians who comment on what they perceive to have been a night of lovemaking. The play ends with the compliments of the high priests on this "chef-d'oeuvre de femme."

R.'s literary and dramaturgical analysis yields that this *mystère* is historically true to its source in spite of significant modifications. In comparison to a traditional mystery play, God, angels, and devils are missing here, as well as typological implications, and the Jews, unlike those of passion plays, are the heroes. Furthermore, the dramaturg has replaced the narrative passages of the Book of Judith by monologues and dialogues, added or suppressed certain characters, changed the order of episodes, and built in comic and vulgar elements, in short, he created a play which would please his fifteenth-c. audience. The conflict opposes Holofernés and Judith, each representing different religions, and — like in the *Chanson de Roland* — a tribal confrontation becomes a struggle between heathens and Christians, evil and good. Their weapons are unequal; but, at the same time, military strength is compared to weakness, the desires of generals standing versus peaceloving people (*le menu peuple*). The army commanders are cast in a negative light: they are greedy and cowardly, like their soldiers who have not seen their salary for quite some time and hope to devastate fields and homesteads of peasants. Holofernés has a comic dimension, and so has Vagao, his servant, who plays a king's jester at times. Judith, a remarkable woman, combines intelligent calculation and psychological realism.

In addition, R. has studied the play's representations in the fifteenth and sixteenth centuries, its iconography, and the staging which would reveal a wealth of gestures and possible *jeux de scène*, lost in reading the 2,490 verses. The versification shows, besides frequent octosyllabic verses, complicated metric forms (nineteen!) so dear to the *grands rhétoriqueurs*, forms which were to provoke certain effects, as, for example, Judith's passionate faith or Holofernés's comic ridiculousness when courting her.

The language of the play is that of Paris in the fifteenth and beginning sixteenth century, of a compiler (or several "authors"), who used manuscripts; and the date is set by R. for 1480-90 (according to his system for linguistic dating, as described in his article of 1976 [*Modern Language Review*, 71, 757-65]). Of special interest is his attempt to defend Jean Molinet's authorship, based on thematic, textual, lexical, and metric similitudes between the rhetorician's works and our *Mystère*. Some of these proofs are not convincing: the fact that both, Molinet's texts and the *Mystère*, have frequent proverbs (*épiphonèmes sententieux*, see pages 61-63) brings little evidence, because this procedure was used by many authors ever since Hélinand's *Vers de la Mort* (twelfth century). The same is true for enumerations, a favorite practice of the *grands rhétoriqueurs* (70). Furthermore, why would Molinet not have signed this play, if he signed his other works? And linguistically, his texts show traces of Picard dialect, while *Judith et Holofernés* is written in pure Parisian French.

R.'s text edition is exemplary, whereas the notes often repeat what has been said in the introduction. Others, like the note to line 461, are superfluous. A list of characters and a glossary of proper names follow (261-64); a general glossary concludes this valuable volume.

Schubert, Ernst. *Fahrendes Volk im Mittelalter*. Bielefeld: Verlag für Regionalgeschichte, 1995, xii, 497.

This excellent work on vagrant people in the Middle Ages sheds light upon a vast group of non-citizens which was, grosso modo, indispensible for urban and rural communities alike. Treating mainly North German regions, the monograph can, without a doubt, be taken as indicative of Germany in general, and even of other European regions, comparable to the pioneering study of Emmanuel Leroy Ladurie for Southern France (*Montaillou, village occitan de 1294 à 1324* [Paris: Gallimard, 1975]).

Interestingly, Schubert has discovered an important change in attitudes toward these wandering individuals or groups during only a few centuries. Deemed indispensible in 1408 in a municipal resolution concerning mainly musicians and town pipers (speakers of news), vagrants would no longer be tolerated in 1586: gipsies, land rovers, discharged mercenaries, performers, thieves, messengers, beggers, tooth breakers, fortune tellers, and devil catchers.

How was such a change possible? Many arts and crafts originally handled by wandering people were professionalized already in the sixteenth century, and, abandoned by society, the vagrants received little remuneration and less gifts. Today, they are called homeless people, isolated, at times ghettoized. The medieval ambulant merchant, craftsman, or druggist was often more educated than his customers or clients, whereas the modern homeless are, frequently, in need of "special education."

We have sought out in S.'s volume especially the wandering performers who changed from minstrels and acrobats to actors and histrionic artists. But already Roman law had considered that one's display on a stage for lucrative purposes was an infamous occupation. In the Middle Ages, actors were despised just as much as prostitutes, and St. Augustine demanded that they were excluded from the sacraments. In theological writings, minstrels and comedians were presented as the very incarnation of evil, allies of the devil. Since the thirteenth century, however, this attitude changed slowly. Traveling entertainers were welcome at courts, at town fairs and in villages alike. Sometimes, musicians stayed in the communities: they were needed for wedding dances, municipal processions, and for bringing news. Johann Sebastian Bach's ancestor was a town piper. While passion-, Christmas-, and carnival plays were staged in cities and played mainly by burghers, wandering minstrels and other histrionic performers, discredited by the Church, put on skits and puppet plays, even with pious content, and with music and acrobatic feats. Students earned their living in wandering troupes, and in the seventeenth century, the latter were hired by territorial princes and brought about a reform of German theater. Foreign troupes were often preferred: Italians since the end of the fifteenth century, English later. But the theologians continued to distrust the theater and actors (in spite of the good reputation of the Jesuit stage), and Protestant reformers chimed in; women were unthinkable as performers still in the seventeenth century, when, also, the stage was finally dissociated from the circus culture and its wandering exhibitors of bears and monkeys. The development of the theater was henceforth guaranteed by princes and burghers alike.

In the late Middle Ages, traveling, i.e., daring to leave the protective walls of a city (or the limits of a village) was evaluated positively, for it created experience: witness the connection between German *fahren* and *Erfahrung*. Mobility was considered a constitutive factor of medieval life and mentality. Pilgrimages had economical advantages for many regions, and the travels of craftsmen were necessary for the mastery of a certain trade. Surgeons, eye doctors, and quacks, and, of course, students, were wandering roads and forests, where they faced considerable dangers and often lived only by their ingenuity, wit, and/ or theft. To help one another, they established fraternities comparable to those of "honorable" professions. (It is astonishing that in his bibliography of thirty-three pages and in the notes S. never mentions *The Medieval Underworld* by Andrew McCall [London: Hamish Hamilton, 1979] or *Unehrliche Leute* by Werner Danckert [Bern: Francke, 1963]).

S. describes in detail the filth, hunger, and sicknesses, to which the vagrants were exposed in an age far removed from the romanticism of Eichendorff's *Good-for-Nothing* (nineteenth century). Traveling clergymen and hungry students lived by the charity of townspeople, and poets like Villon hovered always between books and gallows. There existed a regular clerical proletariat in early modern times, and deception often traveled under a pilgrim's or monk's frock. False relics were exhibited already in *Raynard the Fox* (thirteenth century), and fortune tellers did not have to wait to see their predictions come true. Wandering mercenaries revealed the underside of chivalry and warfare, while very uncourtly prostitutes supplied the demand of citizens and Church councils alike.

It seems impossible to do justice to Schubert's rich volume with all its descriptions and anecdotal matter. However, we would have liked to find more material on traveling performers, on secular pre- or proto-theater activities, such as minstrels' mimes, monologues and dialogues which, of course, may never have survived orality. Nevertheless, from now on, *Fahrendes Volk im Mittelalter* should be part of every university library, as it supplies valuable information hitherto missing in curricula of medieval and early modern studies. The book contains a good index of twenty-two pages (double columns).

Marygrove College

Löwenritter und Teufelsbündler — ein Braunschweiger Herzog auf Abwegen. Überlegungen zur Lokalisierung von Michel Wyssenherres Dichtung[1]

Hans-Joachim Behr

Der Text, der Ausgangspunkt der nachfolgenden Spurensuche ist, befaßt sich in gewisser Weise mit Heinrich dem Löwen. Aber weder seine Persönlichkeit noch seine politische Leistung sind Gegenstand der weiteren Überlegungen, sondern die Umgestaltung des Welfenherzogs zur literarischen Figur in einem Text des 15. Jahrhunderts, als dessen Autor sich ein sonst unbekannter Michel Wyssenherre vorstellt (Str. 98,7).[2] Überliefert ist er in einer Sammelhandschrift der Württembergischen Landesbibliothek Stuttgart (Signatur: Cod. poet. et phil. 2° 4), die sich zu etwa 96 Prozent dem Thema "Reise und fiktiver Reisebericht" widmet. Als ihr Schreiber und Illustrator nennt sich auf Blatt 91ra ein *Hans von Goſzhem tzu disser tzijt tzentgreffe tzu modau* [=Hans von Gochsheim/Gossheim, zur Zeit Zentgraf in Mudau/Modau], der den Codex nach eigenen Angaben in den siebziger Jahren des 15. Jahrhunderts angelegt hat.[3]

Die Identität dieses Mannes ein wenig zu lichten, ist das Ziel der nachfolgenden Überlegungen, die sich in fünf Fragekomplexe aufteilen:

1) Was versteht man unter einem Zentgrafen und welche Aufgaben hat er inne?

2) Wo gibt es einen Ort Mudau oder Modau, der in der zweiten Hälfte des 15. Jahrhunderts Amtssitz eines Zentgrafen gewesen ist?

3) Wer ist Eigentümer dieser Zent und damit "Dienstherr" des dortigen Zentgrafen?

4) Wo gibt es einen Ort Gochsheim oder Gossheim, der zu Mudau/Modau bzw. dem Eigentümer der dortigen Zent in Verbindung steht?

5) Ist irgendwo ein Hans von Gochsheim/Gossheim urkundlich als Zentgraf oder in einer anderen Funktion belegt?

Zu 1):

Unter "Zent" (lat. *centena*, im Deutschen korrekterweise ohne Dehnungs-h geschrieben) versteht man eine erstmals im Hochmittelalter nachweisbare Form niederer Gerichtsbarkeit, die allerdings sehr rasch Aufgaben der Hoch- und Blutgerichtsbarkeit okkupiert.[4] Als Vorsitzender im Zentgericht fungiert der Zentgraf, "gelegentlich ein Adeliger, der dieses Amt als Lehen oder pfandweise innehatte",[5] im allgemeinen aber ein "niedere(r) Beamte(r)", der vom Zentherrn nach Rücksprache mit den Großgrundbesitzern der Region eingesetzt wird.[6] Ihm obliegt es, Klagen entgegenzunehmen und einen Termin für das anstehende Zentverfahren anzuberaumen, ebenso, für einen ordnungsgemäßen Ablauf des Prozesses und für den Vollzug des ergangenen Urteils zu sorgen.[7] Allerdings ist die Zent kein allgemeines Gericht, da Adelige nicht ihrer Jurisdiktion unterstehen.[8]

Zu 2):

Für das in der Handschrift überlieferte "tzu modau" ergeben sich bei Berücksichtigung sprachhistorischer Zusammenhänge und nach Auswertung sowohl mittelalterlicher Quellenwerke als auch des Kartenmaterials eines großen deutschen Automobilclubs nicht weniger als vier verschiedene Zuordnungsmöglichkeiten:

1) Mudau im Odenwald, etwa 20 km südlich von Miltenberg am Main gelegen,

2) Ober- und Niedermodau, ca. 20 km südöstlich von Darmstadt, heute Bestandteil der Stadt Ober-Ramstadt,

3) die Flächengemeinde Modautal,

4) Meudt im Ostwesterwaldkreis, etwa 15 km nordwestlich von Limburg.

Davon scheidet Nr. 3 "Modautal" von Anfang an aus, da der Ort erst durch die Hessische Gebietsrefom zum 1. Januar 1977 aus elf ursprünglich selbständigen Gemeinden gebildet wurde.[9] Schon weniger eindeutig sind die Verhältnisse bei "Meudt" (Nr. 4), denn dort ist immerhin eine Zent bezeugt, die Graf Adolf von Nassau-Diez am 19. Februar 1391 zusammen mit anderen Zentgemeinden an Graf Diether von Katzenelnbogen versetzt.[10] Im Besitz dieses Hauses ist sie gleich mehrmals belegt: 1444, 1453 und 1454,[11] mithin also knapp zwanzig Jahre, bevor der Zentgraf Hans von Gochsheim seine Wyssenherre-Erzählung zu Papier bringt. Trotzdem ist Meudt als dessen Amtssitz eher unwahrscheinlich, da die in den Urkunden ausschließlich verwendete Namensform Mude zu stark von dem überlieferten "tzu modau" abweicht. Ober- und Niedermodau (Nr. 2), seit 1977 in das benachbarte Ober-Ramstadt eingemeindet,[12] gehören seit der Mitte des 14. Jahrhunderts wie Meudt zum Besitz der Grafen von Katzenelnbogen, denen sie auch zu der Zeit, als die Handschrift mit dem Wyssenherre-Text entsteht, noch immer tributpflichtig sind.[13] Indes, eine Zent ist in beiden Orten nachweislich nicht vorhanden.[14] Ganz anders verhält es sich mit Mudau im Odenwald. Schon 1271 ist dort ein Zentgericht mit 28 Dörfern als Einzugsbereich belegt, als Ulrich III. von Durne aus Geldmangel Ort und Zent an das Mainzer Erzbistum verkauft.[15] Damit scheint sich der erste von mehreren Knoten entwirrt zu haben, ist doch Mudau im Odenwald der einzige Ort, für den der sprachgeschichtliche und der historische Befund übereinstimmen.

Zu 3):

Nach Recht und Gesetz wird der Zentgraf vom jeweiligen Territorialherren eingesetzt.[16] Damit bestätigt sich erneut der Charakter der Zent als eines trotz Blutgerichtsbarkeit abhängigen Gerichtes. Für die beiden hier in Frage kommenden Zentorte Mudau bzw. Meudt sind Landesherren die Erzbischöfe von Mainz oder die Grafen von Katzenelnbogen, die einen Erzkanzler und Kurfürsten des Reiches aufweisen und zu den mächtigsten Territorialherren überhaupt gehörend, die anderen erst seit dem späten 11. Jahrhundert belegt und in staufischen Diensten zu Macht und Ansehen aufgestiegen sind.[17]

Zu 4):

Damit stellt sich nunmehr die Frage nach dem Ort Gozhem, den der Zentgraf Hans als seine Heimatgemeinde benennt. Wiederum gibt es dafür mehrere Möglichkeiten:

1) Gosheim, Luftlinie etwas mehr als 10 km südöstlich von Rottweil
2) Gochsheim in Bayern, etwa 6 km südöstlich von Schweinfurt
3) Gochsheim in Baden-Württemberg, heute Teil der Stadt Kraichtal, etwa 30 km nordöstlich von Karlsruhe.

Auch hier konzentriert sich die Entscheidung auf zwei Ortschaften, da der Weiler Gosheim (Nr. 1) doch wohl zu unbedeutend ist, als daß man in dem etwa 250 Straßenkilometer entfernten Mudau auf ihn Bezug nehmen und einen positiven Wiedererkennungseffekt hätte auslösen können. Das bayerische Gochsheim (Nr. 2) hingegen genießt als "Reichsdorf"[18] de iure die gleichen Freiheiten wie die benachbarte Stadt Schweinfurt, d.h. steht unter königlicher Verwaltung und hat mit dem benachbarten Territorialherrn, dem Bischof von Würzburg, nur eine Art Schutzvertrag.[19] Aber der Umstand, daß weder in Würzburg noch in den angrenzenden Territorien irgendwer urkundlich bezeugt ist, der die Bezeichnung "von Gochsheim" als Bestandteil seines Namens auch tatsächlich führt, mahnt zur Vorsicht. Denn als freies Reichsdorf liegt der Ort auf Königsland[20] und ist demnach unabhängig von adeliger Grundherrschaft, so daß es ein Herrengeschlecht derer von Gochsheim wohl nie gegeben hat. Der württembergische Namensvetter indes ist als Gründung und Wohnsitz der Herren von Eberstein von Anfang an dynastisch besetzt.[21] Wie die Grafen von Katzenelnbogen kommen auch sie im 12. Jahrhundert im Herrendienst zu Ansehen, Reichtum und Macht, wobei das Bistum Speyer eine Schlüsselposition innehat.[22] "Noch vor 1250"[23] gründen sie die Stadt Gochsheim. Doch da ist der Zenit ihres Wirkens schon fast überschritten: geringe Ausbaumöglichkeiten ihres Territoriums, übermäßige Spenden an die Kirche, die in keinem Verhältnis zu ihren Einkünften stehen, und die Verwicklung in kriegerische Auseinandersetzungen mit mächtigen Nachbarn zwingen immer wieder dazu, Kernlande zu veräußern, um der drückenden Schuldenlast wenigstens einigermaßen Herr zu werden. Daher sind die Ebersteiner bereits Ende des 14. Jahrhunderts so verarmt, daß sie bis zu ihrem Aussterben im Jahr 1660 "nur noch ein Kümmerdasein"[24] führen. So wird denn Gochsheim, nachdem die Stammburgen Alt- und Neu-Eberstein sukzessive hatten verkauft werden müssen, zwangsläufig Hauptsitz eines ehedem bedeutenden Geschlechts, das freilich schon 1377 seine frühere Selbständigkeit aufgegeben hatte und in fremde Dienste getreten war.[25] Hinzukommt ein weiterer Gesichtspunkt: Wie Mudau liegen Gochsheim und Speyer, Ausgangspunkt des Ebersteinschen Aufstiegs, im Diözesansverband von Mainz,[26] so daß es keinerlei Probleme bereitet, wenn ein Vasall des Bistums Speyer mit oder ohne Vermittlung weiterer kirchlicher Instanzen im knapp 80 Straßenkilometer entfernten, zu Mainz gehörenden Mudau unterkommt, zumal dann, wenn es sich um eine Familie handelt, deren wirtschaftlicher Ruin nicht zuletzt durch ihre Großzügigkeit gegenüber der Kirche bedingt ist.

Zu 5):

Es sei nicht verhohlen, daß das Votum für das württembergische Gochsheim vor allem aus der Annahme, der genannte Zentort sei mit Mudau im Odenwald zu identifizieren, einen großen Teil seiner Absicherung erfährt. Insofern stützen sich hier zwei Hypothesen gegenseitig. Indes, wenn Ortsnamen zur erfolgreichen Kennzeichnung von Personen dienen sollen, müssen entweder der Ort selbst oder die Verbindung von Person und Ort hinreichend bekannt sein. Für Gochsheim und die Herren von Eberstein ist dies der Fall — und tatsächlich ist zwischen 1471 und 1474, den Eckdaten für die Entstehung der Handschrift, ein Hans von Eberstein urkundlich belegt,[27] übrigens der einzige Träger des Namens in diesem Geschlecht. Am 1. Juni 1421 geboren, lebt er trotz reicher Heirat (seine Frau Maria von Eppstein hatte immerhin eine Mitgift von 4000 Gulden eingebracht[28]) in wirtschaftlich derart zerrütteten Verhältnissen, daß er 1451 seinen letzten Anteil an der Burg Neu-Eberstein seinem Bruder Bernhard II. verkauft und von da ab ausschließlich in Gochsheim wohnt.[29] Er ist Vasall des Pfälzer Kurfürsten Friedrich I., in dessen Diensten er sich als Krieger und Heerführer betätigt, wenn er nicht gerade mit eigenen Fehden beschäftigt ist. Die letzte Urkunde sieht ihn 1469 bei Graf Ulrich von Württemberg in Sold,[30] gestorben aber ist er erst 1479.[31] Was er in den letzten zehn Jahren seines Lebens gemacht hat, ist unbekannt, und so könnte es durchaus sein, daß er angesichts seiner chronischen Geldnot in Mainzer Dienste übergewechselt ist und wenigstens zeitweise als Zentgraf in Mudau sein Auskommen hatte. Aber das ist lediglich Vermutung und aus den Urkunden nicht zu belegen, auch wenn die Wahrscheinlichkeit, daß es so gewesen sein könnte, nicht sogleich gegen Null tangiert.

Zusammenfassend läßt sich damit die folgende These formulieren: Hans von Eberstein, seit 1451 ausschließlich wohnhaft im württembergischen Gochsheim, steht zwischen 1471 und 1474 in Diensten des Mainzer Erzbischofs Adolfs II. von Nassau, für den er als Zentgraf im badischen Mudau, einem ländlichen Verwaltungszentrum von nicht unbedeutendem Ausmaß, Hoheitsrechte wahrnimmt.

Allerdings ist damit noch nicht geklärt, warum er nebenher eine Sammelhandschrift anlegt und reich bebildert. Gerade der letzte Umstand spricht für eine Auftragsarbeit. Zudem befassen sich mehr als neun Zehntel des Codex mit dem Thema "Reisen und ferne Länder." Das hängt mit einer im Vergleich zum Hochmittelalter geradezu unglaublich gesteigerten Mobilität zusammen: Nicht nur in Gestalt der großen Entdeckerfahrten eines Vasco da Gama, Christoph Kolumbus oder Fernão de Magalhães, sondern auch in privaten Bildungs- und Pilgerreisen, wie sie sich etwa mit den Namen Georg von Ehingen, Jörg Pfinzing, Albrecht (Achilles) und Johann von Brandenburg oder Albrecht von Sachsen verbinden.[32] Auch Philipp der Ältere von Katzenelnbogen hat 1433/34 Palästina besucht und sich von einem schreibkundigen Augenzeugen, den er vorsichtshalber als Chronisten mitgenommen hatte, einen authentischen Reisebericht anfertigen lassen.[33] 1477, mehr als vier Jahrzehnte später, beauftragt schließlich der Mainzer Erzbischof Diether II. von Isenburg Erhart Wameszhafft, diesen Text in deutschen Verse zu übertragen.[34] Zu keiner Zeit ist das Verhältnis zwischen den reichen Grafen von Katzenelnbogen und der Mainzer Kirche enger als in der zweiten Hälfte des 15. Jahrhunderts, so daß sich hier eine wirtschaftliche und politische Allianz auch auf kulturellem Sektor niedergeschlagen hat. Damit stehen Hans von Gochsheim und seine Handschrift im gleichen geistigen Umfeld wie die Reiseberichte der Palästinapilger oder die Versübertragung des Erhart Wameszhafft. Nun ist bekannt, daß die Grafen von Katzenelnbogen nicht nur reich, sondern auch kulturell ambitioniert waren[35]: Ihre Bibliothek ist zwar nicht erhalten, aber teilweise bekannt. So befanden sich in ihr relativ viele Texte, die sich mit Reisen, fernen Ländern und der Begegnung von Orient und Okzident befaßten: eine (mitteldeutsche?) Version von *Brandans Meerfahrt*,[36] eine deutsche Übersetzung der *Historia trium regum*, der Dreikönigslegende, des Johannes von Hildesheim mit Anklängen an zeitgenössische Pilgerberichte,[37] zwei nicht näher bezeichnete Weltchroniken[38] und vielleicht der *Willehalm* Wolframs von Eschenbach.[39] Auch Augustijns *Herzog von Braunschweig*, eine Kurzerzählung von Liebe und Abenteuer, scheinen die Katzenelnbogener besessen zu haben.[40] Obwohl diesen Stoff nichts mit Michel Wyssenherres Gedicht und schon gar nichts mit irgendeinem realen Braunschweiger Herzog verbindet, ist die hier literarisch konstruierte Amts- und Familiendynastie des Minneabenteurers mit dem Teufelsbündler ein weiteres Bindeglied zwischen der Wyssenherre-Handschrift und der gräflichen Bibliothek. Aber weitere Überlegungen in dieser Richtung sind (momentan) nicht zu beweisen.

NOTES

[1] Der folgende Aufsatz ist die Kurzfassung eines Vortrages, den ich am 6. Mai 1995 im Rahmen der Ausstellung "Heinrich der Löwe und seine Zeit. Nachleben" im Braunschweiger Landesmuseum gehalten habe. Er erscheint in der längeren Version voraussichtlich 1996 in der "Wissenschaftlichen Zeitschrift des Braunschweigischen Landesmuseums."

[2] Michel Wyssenherres Gedicht “Von dem edeln hern von Bruneczwigk, als er über mer fuore” und “Die Sage von Heinrich dem Löwen,” ed. Walther Seehaussen (Breslau: M. & H. Marcus, 1913), 151-173. *Michel Wyssenherre: Eyn buoch von dem edeln hern von Bruneczwigk als er uber mer fuore*. In Abbildungen aus dem Cod. poet. fol. 4 der Württembergischen Landesbibliothek ed., eingeleitet und transkribiert von Iris Dinkelacker und Wolfgang Häring, (Göppingen: Kümmerle, 1977), 16-46 (Faksimile), 47-55 (Transkription).

Neuausgabe des Textes, Übersetzung und Kommentar: *Vestigia Leonis — Spuren des Löwen. Das Bild Heinrichs des Löwen in der deutschen und skandinavischen Literatur*,” Band 1: Mittelalter und frühe Neuzeit. Von Hans-Joachim Behr und Herbert Blume (Braunschweig: Michael Kuhle, 1995).

[3] Blatt 90 und 104. C f. Dinkelacker-Häring, “Michel Wyssenherre,” 8.

[4] Vgl. Karl Kroeschell, “Die Zentgerichte in Hessen und die fränkische Centene,” *Zeitschrift für Rechtsgeschichte. Germanische Abteilung* 73 (1956), 300-360. Karl Kroeschell, *Deutsche Rechtsgeschichte 1 (bis 1250)*, (Reinbek: Rowohlt-Taschenbuch, 1972), 184-187. Heinrich Mitteis, *Der Staat des hohen Mittelalters*, (Darmstadt: Wissenschaftliche Buchgesellschaft, 1986), 188f., 242-244.

[5] Kroeschell, “Die Zentgerichte in Hessen und die fränkische Centene,” 346.

[6] Kroeschell, “Die Zentgerichte in Hessen und die fränkische Centene,” 347.

[7] So z.B. festgelegt im Zentbrief von Möckmühl (1429). C f. Karl Kroeschell, *Deutsche Rechtsgeschichte 2 (1250-1650)*, (Reinbek: Rowohlt-Taschenbuch, 1973), 133-135.

[8] So ausdrücklich formuliert im *Statutum in favorem principum*, cap. 9. C f. Kroeschell, *Deutsche Rechtsgeschichte 1 (bis 1250)*,” 294.

[9] Cf. *Hessisches Gemeinde-Lexikon. Ein Handbuch über die Städte, Gemeinden und Landkreise in Hessen von Aarbergen bis Zwingenberg mit vielen Informationen, Daten und Fakten aus Geschichte und Gegenwart*, ed. vom Hessendienst der Staatskanzlei in Zusammenarbeit mit dem Hessischen Statistischen Landesamt (Wiesbaden: Hessendienst der Staatskanzlei, 1983), 341f.

Für Informationen, Literaturhinweise und tatkräftige Unterstützung bei der Beschaffung heimatkundlicher Literatur (die wenigsten der hier zu behandelnden Orte sind wissenschaftlich hinreichend erforscht), habe ich zu danken: den Stadt- und Gemeindeverwaltungen von Gochsheim, Gosheim, Kraichtal, Modautal, Mudau, Ober-Ramstadt, dem Stadtarchiv Kraichtal und zahlreichen Privatpersonen.

[10] Cf. Karl E[rnst] Demandt, *Regesten der Grafen von Katzenelnbogen. 1060-1486*, 3 Bände und ein Registerband (Wiesbaden: Harrasowitz, 1953, 1954, 1956, 1957). Hier Band I (1060-1418), 549f.

[11] Demandt, *Regesten der Grafen von Katzenelnbogen*, Band II: (1418-1482), 1175f., 1139f., 1341, 1352, 1355.

[12] Cf. *Hessisches Gemeinde-Lexikon*, 381f.

[13] Zahlreiche Belege dazu bei Demandt, *Regesten der Grafen von Katzenelnbogen*, Band IV:Register. Der früheste Beleg stammt aus der Zeit um 1360 (Band I, 366), der jüngste vom 31. August 1472. Cf. Demandt, *Regesten der Grafen von Katzenelnbogen. 1060-1486*, Band III: Rechnungen, Besitzverzeichnisse, Steuerlisten und Gerichtsbücher (1295-1486), 2257.

[14] Auch in der heimatkundlichen Literatur findet sich keine Erwähnung eines Zentgerichtes in Ober- oder Niedermodau. Cf. Arthur Fink und Georg Zimmermann, "Zur Geschichte der Evangelischen Kirche zu Nieder-Modau" (Reinheim/Odw.: Lokay-Druck, o.J.), 5f.

[15] Cf. Theodor Humpert, *Mudau. Wesen und Werden einer Odenwaldgemeinde*, (Buchen (Odenwald), Selbstverlag der Gemeinde Mudau, 1954), 28.

[16] Text und Übersetzung nach Kroeschell *Deutsche Rechtsgeschichte 1 (bis 1250)*, 294f.

[17] Cf. Karl Demandt, "Die Mittelrheinlande (Hessen und Mainz)," in: Georg Wilhelm Sante und A. G. Ploetz-Verlag (Hgg.), *Geschichte der deutschen Länder. Territorienploetz*, 1. Band: Die Territorien bis zum Ende des alten Reiches (Würzburg: A. G. Ploetz, 1964), 178-210. Hier: S. 185-189 (Mainz) und S. 192-194 (Katzenelnbogen). Zum Aufstieg der Grafen von Katzenelnbogen im Königsdienst cf. Karl E[rnst] Demandt, "Die Anfänge des Katzenelnbogener Grafenhauses und die reichsgeschichtlichen Grundlagen seines Aufstiegs," *Nassauische Annalen* 63 (1952), 17-71.

[18] Cf. Alfred Wendehorst, *Das Bistum Würzburg*, Teil 3: Die Bischofsreihe von 1455 bis 1617 (Berlin — New York: de Gruyter, 1978), 144.

[19] So muß etwa der Würzburger Bischof Julius Echter von Mespelbrunn 1575 für Gochsheim die "Wahrung der Konfession" garantieren. See Wendehorst, *Das Bistum Würzburg*, 193.

[20] Cf. die von der Gemeindeverwaltung herausgegebene Broschüre *Gochsheim*, (Kissing: WEKA Informationsschriften- und Werbefachverlage GmbH, 1992), 2.

[21] G[eorg] H. Krieg von Hochfelden, *Geschichte der Grafen von Eberstein in Schwaben. Auf Befehl seiner Königlichen Hoheit des Großherzogs Leopold von Baden aus den Quellen bearbeitet* (Carlsruhe: Hasper, 1836). Alfons Schäfer, "Staufische Reichslandpolitik und hochadelige Herrschaftsbildung im Uf- und Pfinzgau und im Nordwestschwarzwald vom 11.-13. Jahrhundert," *Zeitschrift für die Geschichte des Oberrheins* 117 (1969), 179-244. Hier: S. 229-244. Ob die schwäbischen Herren von Eberstein mit gleichnamigen Geschlechtern in Franken, Thüringen und Sachsen verwandt waren, ist unsicher, kann aber hier außer Betracht bleiben, da im Hoch- und Spätmittelalter keinerlei Verbindungen untereinander bestehen.

[22] Schäfer, *Staufische Reichslandpolitik und hochadelige Herrschaftsbildung*, 232.

[23] Ibid., 242.

[24] Ibid., 244.

[25] Krieg von Hochfelden, *Geschichte der Grafen von Eberstein in Schwaben*, 85.

[26] Cf. "Die Bistümer Mitteleuropas". In: *Großer Atlas zur Weltgeschichte*, ed. von Hans-Erich Stier u.a., Westermann Schulbuchverlag Braunschweig, Sonderausgabe Orbis Verlag für Publizistik (München: Orbis, 1991), 89 unten.

[27] Krieg von Hochfelden, *Geschichte der Grafen von Eberstein in Schwaben*, 110-120.

[28] Ibid., 109.

[29] Ibid., 114 und 116.

[30] Ibid., 120.

[31] Ibid., 120.

[32] Silvia Schmitz, *Die Pilgerreise Philipps d. Ä. von Katzenelnbogen in Prosa und Vers. Untersuchungen zum dokumentarischen und panegyrischen Charakter spätmittelalterlicher Adelsliteratur*, (München: Fink, 1990), 140-190. Anne Simon, " 'Gotterfahrung' oder 'Welterfahrung'. Das Erlebnis des Reisens in Pilgerberichten des 15. Jahrhunderts," in: "*Reisen und Welterfahrung in der deutschen Literatur des Mittelalters*. Vorträge des XI. Anglo-deutschen Colloquiums. 11.-15. September 1989. Universität Liverpool," ed. Dietrich Huschenbett u.a. (Würzburg: Königshausen und Neumann, 1991), 173-184.

[33] *Schmitz, Die Pilgerreise Philipps d. Ä. von Katzenelnbogen*, 130-139. Den Ausführungen der Verfasserin, der Katzenelnbogener Finanzbeamte Siegfried von Gelnhausen sei der Autor der Prosaversion, vermag ich mich nicht anzuschließen.

[34] Cf. *Europäische Reiseberichte des späten Mittelalters. Eine analytische Bibliographie*, ed. von Werner Paravicini, Teil 1: Deutsche Reiseberichte, bearbeitet von Christian Halm (Frankfurt/M. u.a.: Lang, 1994), 76-78. Schmitz, *Die Pilgerreise Philipps d. Ä. von Katzenelnbogen*, 219-236.

[35] Cf. Karl E[rnst] Demandt, "Kultur und Leben am Hofe der Katzenelnbogener Grafen," *Nassauische Annalen* 61 (1950), 149-180. Schmitz, 102-111.

[36] Zur Bibliothek der Grafen von Katzenelnbogen vgl. Demandt, *Kultur und Leben am Hofe der Katzenelnbogener Grafen*, 155f. Schmitz, 104-106. Ulrich Seelbach, "Wolframs 'Willehalm' in der Bibliothek des letzten Katzenelnbogener Grafen Philipp?," in: *Der Buchstab tödt — der Geist macht lebendig*. FS. für Hans-Gert Roloff (60), ed. James Hardin u.a., Band I (Bern u.a.: Lang, 1992), 421-430. Hier S. 422f. Zum Text selbst cf. Walter Haug: "Brandans Meerfahrt," in: *Die deutsche Literatur des Mittelalters. Verfasserlexikon, 2.*, völlig neu bearbeitete Auflage, ed. Kurt Ruh u.a., Band 1 (Berlin — New York: de Gruyter, 1978), 985-991.

[37] Dazu Franz Josef Worstbrock und Sylvia C. Harris, "Johannes von Hildesheim," in: *Verfasserlexikon*, ed. Kurt Ruh u.a., Band 4 (Berlin — New York: de Gruyter, 1983), 638-647. Hier Sp. 644.

[38] Seelbach, "Wolframs 'Willehalm' in der Bibliothek des letzten Katzenelnbogener Grafen Philipp?," 422.

[39] Ibid., 425.

[40] Ibid., 423.

Zum Text selbst cf. Robert Leclercq, "Augustijn" in: *Verfasserlexikon*, ed. Kurt Ruh u.a., Band 1 (Berlin — New York: de Gruyter, 1978), 530f.

TU Braunschweig

Akademisch gebildetes und einfaches Theaterpublikum im Spätmittelalterlichen Polen

Piotr Bering

In der modernen Literaturwissenschaft bestimmt der Begriff *literarisches Publikum* vor allem "die Gemeinschaft der Empfänger der literarischen Werke."[1] Diese etwas unpräzise Definition reicht meines Erachtens für die einleitenden Studien.[2] Der Begriff *Theaterpublikum* ist in demselbem Maße unklar, hat er jedoch im Vergleich zu dem obengenannten literarischen Publikum einen Vorteil: das Theaterpublikum ist relativ leicht nach quantitativen Kriterien zu klassifizieren.[3]

Bei der Forschung der älteren Epochen sollten beide Begriffe modifiziert werden. Das es im Mittelalter kein "modernes Publikum" gab,[4] kann man — ohne Zweifel — von den Zuschauern und Empfängern sagen. Wenn die aus dem zwanzigsten Jahrhundert stammende Terminologie erwähnt wird, soll nur an eine "teilweise Kompatibilität" gedacht werden.

Die Anfänge der polnischen mittelalterlichen Theaterkultur liegen noch im Dunkeln. Nach dem heutigen Stand der Wissenschaft stammen aus der Mitte des 13. Jhs. die ersten Überlieferungen von *Visitatio Sepulchri* und *Processio in Ramis Palmarum*. Der relativ kleine Ertrag wurde bedeutsam im Spätmittelalter vermehrt, und der größte Anteil der aufbewahrten schriftlichen Überlieferungen hatte seinen Ursprung im 14. und 15. Jahrhundert.[5] Es handelt sich nicht nur um einfache Vervielfältigung, sondern auch um die Evolution der Gattung. Der Zeitablauf brachte die Veredelung der szenischen Mittel mit sich und verbreitete das Spektrum der aufgeführten Gattungen. Auch die Formen des Anteils des Publikums änderten sich. Für *Visitatio Sepulchri* ist ein bescheidener Anteil von *laici* charakteristisch. Die lateinische Sprache, in der diese Gattung dargestellt wurde, bildete eine Sprachgrenze für die einfachen Leute. Natürlich konnte der Inhalt des Stückes teilweise, vor allem Dank der Mimik und Bewegung, verständlich werden.[6] In Polen wurde im größten Maße *Visitatio Sepulchri* nach der sogenanten "Zweiten Art" gespielt,[7] die durch den Wettlauf der Apostel für die Zuschauer stark attraktiv war. Die Didaskalien unterrichten darüber, daß die Apostel den Lauf vortäuschen sollten "quasi cursum ostentantes."[8]

Diese Episode war wirklich expressiv, für einige Zuschauer aber nicht akzeptabel. Diverse Meinungen verursachten, daß der Posener Bischof Jan Latalski (gest. 1540) ganz anders dieses Problem in seiner Fassung (das ist die späteste polnische Fassung) gelöst hatte.[9] In allen restlichen polnischen Fassungen traten als die wichtigsten Zeugen der Auferstehung die Apostel auf, und sie zeigten das Grabtuch allen anwesenden Personen vor. In der Posener Fassung übernahmen diese Rolle die Engel: "Tandem pueri in sepulcro eiciant linteamina extra sepulcrum cantans: Cernite o socij ecce lintheamina et sudarium et corpus non est in sepulcro inuentum..."[10] Jetzt bekundigten sie allen Gläubigen aus Posen — durch alle Jahrhunderte — daß Christus auferstanden sei.[11] Die Rolle der Apostel wurde ganz ausgeschlossen. Der Gang wurde durch die Worte ersetzt: "Presbiteri cantent ante sepulcrum: Currebant duo simul et ille alius discipulus precucurrit citius Petro! et venit prior ad monumentum..."[12] Diese Modifikation verlangte ein anderes Niveau der Rezeption. Alle Zuschauer, die Zeuge der Auferstehung sind, mußten sich besonders auf den Wortlaut konzentrieren. Jetzt bildeten die Zuschauer und die Schauspieler eine gewisse Einheit. Sie waren die Gläubigen — *discipuli Christi*.[13] Sowohl die realistischen Elemente, als auch die Bewegung, die als eine komische Einlage in dem wichtigsten Ereignis des Christentums auftraten, konnten für die religiösen Zwecke gefährlich sein. Die Aufmerksamkeit der Zuschauer wurde auf die Nebenmotive, nicht auf die Wahrheit des Glaubens gelenkt. Es gab auch eine anderere Ansicht dieser Modifikation: Jan Latalski lehnte die hundertjährige Tradition der Inszenierung ab. Wie nahm das Publikum diesen Wechsel an, das sich an eine völlig andere Aufführung gewöhnt hatte? Man kann zwar nicht diese Frage beantworten, aber es ist bekannt daß, die traditionellen Formen von *Visitatio Sepulchri* in der ersten Hälfte des 16. Jhs. wesentlich häufiger als die Modifikation von Jan Latalski gespielt wurden.[14]

Eine ähnliche Situation entstand bei den Inszenierungen von *Cena Domini*. Für die ungebildeten Zuschauer spielten plastische Mittel, Bewegung und Mimik eine viel wichtigere Rolle als das Wort. Die mittelalterlichen Verfasser und Künstler wußten davon. Die Sorgfältigkeit, in der verschiedene Requisiten der Bühnenbilder beschrieben wurde, zeugt nicht nur von pastoralen Zwecken, sondern auch von dem Bedürfnis der realistischen Darstellung. Gemäß der Hinweise des Verfassers sollte Wasser in einer Menge vorbereitet werden, damit es fürs Waschen reicht, und das Handtuch für *Cena Domini* war speziell angeschafft worden — "linteum ad hoc per fratres emptum et comparatum."[15] Diese realistischen Elemente sollten vor allem auf die Einbildung der einfachen Zuschauer wirken. Als eine Abwechslung, die mit dem Wort verbunden worden war, auftrat, war sie nur für einen Teil des Publikums verständlich. Manchmal waren es nur die *Leser*. So geschah es bei der Inszenierung *Cena Domini* in Krakau 1520. Diese Fassung empfielt, daß der hl. Petrus mit Jesus einen Dialog führen soll. Der Chor singt die Reden des Apostels, der andere übernimmt die Rolle von Christus.[16] Diese Veränderung war auf der Bühne sichtbar, aber nur die Handschrift unterstrich z.B., daß der Chor lustig singen sollte,[17] deswegen konnte nur ein beschränkter Kreis den ästhethischen Sinn vollkommen verstehen.

Der Anteil des Publikums im Mitwirken der Aufführung war begrenzt. Am Ende von *Visitatio Sepulchri* durften *laici in vulgari* das Lied *Chrystus zmartwych wstał jest* (entspricht dem deutschen Lied *Christ ist erstan-*

den) singen. Viel breitere Möglichkeiten für die Zuschauer bot die Dramatisation *Processio in Ramis Palmarum* an. Diese Form trat in vielen Arten auf, und nach den Studien von Zenon Modzelewski gab es sechs Veränderungen dieser Form in Polen.[18] In allen spielten die Bewegung und das gesungene Wort eine sehr wichtige Rolle. Schritt für Schritt wurde die Rolle der Schauspieler immer wichtiger. Sie unterschieden sich allmählich von der Teilnehmermenge der *Processio*. Die letzten würden ab dieser Zeit nur die Zuschauer sein. Diese Dichotomie wurde durch den Gebrauch von Requisiten verstärkt. Das Kreuz wurde mit der Albe bekleidet. Sowohl die Schauspieler, als auch die Zuschauer wußten, daß das Kostüm in sich einen symbolistischen Inhalt mittrug.[19] Die *laici* durften nur etliche Stellen der liturgischen Lieder singen, und in diesem Moment traten sie als Teilnehmer der Liturgie auf; aber da sie nur sahen oder hörten, waren sie vor allem Zuschauer.[20] Obwohl es verschiedene Evolutionsphasen dieser Form und diverse Proportionen des Anteils von *laici* gab, hat jedoch diese Dramatisierung als erste die Teilung zwischen Schauspielern und Zuschauern angedeutet.

Die Distinktion zwischen Schauspielern und dem Publikum wurde viel deutlicher während der Inszenierungen der Oster- und Passionspiele. Hier sollten die Stücke nicht nur den Glauben vertiefen, sondern auch eine gewisse Unterhaltung bringen. Deshalb mußten sie nicht selten mit trivialen, volkstümlichen Motiven aufgelockert werden. In dem *Wiener Osterspiel* — das, obwohl es zu dem Deutschsprachgut gehört — jedoch aus Schlesien stammt,[21] das mit Polen sehr große und rege kulturelle Bündnisse hatte, richtete *Mercator* sich an seine Frau mit dieser Ansprache:

Sweiget, frawe, vnd lot ewer swanczyn!
zo Breslaw uf dem tume beckit man gute mosanczyn,
czu Othmechaw gar gute weiche kese;
ich getrawe gar wol vor euch czu genesin![22]

Das Publikum fühlte in diesem Moment, daß die Worte auf der Bühne vor allem an sie — an die Mitglieder der lokalen Gemeinschaft[23] — gerichtet wurden. Jeder Prolog war auch ein Versuch der direkten Kommunikation zwischen den Zuschauern und den Schauspielern. Der Anfang des *Wiener Osterspiels* lautet:

Hut vnd tret mir aws dem wege
das ich meyne zache vor lege! [...]
nu horet czu alle gleich
beyde arm vnd reich
horet czu alle gemeyne
beyde groß und cleyne,
ir iungen vnd ir alden [...]
wir wellin haben eyn ostirspil
(das ist frolich vnd kost nicht vil).[24]

Sehr ähnlich sah der Spielbeginn des *Innsbrucker Mariae Himmelfahrtsspiels* aus: "Nû wicht em al glich / Beyde arm und rich."[25] Dieselbe Kommunikationssituation gab es, wenn im *Wiener Osterspiel* der *Praecursor* oder einer der Schauspieler (*Pilatus, Juden*) sich ans Publikum wandte:

> Silete, silete, silete, silete!
> Silentium habete!
> Sweiget, liben gesellin.[26]

Die Worte *beyde groß und cleyne*, die im Stück siebenmal vorkommen,[27] funktionieren als *Appelatio* an die Zuschauer, während dieser eine Doppelkommunikation entsteht: eine, die aus dem Text stammte und die andere, die zwischen dem Publikum und der Bühne geführt wurde. Von hier an gab es nur einen Schritt zum "mitspielenden Publikum.[28]" Dieselben Strukturen und Motive, die den dramatischen Charakter des Spiels unterstreichen,[29] sind in dem altpolnischen Stück *Historie von der glorreichen Auferstehung des Herrn*[30] zu finden. Der *Prologus* richtete sich direkt ans Publikum mit dieser Rede:

> Wciórnastkie rzeczy stworzone,
> Tak niebieskie jako ziemne,
> Krzescijanie mili, wierni,
> W Panu Bogu zgromadzeni
> (Alle Geschöpfe, sowohl himmlische, als auch irdische, nette und treue in Gottes Namen gesammelte Christen).[31]

Später gab *Prologus* eine Zusammenfassung des Inhaltes des Stückes an. Am Ende der "Einführung" appellierte er ans Publikum, daß dieses beurteilen möge, ob das ganze Stück mit dem Evangelium im Einklang stehe.[32] Und das lezte Wort von *Prologus* war eine entschlossene Bitte, damit die Zuschauer ruhig würden:

> Waszmosc sie juz uspokójcie,
> A rzeczy pilno słuchajcie.
> A chcac Waszmosc miec czujniejsze
> I tez w słuchaniu pilniejsze
> Bêdziem uzywac spiewania,
> Które Waszmosc budzic bêdzie
> Miêdzy wierszykami wszêdzie.
> (Die Herrschaften werden gebeten schön ruhig zu sein. Hören Sie fleißig zu, wir möchten, daß Sie wachsamer seien und beim Hören fleißiger seien, wir werden das Singen benutzen, damit Sie in allen Strophen wach bleiben.)[33]

In der Fassung vom Anfang des 17. Jhs., finden wir das Verlangen, wie sich das Publikum benehmen sollte, strikter: Niemand darf angetrunken sein: *Tylko tu zaden nie badz pijany*.[34]

Die alltägliche Realität widersprach sich in dem Stück an vielen Orten. Die jüdischen Erzpriester *Kaiphas* und *Annas* betitelten *Pilatus* als

Starosta. Dieser Titel und dieses Amt war nur in Böhmen und in Polen bekannt. *Starosta* war ein Vertreter des Königs, der eine Verwaltungskraft auf einem Gebiet hatte und der als *brachium regale* von Juristen bezeichnet wurde.[35] *Pilaks*, einer von den Grabwächtern, charakterisierte seine Gesellen als *Hajducy, Junacy*. Diese zwei Termini bedeuten sehr brave Soldaten. Er betitelte die Erzpriester als Bischöfe.[36] Die Szene der Bewachung des Heiligen Grabes ging dem Geschmack des "breiten Publikums" entgegen. Die Grabwächter, die geschwätzig und stolz waren, konnten ohne Schwierigkeiten mit dem Adel assoziert werden. Die Osterspiele wurden in den Städten aufgeführt.[37] In dieser Szene kam auch das Nationalbewußtsein zum Wort. Einer der Wächter, *Tereon*, der vermutlich Deutscher ist, hat Probleme mit der Formulierung und Äußerung seiner Gedanken:[38]

> Uram gazda! Rata! Przebóg! [...]
> Wos ist dos, mayn herr Pilaksie,
> Czemu go wy tak wołacie?[39]

Zu interessanten Schlußfolgerungen kann man kommen, wenn die Hinweise für den Regisseur dieses Stückes — *Do tego, który by sprawował tê historyja* — genauer analysiert werden. Sie schaffen die Möglichkeit der Verkürzung des Textes.[40] Vermutlich wurde diese Änderung durch die Reaktion des Publikums verursacht.

Es soll hier die Frage gestellt werden, wie breit der Wirkungsbereich der polnischen Osterspiele sein konnte. Aus allen polnischen Territorien stammt nur eine *[sic!]* Nachricht über die Aufführung des Spiels. 1377 fand in Kazimierz (damals eine Stadt bei Krakau, heute ein Stadtviertel von Krakau) das *ludus pascalis* statt. Im Ratsbuch wurde die Nachricht über eine Unterstützung notiert: *Nota quantum domini consules super civitatem exposuerunt [...] Item dederunt VI gr[ossos] pro iuvamine ludi pascalis domini.*[41]

Einen Pol bilden die ziemlich allgemeinen Formen wie Passionspiele oder liturgische Dramen, und auf dem anderen befinden sich Überlieferungen der Elegienkomödie und der humanistischen Komödie. Der wichtigste Unterschied zwischen beiden Komödien liegt in ihrer Entstehungszeit (Elegienkomödie in 12. Jhd.; humanistische Komödie in der Frührenaissanceperiode). Auch funktionierten sie anders unter den damaligen Empfängern. In beiden jedoch wird dieselbe erotische Thematik behandelt.[42] Das Theaterwesen dieser Stücke bleibt bis heute in der Wissenschaft offen.[43] Die Analyse der Überlieferungen gibt dem Forscher noch andere Schwierigkeiten zu überwinden. Alle Überlieferungen dieser Art werden in *Codices* aufbewahrt, die anderen umfassen nicht selten sehr diverse Texte. Viele von diesen Handschriften, die Texte der Komödien enthalten, wurden während der Studien ihrer Besitzer (natürlich nicht Autoren) geschrieben, deshalb ist es nicht leicht zu beurteilen, ob das Publikum dieser Stücke als Zuschauer oder als Leser behandelt wurde.

Schon Rolf Bergmann[44] bewies, daß die Form und das Aussehen der Handschrift von ihrer Benutzung zeugt. Da diese Texte häufig zahlreiche Glossen haben, kann man sie auch erforschen und anhand der Ergebnisse zum Schluß kommen.[45] Man sollte auch veranlassen zu erforschen, welche "Umgebung" die Texte der Elegienkomödie haben. Zu weiterer Analyse werden zwei schlesische und eine Krakauer Handschrift verwendet. Alle entstanden in der Zeit der Frührenaissance (Wende des 15. und 16. Jhs.), und in allen befinden sich sowohl die Texte der Komödie als auch literarische Werke von *moderni* und *antiqui*. Die erste Handschrift[46] wurde in der zweiten Hälfte des 15. Jhs. bis zur ersten Hälfte des 16. Jhs. geschrieben. Sie enthält den Text von *Poliscene*, deren Verfasser Leonardo Aretino Bruno war. Diese Komödie war in jener Zeit sehr populär — heute kennt die Wissenschaft siebenundzwanzig Handschriften, davon sieben polnische, und bis 1519 wurde sie fünfzehnmal gedruckt.[47] Die Glossen im Breslauer Exemplar geben leider keine Hinweise über die Ausstattung und die Bewegung, sondern bringen Bemerkungen über die Eigenschaften der Komödie: sie wurde *stilo satirico* geschrieben, und stellte menschliche Schwächen und Mangel wie "luxus et alia insolentia" dar.[48] Eine der zahlreichen Glossen bringt die "Quasi-Definition" der Komödie: *Unde comedia est fabula dicta....*[49] Diese Anmerkungen konnte nur ein kultivierter, gut ausgebildeter Mensch schreiben. Aber was wußte er vom Theater? Sah er vielleicht irgendeine Aufführung? Oder war der Besitzer nur Leser? In diesem Text findet man einen wichtigen Hinweis: *dramatis personae* sind als *persone introducte* bezeichnet,[50] was natürlich nur über die Möglichkeit der Inszenierung zeugen *konnte*. Um diese Stücke zu inszenieren, sollte man ein gutes Wissen über das Theater und die Bühne haben. Eine Spur führt zur Lektüre, eine andere zur Universität.

An der Jagelloner Universität hielt 1451 Andrzej Grzymała von Posen einen Vortrag über Theater, Tragödie, Komödie, und die Unterschiede der beiden Gattungen, über die Bühne und den Dialog. Als Vorlage für diese Vorlesung wurde *Poliscene* gebraucht.[51] Unter vielen verschiedenen Kommentaren befinden sich auch solche, die erklären, wie die Eigenschaften der Helden ihren Namen entsprechen. Der Student notierte u. a. auch ein kostbares Beispiel der damaligen Gelehrsamkeit:

> Gurgulio Parasitus denominatus est a "gurgulione" quod est piscis, nam sicut ille piscis dictus Gurgulio habet magnam et latam gulam ad escam accipiendam, ita iste seruus erat gulosus et leccacitati deditus propter quam lenocinium faciebat solum ut ventrem repleuit.[52]

Ähnlich wurden alle anderen Personen charaktisiert. Noch interessanter sind die Fragmente, in denen die Eigenschaften der Komödie vom Professor erklärt wurden:

> Comedia vero est villanus cantus vel villana laus, que tractat de rusticalibus rebus, id est comedia fabula composita de despectibus hominum privatorum. Et poete, qui tales comedias canebant, vocati sunt poete comici. [...] Item Tragedie stilo humili [!], Comedie alto [!] describuntur.[53]

Diese Feststellungen klingen sehr ähnlich wie die in der Breslauer Handschrift. Der Inhalt der beiden Handschriften ist für die Lektüre der damaligen intellektuellen Elite typisch. Die Krakauer Handschrift enthält u. a. *Liber satrarum Iuvenalis*, Werke von Persius und Tragödien von Seneca; hier ist *Poliscene* als *Comedia noua* (d.h. humanistische) bezeichnet.[54] Die Handschrift IV F 68 umfaßt *Epistolae* und *Carmina* aus dem ersten Buch von Horaz. Es gibt auch hier die *Ecloga prima* von Vergil und *Bellum Catilinae* von Sallust. Viele dieser Werke hatten Glossen. Die zweite schlesische Handschrift stammt aus dem Kloster der Breslauer Dominikaner und entstand 1515. Sie enthält die Überlieferung von *Aulularia* des Plautus.[55] In diesem Text ist es leicht, die Verteilung in Rollen zu beobachten. Die ersten zwei oder drei Buchstaben der Personennamen sind — als Initialen — größer oder wurden mit anderer Tinte geschrieben.[56] Aber für die Forscher ist der interessanteste Text betitelt *De Comedia Collecta*. Zu dem Kreise der Probleme, die für die Tragödien interessant sind, gehört u. a. *fragilitas hominorum*; dagegen *Comedia est private similibus factis sint peracta*.[57] Beide Gattungen wurden in verschiedenen Stilen geschrieben: "comedia [...] in mediocro stilo [...] tragedia [...] altissimo stilo."[58] Schon aus diesen Fragmenten ist es leicht festzustellen, daß das Publikum der Komödie die spezifische "Sprache" des Theaters verstanden hatte. Für es bildeten die szenischen Werke eine wichtige Lektüre, die vielen verschiedenen (ästhetischen, moralischen und wissenschaftlichen) Zwecken dienten. Aber der Anteil dieses Publikums am Mitschaffen des szenischen Lebens war bescheiden. Es äußerte seine Reaktionen selten und diese waren eher "Rezensionen von Kritikern". So war es 1500, als Laurentius Corvinus Rabe mit seinen Schülern in Breslau die Komödie *Eunuchus* von Terenz aufgeführt hatte. Die eingeladenen Domherrn schätzten sein Talent hoch. Diese Aufführung wurde in *Acta Capituli* wie folgend notiert:

> 1500. febr. 28. fer. VI Eodem die scientificus vir magister Laurentius Rabe rector scholae sanctae Elizabeth invitavit d[omi]nos ad comediam Terentii secundum Eunuchi, quam ludere velit proxima dominica carnisprivii in aula praetoriana cum suis scholaribus. Commendata est opera viri doctissimi; d[omi]ni eant qui vellint pro honore illius...[59]

Zwei Jahre später führte Corvinus die Komödie von Plautus auf, und nochmals übernahmen die Domherrn die Rolle der Kritiker.[60]

Am Ende sollen einige Schlußfolgerungen formuliert werden. Der Anteil des Publikums teilweise als Zuschauer, teilweise als Leser hängt vor allem von der Gattung ab. Reger und fast unkontrollierbar war er bei den

Inszenierungen der Osterspiele, beschränkt bei den Inszenierungen der liturgischen Dramen. Die Empfänger der humanistischen Komödien und der Elegienkomödien waren Kenner der Literatur und des Theaters. Im Gegensatz aber gaben ungebildete Schichten der Gesellschaft, die ganz und gar nichts vom Theater wußten, einen viel größeren Beitrag zu aktiver Rezeption, als die kultivierten Empfänger, die den Text erklärten und kommentierten. Jedoch trugen beide Gruppen zur Entwicklung der mittelalterlichen Bühne bei.

NOTES

[1] So definiert Michał Głowinski *literarisches Publikum* [in:] *Słownik Terminów Literackich [Das Wörterbuch der literarischen Begriffe]* pod red. Janusza Sławinskiego, 2. wyd. popr. i uzup. (Wrocław: Ossolineum, 1988), 416-417. Die Diskussion über den Begriff *literarisches Publikum* und seine Rolle gehört heute zu den wichtigsten Forschungsproblemen der polnischen Literaturwissenschaft. Einen anregenden Beitrag brachten hier sowie die Studien der damaligen sowjetischen Semiotiker (Jurij Lotman u. a.) als auch der amerikanischen Soziologen (Amitai Etzioni) mit. Man soll hier erwähnen, daß zu den wichtigsten polnischen Forschern dieser Problematik gehören: Stefan Zółkiewski, Janusz Sławinski, Krzysztof Dmitruk, und Janusz Lalewicz.

[2] Vgl. Krzysztof Dmitruk, "Wprowadzenie do teorii publicznosci literackiej" ["Einführung zur Theorie des literarischen Publikums"], [in:] *Publicznosc literacka* pod red. Stefana Zółkiewskiego i Maryli Hopfinger (Wrocław: Ossolineum, 1982), 21, Anmerkung 1.

[3] Dmitruk, "Wprowadzenie," 47; vgl. auch Maurice Descotes, *Le public de théâtre et son histoire* (Paris, 1964).

[4] Krzysztof Dmitruk, "Problemy publicznosci literackiej w dawnej Polsce" ["Die Problematik des literarischen Publikums im früheren Polen"], [in:] *Publicznosc literacka i teatralna w dawnej Polsce* pod red. Hanny Dziechcinskiej (Warszawa-Łódz: Panstwowe Wydawnictwo Naukowe (weiter: PWN), 1985), 15-16; dieser Forscher benutzt hier den Begriff *wspólnota znakowa [Zeichengemeinschaft]*.

[5] Julian Lewanski, "Dramat i dramatyzacje liturgiczne w sredniowieczu polskim" ["Das Drama und liturgische Dramatisierungen im polnischen Mittelalter,"] *Musica Medii Aevi* 1 (1965), 161. Die umfangreiche kritische Ausgabe der altpolnischen Stücke ist: *Dramaty Staropolskie. Antologia* [Altpolnische Dramen. Antologie], hrsg. von Julian Lewanski, Bd. 1-6 (Warszawa: PWN, 1959-63). Eine ausführliche Charakteristik der Gattungen ist [in:] *Sredniowieczne gatunki dramatyczno-teatralne*, oprac. Julian Lewanski [Die mittelalterlichen dramatisch-theatralischen Gattungen, bearb. von Julian Lewanski], Heft 1 Dramat liturgiczny [Das liturgische Drama], Heft 2 Komedia elegijna [Die Elegienkomödie], Heft 3 Misterium [Das Oster- und Passionspiel] (Wrocław-Kraków-Warszawa: Ossolineum, 1966-69) zu finden.

[6] Vgl. *Sredniowieczne gatunki*, Heft 1, 11.

[7] Der Unterschied zwischen diversen Arten von *Visitatio Sepulchri* wurde zum ersten Mal von Carl Lange, *Die lateinischen Osterfeiern*, (München, 1887)

durchgeführt. In der "ersten Art" treten nur drei Marien auf, in der "zweiten Art" erscheinen auch die Apostel und in der "dritten Art" spricht der auferstande Christus mit Marie Magdalene; vgl. auch Julian Lewanski, *Dramat i teatr sredniowiecza i renesansu w Polsce* [*Das Drama und das Theater im Mittelalter und in der Renaissance in Polen*] (Warszawa: PWN, 1981), 63.

[8] Lewanski, *Dramat i teatr*; die Auswahl der polnischen Texte von *Visitatio Sepulchri* ist [in:] Dramaty Staropolskie, Bd. 1, 98-121 zu finden.

[9] *Agenda secundum cursum et rubricam Ecclesie Cathedralis Posnaniensis*, (Lipsiae, M. Lotter 1533). Hier wurde das Exemplar aus der Bibliothek zu Kórnik, Sign. Cim. Qu 2953, benutzt. Die gegenwärtige Ausgabe [in:] *Dramaty Staropolskie*, Bd. 1, 118-121.

[10] Bibliothek zu Kórnik, Sign. Cim. Qu 2953, Fol. 45r.

[11] Lewanski, *Dramat i teatr*, 61; über die Relativität der Auffassung der Zeit im Mittelalter schreibt ausführlich: Bronisław Geremek, "Wyobraznia czasowa polskiego dziejopisarstwa sredniowiecznego" ["Die Einbildungskraft der polnischen mittelalterlichen Annalistik,"] *Studia Zródłoznawcze. Commentationes* 22 (1977), 1-17.

[12] Bibliothek zu Kórnik, Sign. Cim. Qu 2953, Fol. 44v-45r; über diesen Wechsel vgl. *Sredniowieczne gatunki*, Heft 1, 70.

[13] Vgl. die Bemerkungen von Heinz Kindermann, *Theatergeschichte Europas*, Bd. 1-10 (Salzburg: Otto Müller Verlag, 1957-72), Bd. 1: 62.

[14] Vgl. *Sredniowieczne gatunki*, Heft 1, 69-70.

[15] Diese Hinweise befinden sich in der Überlieferung aus dem Posener Heilige-Marie-Magdalene-Kapitel, von 1562. Sie wurden von Julian Lewanski [in:] Dramaty Staropolskie, Bd. 1, 153-159 und [in:] "Dramat i dramatyzacje liturgiczne w sredniowieczu polskim," 132-133 herausgegeben. Vgl. auch Piotr Bering, "Sztuka aktorska i re¿yserska w swietle przekazów sredniowiecznych i staropolskich" ["Schauspieler- und Regiekunst im Spiegel der mittelalterlichen und altpolnischen Testimonien,"] *Symbolae Philologorum Posnaniensium Graecae et Latinae* 10 (1994), 133.

[16] Bibliothek der Bernhardiner zu Krakau, Hs. Sign. 18/RL, Fol. 38-40; herausgegeben von Julian Lewanski [in:] "Dramat i dramatyzacje liturgiczne w sredniowieczu polskim," 134-135; vgl. auch *Sredniowieczne gatunki*, Heft 1, 42-43; Lewanski, *Dramat i teatr*, 34-36, wo er ausführlich diese Fassung analysiert.

[17] Lewanski, *Dramat i teatr*, 35.

[18] Zenon Modzelewski, "Estetyka sredniowiecznego dramatu liturgicznego (Cykl Wielkiego Tygodnia w Polsce)" ["Die Ästhethik des mittelalterlichen liturgischen Dramas (Zyklus von der Karwoche in Polen),"] *Roczniki Humanistyczne* 12, Heft 1 (1964), 24-30.

[19] Modzelewski, "Estetyka sredniowiecznego," 40-41.

[20] Vgl. Modzelewski, "Estetyka sredniowiecznego," 40.

[21] Hier werden die Forschungsergebnisse von Eduard Hartl, *Das Drama des Mittelalters*, 2. Aufl., Bd. 1-2 (Darmstadt: Wissenschaftliche Buchgesellschaft, 1969), Bd. 2, Osterspiele benutzt. Dort befindet sich auch die moderne kritische Edition der handschriftlichen Überlieferung. Mit dieser Thematik befaßte sich auch Joseph Klapper, "Das mittelalterliche Volksschauspiel in Schlesien," *Mitteilungen der Schlesischen Gesellschaft für Volkskunde* 29 (1928), 181-183.

[22] Vgl. Edition [in:] Hartl, *Das Drama des Mittelalters*, Bd. 2, 101, Zeilen 718-721.

[23] Vgl. Heinz Kindermann, *Das Theaterpublikum des Mittelalters*, (Salzburg: Otto Müller Verlag, 1980), 19-26.

[24] Hartl, *Das Drama des Mittelalters,* Bd. 2, 74-75, Zeilen 1-2, 13-17, 23-24.

[25] Zeilen 4-5; vgl. Kindermann, *Das Theaterpublikum*, 27.

[26] Z. B. Zeilen 171-173, 199-200; vgl. Hartl, *Das Drama des Mittelalters*, Bd. 1, Sein Wesen und sein Werden. Osterfeiern, 72; Lewanski, *Dramat i teatr*, 144.

[27] Zeilen 17, 52, 58, 90, 104, 132, 138; Vgl. Hartl, Bd. 1, 88.

[28] Vgl. Kindermann, *Das Theaterpublikum*, 30.

[29] Über Struktur der Osterspiele, und ihre Merkmale, deren Bündnisse manchmal mit der Liturgie, oder in anderen Fällen mit dem Drama größere sind, schreibt Johan Nowé, "Kult oder Drama? Zur Struktur einiger Osterspiele des deutschen Mittelalters," [in:] *The Theatre in the Middle Ages*, ed. by Herman Braet, Johan Nowé, Gilbert Tournoy (Leuven: Leuven University Press, 1985), 269-313.

[30] Der polnische Titel: *Historyja o Chwalebnym Zmartwychwstaniu Panskim* ist hier in der deutschsprachigen Form nach Kindermann, *Das Theaterpublikum*, 250 zitiert. Das, vermutlich, einzige Exemplar der Ausgabe von 1590(?) befindet sich in der Bibliothek zu Kórnik, Sign. Cim. O. 496. Es war als Vorlage für moderne Editionen gedacht.

[31] Zeilen 1-4; vgl. die beste polnische Edition: *Historyja o Chwalebnym Zmartwychwstaniu Panskim*, oprac. Jan Okon (Wrocław-Kraków: Ossolineum, 1971), 8.

[32] "Ostatek sami osadzcie, / Jesli nie tak jest na swiecie, / Co my tu bêdziem spominac, / Nad Pismo swiête przyczyniac" — Zeilen 105-109.

[33] Zeilen 115-122; der Titel *Waszmosc* (Herrschaften) wurde nur durch den Adel gebraucht. Hier wird er für alle Zuschauer benutzt, um den feierlichen Aspekt der Rede zu unterstreichen — wie Okon richtig bemerkt, [in:] *Historyja*, 14 (Anmerkung).

[34] *Historyja*, 128, Zeile 90; über verschiedene Redaktionen sieh — ebenda, LXI-LXXXIV, v. a. LXVI.

[35] Juliusz Bardach, Bogusław Lesnodorski, Michał Pietrzak, *Historia panstwa i prawa polskiego*, 4. wyd. popr. i uzup. [Geschichte des polnischen Staates und polnischen Rechts, 4. verb. und erg. Ausgabe] (Warszawa: PWN, 1985), 101-102.

[36] Vgl. *Historyja*, Zeilen 183-189.

[37] Vgl. Bemerkungen von Hartl, *Das Drama des Mittelalters*, Bd. 1, 100; auch im polnischen Stück *Kupiec [Der Kaufmann]* von Mikołaj Rej wird der Adel sehr kritisch dargestellt — vgl. die Ausgabe [in:] *Dramaty Staropolskie*, Bd. 1, 508, Zeilen 207-220 und 545-552, Zeilen 7418-7577.

[38] Lewanski, *Dramat i teatr*, 174.

[39] *Historyja*, Zeilen 351, 369-370; die ganze Szene wurde von Zeile 348 bis zu Zeile 390 geschrieben.

[40] Vgl. *Historyja*, 6-7.

[41] Staatsarchiv in Krakau, Akta miasta Kazimierza 1335-1802, Sign. K. 1, 202; veröffentlicht von Adam Chmiel, *Ksiêgi radzieckie Kazimierskie 1369-1381 i 1385-1402 [Die Ratsbücher zu Kazimierz 1369-1381 und 1385-1402]* (Kraków: Wydawnictwo Archiwum Akt Dawnych Miasta Krakowa, 1932). Diese Nachricht veröffentlicht und analysiert zum ersten Mal Stanisław Windakiewicz, "Dramat liturgiczny w Polsce sredniowiecznej" ["Das liturgische Drama im mittelalterlichen Polen,"] *Rozprawy i Sprawozdania Akademii Umiejêtnosci. Wydział Filologiczny* 34 (1902), 355-356; vgl. auch Kindermann, *Das Theaterpublikum*, 250.

[42] Vgl. Lewanski, *Dramat i teatr*, 95-96, 101-102.

[43] Hier soll die Geschichte der Diskussion nicht analysiert werden. Die neueren Studien, die u. a. den Stand der Diskussion zusammenfassen: Ludwig Braun, "Die 'dramatische' Technik des Vitalis von Bloi und sein Verhältnis zu seinen Quellen," [in:] *The Theatre in the Middle Ages*, 60-83; Sandro Sticca, "Sacred drama and tragic realism in Hrotswitha's Paphnutius," [in:] *The Theatre in the Middle Ages*, 12-44; vgl. auch Stichwort 'Elegienkomödie' (bearbeitet von Michele Feo) [in:] *Lexikon des Mittelalters*, Bd. 1-5 (München-Zürich: Artemis Verlag, 1980-91), Bd. 3: 1796-1797, wo weitere Literatur gegeben wird. Die besten polnischen Arbeiten aus diesem Bereich sind: *Sredniowieczne gatunki*, Heft 2 und Julian Lewanski, "Penetracje antyku do sredniowiecznej kultury teatralnej (Na przykładzie losów komedii "Pamphilus" z XII wieku)" ["Die antiken Einflüsse auf die mittelalterliche Theaterkultur (nach dem Beispiel von dem Schicksal der Komödie "Pamphilus" aus dem 12. Jhd.),"] [in:] *Sredniowiecze. Studia o kulturze*, Bd. 1-4 (Warszawa: PWN; ab Bd. 2 Wrocław-Warszawa-Kraków: Ossolineum, 1961-69), Bd. 1: 239-262.

[44] Rolf Bergmann, "Aufführungstext und Lesetext," [in:] *The Theatre in the Middle Ages*, 314-329.

[45] Diese Methode benutzt Lewanski, "Penetracje," 251, 252, 260.

[46] Universitätsbibliothek zu Breslau, Sign. IV F 68.

[47] Julian Lewanski, "Wykład o teatrze w Krakowskiej Akademii w 1451 roku" ["Die Vorlesung über das Theater an der Krakauer Akademie im Jahre 1451,"] [in:] *Pogranicza i konteksty literatury polskiego sredniowiecza*, pod. red. Teresy Michałowskiej (Warszawa: PWN, 1989), 320; A. Stäuble, *La commedia umanistica del Quatrocento* (Firenze, 1968), 271-274.

[48] Universitätsbibliothek zu Breslau, Sign. IV F 68, Fol. 25v.; zum ersten Mal von dieser Handschrift unterrichtete Lewanski, "Wykład," 321. Vgl. auch Bering, "Sztuka aktorska," 131.

[49] Universitätsbibliothek zu Breslau, Sign. IV F 68, Fol. 25v.

[50] Wie oben.

[51] Lewanski, "Wykład," 321-326. Der Forscher benutzte die Handschrift aus der Czartoryski-Bibliothek zu Krakau, Sign. 1315.

[52] Lewanski, "Wykład," 328.

[53] Lewanski, "Wykład," 327.

[54] Lewanski, "Wykład," 323, 331.

[55] Universitätsbibliothek zu Breslau, Sign. IV F 36, Fol. 211-227v.

[56] Vgl. Anmerkungen von Bergmann, "Aufführungstext," 314-318.

[57] Universitätsbibliothek zu Breslau, Sign. IV F 36, Fol. 78.

[58] Wie oben.

[59] Vgl. *Acta capituli Wratislaviensis 1500-1562*. Die Sitzungsprotokolle des Breslauer Domkapitels in der ersten Hälfte des 16. Jahrhunderts, bearb. von Alfred Sabisch, Bd. 1-2 (Köln-Wien: Boehlau Verlag, 1972-76), Bd. 1, 1500-1516, Hlbd. 1, 1500-1513: 10.

[60] *Acta capituli Wartislaviensis*, Bd. 1, Hlbd. 1, 84.

Polnische Akademie der Wissenschaften
Bibliothek zu Kórnik, Poznan

Approaches to Medieval Translation in the Iberian Peninsula: Glosses and Amplifications

Roxana Recio

It is well known how important glosses and amplifications were for medieval education. When dealing with glosses in Spain, Francisco Rico's remarks to Chenu in relation to medieval pedagogy come immediately to mind: it is based on reading the classics, but also on commentary about them. There is no doubt that, even outside the classroom, texts would be circulated with glosses.[1] Both glosses and amplifications are a typically medieval tool.

This paper will be concerned with the role played by glosses and amplifications in translations written in the Iberian Peninsula during the fifteenth century. Before I proceed, it is necessary to clarify two things. First of all, this study, although focused on the fifteenth century, will make reference to other periods. Second, it will analyze only characteristics related to translation, rather than being engaged in poetic tradition or literary theory in general.[2] The concepts of gloss and amplification will be seen from the point of view of translation theory and practice.

Julian Weiss has already shown how significant translations were in literature with didactic purposes, and in some texts with commentary. Throughout the fifteenth century, glossed texts, especially those translating from a document originally written in Latin, were very common. This can be perceived in authors such as López de Ayala, Cartagena, Villena, Fray Alonso de Cristóbal and Gómez García del Castillo, among others.[3]

This fact did not pertain only to teaching or explanatory purposes. In some instances glosses would embellish a particular text, highlighting images and offering psychological explanations.[4] With respect to the field of translation, the act of glossing a text or amplifying concepts was related to two essential factors. The first was the contempt many translators felt towards the vernacular language in comparison to Latin. Romance languages, since they originated from Latin, were automatically considered inferior. Because Latin was regarded as a perfect language and the origin of all Romance languages, other non-Latin languages would be perceived as imperfect and lacking the linguistic subtleties that would enable them to express some Latin concepts. Therefore, any Romance language, including Castilian, would need long explanations when serving as a vehicle to express Latin concepts. Peter Russell has documented this fact extensively.[5] In his work Russell provides several examples, such as Cartagena, as well as other prominent latinists, like Alfonso de Palencia. However, this attitude toward the vernacular and Latin is found not only among latinists and translation scholars, but was also shared by the most famous poets of that time in Castile. As an example, after pointing out that Homer's work was initially translated into Latin and that he made his Castilian translation from the Latin, Juan de Mena, in the prologue to his translation of the *Iliada,* says:

> Such a work [Homer's *Iliad*] all Latin grammar and even Latin eloquence could barely comprehend, and contain in themselves the heroic chants of the foretelling poet Homer. Then, what else the rough and deserted romance cannot do! For this reason it will happen to the Homeric *Iliad* as to the sweet and tasty fruits at the end of the Summer, that with the first rain they are damaged and with the second they are lost. Therefore, this work will receive two offenses: its use in the Latin translation and, the most damaging and the most serious, in the Romance interpretation that I intend to provide.[6]

Mena will make it even more explicit with the following words:

> And for this reason [the imperfection of Castilian language], very powerful master, I arranged not to interpret twenty-four books, which are the extent of the *Iliad*, but to summarize briefly.[...] And I left it off so as not to damage or offend his prominent work, by bringing it down to the humble and low Romance language.[7]

Juan de Mena follows Cartagena in accepting that Latin's *dulzura* (literally sweetness) is inevitably lost in the romance language, as the latter said himself in his *Rhetorica*.[8]

In addition to Mena, the same attitude can be found in the Marquis de Santillana. This author, while admitting his poor knowledge of Latin, agrees with his son:

> I know very well now that, as has already happened to me with you and with some others, you will say that Latin words and terms keep and retain in themselves ... sweetness or gracefulness. [...] Because it would be difficult now that, after quite a number of years and not less hardship, I might desire or prepare myself to struggle with Latin, as Tullius declares that Cato (from Utica, I think) learned the Greek letters when he was eighty years old; but Cato was unique and singular among the human lineage in this and many other things. And, since we cannot have what we want to have, let us want what we can have. And, if we lack the form, let us be content with the subject matters.[9]

Santillana, as we can see, also speaks about Latin "sweetness" and, furthermore, he introduces the second determining factor for the use of glosses above mentioned; that is, the superficial knowledge that many scholars of the time had of classical languages, especially Latin. This insight is important because the circumstances gave origin to obscure vernacular translations requiring additional explanation. In the intellectual scene of the time there are several testimonies of limitations with respect to Latin. A clear example is Fernán Pérez de Guzmán, who in a letter to Gonzalo de Ocaña says:

> It is true that I sometimes read that book composed by the Holy Pope and glorious doctor Saint Gregory, which is the above-mentioned *Diálogos*. As it is written in Latin, because of some obscure words and high style in it, I could not understand it clearly in order to obtain from it all the fruit I desire.[10]

Pero Guillén de Segovia shares this same frustration when speaking about *la Gaya Ciencia*:

> It was written in Latin and in such an elevated style that few readers can draw out true sentences from its assertions.[11]

As it is well known, it was common among latinists to display difficult and obscure texts, addressed only to the cultural elites. It is for this attitude that López de Ayala calls latinists "wise men" in his introduction to *Las Flores de los Morales de Job*. Those wise men:

> Made their writings hard and they used difficult words and even obscure, so that men would read them many times, retain them better and better appreciate them, the more hardships they experienced with them. Because what is won with harder work, is held in greater appreciation.[12]

Authors like López de Ayala, Cartagena and Palencia follow in their translations the philosophical line dictated by those "wise men."

This closed attitude may be contrasted with Saint Jerome's ideas on translation. Several years ago Margherita Morreale spoke of a liberal current sponsored by the saint, which is undeniable if we consider the history of translation in Spain. Saint Jerome refers to "sensum exprimere de sensu" (Saint Jérome 3: 59).[13] His interest was directed to the meaning, rather than the words. The ideas expressed in the original text were the most important thing. For Saint Jerome, the true translator is the one who is capable of understanding in his own language the meaning of the text that he is translating. This position is reflected in the paragraph that Santillana addresses to his son, since he grants much more relevance to the "matter" than to the "form." However, Santillana's attitude toward the inferiority of the romance language eliminates the possibility of an eloquent Castilian translation that could truly be worthy of the original.

As the fifteenth century advances, there is a tendency to eliminate the obscurity from texts and to make translations more clear and familiar for less-educated readers. Within this context some of Enrique de Villena's statements should be reevaluated, since they anticipate some of the new ideas that will later succeed. Many of Villena's techniques have been deemed failures by later scholars. However, translators in some way needed to provide for that lack of "sweetness and grace", that is, the Latin eloquence, because, in Alfonso de Palencia's words, in translations "witty things turn vulgar, and very vivid things faint completely".[14] It is precisely this attempt to follow Saint Jerome without breaking with the authority of latinists that glosses and amplifications are widely used in translations. More and more there is a compulsory need to render translations more intelligible; in other words, clear, familiar and closer to the reader in the Iberian Peninsula.

The use of glosses and amplifications is related to the kind of translation that is undertaken. The new issue here is whether translations adhere to or depart from the original; in other words, whether they are literal or free translations.

In relation to those two types of translation, the best-known document that has survived is Alfonso de Madrigal's preface to his *Tostado sobre Eusebio* (around 1450). "El Tostado," as he was called, distinguished between interpretation, that is, translation close to the original, and gloss, a translation that allows changes, additions and omissions and is "suited for lesser talents." As I have demonstrated elsewhere, this distinction is totally artificial and serves as an act of respect to latinists and their fidelity to the original.[15] When closely examining Madrigal's argumentation on his idea of beauty in translation, it is not difficult to find contradictions. I have already pointed out that, unlike Cartagena, Madrigal wanted a translation that would be "hermosa" (beautiful) in the target language. By that term he only meant that it had to adapt to the codes and rules governing the target language and its culture. The language of the translation (the text being adapted to a code which is different from the code generating the original) becomes the main concern. Thus, the work being translated was considered a separated world and, for that reason, all changes necessary for this transfer are accepted, including among them relevant amplifications and explanations. They become part of the translation framework, which granted translators much more freedom to display their text.[16]

In the Iberian Peninsula two main currents on translation can be distinguished throughout the fifteenth century. The first current advanced more in Aragon. There some translations that are close to the original, were written independently, so to speak, without glosses and amplifications. Examples of this are the translations of Boccaccio's *Fiammetta* and Diego de San Pedro's *Cárcel de amor*. Of course, in translations from one romance language to another, this method is favored because of their linguistic resemblance. Nevertheless, there are other translations departing much more from the original, such as the anonymous Catalan version of the *Decameron* (1429). Other cases worth mentioning are the comments and paraphrases of Dante's *Commedia* in Catalan. Even though works on Dante have not been seriously studied, a very important author for translation techniques is Jaume Ferrer de Blanes, who wrote some comments highlighting the Christian ideology of some passages in the *Commedia*. But what is significant here is the way he does it: his exegesis is totally free, since his recreations are the most relevant part. The recreations sometimes show a clear regionalist character, and there is an obvious attempt to render the original text, and Dante himself, familiar and notorious.

Perhaps these special cases, following the original closely, are possible in Aragon because of the long tradition beginning with the religious preachers, which influenced historians like Antoni Canals and later influenced literary works such as Isabel de Villena's *Vita Christi*.[17] In Villena's case, her explanations about the life of Christ relate not only to matters of translation, amplification or gloss, or to the use of Latin in the structure of a composition in romance, but also to the use of familiar language directed to a very specific audience.

The second current develops especially in Castile, where, in spite of Madrigal's ideas, the authority of latinists prevails and Saint Jerome's views were not really accepted. Among Castilian texts, glosses and amplifications predominate, based on some precepts of how to translate prose and verse.

However, this situation evolves throughout the fifteenth century. Over time there was a growing acceptance of Saint Jerome's perspective in Castile, even among translators of Latin works. Russell provides an example of this. He informs us that the prince of Viana invokes the saint in defense of his translation on Aristotle's *Ética*, which was based on Bruni's Latin version.[18] During this evolving process, glosses and amplifications either move to the background, become part of the translation itself, or just disappear in Castilian texts. Glosses retained their function as explanations, and are often incorporated in the translations.

Enrique de Villena's glosses in his version of the *Eneida* figure among those that are an integral part of the translation. An example of this is the beginning of Chapter 23 of the Second Book, with the title "Do cuenta eneas como el rey priamo tomo armas para se defender:"

> If you demand to know Priam's fate and wonder what he did on that occasion, I certify that, having seen his city taken, the Trojan building demolished, and the enemies inside the fortress, because of his age he was shaking. He took his abandoned arms which long ago he had left; he wore his sword with effort, although he could not strike with it, and he put on his arms and left seeking and daring to die among the numerous enemies.[19]

The gloss corresponding to this paragraph begins in this fashion:

> *If you demand,* etc. Meaning: "If you, queen, have stopped asking other things and you want to know mainly what happened to Priam at the height of his misfortune and how he reacted in such a moment when it was necessary to show the biggest courage." Aeneas said this with dignity,

> assuming that the judicious queen wanted to know Priam's conduct more than all other things occurring later. And that word *fate (hados)* is understood as the cause that his constellation brought him to that end and result. And as the one who paid very good attention to it says and certifies, being also sure about it, the above-mentioned Priam, having seen that decay, Troy being defeated and taken by enemies, demolished its solemn buildings and its fortress, captured by enemies without hope of retrieval, wanted to show his courage as the one who did not expect anything other than captivity or death, notwithstanding his old age and the weakening of his strength; he was over eighty-nine years old, as can be inferred from the chronicles speaking of him.[20]

Villena's explanations are part of his translation, as can be seen with this example. In that sense, translation and glosses are closely united; they form a common entity. If we consider the anonymous Catalan translation of *I Trionfi*, it is clear that the verse lines are kept in Italian while the exegetic text is a translation of Illicino's comments. In this case glosses are not an integral part of translation, since it is totally independent of the translator's personal commentary on the text he is translating. Its difference, with respect to Villena's text, rests on the close relationship between translation and explanation, with the same style by the same author. It must be emphasized that glosses are perceived more and more as an explanatory complement of the text, while amplification became a system that, not being necessarily explanatory, had an embellishing function which was based frequently on repetition.[21]

By the end of the century, the Castilian translation of the *Decamerón*, following the same method as the Catalan version from the first half of the century, offers an interesting example. Here some Castilian songs are added instead of Italian songs, and some stories are incorporated with other omissions and considerable changes. Amplifications are so numerous that, when this translation has been published in the twentieth-century, the editor has "corrected" it with some paragraphs from modern versions of Boccaccio's text. These approaches to medieval translations, with a preconceived idea of what constitutes a good rendition, have no doubt contributed to a distorted picture of translators' skills.

Against this background, it is very important to note how close translations are in relation to the original. Depending on how translators conceive their own work, glosses (with different purposes, such as explanation or embellishment) and amplifications (sometimes also omissions) are essential. It is through this approach that some characteristics of translations made at the beginning of the sixteenth century acquire a new dimension. Examples of this are Antonio de Obregón's idea of fidelity in translation, and Alvar Gómez de Ciudad Real's descriptions and songs incorporated in the main body.[22]

One of the most important documents with respect to the function of glosses and amplifications in translation is Francisco de Madrid's *De los remedios contra próspera y adversa fortuna* (1510):

> The successful have no less need of temperance than of patience, and in the translation I try to profit from the doctrines of the blessed doctor Saint Jerome: translating more the sentence than the letter in some parts, and in some others, through some circumlocution, bringing the obscurity of his Latin to the clarity of our romance, leaving aside sometimes some lost expressions that serve more the abundance of the language than the clarity of the sentence. Other times I add something necessary for the sentences to be linked; because he who wished to translate this book (with its obscurity) by the letter, as in Latin, that would be such a dull and obscure thing that it could not be read nor, if it were, could be understood.[23]

As Alvar Gómez will do later when he introduces explanations and amplifications with many rhetorical changes, Francisco de Madrid eliminates glosses completely. At this point the gloss becomes the translation itself, free to introduce changes when considered necessary. Besides, what is important here is the prominence of the Romance language and not Latin. Now the obscure text is the Latin one. This translator focuses on the reader for whom he is writing. Translators at this period see themselves as mediators who contribute to the spreading of ideas while rendering them familiar to their audience.

Villegas too, in his explanation of how he translates Dante's *Infierno*, explains the kind of translation he has undertaken. He clearly states that he has sometimes transformed the information appearing in glosses for his verse translation:

> It must be indicated that Dante writes his work in three-line stanzas (*tercetos* as the Tuscan writer calls them), rhyming the third line with the first, and later the first of the next *terceto* with the second, so that these four lines would constitute half a *copla de arte mayor*, which, since it has eight lines, would fit very well. But, since he writes in three-line stanzas, in two *tercetos* there are two lines lacking to complete the said *copla de arte mayor*. I tried to make it in *tercetos*, but it seemed to me so unrefined that I stopped. There remained the above-mentioned defect of one line lacking in every *terceto* to complete half a *copla* and two to complete a whole one. These I determined to substitute in the following way: sometimes having the inspiration of a good line that may clarify more of his text or confirm his sentence, I include it; and may Dante endure with patience that in his gold brocade some patches of sackcloth be included to make it look better! As the philosopher says, to use always what is found denotes the most miserable mind. Other times I substitute those lines with what some of his commentators say. And with some others (and most of them when that may be done well) I also take the first and second line of the next *terceto*. And that is the way that his two, and sometimes *three*, *tercetos* make an eight-line *copla*.

> It must be indicated, too, that he who translates from another advances after him with some loose parts and, therefore, cannot advance how, or as much as he wants. Thus, at times, some lines have been forced in, because it was not possible to do it better — or one simply did not know how. Receive this with good disposition, because no one could give more than he has. It must be indicated as well, that to translate one language into another (not only in verse but neither in *oración soluta*, or prose as some people call it) is impossible to do through the same words in such a way that would not be completely dull. For in one language, one thing is more graceful, but said in another through the same words it would be very dull. Therefore, as long as the same words can be used, it is done, but in many parts the intended meaning and sense are taken, rather than the words.[24]

Villegas introduces, in his poetic text, ideas arising from glosses which would help, according to him, to make his translation more explicit. This is one of the best examples for observing the glosses that become part of the translation itself. Here gloss is already diluted within the verses. It is important to point out his denial of a word-for-word rendition as a system; he openly declares the need for translators to pay more attention to the meaning rather than to the words.

Another example of the acceptance of Saint Jerome's approach can be found in the work by Licenciado Peña, translator of Petrarch's *De vita solitaria*, which was published in Medina del Campo in 1553:

> I have been really careful in translating this short piece from Latin into our Castilian and, even though in some places the translation may not correspond with the original, I do not deserve any censure since I follow good masters in many of their translations, such as St. Jerome. And he himself at a certain moment gives as a rule for those who translate to extract the substantial from the original, but not the sound of the words and reasons formally.[25]

As with Villegas, Peña is in favor of ideas and meaning, not words, as the most important things for translators. It seems as if from this moment on it is not necessary to provide an explanation for a translation which has not been rendered word-for-word.

Because of this change that develops in the fifteenth century and reaches into the sixteenth, it is not appropriate to compare, as critics do, translations like Villena's *Comedia* (1427) with Boscán's *El Cortesano* (1534). In between these two works occurs a whole liberating process with respect to the original and to poetic tradition (for example, the verse translation to the eight-syllable verse as the only possible form).

In conclusion, glosses and amplifications are two procedures essential in translation, and they are important factors to better understand the methods of translation used in the fifteenth century. It becomes necessary to distinguish the different meaning translation practices had at particular times, and to abandon those evaluations founded solely on the labels "literal" and "free," since matters are more complex and are based on specific issues. From this perspective, it is urgent to reevaluate many translations of the period that have been deemed as bad, completed in a hurry, or careless, etc. by later critics, when in fact they are the product of how translations were conceived at a particular time and place.

Creighton University

NOTES

[1] Francisco Rico, *Alfonso el Sabio y la General Estoria* (Barcelona: Ariel, 1984) 167.

[2] Julian Weiss, *The Poet's Art: Literary Theory in Castile c. 1440-60* (Oxford: Medium Aevum Monographs, 1990) 107-64.

[3] Weiss, 121.

[4] Rico, 183-87.

[5] Peter Russell, *Traducciones y traductores en la Península Ibérica (1400-1550)* (Bellaterra: Universitat Autonoma de Barcelona, 1985) 5-26.

[6] "La qual obra apenas pudo toda la gramática y aún eloquencia latina conprenhender, y en sí rescebir los eroicos cantares del vaticinante poeta Omero; pues, quánto más fará el rudo y desierto romance! Acaescerá por esta cabsa en la omérica Yliada como a las dulces y sabrosas frutas en la fin del verano, que a la primera agua se dañan y a la segunda se pierden. E así esta obra rescibirá dos agravios: el uso en la traslación latina y, el más dañoso y mayor, en la interpretación del romance que presumo y tiento le dar" [Juan de Mena, *Obras completas*, ed. Miguel Ángel Pérez Priego (Barcelona: Planeta, 1989) 334.]

[7] "E por esta razón [la imperfección del castellano], muy prepotente señor, dispuse de no interpretar de veinte y quatro libros, que son en el volumen de la Yliada, salvo las sumas brevemente de ellos [...] Y aun dexélo de fazer por non dañar nin ofender del todo su alta obra, trayéndogela en la umilde y baxa lengua del romance" [Mena 334.]

[8] Alonso de Cartagena, *La Rhetorica de Marco Tullio Cicerón*, ed. Rosalba Mascagna (Napoli: Liguori, 1969) 31.

[9] "Bien sé yo agora que, según que ya otras vezes con vos y con otros me ha acaescido, diredes que la mayor parte o quasi toda de la dulçura o graçiosidad quedan y retienen en sí las palabras y vocablos latinos [...] Ca difíçil cosa sería agora que, después de assaz años e no menos travajos, yo quisiese o me despusiesse a porfiar con la lengua latina, como quiera que Tulio afirma Catón — creo Uticense — en hedad de ochenta años aprendiesse las letras griegas; pero solo e singular fue Catón del linage humano en esto y en otras muchas cosas. E pues no podemos aver aquello que queremos, queramos aquello que podemos. E si careçemos de las formas, seamos contentos de las materias" [Íñigo López de Mendoza Marqués de Santillana, *Prohemios y cartas literarias*, ed. Miguel Garci-Gómez (Madrid: Editora Nacional, 1984) 128.]

[10] "Es así que yo leí algunas veces aquel libro que compuso el sanctísimo papa e glorioso doctor sant Gregorio, que es dicho Diálogos, el cual como es en latín e yo, por alguna escuridad de vocablos y alteza de estilo que en él es, no le podía así claramente entender para que dél cogiese el fruto que deseo" [Fernán Pérez de Guzmán, *Generaciones y semblanzas*, ed. J. Domínguez Bordona (Madrid: La Lectura, 1924) 215.]

[11] "La pusieron en el latyn y en estilo tanto elevado que pocos de los lectores pueden sacar verdaderas sentencias de sus dychos" [Pero Guillén de Segovia, *La Gaya Ciencia*, eds. O. J. Tulio and J. M. Casas Homs, 2 vols. (Madrid: Consejo Superior de Investigaciones Científicas, 1962) 1: 43.]

[12] "Dificultaron sus escrituras y las posieron en palabras dificiles y aun obscuras, porque las leyesen los hombres muchas veces y mejor las retoviesen y mas las preciasen, quanto en ellas mas trabajo tomasen; ca lo que con mayor trabajo se gana, con mayor prescio se guarda" [Pero López de Ayala, *Las Flores de los Morales de Job*, ed. Francesco Branciforti (Firenze: Le Monnier, 1963) 5.]

[13] Saint Jérome, "À Pammachius: la meilleure méthode de traduction", *Lettres*, ed. Jérome Labourt, 8 vols. (Paris: Les Belles Lettres, 1953) 3: 54-73.

[14] Alfonso de Palencia, *Batalla campal de los perros* (Sevilla: 1490) fol. aij (r).

[15] Roxana Recio, "Alfonso de Madrigal (El Tostado), la traducción como teoría entre lo medieval y lo renacentista", *La Corónica* 19.2 (1992), 112-31.

[16] Roxana Recio, "El concepto de la belleza de Alfonso de Madrigal (El Tostado), la problemática de la traducción literal y libre", *La traducción en España (ss. XIV-XVI)*, ed. Roxana Recio (León: Universidad de León, 1995) 59-68.

[17] Roxana Recio, "Las interpolaciones latinas de Sor Isabel de Villena: ¿traducciones, glosas o amplificaciones?", *Anuario Medieval* 5 (1993), 126-40.

[18] Russell, 29.

[19] "E si requieres los fados de Príamo e quieres saber qué fizo en aquella hora, çertefícote que, vista su çibdat tomada e derribado el hedifiçio troyano e los enemigos dentro en su alcáçar, maguer que era viejo e por antigüedat ya temblava, tomó las armas desusadas que tiempo avía grande ya dexado; e çiñóse su espada con esfuerço, maguer con ella ferir nos pudiese; e tomó las armas sobre sí e fuese con intinçión e osadía de morir entre los enemigos espesos" [Enrique de Villena, *Obras completas*, ed. Pedro M. Cátedra, 3 vols. (Madrid: Turner, 1994) 2: 468.]

[20] "*E si requieres los fados, etc.* Queriendo dezir: "Si tú, reina, dexado de preguntar las otras seguidas cosas e quieres saber prinçipalmente lo que a Príamo acaesçió en el extremo de su desventura e cómo se ovo en aquel paso en do cumplía mostrar la mayor virtud". Esto dizía Eneas dignamente, presumiendo que la entendida reina más quería saber este acto de Príamo que todas las otras cosas ende contesçidas. E aquella palabra *fados* se entiende por los acarreos que su costillaçión le troxo a tal salida e fin. E como aquel que bien a ello paró mientes, dize que le çertifica, ansí como çierto d'ello por occulada fe, el dicho Príamo, visto aquel

decaimiento, vencida e tomada Troya de los enemigos e derribados sus hedificios solempnes e su alcáçar apoderado de los enemigos irrecuperablemente, como quien ya non esperava sinon captividat ho muerte, quiso mostrar su virtud, non obstándole la vejez e debilitaçión de fuerças; que ya pasava de ochenta e nueve años, segúnd collegir se puede de los istoriales que d'él fablan" (Villena 2: 469.)

[21] A. K. Zholkovski, "Sobre la amplificación", *Teoría y práctica del estructuralismo soviético* (Madrid: Comunicación, 1972), 173-82.

[22] Antonio de Obregón, *Francisco Petrarca, con los seys triunfos de toscano sacados en castellano con el comento que sobrellos se hizo* (Logroño: Arnao Guillén de Brocar, 1512); Alvar Gómez de Ciudad Real, *Triunfo de amor de Petrarca traducido por Alvaro Gómez de Ciudad Real* (around 1510).

[23] "Que no tiene menos necesidad de templança el prospero que de paciencia el abatido y en la traslacion del quise me aprovechar de la dotrina del bienaventurado Doctor San Hieronimo: trasladando en algunas partes que lo requerian mas la sentencia que la letra y en otros, por algun rodeo, trayendo la escuridad de su latin a la claridad de nuestro romance, dexando algunas vezes algunos vocablos perdidos que sirven mas a la abundancia de la lengua que a la claridad de la sentencia, y otras añadiendo algo necesario para que las sentencias vayan encadenadas, porque quien quisiese trasladar este libro, (segun su escuridad) letra por letra, como en el latin, ésta seria una cosa tan desabrida y tan escura que ni se podria leer ni, ya que se leyese, se podria entender" [Francisco de Madrid, *De los remedios contra próspera y adversa fortuna de Francisco Petrarca* (Valladolid: Diego de Gumiel) fol. iii.]

[24] "Débese notar que el Dante escribe su obra en coplas de *tercetos* (que ansí los nombra el toscano), correspondiente el tercero pié al primero, y despues el primero del terceto siguiente al segundo: de manera que aquellos cuatro farian una media copla de arte mayor, que, como es de ocho piés, viniera ansí justo al talle; pero como escribe de tres en tres, en dos tercetos faltan dos piés para una copla del arte mayor ya dicha: yo probé á los facer ansí en tercetos, la cual manera no es en nuestro uso; y parescíame una cosa tan desdonada, que lo dejé. Quedó el defeto ya dicho de faltar en cada terceto un pié para la media copla, y dos piés en cada una entera; éstos yo acordé de los suplir desta manera: que algunas veces, ocurriendo de mio algund buen pié, que más aclare su texto ó confirme su sentencia, póngole; y haya paciencia el Dante que en su brocado se ponga algund remiendo de sayal, que más le faga lucir; y el filósofo dice, que de misérrimo ingenio es siempre usar de lo fallado. Otras veces suplo aquellos piés de lo que alguno de sus glosadores dice; y otras también (y las más, cuando buenamente se puede facer) tomo el primero y segundo pié del terceto siguiente, y ansí se facen sus dos, y á las veces tres, tercetos, una copla de ocho piés. Nótese tambien que el que treslada de otro anda tras él con sueltas, y no puede ir cómo ni cuánto quiere; y ansí van, algunas veces, piés algunos forcejados, que no se pudo ó no se supo mejor facer: rescíbase la buena voluntad; que ninguno da más de lo que tiene. Ansimesmo se debe notar que tresladarse una lengua en otra, no solamente en verso, pero ni en oración soluta, ó prosa que algunos llaman, es imposible tresladarse por las mismas palabras, que no fuese la más desabrida cosa del mundo; porque en una lengua tiene una cosa gracia, y dicho en otra por aquellas palabras sería muy frio: por ende aquí, en todo cuanto de las mesmas palabras se puede usar, se face; pero en muchas partes se toma el sentido y intencion, más que no las palabras" [Pero Fernández de Villegas, *La Divina Comedia de Dante*, ed. Juan

Eugenio Hartzenbusch (Madrid: Tomás Rey, 1868) xi.] There are copies of the 1515 edition, *Tradució del Dante de lengua toscana en verso castellano* (Burgos: 1515), in the Cornell University Library (signature Dante PQ 4318.12.lv73) and in the Biblioteca Nacional in Madrid (signature R. 307670).

[25] "Yo he tenido no mediano cuydado en traduzir esta breve obra de latin en nuestro castellano y, puesto que en algunos lugares no conforme en la traduccion con el original, no soy digno de reprehension pues sigo a buenos maestros que es sant Hieronymo en muchas de sus traduciones; y el mismo en cierta parte da por regla a los que traduzen que saquen lo substancial del original aunque no formalmente el sonido de las palabras y razones." Juan Peña, *De la vida solitaria* (Medina del Campo: 1553) fol. v.

Courtly Love and Patriarchal Marriage Practice in Malory's Le Morte Darthur

MaryLynn Saul

As shown in Sir Thomas Malory's *Le Morte Darthur*, two ideological systems restrict medieval women's actions. On the one hand, patriarchal marriage exercised strict control over a woman's sexuality. Because of the necessity of ensuring legitimate male heirs, a woman's adultery was considered much more of a crime than a man's: a nobleman had to be certain that his wife's son, his heir, was in fact his own offspring. On the other hand, courtly love, an ideal which maintains that love must exist outside marriage, appears to break those restrictions on a woman's sexuality; nevertheless, this system also imposes limitations on a woman's actions. Although the ideal of both systems may have been female passivity, numerous female characters in *Le Morte Darthur* show assertiveness in pursuing their own goals. Guenevere's participation in courtly love dictates that she commit adultery, thus disregarding the rules of marriage. Ettard apparently ignores the expectations of courtly love by refusing to accept Pelleas' love. Although Nyneve does actively pursue her own goals, she seems to be accepted by the male characters because of her faithful support of Arthur. Elain of Astolat, paradoxically, behaves both passively and aggressively in pursuing Lancelot. Finally, Morgan le Fay demonstrates the most extreme transgressions of both systems, ultimately embodying medieval gynephobia.

Patriarchal marriage negotiations are represented early in *Le Morte Darthur* by the case of Igraine's marriage to Uther. Previous to this arrangement, King Uther and Igraine's husband, the Duke of Cornwall, had been at war with each other. Upon the Duke's death in battle, the King's barons recommend to him that he marry Igraine for the sake of the country. The arrangements proceed without much mention of Igraine's preference, which should be much in doubt since she has previously acted as a loyal wife to the Duke of Cornwall. At the time of Igraine's wedding, marriages are arranged for her daughters. Malory emphasizes the fact that men control the negotiations: first, by noting the initiative of the barons, and second, by adding that the marriage of the daughters "was done at the request of kynge Uther,"[1] while no mention is made of Igraine's wishes concerning her daughters' futures. As portrayed by Malory, women have no control of even their own marriages, much less those of their daughters.

The pressures of patriarchal marriage practice also come to bear on Arthur: immediately after he is established as king and accepted by the barons, his barons advise Arthur to get a wife. In Arthur's discussion of the issue with Merlin, negotiation and romance seem to be mixed. On the one hand, Merlin asks Arthur, "is there one ... that ye love more than another?" (59), and Arthur instantly responds that he has long loved Guenevere. The emphasis then shifts from love to political negotiation when Merlin speaks on Arthur's behalf to King Leodegrance, who gives not only his daughter but also the Round Table and a hundred good knights to the King. Guenevere herself is never consulted about the marriage and does not speak at all until the court of knights and ladies has been established. In these arranged marriages, therefore, the men's wishes and goals are emphasized while the women have little control over their own fates.

For all Arthur's protests that he loves Guenevere and esteems her highly, Arthur's true loyalty is to his knights. He reveals this loyalty near the end of the work, when the knights of the Round Table have dispersed, by saying that he regrets more

> my good knightes losse than for the losse of my fayre quene; for quenys I myght have inow, but such a felyship of good knightes shall never be togydirs in no company. (685)

In other words, he says, a wife is easily replaceable while "such a felyship of good knightes" is not. By giving Arthur such a speech, Malory emphasizes the value of male friendship over the value of marital love, thus diminishing the relationship with the woman.

As shown in Malory's text, marriages in the Middle Ages were often the result of negotiations made by the betrothed's parents, who frequently searched for a suitable heiress to bring the family more power and land. Such heiresses were especially important to find for younger sons who would not inherit the family estate[2] and who, without such an heiress, might not marry.[3] Because marriage was seen as an advantageous arrangement for the family rather than the fulfillment of a personal relationship, betrothals would be made as soon as children were of age, that is, when they were as young as seven years old,[4] although the actual marriage would not take place until puberty or the age set by the Church — twelve for girls and fourteen for boys.

The Neville family provides an example from the late fifteenth-century, in which one daughter married at the age of nine and was widowed and remarried in less than two years.[5] The most extreme example of marriage contracts for the family's political or financial gain involving very young participants comes from the same period as the previous example. In this case, one of the participants had not even been conceived at the time of the contract, which stated that a daughter "to be born within the next five or six years" will be married, and included subsitution of of a niece or sister if such a child was never born (132). The belief that these families are negotiating for influence and not the emotional fulfillment of their children is supported not only by the fact that one of the participants to the marriage does not yet exist, and may never exist, but also by the fact that alternative provisions are made, substituting brothers and cousins, in order to fulfill the specified arrangements including mention of manors, possessions, rents and profits, as well as 500 marks.[6] Money and possessions are emphasized in much the same fashion when Arthur negotiates to wed Guenevere.

Although these examples appear to suggest that daughters and sons were equally powerless in the arrangements made by their parents, Ann S. Haskell explains that, while technically the right of refusal would belong to both participants,[7] daughters were subjected to considerably more pressure than sons.[8] Letters from the Paston family provide an example of such "pressure" in the case of Elizabeth Paston, who in her teens refused to marry Stephen Scrope, a man of around fifty who was "permanently disfigured" (466-7). A family friend, Elizabeth Clere, writes to John Paston of his sister's suffering due to her defiance:

> ... for sche was never in so gret sorow as sche is now-a-dayes; for sche may not speke wyth no man, ho so euer come, ne not may se ne speke wyth my man ... And sche hath son Esterne the most part beteyn onys in the weke or twyes, and som tyme twyes on o day, and hir hed broken in to or thre places.[9]

Besides patriarchal marriage considerations, examination of Guenevere's character reveals the tension between marriage and courtly love. While Guenevere's love of Lancelot may be idealized in texts such as that of Chrétien de Troyes, in Malory Guenevere inspires male criticism. Modern medievalists have interpreted the idea of courtly love in many different ways, including as a psychological fantasy, as a game, as a stylistic convention, and finally as a myth not to be seriously considered.[10] Various critics have examined courtly love in *Le Morte Darthur*, and have expressed various, sometimes contradictory opinions. For example, Charles Moorman believes that Malory "unequivocally condemns courtly love throughout the book."[11] Moorman can make such an "unequivocal" claim by neatly ignoring the passage in which Malory calls Guenevere a "trew lover."[12] R. T. Davies, who does not ignore this passage, sees Malory as inconsistent on the subject of courtly love. While he says that the author views the love of Lancelot and Guenevere as a sin, he believes that we are told that Guenevere meets a good end because she finally repents and joins a nunnery; in this case, a "good end" means that she will go to heaven.[13] At the other extreme, Peter Waldron maintains that Malory makes a distinction between "trew love" (for a person) and "vertuouse love" (for God) and sympathizes with and forgives Lancelot and Guenevere in the end even though they did not follow the higher road of "vertuouse love." These various critics' comments reveal the difficulty of defining a "good" or "true" lover in courtly love: to whom should a "true lover" be faithful — the husband, the lover, God? While Guenevere seems loyal to Lancelot, she also is portrayed as selfish and jealous, as when she falsely accuses Lancelot of betraying her when he wears the favor of Elaine of Astolat.

The claim that courtly love meant an improvement for women, even in theory, has often been questioned recently. Howard Bloch calls courtly love a disguised form of misogyny:

> no less than the discourse of salvational virginity does it place the burden of redemption upon the woman who ... finds herself in the polarized position of seducer and redeemer — always anxious, always guilty, never able to measure up, vulnerable.[14]

In other words, when the love affair does not end happily, the woman may find herself receiving all the blame. Although the man in courtly love may submit to his lady's wishes, it was not true that a woman even in courtly love was really free to exercise this power over the man in any manner she wished. As Georges Duby explains,

> From the moment she joined the game she could no longer violate its laws, whether by withholding herself too stubbornly or surrendering too quickly, without incurring penalties: loss of 'courtly' status and exclusion from the court by the judgment of other women, her rivals.[15]

Guenevere, on the other hand, suffers from the judgment of the men at court. Although Malory may call Guenevere a "trew lover," various male characters criticize her behavior, and in each of her trials she inspires very little male support. The first, though indirect, criticism of Guenevere comes from Lancelot's relative Sir Bors, who encourages him to accept Elaine of Astolat's offer of love, and suggests that everyone would be better off if he could love such an admirable, unattached maiden rather than the Queen.[16] When Guenevere needs a champion to defend her honor, Bors shows her little sympathy, admonishing,

> "I mervayle how ye dare for shame to requyre me to do onythynge for you, insomuche ye have enchaced oute of your courte by whom we were up borne and honoured." (616)

If Guenevere has no one to defend her, Malory implies here, she has no one to blame but herself. Furthermore, Bors's criticism implies that not only has Guenevere lost a champion, but through her jealousy she has also deprived the court of its best knight; therefore everyone will suffer for Guenevere's instability in love. Not only Guenevere, but also other female characters in *Le Morte Darthur* violate the laws of the game of courtly love and are judged harshly by other characters for these violations.

For example, the belief that the woman should hold out neither too short nor too long a time is illustrated in the Pelleas-Ettard episode. In this case, the knight Pelleas is hopelessly in love with the Lady Ettard, who steadfastly rejects his love. Here there is the implication that Ettard is in the wrong since Pelleas is such a worthy knight. Nyneve, the Lady of the Lake, says, "hit is no joy of suche a preude lady that woll nat have no mercy of suche a valyaunte knyght" (104). The issue of Ettard's pride is introduced from the beginning of the tale, when a knight explains the situation to Gawain, saying Ettard rejects Pelleas and that:

> "all ladyes and jantellwomen had scorne of hir that sche was prowde, for there were fayrer than sche, and there was none that was there but and sir Pelleas wolde have profyrde hem love they wode have shewed hym the same for his noble prouesse." (100)

In addition to the judgment of Nyneve as well as "all ladyes and jantellwomen," Ettard herself appears to damn her own behavior by commenting to Gawain, who loves a lady who will not return his love, "Sche is to blame ... and she woll nat love you, for ye that be so well-borne a man and suche a man of prouesse, there is no lady in this worlde to good for you" (102). Although she is speaking of Gawain and not Pelleas, Ettard herself implies that the woman in romance only has one legitimate reason to turn down a worthy man, because she believes she deserves a better one. By violating the implicit rules of courtly love, the woman always bears the guilt for a troubled relationship: either she seeks love from a knight who will not return it and is therefore interpreted as forcing the relationship (as Morgan often does with Lancelot), or she refuses an admirable man because of her own pride.

Pelleas is rescued from Ettard's supposed pride by receiving justice according to Nyneve, who declares, "He shall nat dye for love, and she that hath caused hym so to love she shall be in as evylle plyte as he is or hit be long to" (104). Again, Nyneve claims that the woman caused the situation (Ettard caused him to love her even though she had no interest in loving him) and therefore must bear the responsibility. To solve the problem, Nyneve causes Ettard to be as hopelessly in love with Pelleas as he with her, then causes Pelleas to be in love with herself. Malory appears to consider Nyneve's solution just deserts, yet one must question this opinion. First, the claim that Ettard was motivated by pride in refusing Pelleas is the interpretation of others and not Ettard's own statement of her feelings. Discussing her situation, she tells Gawain, "[Pelleas' infatuation] is grete pyte for he was a passynge good knyght of his body. But of all men on lyve I hated hym moste, for I could never be quytte of hym" (102), thus indicating that while she sympathizes with his suffering and does consider him a good man, nevertheless, she cannot love him. In stories of courtly love, the woman who does not capitulate at the proper time receives a harsh judgment.

Here we should note the similarity to Nyneve's earlier predicament, since Nyneve also has a suitor, Merlin, whom she refuses. The difference in the two romances, which leads to the portrayal of Nyneve as justified and Ettard as overly proud, is that Malory does not give Ettard the excuse of being afraid of a "devyls son," an excuse Nyneve has in refusing Merlin.[17] Overall, Nyneve is portrayed positively in the text, most likely due to her support of men's goals over those of women. Although Nyneve does act in her own interests initially in causing Pelleas to love her and imprisoning Merlin (Arthur's most trusted advisor), nevertheless she is given justification in these actions, as previously explained. After this early selfish behavior, all her subsequent actions protect Arthur. The implications of hostility between women, as between Nyneve and Morgan, will be discussed below.

Besides Ettard, other examples of the restrictions of courtly love can be seen in the many maidens who hopelessly love Lancelot. Bloch questions the motives of men such as Lancelot in courtly love: "the gaze is not upon the woman so much as on the reflection of the man in her eyes."[18] The benefit of loving Lancelot goes not to the women but to Lancelot, who receives their praise and gains in reputation by the number of women who love him. The benefit to a man of a woman's love can be seen in the case of Elaine of Astolat, who loves Lancelot without having her affection returned. In accordance with the submissive feminine role in courtly love, Elaine of Astolat confines herself to a primarily passive role. In defining passive women, Elaine Tuttle Hansen describes their typical behavior: "They put the love of a man above all other responsibilities, even life itself. As a direct consequence of this 'love' they endure great suffering ... [A]lmost all die ..."[19] Elaine exhibits all three types of behavior. As is often true in romances, she apparently has no responsibilities to home or family but instead devotes all her attention to helping Lancelot prepare for battle or nursing him afterwards. Thus, Malory portrays a woman who neglects her own concerns, to devote herself totally to assist the man she loves as normal. As a result of her total devotion to a man, Elaine endures great suffering. Upon Lancelot's rejection, "she shryked shirly and felle downe in a sowghe; and than women bare hir into her chambir, and there she made overmuche sorowe."[20] The use of "overmuche sorowe" contains the double meaning of unbearable sorrow and an inappropriate amount of sadness and pain, as we see when she expires for love. Through Malory's description of her emotions, she is subtly criticized for expecting too much from Lancelot.

Although Elaine may seem passive because she dies of her unrequited love for Lancelot, her death may be more of a passive-aggressive move since she does not do so quietly and invisibly, as do many of the other maidens who, Malory tells us, find a priest, confess and meekly pass away. Instead, Elaine of Astolat plans a great funeral barge to greet her intended love (and his lover, the Queen) at Camelot. Her requirements for her treatment after death are quite detailed, including that a letter be written explaining how she died, that she be dressed in rich clothes, that she be put in a barge with one person with her, and that the barge be covered with black samite (640). In making these arrangements for her death scene, she takes an active role in announcing her love of Lancelot to the court and portraying Lancelot as cruel. At the same time, she has shown the ultimate in passivity by dying for love. While the ideology of courtly love may portray such passivity as romantic, dying for love seems to be the position taken more often by the woman than the man. After all, Nyneve does not rescue Elaine as she did Pelleas. Overall, Elaine may be said to be using her passivity as an aggressive act.

Although she is viewed sympathetically by the court, Elaine is still questioned for exceeding the limited role prescribed for women in courtly love by asserting her love of Lancelot despite his rejection. In contrast to Elaine's desperate love of him, Lancelot defines his own idea of love, which cannot be forced but arises freely — "I love nat to be constrayned to love, for love muste only aryse of the harte self, and nat by none constraynte" (641). What apparently is meant by this is that women should not pursue men and "force" them to return their affections. That is, men are not criticized for pursuing women who do not love them; no one, for example, disapproves of Pelleas for his hopeless infatuation for Ettard. Yet women who pursue men who do not love them are criticized, as is Elaine of Astolat.

Morgan pursues love even more aggressively than Elaine of Astolat, transgressing the limits of both patriarchal marriage and courtly love. Her behavior clearly threatens men, as when she imprisons Tristram and Lancelot. In company with three other sorceresses, Morgan discovers the sleeping Lancelot, puts an enchantment on him and transports him to her castle. There the sorceresses demand that he "choose one of us, whyche that thou wolte have to thy peramour, other ellys to dye in this preson" (152). He, of course being loyal to Guenevere, refuses to take a lover and escapes with the help of one of Morgan's disloyal maidens. Frequently throughout the text, Morgan's own maidens betray her instructions and sabotage her goals. One might speculate that Morgan could have been much more successful in her plots if her maidens were more loyal. Instead of female characters supporting and encouraging each other, Malory more often portrays them as competition for each other. The maidens betray Morgan because of their own goals or desire for Lancelot, and Morgan and Guenevere are rivals for Lancelot's affection.

Morgan is judged harshly by the characters in the text not because she seeks Lancelot's love; rather, the others revile her for directing her anger and sorrow in the wrong direction. Although Elaine chooses the traditional self-sacrificing role, Morgan, as Lancelot notes, has "destroyed many a good knyght" (152). Not only does Morgan imprison Lancelot, but she also does not accept his rejection of her, attempting revenge by two methods. First, she plans for her knights to kill Lancelot, and second, she plans to expose her rival, Guenevere, as an adulteress in front of the court. The threat of Morgan to men such as Lancelot illustrates the medieval male's need to control women. This need may have arisen from various motivations. First, marriage was seen as necessary to restrain man's tendency towards sensuality. Since sensuality was embodied by woman in the eyes of medieval men, women's sexuality must be limited and controlled. In order to achieve this control, in order for "marriage [to] restore the original hierarchy, the domination of flesh by spirit,"[21] the husband believed he must dominate his wife.

Gynephobia also motivated medieval men to control women. Men feared a woman's supposedly insatiable physical desires as well as her ability to harm a man. For example, in the medical treatise *De Secretis Mulierum* from the later Middle Ages, the author explains the treachery of women.[22] In an expanded manuscript of the text, the author insists that a woman has a greater desire for sex than a man because "something foul is drawn to the good" (51), "foul" meaning the woman, "good" meaning the man. According to *De Secretis Mulierum*, not only do women desire intercourse more often, but their health benefits from it since,

> [t]he more women have sexual intercourse, the stronger they become ... On the other hand, men who have sex frequently are weakened by this act... (127)

In *Le Morte Darthur*, Morgan le Fay, who seeks sexual satisfaction outside of her marriage with lovers such as Accolon and Hemison, represents woman's insatiability, and accordingly men fear her. In addition, the author of the treatise also advises men to find tests to determine important information — whether the woman is a virgin or whether she is pregnant, for example. Even these tests are not foolproof, since "Some women ... are so clever and so aware of the trick that they refuse to tell the truth, but rather say something else instead" (125).

Morgan certainly "proves" this idea of the deceitfulness of women when she sends the burning mantle to Arthur, with the message that she wishes to make peace after her unsuccessful rebellion. Although she sends the mantle in the guise of a gift, as a gesture of peace, she plans for it to destroy him. Nyneve suspects her motives and warns Arthur, who orders the maiden bringing the mantle to wear it first: she is burnt to death. This episode underscores the danger to men of such deceit, since Morgan's word cannot be trusted, and the outcome of her plot would have been Arthur's death. Luckily for Arthur, not all women desire men's destruction, and he can rely on Nyneve to warn him of other women's treachery. Yet apparently only another woman can discover the deceitfulness of a woman like Morgan.

Besides showing unfeminine aggressiveness in pursuing Lancelot and attempting to harm men, Morgan violates the boundaries of courtly love in her relationship with Accolon. She has not stopped at merely taking a lover in order to experience the romantic fulfillment which medieval marriage arrangements did not offer; she has gone beyond this role by projecting her adulterous relationship into a ruling partnership in hoping to wrest the crown from her brother. She arranges a fight between her lover Accolon, one of Arthur's own knights, and the King himself, with the expectation that Accolon will kill Arthur, giving her the opportunity to rule in his place. By transforming the personal love relationship into a political one, Morgan has aspired to a role well beyond the boundaries of courtly love.

Although Morgan has clearly used Accolon in her plot against Arthur, a plot which results in Accolon's death, his death is not the outcome Morgan expects. She is not, in other words, a merciless lover who considers her knight expendable as long as she realizes her own ambition. In fact, according to Accolon in his confession to Arthur, she planned for Accolon to rule alongside her and hoped to ensure this outcome by giving him the magical Excalibur and the even more valuable scabbard, which prevents the bearer from losing blood. She demonstrates the strength of her affection for Accolon after his death when she "was so sorowfull that nye hir herte to-braste" (91). Because Morgan is a sympathetic character in grief and an unsympathetic one in her ambition, she proves to be a very complex character. In fact her actions complicate the story itself when she uses the contradiction of the marriage laws' rejection of female adultery and the courtly love's acceptance of it in pursuit of her ambitions.[23]

A good example from *Le Morte Darthur* of how the two ideals conflict on the issue of adultery and how Morgan makes use of the conflict can be demonstrated by the story of Tristram and Isolde. Before Mordred initiates the destruction of the Round Table in the end, Morgan attempts a similar rebellion: Morgan wishes to expose Guenevere's adultery before the court and sends a drinking horn, from which only faithful wives can drink without spilling a drop, to Arthur's court. The "gift" is intercepted by Lamarak, who, bearing a grudge against Tristram, redirects the horn to the court of King Mark. Mark's wife Isolde, in the company of a hundred other ladies, is proven unfaithful to her marriage vows. King Mark wishes to burn Isolde and the other ladies immediately; however, the barons refuse to permit this since the horn was sent by Morgan, whom they believe to be an enemy to true lovers. The barons apparently believe she is an enemy since she is trying to expose lovers such as Lancelot and Guenevere and Tristan and Isolde, rather than helping them to maintain their secrecy.

Because advisors to the king would normally be concerned that an acceptable heir be produced, necessitating control over female sexuality, the behavior of the barons seems incomprehensible. Instead of upholding male power by enforcing marriage laws, they instead side with the women in protecting the women's adulterous relationships. Their refusal may be explained as a wish on the part of the author (whether Malory or one of the writers of his sources) to avoid depicting the destruction that would result from an overt confrontation of the adultery of so many women including Isolde. In this way, the revelation of Isolde's adultery and its possible consequences foreshadows the fate of Guenevere and Lancelot. Morgan uses the contradictions between patriarchal marriage and courtly love as access to the power to destroy her enemies. Although she may not be successful in the attempt, the threat to the court from this tension between the two systems is real and will be exploited successfully by Mordred.

Since her first plot to disrupt the love affair of Guenevere and Lancelot fails, Morgan tries again by providing a shield that she requires Tristram to carry in a tournament at Arthur's court. Malory describes the shield as being painted in this way: "the fylde was gouldes with a kynge and a quene therin paynted, and a knyght stondynge aboven them with hys one foote standynge uppon the kynges hede and the othir upon the quenys hede."[24] When Tristram asks her what it means, she replies, "Hit signyfieth kynge Arthure and quen[ne] Gwenyver, and a knyght that holdith them bothe in bondage and in servage," and Malory then explains that she does this "to put sir Lancelot to rebuke, to that entente, that kynge Arthure myght undirstonde the love betwene them" (340). Morgan has implied through the shield not only that Guenevere is unfaithful, but also that Lancelot is betraying the trust of Arthur, that he is in fact "holding them both in bondage" by threatening to undermine the power represented by the traditional marriage. In other words, the love relationship of Guenevere and Lancelot interferes with the traditional transference of power from one generation of males to the next by calling into question the parentage of any children Guenevere may have. Perhaps luckily for the lovers, Guenevere has no children whose parentage may be questioned. Although Arthur does ask about the shield, Tristram answers that he does not know the meaning, and therefore nothing comes of this plan. Once again, disaster is foreshadowed, not only for Guenevere and Lancelot but also for the whole court.

Morgan's attacks on men are not limited to Lancelot and Arthur; she also tries to kill her husband with his own sword, but is stopped at the last moment by her son. Her motivation for wanting her husband dead may be found in medieval women's position regarding property. In the Middle Ages, a woman's marital status determined how much power a woman had. Although a married woman had more power than an unmarried woman, even a married woman's power would be limited. The time a woman had the most power over property (even property that she brought to a marriage) was as a widow, or when she brought property to a marriage from a previous union. In studying court records in Brigstock in Northamptonshire in the early fourteenth century, Judith M. Bennett discovered that widows "acquired public opportunities that surpassed those of all other women."[25] In fact, she notes that new opportunities for widows included the following:

> independently trading, exchanging, and selling small parcels of property ... They, unlike daughters, owed suit to the Brigstock court and answered complaints and pursued litigation without the *couveture* of a male. In addition, they, like husbands, could be legally liable for the actions and problems of their dependents. (23)

Women, then, gained much more power upon widowhood than they were allowed at any other time of their lives. This greater control of property upon widowhood may partly explain Morgan le Fay's motive for violence against her husband. Although she does not seem to be restricted in her activities while he is alive, her legal power would have grown with her husband's death. It is difficult to say why Morgan seems to be the only woman in *Le Morte Darthur* who is not restrained by marriage. However, it may be one of the reasons she is seen as being an "evil sorceress": a medieval woman who is not submissive was considered to be in some way "unnatural."

Elaine of Astolat, Guenevere, Nyneve, and Morgan le Fay all violate the boundaries of either medieval marriage practices or the ideal of courtly love. Although not successful in her ultimate goal to take Arthur's place as ruler of the country, Morgan is successful in transgressing the limitations placed on medieval women with impunity. She survives partly because of her magical powers, which can protect her from retribution, such as when she temporarily transforms herself into stone to escape capture by Arthur: she is invincible. Although not invincible, all of the women have difficulty fulfilling their desires just as Morgan does. For example, even Guenevere, who does enjoy the love of Lancelot, cannot escape the exposure of her infidelity and the resulting chaos of the court. The lesson of *Le Morte D'arthur*, primarily for medieval women but perhaps also for medieval men, appears to be that women cannot prevail against the restrictions of their society.

NOTES

[1] Malory, *Works*, ed. Eugene Vinaver, (New York: Oxford UP), 5.

[2] Jennifer Ward, *English Noblewomen in the Later Middle Ages* (New York: Longman Publishing, 1992), 17.

[3] Georges Duby, *The Knight, the Lady and the Priest: The Making of Modern Marriage in Medieval France*, trans. Barbara Bray (New York: Pantheon Books, 1984), 268.

[4] Ward, *English Noblewomen in the Later Middle Ages*, 13.

[5] J. R. Lander, "Marriage and Politics in the Fifteenth Century: The Nevilles and the Wydevilles," *Bulletin of the Institute of Historical Research* 36, 121.

[6] *Ibid.* For more on marriage practices, see Joel T. Rosenthal, "Aristocratic Marriage and the English Peerage, 1350-1500: Social Institution and Personal Bond," *Journal of Medieval History* 10 (1984), 181-194.

[7] See John T. Noonan, "Marriage in the Middle Ages I: Power to Choose," *Viator* 4 (1973), 419-434.

[8] Ann S. Haskell, "Marriage in the Middle Ages III: The Paston Women on Marriage in Fifteenth-Century England," *Viator* 4 (1973), 467-9.

[9] *Paston Letters and Papers of the Fifteenth Century*, vol. II, ed. Norman Davis (Oxford: Clarendon Press, 1976), 31.

[10] As summarized in Roger Boase, *The Origin and Meaning of Courtly Love: A Critical Study of European Scholarship*, (Manchester: Manchester UP, 1977), chapter three. For more information on courtly love see Andreas Capellanus, *The Art of Courtly Love*, trans. John Jay Parry, (New York: Columbia UP, 1990); Toril Moi, "Desire in Language: Andreas Capellanus and the Controversy of Courtly Love," in *Medieval Literature: Criticism, Ideology and History,* ed. David Aers (Southampton: The Camelot Press, Ltd., 1986); Julia Kristeva, *Tales of Love*, trans. Leon S. Roudiez (New York: Columbia UP, 1987); and June Hall McCash, "The Flowering of Romance: Women and the Development of Medieval Arthurian Literature," *Avalon to Camelot* 3 (1984), 5-8; and "Mutual Love as a Medieval Ideal,"in *Courtly Literature: Culture and Context*, Keith Busby and Erik Kooper, eds. (Philadelphia: John Benjamin's Publishing Company, 1990), 429-438.

[11] Charles Moorman, "Courtly Love in Malory," *ELH* 27: 176.

[12] Malory, *Works*, 649.

[13] R. T. Davies, "Malory's 'Vertuous Love,'" *Studies in Philology* 53 (1956), 468-9.

[14] Bloch, *Medieval Misogyny and the Invention of Western Romantic Love* (Chicago: Chicago UP, 1991), 196.

[15] Duby, "The Courtly Model," trans. Arthur Goldhammer, in *A History of Women in the West, II Silences of the Middle Ages*, ed. Christiane Klapish-Zuber (Cambridge, Massachussetts: The Belknap Press of Harvard UP, 1992), 262.

[16] Malory, *Works*, 635.

[17] Compare Malory's version to earlier versions of Merlin's love of the Lady of the Lake in the *Huth Merlin* and *Les Prophecies de Merlin*. In these versions Merlin is not called a devil's son and she is portrayed as manipulative, using his love for her to learn all his secrets, then using those secrets to imprison him.

[18] Bloch, *Medieval Misogyny*, 149.

[19] Elaine Tuttle Hansen, "The Powers of Silence: The Case of the Clerk's Griselda" in *Women and Power in the Middle Ages*, ed. Mary Erler and Maryanne Kowaleski (Athens, Georgia: The University of Georgia Press, 1989), 238.

[20] Malory, *Works*, 628.

[21] Georges Duby, *The Knight, the Lady, and the Priest: The Making of Modern Marriage in Medieval France*, 28.

[22] Helen Rodnite Lemay, *Women's Secrets: A Translation of Pseudo-Albertus Magus's De Secretis Mulierum with Commentaries* (Albany: SUNY UP, 1992). Although the work was first written in the thirteenth century, more than fifty printed manuscripts survive from the fifteenth century, demonstrating its continued popularity; see Lemay, page 1.

[23] See Alexander J. Denomy, *The Heresy of Courtly Love* (Gloucester, Massachusetts: The Declan X. McMullen Company, Inc., 1947), 34-5.

[24] Malory, *Works*, 340.

[25] Judith M. Bennett, "Public Power and Authority in the Medieval English Countryside," in *Women and Power in the Middle Ages*, ed. Mary Erler and Maryanne Kowaleski (Athens: University of Georgia Press, 1988), 23.

Worcester State College

*Zwischen politischer Funktion und Rolle der 'virgo docta': Weibliche Selbstzeugnisse im 15. Jahrhundert**

Sabine Schmolinsky

Ein Mensch gibt Einblick in Ereignisse, Entwicklungen und Einstellungen in seinem Leben: solche als Selbstzeugnis[1] charakterisierbare Quellentypen sind für Fragen nach weiblicher und männlicher Präsenz in der historischen Überlieferung in besonderem Maß offen, und sie antworten ihnen offensichtlicher als andere Quellensorten, da das geschlechtsspezifische Ich nicht nur Autor, sondern auch Objekt der Quelle ist. Selbstzeugnisse mittelalterlicher Frauen sind, wenn man von den Mystikerinnen absieht, deutlich seltener als solche männlicher Provenienz und setzen erst im 15. Jahrhundert ein. Formen und Bilder weiblicher Existenz, die sie produzieren, sollen im folgenden untersucht werden.

"... Eine ... Erzählung, in welcher Leben und Seelenbewegung einer klugen und willensstarken Frau kenntlich werden;" — so nannte Gustav Freytag 1866 im zweiten, *Vom Mittelalter zur Neuzeit* betitelten Band der *Bilder aus der Deutschen Vergangenheit* die Aufzeichnungen der Wiener Bürgerin Helene Kottanner (um 1400 – nach 1470),[2] die heutigen Tages vor allem als "die ältesten Frauenmemoiren des deutschen Mittelalters" bekannt sind.[3] Die Überschrift — "Eine deutsche Frau am Fürstenhofe. (Um 1440)"—, der Kontext — böhmisch-hussitische Geschichte sowie Reflexionen über das Leben an deutschen Fürstenhöfen im 15. Jahrhundert — und die gewählten und teils neu gruppierten Ausschnitte verdeutlichen jedoch, daß Freytag eine andere Lektüre dieses Textes vorschwebte: aus der Geschichte vom Raub der ungarischen Krone und der Krönung des gerade geborenen Ladislaus wählte er Abschnitte aus, die "Bilder vom ungarischen Königshofe" zur Zeit eines deutschen Königsgeschlechtes sein sollten,[4] jedoch gerade das nicht Alltägliche, das unerhörte Ereignis erzählten. Darüberhinaus zielte Freytag im Sinn der Konzeption seiner *Bilder*, die den Schluß vom Einzelereignis und Einzelmenschen auf die Seele eines ganzen Volkes erlauben sollten,[5] auf psychologische Aussagen: die — in der Tat sehr spannend geschilderte und einen erzählerischen Höhepunkt bildende — nächtliche Szene des sorgfältig vorbereiteten, eigentlichen Raubes "interessiert am meisten ... und die Gemütsbewegungen eines starken Frauencharakters", d.h. die Art und Weise, in der "in Todesgefahr ... Angst und Gewissen in ihrer Seele arbeiten" und "bei der Tochter des 15. Jahrhunderts sogleich eine sinnlich wahrnehmbare Gestalt" annehmen, eine "Art von Sinnentätigkeit", die in Freytags Vorstellung "allgemein und vorzugsweise kennzeichnend für das Jugendleben jedes Volkes" ist.[6]

Auch wenn Freytags geschichtsphilosophischer Hintergrund und seine Methodik heute nur noch historisch betrachtet werden können, so ist doch sein nicht an der politischen Ereignisgeschichte orientierter Umgang mit den Quellen gegenwärtigen Konzepten der Mentalitätsgeschichte nicht gänzlich fremd, und die erwähnte Szene der Schrecken eines nächtlichen Raubes unter Todesgefahr fände ihren Platz zum Beispiel in einer Geschichte der Angst. Den Aspekt des persönlichen Zeugnisses hat Freytag trotz seiner Suche nach dem Potential an Verallgemeinerbarem in den Quellen durchaus gesehen,[7] wenngleich er ihm in seiner Textvorlage nicht unbedingt nahegelegt wurde, denn 1846 hatte der erste Herausgeber Stefan Ladislaus Endlicher seinem sprachlich modernisierten Druck den Titel *Denkwürdigkeiten der Helene Kottannerin* gegeben,[8] eine Formulierung, die dem Text auch in der kritischen Ausgabe von Karl Mollay 1971 geblieben ist[9] und zunächst allgemein das des Gedenkens Würdige und gegebenenfalls dessen schriftliche Fixierung bezeichnet.

Was denn das sei, war im historischen Verständnis, wie es sich zum Beispiel in Quellenkunden dokumentiert, rasch geklärt: "Narratio casuum et periculorum, quae Elisabetha, fugiens cum corona Hungariae in Austriam a. 1439–1440, superaverat" beschreibt das jüngste Werk dieser Gattung, das *Repertorium fontium historiae medii aevi*, den Inhalt im Jahre 1990.[10] Helene Kottaner kommt darin nicht vor; daß es sich um einen Bericht in der Ich-Form handelt, wird nicht erwähnt.

Zweifelsohne ist die wohl bald nach 1442 entstandene Schrift eine historisch verläßliche Quelle, aber darüberhinaus erzählt sie mit Geschick eine spannende Geschichte, deren eigentlicher Held die heilige ungarische Krone, die Stephanskrone, ist. Diese befindet sich, wie in einer Kette von Szenen eindrücklich vorgeführt wird, wohlverwahrt auf der Plintenburg / Visegrád; sie soll allerdings in größtmöglicher Nähe sein, wenn Elisabeth von Luxemburg, die einzige Tochter Kaiser Sigismunds, deutsche Königin und Königin von Ungarn und Böhmen und gerade (am 27. Oktober 1439) verwitwete Frau des deutschen Königs Albrechts II., ein Kind zur Welt bringen wird. Daher beauftragt sie ihre Hofdame Helene Kottaner, die Krone zu entwenden, was dieser in der erwähnten nächtlichen Aktion mit der Hilfe eines ins Vertrauen gezogenen Ungarn gelingt. In Komorn und nicht, wie vorgesehen, in Preßburg / Bratislava wird am 22. Februar 1440 Ladislaus Postumus geboren, zur großen Freude aller Anhänger der deutschen Partei, da die Existenz eines Thronerben nun endgültig die von der ungarischen Seite favorisierte Verheiratung Elisabeths mit dem polnischen König Władisław Jagiełło obsolet erscheinen läßt. Auch nach seiner — völlig ordnungsgemäßen, aber unter abenteuerlichen Umständen inszenierten — Krönung an Pfingsten (15. Mai 1440) in Stuhlweißenburg / Székesfehérvár ist der kleine König nicht allgemein anerkannt, und im Kreis der Ratgeber wird beschlossen, daß die königliche Familie zu trennen sei und Elisabeth, ihre jüngste Tochter Elisabeth im vierten Lebensjahr und der neugeborene Sohn Ladislaus sich an verschiedenen Orten aufzuhalten hätten. Der Kottannerin als seiner Pflegerin und

Bezugsperson fällt zu, den König zu begleiten. Ihre Schilderung bricht nach der Ankunft in Ödenburg / Sopron ab, mitten im Bericht über Gewalttätigkeiten des ungarisch-polnischen Lagers.[11] Da der Text allein als Handschriftenfragment erhalten ist,[12] könnte über seinen Fortgang und Schluß nur spekuliert werden.

Die Kottannerin bietet jedoch mehr, als Politikgeschichte aus denkbar authentischer Perspektive. Ihre kultur- und mentalitätsgeschichtlich aufschlußreichen Bemerkungen sind — in anderer Terminologie — schon früher wahrgenommen worden;[13] ihr Werk als Selbstzeugnis einer Frau ist allerdings hinter der Kategorie "älteste deutsche Frauenmemoiren" verschwunden, wie sie Karl Mollay 1971 in der Überschrift des Nachwortes zu seiner Edition des Textes erscheinen ließ.[14] Da "Frauenmemoiren" nirgends erläutert wird, sollte offensichtlich nur die literaturgeschichtliche Tatsache weiblicher Autorschaft mit dem Begriff bezeichnet werden, was allerdings denselben Karl Mollay nicht hinderte, am Ende dieses Nachwortes im Kontext der Frage nach der Originalität der Handschrift festzustellen:

> Es ist aber schwer zu glauben, daß im 15. Jahrhundert eine Frau, auch wenn sie so erfahren und schlagfertig war wie die Kottannerin, diese Denkwürdigkeiten ohne Zuhilfenahme einer gelehrten Feder vom Anfang bis zum Ende wie eine einfache Erzählung diktiert hätte. Der Aufbau und die unleugbare Tendenz scheinen das zu bestätigen.[15]

In analoger Weise ist 1988 in der Literaturgeschichte *Deutsche Literatur von Frauen* der wissenschaftliche Blick nur inhaltsbezogen auf die weiblichen Handlungsträger gerichtet:

> Die Denkwürdigkeiten der Kottannerin sind ein einzigartiges Dokument: Zwei Frauen gehen als Siegerinnen aus einer machtpolitischen Auseinandersetzung hervor, die eine der beiden Frauen aus ihrer Sicht darstellt.[16]

Nimmt man die oben zitierte quellenkundliche Inhaltsangabe hinzu,[17] so ist die Frage berechtigt, was denn Helene Kottanners Werk auch als ein Selbstzeugnis lesen läßt. "Do was Ich, Helene Kottannerin auch da vnd ward ich auch mit gesandt ..." führt sie sich ein, nachdem sie das Zusammentreffen des Königs und der Königin mit Albrecht von Österreich sowie der jüngsten Tochter Elisabeth in Preßburg berichtet hat,[18] eine Form der Selbstnennung, die öfters begegnet, insbesondere beim Bericht über Situationen, die der Namensträgerin Reputation garantierten, sie als bevorzugte Ratgeberin ihrer königlichen Herrin oder als Verantwortliche für das königliche Baby in der Mitte des Geschehens zeigten. Als gute Erzählerin folgt Helene trotzdem ihrem Plot, ohne die eigene Person zum Erzählgegenstand *sui generis* zu erheben, so daß man von autobiographischem Schreiben[19] nicht sprechen kann. Nicht privates, sondern öffentliches Leben wird dargestellt; daher trifft die Bezeichnung Memoiren zu.[20]

Dennoch erfährt man über Helene etwas mehr, als nur den Stolz einer königsnahen Bürgerin sowie ihre Angst und ihre religiös genährten Gewissenszweifel beim Raub der Krone: sie hat kleine Kinder, um die sie angesichts ihres Auftrages Angst hat,[21] ihr Beruf fordert sie in arbeitsintensiven Zeiten, wie nach der Geburt des Thronfolgers, Tag und Nacht,[22] Zeit und Raum für Familienleben erscheinen nicht, ihr Mann taucht erst auf, als er vor der Separierung der königlichen Familie, wie alle Welt, einen Treueeid ablegen muß (den seine Frau als einzige, wie sie hervorhebt, nicht schwören muß),[23] ihren Mann und ihre Tochter Katharina muß sie zurücklassen, als sie mit dem kleinen König aufbricht.[24] Ihre Gläubigkeit äußert sich in den Formen ihrer Zeit: der Teufel kann real eingreifen, nur mit Gott kann — und soll — man angesichts einschneidender Entscheidungen zu Rate gehen.[25] Ihre intellektuellen Fähigkeiten sind schwer einzuschätzen: einerseits schreibt sie — in welcher Form auch immer — ein Werk wie das vorliegende, andererseits kann sie trotz ihrer ersten Ehe mit dem Ödenburger Patrizier Peter Székeles Ungarisch nur verstehen, nicht sprechen, ist also nicht zweisprachig geworden.[26]

Im Sinn der Frage nach weiblichen Selbstzeugnissen ist der Bericht der Kottannerin mithin einschlägig — und vor allem selten, denn im 15. Jahrhundert kennt er kaum seinesgleichen. Ihm zur Seite stellen lassen sich die wohl nach 1412 entstandenen[27] kastilischen Aufzeichnungen der andalusischen Adeligen Doña Leonor López de Córdoba (1362/63 — nach 1412), die ebenfalls vor allem als Quelle der politischen Geschichte, hier zur Zeit der kastilischen Könige Pedro I. und seines Stiefbruders Enrique de Trastámara in der zweiten Hälfte des 14. Jahrhunderts, gelesen werden.[28] Sie sind mehr Autobiographie als Memoiren, da sie — zwar chronologisch sprunghaft, aber alle wichtigen Stationen enthaltend — einen Lebensabriß bis etwa zum Berichtszeitpunkt, der in ihrem letzten, historisch unbekannten Lebensabschnitt angenommen wird, bieten. Die Form verweist jedoch auf einen möglicherweise auch rechtlich gearteten Gebrauchszusammenhang, denn Doña Leonor läßt den Text als ein Notariatsinstrument ("Escriptura") aufschreiben, führt sich selbst dem Urkundenformular entsprechend ein ("... yo Doña Leonor Lopez de Cordoba, fija de mi Señor el Maestre Don Martin Lopez de Cordoba, é Doña Sancha Carrillo ...") und beschwört mit dem Kreuzeszeichen die Wahrheit des Folgenden als selbst Erlebtem. Die von ihr befohlene Niederschrift nennt sie "relacion ... por memoria".[29]

Wie bei der Kottannerin bilden außergewöhnliche Ereignisse den Anlaß zur Niederschrift, im Gegensatz zur Kottannerin allerdings meist katastrophaler Natur. Doña Leonor lebte als Tochter des Großmeisters von Calatrava, durch ihre Mutter und ihren Ehemann mit dem Königshaus verwandt, im Umfeld des Hofes Pedros I., bis sie durch den Sieg Enriques II. ihren Vater und Teile ihrer Familie verlor und neun Jahre bis zum Tod Enriques im Gefängnis saß. Während sie nach der Freilassung Aufnahme bei ihrer Tante María García Carillo in Córdoba fand, durchwanderte ihr Mann sieben Jahre lang erfolglos die Welt ("por el mundo, come Desbenturado"[30]), um seinen Besitz wiederzuerlangen; schließlich wohnen beide in einem Haus der Tante, allerdings angefeindet, und als Doña Leonor einmal verzweifelt ihre Geduld verliert, stirbt eines der Mädchen in ihren Händen.[31] Mit der finanziellen Hilfe ihrer Tante gelingt es ihr, einen ihr zuvor im Traum offenbarten Platz für ein Haus zu erwerben; sie interpretiert diese Erfüllung ihres sehnlichsten Wunsches als Gottes Gegengabe dafür, nach einem Judenpogrom eine jüdische Waise aufgenommen und getauft zu haben, und verbindet dies darüberhinaus mit ihren über längere Zeiten hinweg immer wieder rituell durchgeführten Gebeten zu Maria. Erst nach dieser Etablierung — ihr Mann ist aus der Erzählung verschwunden — erwähnt sie ihre Kinder, allerdings im Zusammenhang mit einer Pestwelle, der, nicht ohne ihre Schuld, neben vielen anderen ihr ehemals jüdischer Pflegesohn und ein anderer Sohn zum Opfer fallen — ihrer Sünden wegen, wie sie in diesem letzten Teil ihrer Autobiographie fast topisch ihr Unglück wiederholt begründet; diverse Frömmigkeitsübungen verändern ihre Lage nicht.

Die Verfolgung ihrer Familie und Verwandtschaft, der mühsame Erwerb eines eigenen Hauses und die zahlreichen Tode durch die Pest: das sind die drei Themen Doña Leonors, und mindestens einen Anlaß für ihr Diktat dürfte sie beim Begräbnis ihres Sohns dem Volk in den Mund gelegt haben: "Salid Señores, y vereis la mas desventurada desamparada, é mas Maldita muger del mundo ...."[32] Der Schlußsatz allerdings lautet: "y asi Vineme á mis Casas á Cordoba."[33] Zudem hatte sie ihren Bericht unter das Zeichen der tröstenden und hilfreichen Jungfrau Maria gestellt: alle Leidenden sollten an ihrem Beispiel Marias Unterstützung der an sie Glaubenden ablesen können. Entsprechend sollte die "relacion" Doña Leonors Taten, aber auch die durch Maria geoffenbarten Wunder umfassen.[34]

Trotz aller Unterschiede berühren sich die volkssprachlichen Memoiren der Helene Kottanner und die volkssprachliche Autobiographie der Doña Leonor López de Córdoba in zwei Punkten: zum einen in der Teilhabe am höfischen Leben, die mit dem fast gänzlichen Ausschluß privater Mitteilungen einhergeht; auch Doña Leonors Erfahrungen mit der Pest sind stark von ihrer — teils ehemaligen — öffentlichen Position bestimmt; und zum anderen in der Bedeutung der Religiosität für Entscheidungen und Handlungsweisen. Natürlich ist diese in den geschilderten Zusammenhängen praktischer Natur und in nichts zu vergleichen mit der einer in mystischen Erfahrungen lebenden Frau wie — in diesem Zeitraum — Margery Kempe, deren — *sit venia verbo* — Autobiographie am gesamten Leben der Diktierenden orientiert ist.[35]

Virgines doctae sind mit diesen Namen nicht bezeichnet, und es fällt auf, daß gelehrte Frauen, die von ihren Zeitgenossen mit diesen Worten geehrt wurden, wie beispielsweise die Italienerin Isotta Nogarola,[36] sich im Bereich der Selbstzeugnisse in anderen als autobiographischen Medien, nämlich insbesondere Briefen, geäußert haben; das dürfte durch ihre Teilhabe am humanistischen Diskurs bedingt sein. In Deutschland treten gelehrte Frauen im 15. Jahrhundert wieder anders auf: als Romanautorinnen wie Elisabeth von Nassau-Saarbrücken und Eleonore von Österreich[37] oder Mäzeninnen wie Mechthild von der Pfalz[38] oder Margarethe von Österreich.[39] Erst mit Caritas Pirckheimer als von Konrad Celtis und anderen deutschen Humanisten seiner Generation so apostrophierter "virgo docta"[40] beginnt eine Reihe deutscher gelehrter Humanistinnen, die Ursula Hess in der Literaturgeschichte *Deutsche Literatur von Frauen* exemplarisch mit der "uxor docta" Margarete Peutinger und der schon von den Zeitgenossen als Genie und Wunder angesehenen Olympia Fulvia Morata fortsetzt.[41] Die vom ersten Herausgeber Constantin von Höfler 1852 mit *Denkwürdigkeiten* benannten Aufzeichnungen der Äbtissin Caritas Pirckheimer über die reformatorischen Ereignisse der Jahre 1524 bis 1528 im Kloster S. Klara in Nürnberg[42] liegen jedoch ob dieser Daten jenseits des hier zu betrachtenden Zeitraums, wiewohl Barbara / Caritas ihre Karriere als gelehrte Nonne vor der Jahrhundertwende begann: 1479 wurde sie als Zwölfjährige in das erwähnte Kloster gegeben und fiel als noch nicht Vierzehnjährige im Winter 1481 durch ihre Lateinkenntnisse auf.[43] Bei ihr und anderen Genannten ist augenfällig, daß sie nicht als Hausfrau und Mutter oder Berufstätige erscheinen; sie sind, beispielsweise als geistlich lebende Frau, "abkömmlich" im Sinne Max Webers.

Ein wichtiger Bereich der Selbstzeugnisse ist bisher fast außer Acht geblieben: Briefe. Einzelne Briefe und Briefwechsel von und mit Frauen des 15. Jahrhunderts sind bekannt, aber erst die Aufarbeitung größerer Bestände, wie Katherine Walsh sie gefordert hat,[44] wird sie als Mittel der privaten Mitteilung auszuwerten erlauben.[45] Dabei werden, so ist zu hoffen, auch Selbstzeugnisse der zahlreichen, vor allem in den Städten ihre Berufe ausübenden — mithin nicht abkömmlichen — Frauen auftauchen, denn diese sind bisher nur mit den in der Sozial- und Wirtschaftsgeschichte üblicherweise genutzten Quellentypen zu erfassen. Die Probleme der Kategorisierung werden allerdings nicht kleiner: so wie die Grenzen zwischen Autobiographie, Memoiren und chronikalischem Bericht oft fließend sind, so kann eine topische Aussage in einem Brief schwer von einer authentischen zu trennen sein oder in sie übergehen. Mit Blick auf Fragen der Genderforschung wäre es interessant, falls, offen oder latent, die Kategorisierung geschlechterbezogen ausfiele, etwa ein historischer Bericht einer Frau mit autorenbezogenen Inseraten rascher als Autobiographie qualifiziert würde als ein solcher eines männlichen Autors.

Wie bei den sogenannten "Frauenmemoiren" der Kottannerin zu erkennen war, spiegelt die Vergabe qualifizierender Begriffe auch (vergangene) geschichtswissenschaftliche Forschungstrends und — vorlieben, so daß nur zu hoffen bleibt, daß die gegenwärtige lebhafte Beschäftigung mit Selbstzeugnissen unterschiedlichster Zeiträume und Provenienzen die sorgfältige Differenzierung der Textsorten — gegebenenfalls im Sinne von Kategorisierungen einer Quelle nach Aspekten — immer mit umfassen wird.

NOTES

* Mit Belegen versehene Fassung des auf dem Internationalen Kongreß der Fifteenth Century Studies in Kaprun (Österreich) am 6. Juli 1995 unter dem Titel: "Zwischen 'virgo docta' und Kauffrau. Weibliche Selbstzeugnisse des 15. Jahrhunderts" gehaltenen Vortrags.

[1] Selbstzeugnis sei hier als weitgefaßter, verschiedenste Quellensorten umfassender Begriff verwendet, ohne daß auf die zur Zeit lebhafte Forschungsdiskussion eingegangen werden soll: vgl. Benigna von Krusenstjern, "Was sind Selbstzeugnisse? Begriffskritische und quellenkundliche Überlegungen anhand von Beispielen aus dem 17. Jahrhundert", *Historische Anthropologie* 2 (1994), 462–471, sowie die Beiträge des von Winfried Schulze herausgegebenen Tagungsbandes "Ego-Dokumente. Annäherung an den Menschen in der Geschichte" (Berlin: Akademie Verlag, 1996) und: ders., "Ego-Dokumente: Annäherung an den Menschen in der Geschichte?" in *Von Aufbruch und Utopie. Perspektiven einer neuen Gesellschaftsgeschichte des Mittelalters. Für und mit Ferdinand Seibt aus Anlaß seines 65. Geburtstages*, hg. von Bea Lundt und Helma Reimöller (Köln, Weimar, Wien: Böhlau, 1992), 418–450. Zur nicht der Intelligenz oder Oberschicht zugehörigen Schreibpraxis vgl. Jan Peters, "Wegweiser zum Innenleben? Möglichkeiten und Grenzen der Untersuchung populärer Selbstzeugnisse der Frühen Neuzeit", *Historische Anthropologie* 1 (1993), 235–249, hier 235.

[2] Gustav Freytag, *Bilder aus der Deutschen Vergangenheit*, II. Band: *Vom Mittelalter zur Neuzeit*, hg. von G. A. E. Bogeng (Leipzig: Paul List Verlag, [um 1924]), 367.

[3] Winfried Stelzer, "Helene Kottanner", in *Die deutsche Literatur des Mittelalters. Verfasserlexikon*, 2., völlig neu bearbeitete Aufl., hg. von Kurt Ruh, Bd. 5 (Berlin, New York: Walter de Gruyter 1985), 326–28, hier 328, nach den Worten des Herausgebers: *Die Denkwürdigkeiten der Helene Kottannerin (1439–1440)*, hg. von Karl Mollay (Wien: Österreichischer Bundesverlag für Unterricht, Wissenschaft und Kunst, 1971), Wiener Neudrucke 2: 7. Vgl. ders., "Kottanner(in), Helene", in *Lexikon des Mittelalters*, Bd. 5 (München und Zürich: Artemis Verlag, 1991), 1463.

[4] Freytag (wie Anm. 2), Zitat 368, sowie 319–68; Text 370–81.

[5] Freytag (wie Anm. 2), I. Band: *Aus dem Mittelalter*, Einführung von Georg von Below (XV–XVI) und Einleitung Freytags (1–16, bes. 13–15).

[6] Freytag (wie Anm. 2), 381–82.

[7] "Und nicht am wenigsten merkwürdig ist, daß dieselbe Frau in einer Zeit des rührigen Handelns, wo auch den Männern das Schreiben lästig oder unmöglich war, die wichtigen Ereignisse ihres Lebens und ihren Anteil an der Politik in Memoirenform niederschrieb. Die Verwunderung über einen so ungewöhnlichen Einfall steigert sich ..." Freytag (wie Anm. 2), 369.

[8] Mollay, *Denkwürdigkeiten* (wie Anm. 3), 69–70.

[9] Trotz des spätestens seit Freytag erkennbaren Zusammenhangs mit der Textsorte Memoiren ist der Text nur als historische Quelle rezipiert worden. Vgl. den modernen Titel *Denkwürdigkeiten* eines zeitgenössischen historiographischen Werkes, das die eigene Biographie als Rahmen setzt: *Eberhart Windeckes Denkwürdigkeiten zur Geschichte des Zeitalters Kaiser Sigmunds*, hg. von Wilhelm Altmann (Berlin: R. Gaertners Verlagsbuchhandlung, 1893). Windecke spricht von "buch" oder "geschichten, was harnoch geschriben stot" (1–2).

[10] *Repertorium fontium historiae medii aevi* primum ab Augusto Potthast digestum, nunc cura collegii historicorum e pluribus nationibus emendatum et auctum, Bd. 6 (Rom: Istituto Storico Italiano per il Medio Evo, 1990), 645. Alphons Lhotsky, *Quellenkunde zur mittelalterlichen Geschichte Österreichs* (Graz, Köln: Verlag Hermann Böhlaus Nachf., 1963), Mitteilungen des Instituts für österreichische Geschichtsforschung, Ergänzungsbd. 19: 345. Vgl. Karl und Mathilde Uhlirz, *Handbuch der Geschichte Österreich-Ungarns*, 1. Band — 1526, 2., neubearb. Aufl. von Mathilde Uhlirz (Graz, Wien, Köln: Verlag Hermann Böhlaus Nachf., 1963), 57 mit 66, 437 mit 433.

[11] Mollay, *Denkwürdigkeiten* (wie Anm. 3), 9–35; Inhaltsangabe 78–82. Vgl. Ursula Liebertz-Grün, "Höfische Autorinnen. Von der karolingischen Kulturreform bis zum Humanismus", in *Deutsche Literatur von Frauen. Erster Band: Vom Mittelalter bis zum Ende des 18. Jahrhunderts*, hg. von Gisela Brinker-Gabler (München: Verlag C. H. Beck, 1988), 39–64, hier 60–63. Erika Uitz, "Zeitlicher Frieden im Denken von Frauen des Spätmittelalters", in *Von Menschen und ihren Zeichen. Sozialhistorische Untersuchungen zum Spätmittelalter und zur Neuzeit*, hg. von Ingrid Matschinegg, Brigitte Rath, Barbara Schuh (Bielefeld: Verlag für Regionalgeschichte, 1990), 61–76, hier 71–72.

[12] Mollay, *Denkwürdigkeiten* (wie Anm. 3), 90: Wien, Österreichische Nationalbibliothek, Hs. 2920. Vgl. Hermann Menhardt, *Verzeichnis der altdeutschen literarischen Handschriften der Österreichischen Nationalbibliothek*, Bd. 1 (Berlin: Akademie-Verlag, 1960), Deutsche Akademie der Wissenschaften zu Berlin. Veröffentlichungen des Instituts für deutsche Sprache und Literatur, 13: 618–619.

[13] Mollay, *Denkwürdigkeiten* (wie Anm. 3), 83–85.

[14] Mollay, *Denkwürdigkeiten* (wie Anm. 3), 69; vgl. 86 und 92.

[15] Mollay, *Denkwürdigkeiten* (wie Anm. 3), 92.

[16] Liebertz-Grün (wie Anm. 11), 62. Vgl. den ersten Satz des Kapitels (60), "Wie eine wagemutige und tatkräftige Königinwitwe mit Hilfe ihrer Kammerfrau die Anschläge und Machenschaften ihrer Landesherren durchkreuzen und ihren Willen durchsetzen konnte, hat Helene Kottanner in ihren Memoiren erzählt."

[17] Walther Killys 1988–1993 erschienenes *Literaturlexikon. Autoren und Werke deutscher Sprache* (Gütersloh, München: Bertelsmann Lexikon Verlag) hat die Kottannerin nicht aufgenommen.

[18] Mollay, *Denkwürdigkeiten* (wie Anm. 3), 9, Zitat Z. 10–11.

[19] Darunter seien Berichte des eigenen Lebens verstanden, die den bisher gelebten Lebenslauf als Ganzes oder im Überblick nach – offensichtlich für wichtig gehaltenen — Stationen beschreiben, also einen Berichtszeitraum umfassen, der die eigene Lebensdauer allenfalls durch den Rückblick auf die Herkunft überschreitet, und die als Berichtsziel die Darstellung von Ereignissen und Merkmalen des individuellen Lebens haben und nicht oder kaum die äußerer, überindividueller, z.B. politischer Ereignisse. Zu Definitionen von Autobiographie vgl. Rainer H. Goetz, *Spanish Golden Age Autobiography in Its Context* (New York u.a.: Peter Lang, 1994), American University Studies II, 203: 1–10.

[20] Diese Unterscheidung bei: Horst Wenzel, "Zu den Anfängen der volkssprachigen Autobiographie im späten Mittelalter", in *Daphnis* 13 (1984), 59–75, hier 65.

[21] Mollay, *Denkwürdigkeiten* (wie Anm. 3), 13, Z. 38–39.

[22] "... vnd ich mst swërlich vnd herttikleich dienen meiner gnedigen frawn vnd auch irn kindern Vnd all die weil ir gnad in den kindelpetten lag, kam ich n aus meinem gebant, weder tag noch *nacht*." Mollay, *Denkwürdigkeiten* (wie Anm. 3), 22, Z. 2–5.

[23] Mollay, *Denkwürdigkeiten* (wie Anm. 3), 32, Z. 26–28; 33, Z. 26–28.

[24] Mollay, *Denkwürdigkeiten* (wie Anm. 3), 33, Z. 35–36.

[25] Mollay, *Denkwürdigkeiten* (wie Anm. 3), 11, Z. 14–15; 24, Z. 3 und 13–14; 13, Z. 40 – 14, Z. 2; vgl. 16, Z. 6–11.

[26] Mollay, *Denkwürdigkeiten* (wie Anm. 3), 83.

[27] Amy Katz Kaminsky, Elaine Dorough Johnson, "To Restore Honor and Fortune: The Autobiography of Leonor López de Córdoba", in *The Female Autograph. Theory and Practice of Autobiography from the Tenth to the Twentieth Century*, ed. by Domna C. Stanton (Chicago and London: The University of Chicago Press, 1987, zuerst 1984), 70–80, hier 70. Dietrich Briesemeister, "Die Autobiographie in Spanien im 15. Jahrhundert", in *Biographie und Autobiographie in der Renaissance*, hg. von August Buck (Wiesbaden: Harrassowitz, 1983), Wolfenbütteler Abhandlungen zur Renaissanceforschung 4: 45–56, hier 45, datiert — ohne Begründung — auf 1400. María-Milagros Rivera Garretas, "Orte und Worte von Frauen. Eine feministische Spurensuche im europäischen Mittelalter", übers. von Barbara Hinger (Wien: Wiener Frauenverlag, 1993), Reihe Frauenforschung 23: 177–201, hier 197, bevorzugt eine Datierung zwischen 1401 und 1406, da Doña Leonor ihren Bericht vor Beginn der Zeit als Vertraute der Königin Katharina von Lancaster enden läßt.

[28] Reinaldo Ayerbe-Chaux, "Las memorias de Doña Leonor López de Córdoba", in *Journal of Hispanic Philology* 2 (1977), 11–33. Engl. Übersetzung Kaminsky / Johnson (wie Anm. 27), 73–80. Kaminsky und Johnson kennzeichnen den Text als Quelle für die

Lebensumstände spanischer adeliger Frauen des 14. Jahrhunderts (72), aber auf Grund des Abfassungszeitraums kann er (auch) als dem 15. Jahrhundert zugehörig betrachtet werden. Zur politischen Geschichte vgl. *Historia de España*. Dirigida por Ramón Menéndez Pidal. Tomo XV: *Los Trastámaras de Castilla y Aragón en el Siglo XV*. ... Por Luis Suárez Fernández, Ángel Canellas López, Jaime Vicens Vives, Tercera Edición (Madrid: Espasa-Calpe, S.A., 1982). Doña Leonors Biographie über ihr Werk hinaus rekonstruieren Alan Deyermond, "Spain's First Women Writers", in *Women in Hispanic Literature. Icons and Fallen Idols*, ed. Beth Miller (Berkeley, Los Angeles, London: University of California Press, 1983), 27–52, hier 31–37 und Rivera-Garretas (wie Anm. 27), 189–196.

[29] Ayerbe-Chaux (wie Anm. 28), 16. Briesemeister (wie Anm. 27), 46. Goetz (wie Anm. 19), 23–24; zu relación vgl. 59–60.

[30] Ayerbe-Chaux (wie Anm. 28), 20.

[31] Die Formulierung ist nicht eindeutig in Hinsicht auf die Todesart: "... y fui tan desconsolada, *que* perdi la paciencia, é la *que* me hizo mas contradicion con la Señora mi tia se murió en mis manos, comiendose la lengua ...": Ayerbe-Chaux (wie Anm. 28), 21. "... and I was so disconsolate I lost my patience, and the one who had most set my lady aunt against me died in my hands, swallowing her tongue." Kaminsky / Johnson (wie Anm. 27), 77.

[32] Ayerbe-Chaux (wie Anm. 28), 24. "'Come out good people and you will see the most unfortunate, forsaken and condemned woman in the world' ...": Kaminsky / Johnson (wie Anm. 27), 80.

[33] Ayerbe-Chaux (wie Anm. 28), 24–25. "And thus I came to my houses in Córdoba." Kaminsky / Johnson (wie Anm. 27), 80. Vgl. Goetz (wie Anm. 19), 35–39, 42; Briesemeister (wie Anm. 27), 48.

[34] Ayerbe-Chaux (wie Anm. 28), 16.

[35] *The Book of Margery Kempe*, ed. Sanford Brown Meech and Hope Emily Allen (Oxford: Oxford University Press, 1940, repr. 1961), EETS OS 212. Jüngst hat Lynn Staley die Unterscheidung zwischen "Margery, the subject, and Kempe her author" in die Debatte um den autobiographischen Status des *Book* eingeführt: *Margery Kempe's Dissenting Fictions* (University Park, PA: The Pennsylvania State University Press, 1994), 3. Vgl. Lesley Lawton, "Margery Kempe: The Flesh, the Word and the Text", in *L'Auto/ Biographie* (Toulouse: Presses Universitaires du Mirail, 1994), Caliban 31: 75–83, der das *Book* durch zwei gleichermaßen präsente Stimmen übermittelt sieht, die Margerys und die ihres Schreibers, der sich erst durch vergleichende Lektüre, also andere Texte, von Margerys Authentizität überzeugen kann (82–83).

[36] Katharina Fietze, *Spiegel der Vernunft. Theorien zum Menschsein der Frau in der Anthropologie des 15. Jahrhunderts* (Paderborn, München u.a.: Schöningh, 1991), 115–134.

[37] Liebertz-Grün (wie Anm. 11), 54–59 und 59–60. Hans-Hugo Steinhoff, "Elisabeth von Nassau-Saarbrücken" und "Eleonore von Österreich (Eleonore Stuart, Eleonore von Schottland)", in *Die deutsche Literatur des Mittelalters* (wie Anm. 3), Bd. 2 (1980),

482–88 und 470–473. Volker Mertens, "E[lisabeth] v. Nassau-Saarbrücken", in *Lexikon des Mittelalters* (wie Anm. 3), Bd. 3 (1986), 1836–37. Brigitte Schöning, "E[leonore] v. Österreich", ebd.: 1809.

[38] Renate Kruska, *Mechthild von der Pfalz. Im Spannungsfeld von Geschichte und Literatur* (Frankfurt a.M. u.a.: Peter Lang, 1989), Europäische Hochschulschriften, Reihe 1, Bd. 1111. Martina Backes, *Das literarische Leben am kurpfälzischen Hof zu Heidelberg im 15. Jahrhundert. Ein Beitrag zur Gönnerforschung des Spätmittelalters* (Tübingen: Max Niemeyer Verlag, 1992), Hermaea, N.F. 68: 184–190 u.ö. Hugo Ott, "Aus der Frühgeschichte der Freiburger Universität", *Freiburger Universitätsblätter*, Heft 127, März 1995, 27–28. Immo Eberl, "Mechthilde von der Pfalz", in *Lexikon des Mittelalters* (wie Anm. 3), Bd. 6 (München: Artemis und Winkler Verlag, 1993), 438.

[39] Liebertz-Grün (wie Anm. 11), 63–64. Willem P. Blockmans, "M[argarete] v. Österreich", in *Lexikon des Mittelalters* (wie Anm. 38), 238.

[40] Ursula Hess, "Oratrix humilis. Die Frau als Briefpartnerin von Humanisten, am Beispiel der Caritas Pirckheimer", in *Der Brief im Zeitalter der Renaissance*, hg. von Franz Josef Worstbrock, Mitteilung IX der Kommission für Humanismusforschung (Weinheim: VCH Verlagsgesellschaft, 1983), 173–203, hier 183. Vgl. Stephan Füssel, "Einleitung", in *Deutsche Dichter der frühen Neuzeit (1450–1600). Ihr Leben und Werk*, hg. von Stephan Füssel (Berlin: Erich Schmidt Verlag, 1993), 29.

[41] Ursula Hess, "Lateinischer Dialog und gelehrte Partnerschaft. Frauen als humanistische Leitbilder in Deutschland (1500–1550)", in *Deutsche Literatur von Frauen* (wie Anm. 11), 113–148. Stephan Füssel (wie Anm. 40) nimmt diese Frauen — unter Hinweis auf die Notwendigkeit künftiger Forschung — nur in seine Einleitung auf (29–30).

[42] *Die "Denkwürdigkeiten" der Caritas Pirckheimer (aus den Jahren 1524–1528)*, hg. von Josef Pfanner (Landshut: Solanus-Druck, 1962), Caritas Pirckheimer — Quellensammlung 2: VI. Photomech. Nachdr. mit Veränderungen: *Die Denkwürdigkeiten der Äbtissin Caritas Pirckheimer*, hg. von Frumentius Renner (St. Ottilien: EOS-Verlag, 1982).

[43] Lotte Kurras, "Pirckheimer, Caritas OSCl", in *Die deutsche Literatur des Mittelalters* (wie Anm. 3), Bd. 7 (1989), 697–701, hier 697. Vgl. Paula S. Datsko Barker, "Caritas Pirckheimer: A Female Humanist Confronts the Reformation", *The Sixteenth-Century Journal* 26 (1995), 259–272.

[44] Katherine Walsh, "Ein neues Bild der Frau im Mittelalter? Weibliche Biologie und Sexualität, Geistigkeit und Religiosität in West- und Mitteleuropa. Ist-Stand und Desiderata der Frauenforschung", *Innsbrucker Historische Studien* 12/13 (1990), [Einzelveröffentlichung aus den Innsbrucker Historischen Studien 2]: 395–580, hier 579.

[45] Wie dies — auch im Blick auf Alltagsgeschichte — geschehen kann, hat Claudia Märtl gezeigt: "Aus dem Familienbriefwechsel eines bayerischen Adelsgeschlechts im 15. Jahrhundert", in *Regensburg und Ostbayern. Max Piendl zum Gedächtnis*, hg. von Franz Karg (Kallmünz: Laßleben, 1991), 71–89.

Universität der Bundeswehr Hamburg

The Search for Power: A Female Quest in Antoine de la Sale's Petit Jehan de Saintre

Anne Caillaud

> Courtly love is disturbing ... it justifies and legitimizes adultery. It also places women in a position of supreme power. There are two unbearable transgressions of the masculine order and its morals ... In the courtly world, the lady is granted these two privileges: freedom and power.[1]

If courtly love rests partly on the notion of power, its complexity lies in the relationship between a literary genre and the real social structure of the feudal society. While the idyllic literary vision of the lady on a pedestal with the knight kneeling at her feet suggests the idea of feminine empowerment, flesh and blood women of the nobility actually lost part of their power in the public domain during the period between the creation of courtly literature and the transition from the Middle Ages to the Renaissance.

According to Merry Wiesner,[2] the fifteenth century brought with it an increased awareness by women of men's authority, as well as the desire not to be subjected to its restrictions. Joan Kelly Gadol[3] suggests that women's active participation in promoting a courtly ideal reflected a desire for interaction with men as their peers rather than their inferiors. However, in a patriarchal society which constantly subjected women to male rules and domination, the superiority of the courtly lady was nothing but an illusion. The literary ideal of courtly love granted women a power which they, in reality, were far from possessing.

This irony of courtly love was never more obvious than in *Le Petit Jehan de Saintré*: in this fifteenth-century narrative work, La Belle Dame des Belles Cousines, the main female protagonist, attempts to reproduce the model of courtly love as a basis for her relationship with her young lover, but fails. When the young and idle aristocratic widow decides to take a young page, Jehan de Saintré, under her protection, her ultimate goal is to help him become the most valiant knight of the kingdom. As Saintré accepts the role of Belle Cousine's knight, he agrees to keep this relationship a secret. Urged on by his lady, he rapidly climbs the social ladder: the page becomes the king's "varlet tranchant," then his first chamberlain. Once a knight, he participates, always under the lady's supervision, in several tournaments. His chivalric exploits earn him fame and respect in the court. The lady at this point seems to have achieved her goals. Yet, just as Belle Cousine and Saintré's courtly idyll seems to be at its height, the young man decides to go on his own quest without the approval of his lady. His sudden decision marks the end of their relationship.

In order to understand why Belle Cousine attempts and fails to emulate the perfect relationship between a knight and his lady, I propose to analyse and compare the different steps of their liaison with the guidelines set by Andreas Capellanus in his twelfth-century treatise *De Amore*. Capellanus codifies courtly love and provides guidelines for the lovers to follow. Belle Cousine, as a prominent Lady of the court, is bound to know the main "rules" of courtly love which are described in *De Amore* (if not the treatise itself). She genuinely hopes to emulate a perfect "traditional" courtly relationship, yet she is confronted with the reality of a different situation: Belle Cousine is very aware of her own needs as a woman; she is as eager to fulfill these needs as she is to build up her new relationship with Saintré. Unable to reconcile both tasks, she is at times forced to deviate from the "ideal model" of courtly love. An analysis of the liaison between Belle Cousine and Saintré shows how the lady fails on several instances to follow Capellanus's guidelines. Her failure will be the indirect cause of her decline.

Since she is related to the Queen, Belle Cousine is already a very powerful figure at the court. Yet, even though she is a strong authoritarian individual, she remains limited by her status as a female. In the Middle Ages, authority is viewed as a masculine quality; it is an important asset for men, who are expected to rule their household or govern their estate. This quality may be necessary for women who are left in charge of the estate in the absence of their spouse; however, since restraint is also a most valued female quality, women are constantly reminded that they should always remain moderate in their use of power. Belle Cousine seeks in courtly love the vehicle to power: she can act as a powerful suzerain when the knight is reduced to the role of a vassal. She appropriates the rules of courtly love in order to satisfy her desires as a woman, and uses this ideology to try to overcome the limitations of a society which confines her to a decorative rather than an active role. This lady's actions and reactions are often excessive because her need to dominate is real and not conventional. Her behavior results from a personal interpretation of the courtly conventions and can be viewed as a response to her frustrations. Since it is difficult for a woman to impose herself at the court, Belle Cousine tends to act in a non-traditional manner: in order to seduce Saintré and enjoy power, she assumes on several occasions a role which is traditionally reserved for a man.

At the time of their first encounter, the young Saintré is only a thirteen-year old page who has had little practice in the social life of the court. The narrator explains that the lady has observed him on *several* occasions, has addressed him *several* times in public about *several* topics, and that *the more* she talked to him, *the more* she found pleasure in these encounters.[4] The repetition of the words "several" and "more" emphasize the frequency of their meetings and accentuate the "pleasure" the lady experiences during these meetings. It also underlines the fact that she is always the one who initiates their conversations.[5] This suggests that even before their first "official" encounter, the pattern of the aggressive lady and the passive young man is already in place.

This first "official" encounter sets the tone for the following ones. As the lady and her maidens are retreating to her bedroom one night, they meet Saintré who immediately kneels to salute them. Far from being satisfied with this display of good manners, Belle Cousine unfairly accuses the young man of behaving improperly, and orders him to accompany the ladies to her chamber. The lady's harsh tone contrasts with her enjoyment of the situation and leads the reader to wonder what sort of pleasure she actually experiences in meeting Saintré. His shame and confusion seem to delight Belle Cousine whose cruelty increases once they get to her bedroom. Guy Mermier stresses the fact that Belle Cousine's actions are contrary to what one would expect in a courtly setting as he underlines the sadistic as well as the erotic nature of the game Belle Cousine intends to play.[6]

In fact, Belle Cousine herself compares their first meeting to a battle. Saintré is first subjected to the mockery of the ladies, then he remains alone, trapped with Belle Cousine in her bedroom. Saintré has no choice but to surrender and become her protegé. Once he is released, we are told that Saintré runs away as if he were being chased by fifty wolves. This comparison of the women to wolves evokes the dangerous and destructive character commonly attributed to women in the Middle Ages.[7] In this hunt, it is not the conquering man who chases after the wolf but a fierce pack of females who pursues a feeble prey. Saintré is obviously disoriented by his lack of understanding of the situation. The inequality of the battle is obvious; what makes it interesting is that in this game of cat and mouse the usual roles are reversed. The man no longer plays the role of the cat nor is the lady the besieged mouse. It is upon this inverted foundation that Belle Cousine builds her love story. There are several disturbing elements which contribute to the failure of Belle Cousine and Saintré's relationship. Georges Duby compares the interaction between a lady and her knight in a courtly setting to a joust, and Belle Cousine herself refers to it as a battle. A joust supposes a winner and a loser. Duby implies that, according to the laws of sexuality, the loser cannot be other than the lady herself.[8] The lady must, moreover, become a master in the art of making this game last as long as possible. Duby adds: "The woman was invited to adorn herself, to conceal, then reveal her charms, to give herself parsimoniously so that the young man would learn to dominate himself" (77). The fight is faked on both sides; it is a convention and each partner, or opponent, knows its results in advance. The woman has to be simultaneously direct and passive since she remains, after all, the young man's prey, and sooner or later she will submit and grant him his will. In the case of *Le Petit Jehan*, Belle Cousine conceals her intentions only to insure that Jehan's heart is free. As soon as she is certain of it, she reveals her intention to become his benefactress and his lover and forces the young man to comply to her wishes. Belle Cousine, moreover, never has to adorn herself, nor does la Sale allude in the text to any special effort concerning her clothing or appearance. Jehan, on the other hand, is constantly invited to change garments and wear more and more sumptuous clothes. At the sight of him, Belle Cousine is filled with the same sensual satisfaction a man would experience upon viewing a beautiful woman.

Since Capellanus states that the young suitor should be patient and persuasive, one would expect Belle Cousine, acting in the place of the man, to show patience, sweetness and courtesy in order to seduce Jehan. Far from judging and humiliating him for not having a lover yet, she should try to win his heart by praising him. Andreas Capellanus suggests that the suitor might speak as follows:

> "When the Divine being made you there was nothing he left undone. I know there is no defect in your beauty, none in your good sense, none in you at all except, it seems to me that you have enriched no one by your love. I marvel greatly that Love permits so beautiful and so sensible a woman to serve for long outside his camp."[9]

The suitor's discourse is humble and non-aggressive. It contrasts with Belle Cousine's harsh language.

Cappellanus's example shows how the woman should reply to her suitor's declaration; she should pretend to doubt his truthfulness:

> "You seem to be telling fibs, since although I do not have a beautiful figure you extol me as beautiful beyond all other women and although I lack the ornament of wisdom you praise my good sense" (37).

Her realism contrasts with his idealism and gives a playful aspect to the debate. The exchange becomes a "joust of words" where each argument is carefully weighed and appraised by both opponents.

These elements are absent from la Sale's text. If Belle Cousine compares their first encounter to a battle, it is obviously an uneven match. Jehan demonstrates his ignorance of courtly customs through his silence and his tears. However, despite the inversion of roles, Belle Cousine retains certain feminine characteristics which are present in Capellanus's female protagonist: her discourse is down to earth. According to Joan M. Ferrante,

> The woman as a realist ... is a counterbalance in courtly literature to the woman as image ... when a real woman intrudes on the fantasy, she is likely to point up its most vulnerable areas.[10]

In spite of herself and her desire to experience a courtly relationship, Belle Cousine becomes the element which disrupts all the patterns of traditional courtly love.

From a courtly point of view, age difference should not be an obstacle to love. The Countess of Champagne had herself resolved this question by stating that it was logical for an older woman to prefer a young and more ardent lover, whereas a mature man would naturally prefer the company of a young maiden (176). However, if it is established that in a courtly relationship the lover should be young and single, he should not be a child. What seems abnormal in the case of *Le Petit Jehan* is the extreme youth of the page and his childish behavior; he hides from Belle Cousine and her ladies in waiting, then cries when admonished. La Sale's protagonist is not a very young knight, but rather an inexperienced child: Jehan is only thirteen when Belle Cousine proposes to become his lady. His youth explains his obvious lack of desire to have a "Dame d'amour" and why he does not see the necessity to have one. According to Capellanus, "A girl before the age of twelve and a boy before the age of fourteen cannot enter the service of love" (51).

In a courtly setting, the social rank of the lovers should also be taken into consideration. Nevertheless, Capellanus states that social difference should not be an obstacle to love provided that the lovers are worthy of each other. A woman should accept the love of a man who proves to possess superior qualities:

> If a man of the middle class seeks the love of a woman of the higher nobility, he ought to have a most excellent character, for in order that a man of this class may prove to be worthy of the love of a woman of the higher nobility he must be a man with innumerable good things to his credit, one whom uncounted good deeds extol (53).

La Sale stresses Jehan's promising qualities and Belle Cousine notices the young man's potential as a future knight. However, when she meets him, he is nothing but a page; although from a noble family, he has yet to perform any act of prowess, he has not been noticed by the king, and is far from becoming a valiant knight. Can we then overlook Saintré's deficiencies? The lady's choice is justifiable only inasmuch as Saintré is presented to the reader in his reality of the moment (a thirteen-year-old child, charming, but shy and ignorant) as well as a future projection. The reader is assured in advance that Saintré will indeed become the most valiant knight of the kingdom and that he will acquire all the necessary qualities he now lacks. As their relationship develops, Belle Cousine passes through different stages; from conqueror to benefactress, educator, tutor, mother and lover. She adapts her role to meet the changing needs and social status of her protégé.

Capellanus treats the topic of the formation of a knight by a lady in the response of a young lover to his lady's objections:

> "The height of courtesy seems to be contained in your remarks, in which you are so clearly concerned that all my actions should be laudable. And so, since I see that you are thoroughly instructed in the art of love, I ask you to give me a lesson — that is, I ask that Your Grace may see fit to teach me those things that are specially demanded in love, those which make a man most worthy of being loved, because after I have been instructed, I shall have no defense for any mistakes I make and no opportunity to excuse myself" (58).

The education, or rather the initiation of the young man, is explicitly recommended. In this case, Belle Cousine and Jehan seem to follow the courtly model. However, once again, they deviate from it, since it is not Jehan who begs the lady to instruct him, but the lady who makes this proposition to him.

The traditional courtly relationship presupposes that the young knight fall in love with a married lady. If Jehan de Saintré, being a page instead of a knight, does not follow the regular courtly pattern, neither does Belle Cousine, who is now a widow. Free from the social constraints of marriage, she should be able to choose her lovers. Her liaison does not possess the adulterous quality of courtly love. The sense of the forbidden, however, is not totally absent from the relationship between Belle Cousine and Jehan de Saintré. It manifests itself in a more subtle manner.

When first questioned by Belle Cousine about the woman he loves, Saintré answers: "the one I love the most ... is my mother, and then it is my sister Jacqueline"(8). It is obvious at this point that Jehan cannot fully comprehend the concept of courtly love which explains why, at the beginning of their relationship, Belle Cousine assumes the role of his mother. This substitution is at first unconscious, yet present, on both sides. Once Jehan has entered into her "service d'amour", Belle Cousine takes on a more maternal tone; she teaches him how to spend his money, dress, speak and behave, just as a mother would. When, as instructed by his benefactress, Jehan buys new clothes, he pretends without consulting Belle Cousine, that it is his mother who sent him money to purchase a new attire. This suggests that at the time, he actually sees in Belle Cousine a second mother. When Belle Cousine, in the company of the other ladies, asks why he is so well dressed, Jehan, bound by their secret, uses that same subterfuge and answers: "My lady it is, thanks to the Lord, my mother who made me look so handsome" (56). The protagonist's age difference combined with the fact that Jehan is only a child, naturally provokes this imaginary mother-son link which gives their relationship not only an adulterous overtone, but also an incestuous one. The forbidden aspect of the courtly relation is still present but its nature has shifted, which indicates another deviation from the original courtly model.

Belle Cousine does not actually becomes Saintré's mistress until he has reached both physical and intellectual maturity. She finally respects the precept of courtly love which stipulates that the young man should prove to be an accomplished knight before the lady grants him any favor. The number of kisses exchanged between the lovers grows at each proving of the young man. A traditional exchange between the partners seems to have been reestablished. Yet, as the kisses multiply, the lady's ardor increases whereas Saintré remains shy and reserved in demonstrating his affection. His lack of interest may confirm that he is not in love with the lady and considers her a mother and a benefactress rather than a mistress.

Conscious from the start that their liaison differs in many aspects from an ideal courtly model, the lady attempts on several occasions to re-establish this model. By suggesting that Saintré choose a lady, she avoids proposing herself as his lady with the secret hope he will have the good sense to choose her. Unfortunately, her suggestion comes up against his ignorance, obstinance and lack of desire:

> "Who would such a lady be, who would like me to serve her and who would love me as I am ... My lady, I would rather die than offer myself and be rejected, than be an object of mockery ... therefore my lady, I would rather stay as I am now." (34-5)

Confronted with his naiveté, Belle Cousine has little choice but to take over; she had hoped Saintré would avow his love for her. He would have then assumed the role of the male and she would have become the desired and unattainable lady. Jane Burns and Roberta Krueger explain that:

> It is not appropriate for the woman to say: "*Je vœul devenir votre amie.*" If courtly love is typically defined as the exclusive domain of the ladies, it is also frequently characterized as an emotion reserved ultimately for men ... Love and the woman who speaks it pose a clear and present danger to the system of courtliness which is designed ostensibly to promote just such an exalted emotion.[11]

A transfer of roles is evident from the outset of the story and the reader, like Belle Cousine, is forced to accept a modified copy of courtly love. The lady is not entirely responsible for the unconventional nature of their relationship; Saintré's attitude, on the other hand, is a constant obstacle to its progress. Belle Cousine's and Saintré's behavior result from a distorted beginning: the lady, who wants to insure that no one at the court will be suspicious of their relationship, simulates an argument between herself and Saintré during their first official encounter. Saintré is obviously her victim as he is constantly subjected to strong psychological and financial pressure: she gives him large amounts of money to be repaid in the form of service. By playing Belle Cousine's game, the young page recognizes his inferiority. In the public eye, he loses all self-esteem, whereas Belle Cousine affirms her superiority and power.

Conscious of the taboos of a misogynous society, Belle Cousine is not able openly to express her desire for power. By molding Saintré, she projects herself through the young man who becomes her alter ego, the instrument which allows her to express herself more openly in a patriarchal society. Jane Burns and Roberta Krueger note that women

> become, in many courtly scenarios, the silent initiators and recipients of male exploits on the fields of battle as in the field of literature. Although women are routinely billed as central players in courtliness and its historical development, they are often made to play more peripheral roles, serving as the audience that will receive and authenticate heroic feats and clerkly tales about them (210-211).

Obliged to remain socially passive, Belle Cousine does not give up her ambitions; since she cannot wear armor, she has someone else wear it and chooses a very young man since a child is more malleable than a grown man. Belle Cousine has decided to mold the page to the image of her masculine ideal: Saintré must represent what she would have been, had she enjoyed masculine privileges. The exactness of the commands the lady gives to Saintré reveals her knowledge of knighthood and the importance she grants to her enterprise.

She first focuses on his social behavior and his clothing which is traditionally a female task, and follows with his military education which is a prerogative usually reserved for the masculine domain. Belle Cousine assumes at that point the competence of a man, and her advice is necessary to the young man who, as we know, is ignorant. However, her concern over every detail betrays her intention to rule over everything. Belle Cousine knows exactly what she wants; she considered this enterprise for a long time before selecting Saintré as her protégé, and she minutely directs every action of the future knight; his exploits and praise will indirectly reflect on her. Since their liaison is a secret (a given in a courtly relationship), she is unable to share her success with anyone. Yet, what matters is the personal satisfaction of having produced Saintré on her own. To control a page is not in itself extraordinary, but to control the best knight of the kingdom is proof of power, and Saintré is her creature.

As long as Saintré follows her directions, the lady is satisfied. Nevertheless, at the time she believes her goal has been reached, their relationship suddenly collapses: Saintré decides to be in charge of his own destiny, and Belle Cousine cannot retaliate for she is a prisoner of the secret she has so carefully elaborated. After Saintré frees himself from Belle Cousine, she can no longer relate to the knight, since she has lost control over him and she becomes aware that his future exploits will not belong to her anymore. Despite Belle Cousine's threats, Saintré's decision is irrevocable.

The formation of the young man represents several years of elaborate work without a tangible result and his estrangement marks Belle Cousine's failure. Courtly love could have served as a palliative for Belle Cousine's frustrations. However, in attempting to emulate courtly love, Belle Cousine makes the mistake of exaggerating the domineering attitude granted by convention to the lady over the knight. When she realizes that her expectations of courtly love are not met, she rebels against a system which seeks to confine her to the literary "type" of the "good" lady. She leaves the court and its obligations for her domain in the countryside where her authority is not challenged and, disappointed with courtly love, finds satisfaction in the arms of the local Abbot. This contemptuous liaison, from the point of view of the court, actually fulfills Belle Cousine. Away from Paris and the court, she appears to be oblivious to her peers' judgement. Only once she is brought back to a courtly setting, does she becomes aware of the extent of her mistake. After her former lover Saintré recounts their tale to a courtly audience, La Sale insures that Belle Cousine is judged, condemned by her peers and expelled from the court.

The lady's final humiliation marks the conclusion of *Le Petit Jehan de Saintré*. Indeed, Belle Cousine's exile from the courtly world confirms the fact that Belle Cousine's authority and power was illusory and confirms Margaret Wade Labarge's belief that

> In a society fundamentally based on force, women were always at a disadvantage and could easily be driven outside the accepted boundaries of their society.[12]

One might ponder on La Sale's motives for denigrating, humiliating his heroine and finally banning her from noble society. Does the author merely embrace a misogynistic tradition or, as the author of several didactic works[13], does he intend to deliver a message, a warning to his readers? Simon Gaunt contends that "one cause of misogyny in romance is fear of female power" and adds: "lyric poetry elevates women within courtly discourse and turns a blind eye to consequences; romance has to portray the reactions of women to courtly rhetoric."[14] In the case of Belle Cousine, her reaction to courtly rhetoric and her interpretation of the courtly ideal in terms of its relation to women and power proves to have disastrous consequences. La Sale uses Belle Cousine, an unusual and unpleasant female protagonist, as a powerful deterrent to condemn the concept of courtly love and denounce its aberrations. It is a warning to women who would view courtly love as the means by which to control and shape a lover. Through Belle Cousine's failure, La Sale seeks to prove the impossibility and show the dangers of renegotiating gender roles within an established male hierarchy.

NOTES

[1] Sarde Michelle, *Regard sur les Françaises* (Paris: Stock, 1983), 142. Translations are mine.

[2] Merry E. Wiesner, "Women's Defense of their Public Role," *Women in the Middle Ages and the Renaissance* (Syracuse: Syracuse UP, 1986), 1.

[3] Joan Kelly Gadol, "Did Women Have a Renaissance?" *Women in the Middle Ages and the Renaissance* (Syracuse: Syracuse UP, 1986), 146.

[4] Antoine de la Sale, *Le Petit Jehan de Saintré*, eds. Jean Misrahi and Charles Knudson (Genève: Droz, 1978), 6. Translations are mine.

[5] Although it is unlikely that a page would initiate a conversation with a lady, the fact that the lady takes it upon herself to initiate the dialogue marks a challenge to the traditional courtly pattern. This case was not anticipated by Capellanus who proposes several examples of courtly rhetoric in which the dialogue is always initiated by the man.

[6] Guy Mermier, "Le Message Paradoxal du petit Jehan de Saintré à courtoisie et à chevalerie au XVe siècle," *Studi Mediolatini e Volgari* 26 (1978-79), 151.

[7] According to Michelle Sarde, women are commonly seen as a threat in medieval society: "Woman is evil, as lecherous as a viper, she is also nosey, indiscreet, shrewish ... all evil comes from her. She is doomed to sexuality, to the devil, she arouses horror, repugnance, fear, rejection ... The horror inspired by women is not limited by religious propaganda ... The truth is that women terrorize" (161).

[8] Georges Duby, *Mâle moyen-âge* (Paris: Flammarion 1988), 76.

[9] Andreas Capellanus, *The Art of Courtly Love*, trans. John Jay Parry (New York: Columbia UP, 1959), 37.

[10] Joan M. Ferrante, "Male Fantasy and Female Reality in Courtly Literature," *Women's Studies* 11 (1984), 67.

[11] See Jane Burns and Roberta L. Krueger's Introduction to *Romance Notes* 25.3 (1985), 208-9.

[12] Margaret Wade Labarge, *Small Sound of the Trumpet* (Boston: Beacon Press, 1986) 218.

[13] La Sale is the author of *La Salade* (1445) and *La Salle* (1448) both didactic treatises written respectively for his protectors, the prince of Anjou and the Comte de Saint Pol.

[14] Simon Gaunt, *Gender and Genre in Medieval French Literature* (Cambridge: Cambridge UP, 1995). As the author points out, the interaction between romance and the courtly lyrics "is in many respects evident and the influence of the love casuistry of the troubadour and the trouvère lyric on romance is well documented" (121).

Grand Valley State University

Bernardino of Siena, Popular Preacher and Witch-Hunter: A 1426 Witch Trial in Rome

Franco Mormando

Before the sixteenth-century and the outbreak of the great witch craze, documentation illustrating the history of European witchcraft is rare. Yet, among extant sources from the late-medieval and early Renaissance period are the sermons of Franciscan friar Bernardino of Siena (1380-1444). Bernardino was one of the most successful and most influential popular preachers of the century, and his sermons shed much light on this whole realm of European lived, daily experience. In this study I will examine some of the most important witch-related pages in the Bernardino sermon corpus that summarize his involvement in what he describes as a sensational witch trial held in the city of Rome, most likely in the year 1426. I shall also include in my examination five other fifteenth-century sources (Italian, German, and Swiss) which mention the trial, thereby testifying to the notoriety of this episode in the early history of the European witch hunts.[1]

Bernardino's account of the witches of Rome affords us a good idea of what the Christian faithful in the pre-witch craze era believed or, rather, were taught to believe about the figure of the witch and her (or his) activities. The friar's public instruction also represents an important stage in that slow transformation in the collective European imagination of an inchoate body of disparate beliefs and vague notions regarding superstition, simple sorcery, pagan ritual, and demonology into what Jeffrey Burton Russell calls "the classic formulation of the Witch Phenomenon,"[2] namely, the witch as a devil-worshipping, evil-working woman belonging to a massive, well-organized, international company of moral-social subversives who gather weekly at their sabbaths in remote parts of the countryside.

First of all, the date of the trial. Regrettably, despite the clamorous and fully public nature of this episode right in the heart of a major city, we possess no definitive information about the exact year in which the trial occurred. In recounting the episode, the preacher gives no indication of chronology. Bernardino's principal account of the witch trial occurs in a sermon which he preached to the people of Siena on Sunday, September 21, 1427.[3] The preacher simply introduces the narrative by saying, "I want to tell you what we did in Rome,"[4] omitting his customary time-setting *exemplum* preamble ("A short while ago," "There was once," "Eight years ago"). However, as explained in the Appendix below, there is good reason to believe that the trial during the summer of 1426.

I now take up the simple facts of the case, according to Bernardino.[5] When he first broached the topic of witchcraft in his public preaching in

Rome, Bernardino says he received no response at all; people thought he was "dreaming" it all up.[6] However, a bit of spiritual coercion applied by the friar bestirred their consciences: "At one point it occurred to me to tell them that if anybody had information on any man or woman who practiced these things [*i.e.*, witchcraft] and did not report them to the authorities, he or she would be guilty of the same sin."[7] The results of his challenge were immediate: "And once I had finished preaching," the friar reports, "a multitude of witches and sorcerers were reported." (In his 1443 version of the story, he will specify that "one hundred accusers came forward," adding the fact that his information about what occurred after his preaching came to him through the Franciscan Inquisitor.)[8] Bernardino was soon informed by his Franciscan superior that "[t]hey're going to burn the whole lot of them!" However, given the great number of accusations, "a consultation was held with the Pope, and it was decided that only the worst of these women (*le maggiori*) would be arrested, that is, those women (*quelle*) who had committed the greatest crimes."[9]

Let us stop here to take brief note of certain details of the case thus far: the initial reluctance of the public to denounce the so-called criminals, the involvement of the Pope, the number and gender of the culprits. First, why did Bernardino's Roman audience respond with such initial incredulity or, better, with feigned ignorance? They thought he was "dreaming" it all up. (As the friar confessed in Padua in 1423, other audiences had responded the same way to his sermons on witchcraft.)[10] I am reluctant to believe that it was out of genuine ignorance of the phenomena in question. Was it instead due to fear of accusing their witch-neighbors and thereby perhaps suffering retaliation on the part of such powerful and often malicious practitioners of the occult? Or was it because they really did not share Bernardino's opinion that such activity — the practice of witchcraft in its various modes — was really so harmful, sinful or diabolical? As we saw, it was only Bernardino's terror tactic (added to an already thoroughly demonized characterization of sorcery and superstitious practices) that moved them to action. What we have here may be the same phenomenon observed by scholars regarding the growth and development of the witch craze in other parts of Europe; it was only with the intrusion on the part of intellectual elites with their learned notions of diabolical witchcraft that certain practices of simple sorcery and superstition and certain practitioners — among them innocent folk healers — long tolerated as harmless and indeed necessary by the ordinary citizens of Europe came to be seen, respectively, as heinous acts of subversive evil and as malicious servants of Satan. If correct, what this thesis means, in effect, is that the witch craze was to a large extent the creation of inquisitors, theologians, and preachers like Bernardino.[11] We shall return to this topic of audience response at the conclusion of this paper, for, in the case of Siena in 1427, Bernardino's attempt at instigating a witch hunt appears to have been received with utter indifference (while, as we shall also see, in Todi, 1428, his preaching did enjoy some measure of success).[12]

Another small but noteworthy detail (repeated in the friar's 1443 account of the trial) is the consultation held with the Pope on the matter.[13] The pontiff in question is Martin V, the Roman nobleman, Oddo Colonna. Martin's name does not usually figure in the documents and histories of late-medieval witchcraft, apart from the brief mention of his 1418 reissuance at the Council of Constance of Alexander V's 1409 bull giving the Inquisitor of Avignon jurisdiction over cases involving witchcraft.[14] Bernardino's statement is here an indication that the witchcraft problem had indeed once again reached the personal attention of the highest office of Christendom, and, specifically, Martin V. Though Martin's involvement in the matter did not reach the same intensity as that of, for example, the earlier John XXII or the later Innocent VIII, he did consider the problem serious enough to order the burning of the worst of the culprits. As already mentioned, after his own IHS heresy trial, Bernardino preached in St. Peter's an extensive series of sermons at papal invitation; we wonder how influential Bernardino's own oratory was in sensitizing this pontiff (now a friend and ally to the friar) to the gravity of this crime?[15]

Finally, let us consider the number and gender of the accused. As far as quantity is concerned, though some of the accusations may have been false and though we have no idea of the range of activity included in these denunciations, the picture here is that of widespread involvement in witchcraft-related practices, not in a remote mountain village or isolated agricultural community but in the heart of one of the major cities of Europe, and, as Ginzburg points out, "in the very heart of Christianity."[16] Another impression here transmitted is, however, one of relative leniency toward the phenomenon: the majority of the accused were never even apprehended, and of those apprehended — if Bernardino is accurate — only two are mentioned here as having been given the death sentence. Later, during the height of the witch craze, such leniency will again be the mark of Italy in general, where relatively few witch trials were held in comparison with the rest of Europe.[17]

Next, as far as gender is concerned, Bernardino first says in the same paragraph quoted above that "a great quantity of men and women were accused." Yet, immediately thereafter in the preacher's account, the group that is rounded up consists simply of "those women who had committed the worst crimes" and later, only two executions will be specifically mentioned, both of unnamed women. We see then that those involved in such activity were both men and women, but that only women ended up being implicated as the worst of the practitioners.[18] This — the preponderance of women among the suspects — squares with what we read in the rest of Bernardino's preaching on the subject and confirms what we encounter in studies of the witch craze in the rest of Europe across the centuries. Whether as innocent victims or as true practioners, women seem to have made up the large majority of the cases involved. Here as everywhere else in his denunciation of witchcraft, Bernardino uses both masculine and feminine references; yet, it is the latter which dominate, leaving audiences with the distinct impression that witchcraft is, above all, the domain of women, especially old women, the vetulae or, as Bernardino usually refers to them, "le vecchie rincagnate," the dog-faced old women.[19] (However, in the case here under examination, Bernardino does not describe the culprits as old women, and of our other five sources, only two, Giacomo della Marca and Chraft, do so.) In fact, according to Bernardino, the female connection with witchcraft goes back all the way to the first woman, Eve. It is "because she wanted to be a sorcerer," says the preacher, that our first mother fell to the temptation of the serpent.[20]

Let us proceed with the further details of these events in Rome. Bernardino describes the case of one woman in particular:

> And among all of these women, there was one woman arrested who said and confessed without any torture that she had killed at least thirty young babies by sucking their blood; and she also said that she had freed sixty of them; and she said that every time she freed one of them, she had to offer a limb up to the devil, and she would use the limb of some animal; and this is how she operated for a long time. And what's more, she confessed that she had killed her own son and had made a powder out of his body and used to give this powder to be eaten in her various activities.[21]

The above motifs — infanticide by blood-sucking and the preparation of witchly powder from infant cadavers — are ancient elements in European folklore.[22] In his earlier preaching against witchcraft, Bernardino had already made references to blood-sucking and, though magical powders made from the cadavers of the infant victims are not mentioned in these earlier sermons, I suspect, nonetheless, that Bernardino was already aware of this element, which was to become a classic item of the witch's baggage.[23] The same can be said of another motif here only implied — that of the formal pact between demon and witch ("she said that every time she freed one of them, she had to offer a limb up to the devil"). In his 1425 *exemplum,* the "Godmother of Lucca," Bernardino makes explicit the existence of the same type of tit-for-tat agreement (the devil will reveal to the godmother-witch the location of her godson's lost gold florins on the condition that she create scandal by telling him that his wife is having an affair with the village priest). The devil grants no favors free of charge, not even to members of his own sect.[24]

The detail about "freeing the babies" calls for some comment. Freed from what, we might ask? The power of the devil? Her own possession? Why so in some cases and not others? Bernardino never explains these remarks of his, taking for granted that his audience will understand to what he is referring. As Carlo Delcorno, the latest editor of this Siena

1427 sermon cycle, rightly observes, the reference most likely means that the "witch" was actually a healer (and perhaps also a midwife) whose acts of "liberation" consisted in curing the child from its illness — the illness understood perhaps by both parent and witch as being the result of some act of *maleficium*, an evil spell.[25] As we know from other trial records, many women accused of witchcraft were also practicing folk medicine and were often referred to as medica or its equivalent, such as the woman of Brescia, "Maria la Medica," tried in 1480 for crimes similar to those of Bernardino's witch[26] In a draft for another sermon against witchcraft, Bernardino makes ironic note of the competition between these unlicensed female practitioners (whom he stereotypes again as *vecchie rincagnate*) and the university-trained doctors: "O doctors, how much you have studied your grammar, logic, philosophy, medicine, amidst much expense, peril, and labor, but it's the dog-faced old woman who gathers all the honor!"[27]

Bernardino here (and in his 1443 account of the trial)[28] specifically notes that the woman confessed to all of these deeds "without torture," thereby implying that her account was the spontaneous truth, and not the desperate invention of someone attempting to escape pain. Yet, this may not be the case at all. Commenting upon the 1438 witch trial of a certain Frenchman, Pierre Vallin of Dauphiné, whose trial record states that his confession was likewise made "voluntarily," Jeffrey Burton Russell explains that this "simply means that he was tortured, removed from the place of torture, and then given the choice of confessing voluntarily or of being returned to the torture chamber."[29] Hence, Bernardino's emphasis on the absence of torture in this Roman case is no reassurance of the truth of her confession at all. Whether the woman — who could have easily been psychotic or senile — actually did any of what she confessed to is something we will probably never be able to determine.

The preacher's account continues, giving us further details about the modus operandi and paraphernalia of the so-called witch: "And she told of the way she used to go before daybreak to St. Peter's Square, and she would have with her certain little jars of ointments made out of plants that had been gathered on the feast of St. John the Baptist and on the Assumption."[30] All of Bernardino's sermons on witchcraft are rich depositories of detailed information on witchly and other superstitious practices, and here the preacher reports yet another specific feature of popular belief, that of the special powers of plants harvested on certain, auspicious days of the year, in this case, June 24 (the feast of John the Baptist) and August 15 (the Assumption of Mary). The former date, June 24, figures widely in previous and ensuing accounts of witchcraft and related topics as a popular festival day for witches. Bernardino himself mentions it as well to both the Florentines and the Paduans in 1424, again as a propitious day for gathering magical herbs at dawn.[31] This traditional witches' feast day, June 24, coincides with the date of one of the ancient pagan seasonal festivals, in this case, that of Midsummer; on the eve of this day came the "climax of the fire and fertility rites celebrating the triumph of the sun and renewed vegetation."[32]

The second date mentioned by Bernardino, August 15, is also fraught with significance: it is one of the great feasts of Mary, the virgin "Mother of God," whose stature in popular medieval Mariology was little less than that of a goddess. It is no wonder that the feast of the Assumption, celebrating her bodily entry into heaven (a distinction she shares only with Jesus Christ and no other mortal) would have been considered a particularly auspicious one by witches. Most witches, as we have said, appear to have been women, and their earliest identity as a distinct subculture within Christendom connected them to the so-called Society of Diana, another virgin divinity like Mary.[33] In ancient times, the festival of Diana (in Greek, Artemis) was celebrated on the Ides of August, that is, August 13, two days before the feast of Mary's Assumption.

Bernardino himself does not comment on the significance of these dates but does explain the purpose of the ointments connected with them: "And they said that they would smear these ointments all over themselves and once they were covered, they believed that they were turned into cats, but that's not true. They only thought their bodies changed into something else, but it was only all in their head."[34] The friar cites as his authority for this disclaimer the central canon law text regarding witchcraft, the canon *Episcopi* which, in truth, refers not to shape-shifting, but to night-flight on the backs of animals.[35] Though, in a spirit of "rationality," this canon relegated the night-flight belief to the realm of mere diabolical illusion, nonetheless, it also served to publicize the existence and fear of witches and diabolical possession, as did Bernardino's sermons.[36] According to the canon and to Bernardino, witches may not really turn into cats or fly through the night, but that does not mean they are not under the spell of Satan (whom they can conjure up at will, like Bernardino's Godmother of Lucca)[37] and not able to be instruments of harm and death to their neighbor. Thus, as Franco Cardini points out, when Bernardino exhorts his audiences not to "believe" or "place their faith" in sorcerers, witches, and the like, what he means is: Do not seek the services of or become involved in any way with such people, not because their sorcery is bogus and impotent but because it is precisely the opposite — completely real and completely potent, thanks to their alliance with the devil himself.[38]

The friar then explains to his audience that it is really the devil, not the deluded, possessed witch, who visits the home of the innocent child victim and sucks the infant's blood. With a tone of scientific expertise, he then discourses on the power of the devil to delude these women and the easy susceptibility of the human mind to optical illusion. He gives the example of a mirror, a popular tool in the working of the occult arts.[39]

Bernardino further explains that when the devil arrives at the homes of his victims, it is in the guise of a cat:

> There are those who said they saw a female cat when he [the devil] went to do these things; and some have even taken preventative action against it by throwing whatever they had in their hand at this cat, even managing to strike it. And there are some of these cats that, being struck, got their leg broken. And who do you think ended up with a broken leg? Not the devil, but the possessed woman.[40]

Again, even though it is the woman who suffers the broken leg and not the cat-devil, the illusion is that it is the woman who does the deed, not that such frightful things as demonic possession and demonic infanticide do not occur.

This same detail of the malevolent and/or infanticidal cat figures prominently as well in the three non-Italian contemporary sources describing this Roman witch case, that is, Felix Hemmerlin, Johann Hartlieb, and Johann Chraft.[41] (The cat is missing in the two Italian sources, Stefano Infessura and Giacomo della Marca.) Hemmerlin's brief report explains that a clever mulier strega from Trastevere (a detail unique to this account) used to transform herself into a cat in order to create a need for her services as healer (likewise, a unique detail). Once a cat, she used to "poison with evil spells children lying in their cribs; afterwards, transforming herself back into human shape, she would cure them, collecting a fee [for her medical services]."[42]

Both Hartlieb's and Chraft's accounts agree with Bernardino's in the further detail of the wounding of the cat-witch by a quick-acting eyewitness. (In Bernardino, this witness is unidentified; in Hartlieb it is the father of the child; in Chraft, simply "a wise old man.") Hartlieb's *Buch aller verbotenen Kunst, Unglaubens und der Zauberei (Book of All Forbidden Art, Superstition and Magic*), written in a crude, archaic German, gives the following story, the most elaborate among the five accounts:

> A great sign of magic. Honorable prince, I will tell you something, which I and many people in Rome have seen and heard. It was in the sixth year of Pope Martin, that an unbelievable thing happened in Rome, namely, that a certain woman and man turned themselves into cats, and killed very many children in Rome. One time, a cat came into the house of a citizen, and bit his child in the cradle. The child cried out, the father got up quickly and took a knife and stabbed the cat in the head as she tried to go out the window. The next morning very early, the woman sent for the holy sacrament [because she feared she was dying?]; her neighbors bewailed her illness, as is the custom there. The neighbor [the father of the child] also commiserated with her; she answered him: if you were sorry for my sickness, you wouldn't have done that to me. On the third day, it happened that the woman developed a wound in her head. The neighbor remembered the cat and her words as well; he brought the matter to the

> Senate. The woman was arrested and confessed; she said before the Capitol in a very loud voice that if she had her ointment [which would allow her to escape], she would be willing to leave. O how gladly would I and many a courtier have loved to have seen the ointment given to her! Then a doctor stood up and said that the ointment should not be given to her, since the devil would like to cause great confusion with God's plan. The woman was burned at the stake, that I saw myself. Likewise many other people in Rome [saw it] as well.[43]

Note that Hartlieb initially specifies that both a man and a woman were responsible for the child murders, even though, as with Bernardino, the narration abruptly shifts to the feminine gender alone, with no further word of the male offender.

From Johann Chraft's continuation of Andreas of Regensburg's "chronicle of the Roman pontiffs and emperors," we have the following version of the story. It comes up in the chronicle after a reference to Martin V:

> In whose time [there was] a certain feline [murilegus] or cat in Rome [which] had been killing many babies lying in their cribs, seizing the opportunity [to do so] when they were not being properly watched by their nurses. Finally, a certain wise old man, who was watching a little boy entrusted to him, pretending not to notice the cat entering the window in order to suffocate the boy, wounded this cat with a sword to the point of drawing blood. It was subsequently discovered, thanks to the traces of the blood and the presence of the wound, that this cat was an old woman living nearby who was being treated by a surgeon; whenever she wished, she would transform herself into a cat and thus kill the children, in order to sustain her life [by sucking their blood?].[44]

In Chraft, the one unique detail of note, as far as witch-lore is concerned, is the final explanation of the witch's need for (I assume) the infant's blood for the prolongation of her own life. In this account, furthermore, the mode of her discovery differs slightly from what we read in Hartlieb. (Hemmerlin does not discuss the unmasking of the culprit.) In substance, however, the account coincides with the other two non-Italian sources, again, making it reasonable to conclude that the three authors are likely referring to the same episode in Roman history.

Some further word about our other two fifteenth-century sources, Stefano Infessura and Giacomo della Marca, is here appropriate.[45] Like the three non-Italian sources, neither Italian report specifically links the execution of the Roman witch to the activity of Bernardino. (Infessura gives her the name, Finicella, whereas, in Giacomo della Marca, she is Funicella.) In Infessura, the link is made by mere juxtaposition: the news item about the execution of Finicella is given in a separate paragraph inserted between two other news items regarding Bernardino's activities in Rome.[46] In Giacomo's sermon, Bernardino's name (strangely enough since the two were such close friends) is completely absent. Of all our sources,

Infessura is the most sparing in his details regarding the witch's *modus operandi;* he simply tells us that "Finicella" was burnt at the stake because "she diabolically killed many children and put spells on many people." Giacomo, on the other hand, supplies a few more details: "Funicella" is specifically an old woman (as she is in only one other account, that of Chraft); she killed specifically sixty-five children, including her own son, whose arm was used for the preparation of her witchly brews (as in Bernardino's account, except for the detail of the arm); and she did all of this, it is implied, under the direction of the devil, who convinced her with a bit of theological sophistry. Giacomo also names as the source of this information the same Franciscan inquisitor, Nicholas of Rome, who had been Bernardino's authority.[47] Neither of these two accounts relates any information about a wounded cat, the unmasking of the culprit, or the trial itself.

The similarity between the names of the witches, Finicella/ Funicella, makes it reasonable to conclude that Giacomo della Marca and Stefano Infessura are probably talking of the same person, while Infessura's placement of the trial during Bernardino's visit to Rome would indicate that, in all likelihood, the three Italians are speaking of one and the same episode. We have already concluded that the three non-Italian sources are describing the same case; the question is now: Are our Italian sources referring to the same case as our non-Italian sources? In his annotated "Calendar of Witch Trials," Kieckhefer cautions against this identification, but I, instead, believe it is reasonable to maintain.[48] The agreement among the texts, as we have seen, is substantial. Furthermore, until the late fifteenth century, witch trials, especially in Italy, were simply few and far between. It seems unlikely (though, admittedly, not impossible) that there be more than one such case even in Rome within the space of a few years. Infessura's *Roman Diary*, whose entries cover the whole of Martin's pontificate, in fact, only gives notice of this one trial.

We now return to Bernardino's text. The preacher concludes his account with a brief description of the fiery end of this woman, which according to Infessura, "all of Rome went to see." She was "condemned to the stake, and burned so that there was nothing left of her but ashes."[49] Another of her (female) colleagues in the profession, "who confessed to having done similar things" was also sent to the stake at the same time. The friar specifies, however, that this second woman was not strangled to death before being consigned to the flames, as was customary; she was still alive when they set her on fire, a gruesome specification, presumably meant to instill the fear of God in Bernardino's audience.

Bernardino's account of the trial ends here. By way of summary and conclusion, let us note that the above account contains nearly all of the classic components of the witch scenario that had been slowly coalescing in the collective imagination over the centuries as a mass of disparate folkloric beliefs metamorphosed into the complex drama of diabolical witchcraft. The culprits here are for the most part old women; they are in a pact with Satan and do his every bidding; this bidding frequently involves the kidnapping, blood-sucking, and murder of babies; and they have knowledge of secret herbal potions and creams that assist them in the working of their spells and various other acts of *maleficium*.[50] These women furthermore believe that they can transform themselves into cats with the help of their witchly ointments, but this is simply a diabolically induced delusion; it is the devil who transforms himself into a cat in order to stalk his infant victims.

From other sources, we learn that these magic ointments also "enable" the witch to fly through the air to arrive at the appointed time and place for their regularly scheduled secret nocturnal assemblies under the direction of Satan, their master. This notion of the assembly is yet another universal item in "the classic formulation of the Witch Phenomenon."[51] Like much else in the baggage of the European witch, it, too, has its roots in pagan mythology, specifically, in the un-Christian but non-diabolical "Society of Diana," an innocuous, festive ride and gathering of women under the tutelage of the pagan goddess of the moon and the hunt.[52] (A variant of this same widely disseminated item of folklore forms the nucleus of one of the stories in Boccaccio's *Decameron.)*[53] Turned into a demonized witch phenomenon by the theologians and canonists of Christian Europe, the assembly was eventually to be known by the end of the fifteenth century as the witches' "sabbath," acquiring ever more heinous, orgiastic characteristics with the passing years. During Bernardino's lifetime, it was called by various names; the preacher himself, in one of his 1424 sermons to the Florentines, refers to it by the Italian term, *tregenda*.[54]

As to exactly what Bernardino imagined as occurring during the *tregenda*, we cannot be completely sure, since the notion of the "sabbath" was still in its developmental phase, albeit far advanced in it. The friar's 1424 sermon does not describe this convocation of witches. His later treatise on witchcraft and superstition, De *idolatriae cultu* (1430-36), contains a reference to the *tregenda*, though the word itself does not appear in the text. This Latin work, nonetheless, gives us some idea of his conception of the "sabbath." It is, however, merely a repetition of the classic description supplied by the famous canon Episcopi. Making its first appearance in a tenth-century anthology of legal documents compiled by Regino of Prüm for the archbishop of Trier, Episcopi represents the Church's principal position statement with respect to the witch phenomenon. Most of Bernardino's own passage is a verbatim quote from this canon:

> Among these most impious wild brutes are some most wicked women and even sometimes men who believe and openly profess that they go riding on certain beasts along with Diana (or Iobiana[55] or Herodias) and countless other women, traveling over great distances in the silence of the dead of

> night, obeying her commands as if she were their mistress and are pressed into her service on certain nights, such as Thursday and Sunday. They also claim that some children, especially small boys, can be changed by them into a lower or higher form (in deterius vel in melius) or transformed into some other appearance or likeness.[56]

The *tregenda*, it would seem, is what Bernardino intends at least to allude to when later, in a somewhat confused passage in the same Siena 1427 sermon containing his report on the witches of Rome, he tells of a cardinal's page who stumbled across a "wild" nocturnal assembly near Benevento in southwest Italy:

> Hey, do you know what these enchanters do, huh? Let's look at the facts. Once, in Rome, there was a page of one of the cardinals who, going to Benevento at night, saw a crowd of people — women and children and young people — dancing in an open field; the sight filled him with fear. Then after looking for a little while, he took courage and went, with a bit of fear, to the place where these people were dancing, and little by little he got closer to the spot and he saw that they were all very young people. He actually got up the courage to join in the dancing. And so the whole gang went on dancing till the ringing of matins. As soon as the bells struck matins, all of these women [Bernardino switches to the feminine here, "tutte"] left in an instant except one girl, that is to say, the girl whom this guy was holding by hand. She wanted to leave with the other women but this guy kept her back: she pulled and he pulled. He held onto her in this way for so long that daybreak soon arrived. Seeing how young she was, he brought her to his own house. And listen to what happened next: he kept her for three years with him and she never spoke a word. And it was discovered that this girl was from Slavonia. Just think about that, what a fine job that was, taking a little girl away from her father and mother in that way.[57]

This account is followed immediately by the friar's injunction to "exterminate" any "enchantress or sorceress, or enchanters or witches."[58] Yet, taken by itself, this story (as we shall see, probably appropriated by the preacher from an older source) offers absolutely no grounds for seeing in it a description of the witches' sabbath — to begin with, the devil or his surrogate in the form of the usual female divinity is completely absent. As it stands, all this scene really describes is a night of dancing by a group of young men and women; there is nothing explicitly supernatural, let alone diabolical, in what Bernardino describes. Of course, our otherwise seemingly verbatim *reportatio* may be here at fault by failing to record all of the preacher's narration or it could be that Bernardino, improvising his re-telling of the tale, simply forgot in the heat of the moment to supply all the necessary facts to convey the true nature of this assembly.

Nonetheless, if we pay close attention, there are certain details in this story of "the cardinal's page" which do at least insinuate the presence of evil, and would have most likely raised the suspicions of contemporary audiences. The mention, first of all, of the town of Benevento in this passage is significant; the association of that area with magic and pagan rites was one already long established. By the age of the Lombard domination of Italy, a special cult had developed around a certain ancient walnut tree, cut down in the seventh century by the bishop, Saint Barbato.[59] At least some of Bernardino's public is likely to have been attuned to this allusion and thus assumed that any nocturnal gathering in that vicinity could only imply the practice of witchcraft. The friar's second geographic specification is also an important detail in this regard. The alien land of "Slavonia" (in Italian, *Schiavonia,* that is, the Balkans) was thought to be home to the Bogomils, a notorious heretical sect of the earlier Middle Ages who strongly influenced and abbetted that of the even more notorious Cathars of southern France, the Rhineland, and Lombardy.[60] Heretics — Bogomils, Cathars, Waldensians, Nicolaitans — were all still feared and believed to be living in northern Italian, as Bernardino himself teaches. For the preacher and his contemporaries, where there was heresy, there was also likely to be sorcery, diabolism, and allied aberrations, for the sins of the heretic and of the witch frequently overlapped.[61]

Finally, the predominant role played by women in this story would have been yet another cause for suspicion on the part of Bernardino's audience. Though the passage is confusing on this point — as in his account of the witches of Rome, Bernardino here too starts out using both masculine and feminine pronouns but then inexplicably switches to the feminine alone — the overall impression conveyed is that women indeed formed the more conspicuous part of this night-time assembly. Bernardino's was a society in which women, married or unmarried, were usually restricted to the home and, hence, "there were so very few gatherings to which an honest woman could go."[62] This was clearly not one of them. As with heretics, where there were women, the misogynistic premises of the age assumed, there was bound also to be mischief, if not outright evil such as that of witchcraft, the quintessentially female crime. The real crime in this story, however, is perpetrated by the male intruder, the cardinal's page, who ends up kidnapping the girl! (It is not clear, however, at whom Bernardino's concluding reproach is directed: at the "witches" for bringing the young girl from "Slavonia" to Italy or at the page for taking her home with him.)

Bernardino relates this story as if it were a fact of fairly recent occurrence. But let us not be deceived by assurances of historical veracity on Bernardino's part in such cases. In the preacher's sermons, even the most fantastic accounts of the supernatural are introduced in the same realistic, "historical" fashion — stories that have been subsequently traced back to the usual collections of legends, fables, and *exempla* in widespread circulation in the Middle Ages such as the *Gesta romanorum,* the *Thousand and One Nights,* and Peraldus' *Summa virtutum et vitiorum.*[63] As far as his tale of the cardinal's page, I suspect that Bernardino has, in fact, recast the story of "Eadric Wild, lord of Lydbury North" included in

Walter Map's *De nugis curialium* (ca. 1180), "one of the most famous collections of gossip, lore, and satire of the twelfth century."[64] In this tale, Eadric, returning home after a day of hunting with his page, loses his way late one night in a wild landscape. On the edge of a forest, he stumbles across a house in which he sees a large number of noble, comely ladies dancing and singing. (Despite their noble appearance and outwardly innocent comportment, the ladies, we are told, are actually demonic spirits.) In love at first sight with one of them, Eadric enters the house to join the party and ends up, after a fierce struggle with her companions, running off with the nubile object of his desire. Three days and nights of total silence on her part ensue while Eadric has his sexual way with her. The story goes on from there, but what remains is irrelevant to our present concerns. What is sufficiently clear is the kinship between Map's tale and that of Bernardino. Bernardino, of course, did not necessarily encounter this story directly in Map; he may have heard or read it from some source and/or in some other version. The essential plot of "Eadric Wild," in turn, is a traditional one in the folktale repertory, that of the "Swan Maiden," according to Stith Thompson's classification. [65]

Though, as in Bernardino's tale, nothing explicitly diabolical or immoral ever occurs in "Eadric Wild" (except, again, the kidnapping and raping of the unconsenting young lady by the Christian male intruder!), the narrator's comments cast the story as such, namely, as a tale of an encounter with the diabolical. His introduction to the story makes reference to "Dictynna and the bands of Dryads and Lares," that is to say, the pagan goddess Diana and her "society" of wood-nymphs and other mysterious companion spirits whom Christian Europe had long since demonized, amalgamating them into the witch phenomenon. Then, at the end of the tale, the narrator informs us that the story has been about "demons that are *incubi* and *succubi,* and of the dangers of union with them." (Yet, in fact, Eadric and the supposed *succuba* go on to have a seemingly happy, normal marriage, producing a son who grows to become "a man of great holiness and wisdom"!)[66] As for Bernardino's own version of the legend, although it likewise offers very little by way of actual evil, that is how our preacher means it to be understood: as a tale of evil, diabolical women, "enchantresses" (a label in Bernardino's usage, synonymous with witches).

The "one hundred accusations" filed with the inquisitor after Bernardino's preaching in Rome would suggest that the preacher's audience there was immediately persuaded by his anti-witch oratory. Did he meet the same response elsewhere? Unfortunately we do not have a complete record of the preacher's successes and failures in this regard and, in fact, can only cite two other examples, contrary in their outcomes. Earlier in the same year (1426) Bernardino had preached on the same topic in the Umbrian hill town of Todi. The concrete results of that preaching mission were to surface only two years later when, on March 20, 1428, a woman from the nearby castle of Ripabianca, Matteuccia Francisci (di Francesco), disciple of "the Enemy of Mankind," after being led through town "on a donkey with a paper hat on her head and her hands tied behind her back," was burnt at the stake.[67] The charge: a whole series of crimes of witchcraft "documented" for the years 1426, 1427, and 1428 not by "malignant and suspicious people" but by "honest and truthful citizens," many of whom were former clients, willing beneficiaries of her expertise. The complete text of this trial, "one of the oldest of its kind for Italy," has survived and is filled with intimate detail as to the witch's activities, clients, recipes, incantations, and so forth.[68]

Bernardino is explicitly mentioned in the records of this trial: in two separate paragraphs, some of Matteuccia's crimes are dated specifically "before the coming of friar Bernardino."[69] The friar, in fact, did deliver a course of sermons to the people of Todi in early 1426, arriving in that town in mid-January and remaining until early March.[70] (His preaching apparently met with great popular success, for, according to one chronicler, at its termination, the friar was escorted from the town by a procession of 1,800 citizens, "not counting women and children").[71] There is no explanation in the text itself why "the coming of friar Bernardino" is significant here, significant enough to warrant inclusion in the official record. At first glance, the inclusion might seem inappropriate or irrelevant. But, given what we know of the zealous anti-witchcraft campaign of the itinerant preacher (it is a theme represented in some shape or form in every one of the extant Bernardinian sermon cycles), we are probably safe in concluding that it was thanks to the public harangues of Bernardino that such a servant of "the Enemy of Mankind"[72] was finally brought to "justice." It was most likely he who opened the town's eyes to the grave "evil" and "danger" this woman represented, a woman who apparently until that point had been peacefully tolerated, and, indeed, actively patronized by her neighbors and by clients from near and far.

What we do know for certain, however, is that as a concrete memorial of his preaching mission there, Bernardino proposed a series of penal code reforms which were approved and adopted as official law by the government of Todi. These new *reformationes* do not mention Bernardino's name, but the minutes of a town council meeting held on January 27 (while Bernardino was still in Todi) speak explicitly of "some statutes, laws, and ordinances" that the friar had proposed to the government. Thus we can assume that these 1426 reformationes, which became law on the day of (or the day before) the friar's departure from the city, are the same as or somehow incorporate Bernardino's original proposals.[73] Among the ten items legislated by the Priors of Todi at this time is the brief, simply worded ordinance, *"De pena incantatorum et facturariorum,"* against "enchanters and sorcerers": "that no one must conjure up devils or carry out or cause to be carried out any spells or acts of witchcraft."[74] The same ordinance goes on to mandate death by fire as punishment for such criminals (*dictos incantatores, maliarios sive facturarios*), expressly allowing the use of torture "according to the nature of the crime and the condition of the persons involved." So, not only did Bernardino leave an imprint on the imaginations of the citizens of Todi, he also left his enduring mark on the very law of the land, a law which two years later was used to bring Matteuccia to trial.

Back in Siena in 1427, alluding to his successful solution to the witch problem in Rome, Bernardino encouraged his audience to "send up a little bit of incense to the Lord God here" as well — that is, to send to the stake the witches, sorcerers, and other devotees of the black arts practicing in the city and surrounding territory. Yet, surprisingly and ironically, in his own home town, according to the research of Bernadette Paton, Bernardino's oratory fell on completely deaf ears:

> Bernardino's denunciations of witches in 1427, like the earlier sermons of 1425 on the same subject, appear to have aroused little local response from either populace, authorities or clergy. The medieval inquisitorial and secular courts of Siena have attracted enough attention to enable us to trace their activities with some degree of accuracy, and the pattern of trials does not suggest an upsurge of interest in heresy or witchcraft in the fifteenth century. The case is, indeed, the reverse.[75]

We cannot be completely certain as to why the Sienese reacted with such indifference but one important reason is likely to have been what Paton calls the traditional "conservatism" of most Sienese theologians, catechists, and preachers with respect to the topic of witchcraft, namely, their tendency to dismiss the issue as having to do with mere superstition and illusion, unwilling to ascribe to it either the epidemic proportions, malevolent, heretical nature or demonic peril that the "radical" Bernardino alone preached in Siena. "Even among Bernardino's Franciscan Observant followers in Siena the subject of the witch/heretic appears to have aroused little interest or concern."[76]

In any case, Bernardino may have failed in Siena, but he succeeded, as we have seen, in Rome and Todi (the only two towns for which we have documentary evidence linking Bernardino to witch trials).[77] He succeeded not only in sending to the stake for the crime of diabolical witchcraft women who may very well have been guilty merely of simple sorcery and harmless superstition but also in intensifying the general climate of fear and suspicion which permeated the cities and towns of Italy regarding the figure of the witch. Now, by any standard, Bernardino was one of the most influential popular preachers of medieval and early Renaissance Italy: he and his band of preaching disciples combed the Italian peninsula for most of the fifteenth-century and where they did not arrive personally, their written word did, diffused over the vast international Franciscan network.[78] It will therefore come as no surprise to learn that historians charting the growth and development of the European witch craze all point to a dramatic rise in anti-witch literature and prosecution beginning in the second quarter of the fifteenth-century, that is to say, precisely in those years in which Bernardino, at the height of his career, was preaching sermons such as the one we have examined in this essay.[79]

The contribution of our friar to this crescendo is unquestionable: as we have seen, a report of the 1426 witch trial instigated by Bernardino and which "all of Rome went to see" (in the words of Stefano Infessura) reached Germany and Switzerland and all those lands where the original eyewitnesses may have had their home, as well as where Bernardino and his extensive band of Franciscan disciples (like Giacomo della Marca) were to bring their preaching campaigns. "Witch trials inspired more witch trials, because the report of action in one place would stimulate passions elsewhere. Oral report alone might have sufficed for this effect, but it was supplemented by inflammatory written accounts."[80] Included among such accounts were the writings and reported sermons of Bernardino disseminated after his death, as already mentioned, throughout Europe and beyond. By the close of the fifteenth century, the fear inspired by preachers such as Bernardino would become paranoia and the suspicion, aggressive intolerance. The result was the great witch mania which was to plague Western Christianity for the next two centuries.[81]

APPENDIX

The Date of the Trial

As already mentioned, Bernardino gives no indication of the date of the trial, stating simply that it occurred when he was in Rome ("Let me tell you what we did in Rome"). The important question becomes: when was Bernardino in Rome? Unfortunately, given the present state of evidence, it is impossible to reconstruct the friar's itinerary with complete certainty.[82] We know that at one point in the late 1420s Bernardino had been summoned to Rome by Pope Martin V to stand trial for heresy, a charge deriving from his propagation of the "novel" cult of the Holy Name of Jesus with its public veneration of the "IHS" monogram. Bernardino was not only acquitted of the charge but was asked to remain in the city to deliver a series of sermons — 114 of them — in St. Peter's and elsewhere.[83] In the past, scholars were divided between a 1426 and a 1427 date for this heresy trial and ensuing public preaching, most accepting Longpré's persuasive, well-documented chronology which argues for the later of the two dates. However, subsequent evidence from the extensive 1427 correspondence between the Roman Curia and the government of Siena (regarding Bernardino's nomination as bishop of that city) and the 1445-48 canonization trial depositions all but establishes the year of the heresy trial as 1426.[84]

As for the burning of Finicella and companion, testimony from Bernardino's canonization trials places that event as well in the year, 1426. Leonardo

Benvoglienti, Sienese diplomat, childhood friend and biographer of Bernardino, stated in his 1448 deposition that he had heard Bernardino preach in Rome in 1426, "adding that in Rome and also in Perugia ... he [Bernardino] had several witches burnt at the stake." Unfortunately, this assertion is followed by the troubling line: "Interrogated as to how he knew this, [Benvoglienti] answered that he had heard it said (dixit audivisse)." Thus, what we have is Benvoglienti in 1448, trying to remember events of at least twenty years previous, notice of which, at least in part, came to him by hearsay. Precisely what information Benvoglienti received by hearsay is unclear — the burning of the witches both in Rome and Perugia or just in Perugia (where by his own account he does not seem to have witnessed Bernardino's preaching)? It may indeed be the case that Benvoglienti heard Bernardino preach in Rome in 1426, as he declares to the papal canonization committee, but he may not have remained in the city long enough to be present at or to at least learn firsthand of the burning of the witches itself.[85]

As for the other fifteenth-century primary sources which tell of this witch trial, they are of little real help to us in establishing the date of the event. Stefano Infessura tells us that the Finicella witch trial took place in 1424; however, the dates contained in Infessura's diary are highly unreliable, as with many early chronicles.[86] There is no other evidence indicating a 1424 visit to Rome by Bernardino; any scholar asserting such a visit does so only on the unsteady ground of the Infessura diary.[87] Another consideration which would tend to eliminate 1424 as a date for the Roman preaching and witch trial is the fact that Bernardino preached a whole sermon on the topic of witchcraft during his 1425 mission to Siena (April 20-June 1), and there is not the least mention of this trial in this or any of the sermons from this series. Thus, one is led to suspect that the "Finicella" episode had not yet occurred.

Johann Hartlieb, a supposed eyewitness to the trial, places the event "in the sixth year of Pope Martin," that is, 1423, whereas in Felix Hemmerlin, the assigned date is, instead, 1420.[88] Johann Chraft simply says the episode took place during the reign of Pope Martin, while Giacomo della Marca gives no indication of time at all. Thus, as we see, none of these five sources confirms the 1426 date for which the previously cited evidence argues; yet at the same time, none of them is of such reliability with respect to their dating of events so as to oblige us to alter our conclusions thus far, namely, that after his own heresy trial in the spring of 1426, Bernardino went on to preach his 114 sermons in Rome, resulting (after his departure from the city?) in the trial and burning of Finicella and another anonymous witch, sometime, most likely, in the summer of that same year.[89]

It is, of course, possible that Leonardo Benvoglienti's memory was wrong, i.e., that the Bernardino-provoked witch-burning did not take place in 1426; in which case there is no evidence at all to support the traditional assumption that that Bernardino's own heresy trial and the "Finicella" witch trial occurred during the same Roman trip. The latter could easily taken place during another of the preacher's visits to the city, even though we cannot be certain as to precisely how many visits to Rome Bernardino made and what, if any preaching he did on those occasions. We do know that, as of September 1427 (the date of the sermon examined above), Bernardino's most recent visit to the city had been earlier that same summer of 1427: on July 12, we can place him securely in Rome, renouncing before Martin V his nomination as bishop of Siena. However, again, we do not know whether he did any public preaching while in Rome on this occasion; the precise dates of his arrival and departure are themselves unknown.[90] There is no evidence of any other Roman preaching mission by Bernardino beyond the one immediately following his heresy trial; thus, the traditional placement of the two trials in the same year remains a reasonable though, of course, tentative conclusion.

Abbreviations

All citations from Bernardino's sermons and treatises are to the following editions with their respective abbreviations:

OOH	*Opera omnia*, ed. Jean De la Haye, 5 vols. (Venice: Poletti, 1745). Cited by volume, page and column: e.g., OOH.III. 217b.
OOQ	*Opera omnia*, 9 vols. (Quaracchi: Collegio San Bonaventura, 1950-65).
A, B	*Le prediche volgari* (*Firenze 1424*), ed. Ciro Cannarozzi, 2 vols. (Pistoia: Pacinotti, 1934).
C, D, E	*Le prediche volgari (Firenze 1425)*, ed. Ciro Cannarozzi, 3 vols. (Florence: Libreria Editrice Fiorentina, 1940).
F, G	*Le prediche volgari (Siena 1425)*, ed. Ciro Cannarozzi, 2 vols. (Florence: Rinaldi, 1958).
R	*Prediche volgari sul Campo di Siena 1427*, ed. Carlo Delcorno, 2 vols. (Milan: Rusconi, 1989).

All translations from the original languages are mine, unless otherwise noted. The witch trial here discussed is at R.1006-13.

NOTES

[1] Though it is not demonstrable beyond a doubt that Bernardino and all of these five authors are referring to the same trial, as we shall see, the evidence points entirely in this direction. These other fifteenth-century references to the trial are to be found in:

a. The diary of Roman Senate scribe, Stefano Infessura, *Diario della città di Roma*, ed. Oreste Tommassini (Rome: Istituto Storico Italiano, 1890), 25.

b. The sermon, "De sortilegiis" (before 1476) by Bernardino's Franciscan confrere and disciple, Giacomo (or Iacopo) della Marca (James of the March), in Iacobus De Marchia, *Sermones dominicales*, ed. Renato Lioi (Falconara Marittima: Biblioteca Francescana, 1978), 424.

c. The *Dialogus de nobilitate et rusticitate* (1444-50) by ecclesiastical diplomat, Felix Hemmerlin (Malleolus) of Zurich, excerpted in Joseph Hansen, *Quellen und Untersuchungen zur Geschichte des Hexenwahns und der Hexenverfolgung im Mittelalter* (Bonn: Carl Georgi, 1901), 109-10.

d. The *Buch aller verbotenen Kunst, Unglaubens und der Zauberei* (1456) by Johann Hartlieb, personal physician to Duke Albrecht III of Bavaria, excerpted in Hansen, *Quellen und Untersuchungen*, 130-31.

e. The *continuatio* (after 1490) by Johann Chraft, "praedicatore Cambensi," of the *Chronica pontificum et imperatorum romanorum* of the Augustininian chronicler, Andreas of Regensburg (Andrea Ratisbonensis, ca. 1380-ca.1438). Andreas' *Chronica* ends at 1422 (see the 1903 edition by Georg Leidinger in Andreas von Regensburg, *Sämtliche Werke* [Munich: M. Riegersche Universitäts-Buchhandlung]) but was subsequently "interpolatum et usque ad annum 1490 continuatum" by Chraft (whom I have been unable to identify. "Cambensis" most likely refers to Cham, in eastern Bavaria). I quote the 1723 edition published by Eccardus (Johann Georg Eckhart) in his *Corpus Historicum Medii Aevii*, 2 vols. (Lipsia: apud Jo. Frid. Gleditschii), 1.2159. Henry Charles Lea paraphrases this report (naming its source somewhat innacurately as Andreas) in his *Materials Toward a History of Witchcraft*, ed. Arthur C. Howland, 3 vols. (Philadelphia: University of Pennsylvania Press, 1939), 3.1071.

[2] Jeffrey Burton Russell, *Witchcraft in the Middle Ages* (Ithaca: Cornell University Press, 1972), 227. Russell's work (a most thorough study of medieval witchcraft to which the present essay is greatly indebted) traces this transformation as does Norman Cohn, *Europe's Inner Demons* (New York: New American Library, 1975). See also Russell's *A History of Witchcraft* (London: Thames and Hudson, 1980), 37-89. In addition to the preceding, the following works are most useful to the study of medieval witchcraft in Italy: Giuseppe Bonomo, *Caccia alle streghe. La credenza nelle streghe dal secolo XIII al XIX con particolare riferimento all'Italia* (Palermo: Palumbo, 1971, orig. pub. 1959); Franco Cardini, "Magia e stregoneria nella Toscana del Trecento," *Quaderni medievali* 5 (1978), 121-55; *Magia, stregoneria, superstizioni nell'Occidente medievale* (Florence: La Nuova Italia, 1979); and "*La predicazione popolare alle origini della caccia alle streghe*" *in La strega, il teologo, lo scienziato: Atti del convegno "Magia, stregoneria e superstizioni in Europa e nella zona alpina*." Borgosesia, 1983, ed. Maurizio Cuccu and Paola Aldo Rossi (Genoa: ECIG, 1986), 277-93; Carlo Ginzburg, *Ecstasies: Deciphering the Witches' Sabbath* (New York: Pantheon, 1991); Richard Kieckhefer, *European Witch Trials: Their Foundations in Popular and Learned Culture, 1300-1500* (Berkeley: University of California Press, 1976) and *Magic in the Middle Ages* (Cambridge: Cambridge University Press, 1989); Henry Charles Lea, *Materials Toward a History of Witchcraft* (see previous note); Brian P. Levack, *The Witch-hunt in Early Modern Europe*, 2nd ed. (London:

Longman, 1995); and Raoul Manselli, "Le premesse medioevali della caccia alle streghe" in *La stregoneria in Europa (1450-1650)*, ed. Marina Romanello (Bologna: Il Mulino, 1975), 39-62. In addition, Carlo Delcorno's copious notes to his 1989 edition of the Siena 1427 sermon here in question (R.1006-13) have been most valuable to me in this study. There has been no thorough study of Bernardino's account of this case before; brief discussions of it can be found in Bonomo, *Caccia alle streghe*, 118-20, 262-63; Ginzburg, *Ecstasies*, 297-300; Kieckhefer, *Magic in the Middle Ages*, 194-95. The trial (but not Bernardino) is also mentioned in Russell, *Witchcraft in the Middle Ages*, 217. On Bernardino and witchcraft-related ideas in general, see Giovanni Battista Bronzini, "Le prediche di Bernardino e le tradizioni popolari del suo tempo" in *Bernardino predicatore nella società del suo tempo* (Todi: *Centro di Studi sulla Spiritualità Medievale*, 1976), 121-34; and Cleto Corrain and Pierluigi Zampini, "Spunti etnografici nelle opere di S. Bernardino da Siena," *La palestra del clero* 44 (1965), 882-905.

[3] The thirty-fifth of forty-five sermons delivered on the Piazza del Campo between August 15 and October 5 of that same year, the sermon is entitled "*Qui tratta delli tre peccati capitali*" (Herein are treated the three capital sins, R.992-1042), and focuses on the evils of pride, lust, and greed. The account of the Roman witch trial is given under the rubric of the sin of pride, for it is in this category that is classified all variety of belief in or practice of any of those "magical," superstitious, person- or environment-manipulating and future-predicting activities which, for convenience's sake, we gather under the term witchcraft. As the preacher tells his listeners, it is pride which drives us to want to do or see what is not ours, but rather God's, to do or see (R.1005). This famous sermon cycle has come down to us in a near-miraculous, seemingly verbatim transcription thanks to an industrious scribe, Benedetto di maestro Bartolomeo, cloth-cutter. See the Prologue to this transcription, R.81-84. There is another account of this trial by Bernardino in one of his unpublished 1443 Paduan sermons, which I have not been able to consult; excerpts from it are to be found in Delcorno's notes (R.1006-07, 1008). Strangely enough, there is no mention of this trial in Bernardino's Latin treatise on witchcraft, "*De idolatriae cultu,*" composed in the years 1430-36 for the benefit of future preachers (OOQ.I.105-18). (For date of the treatise, see Dionisio Pacetti, *De sancti Bernardini Senensis operibus ratio editionis critica* [Quaracchi: Collegio San Bonaventura, 1947]: 3-4.)

[4] *Io vi voglio dire quello che a Roma si fece* (R.1007).

[5] In the unpublished *reportatio* of Bernardino's Padua 1443 preaching, we find another account of this same case, which, as far as one can judge from the extracts provided by Delcorno, agrees in substance and detail with his 1427 version of the episode, again, with no date provided and with some slight variation which will be pointed out as we proceed in our analysis: "*Unde me predicante Rome de istis feci conscientiam omnibus scientibus strigones et dyabolicas strigatrices quod irent ad inquisitorem.... Unde accidit quod post illam admonicionem quam feci Rome, prout retulit nostri ordinis inquisitor, inde ad paucos dies venerant bene centum accusatores. Unde consilium quatenus diceret papa Martino, qui ordinavit ipsas capi et sic capte fuerunt multe strige, inter quas fuerunt tres pessime capte, quorum una confessa fuit sponte quod interfecerat triginta infantulos et liberassse sexaginta.*" (Wherefore while I was preaching in Rome about these people, I aroused the consciences of all those knowing male witches [*strigones*] or diabolical female witches [*strigatrices*], that they were to go [report them] to the inquisitor.... Wherefore it

happened that after this admonition which I gave in Rome, according to what the inquisitor of our order relates, a few days later no less than one hundred accusers came forward. Wherefore a consultation was held with Pope Martin who ordered these women to be arrested and many witches were thus arrested, among whom there were three women who were the worst cases, one of whom confessed of her own accord that she had killed thirty little babies and had set sixty free" (R.1006-07, n.123). I avoid translating Bernardino's masculine noun *strigones* with the later English term, "warlock," on the basis of Russell's observation that the word, "witch," "always applied to female as well as male witches, and there is no justification for using 'warlock' as the male equivalent of female 'witch'" (History of Witchcraft, 12). Note, further, that in reproducing Bernardino's Paduan sermon quote from an unpublished *reportatio*, Delorno (R.1006, n. 123) mistakenly refers to its source as the "Seraphim" cycle. In fact, the 1443 Padua cycle is distinct from the "Seraphim" Lenten cycle which Bernardino preached (also in Padua) in 1423, as Delcorno himself points out (R.55 and R.59). The later ("Seraphim") cycle can be found in the 1650 and 1745 editions of Bernardino's *Opera omnia*, edited by Jean De la Haye.

[6] *Avendo io predicato di questi incantamenti e di streghe e di malie, el mio dire era a loro come se io sognasse* (R.1007).

[7] *Infine elli mi venne detto che qualunque persona sapesse niuno o niuna che sapesse fare tal cosa, che, non accusandola, elli sarebbe nel medesimo peccato* (R.1007).

[8] See n. 6 above.

[9] *E come io ebbi predicato, furono accusate una moltitudine di streghe e di incantatori. E per la tanta quantità de li accusati, elli venne a me el guardiano* [i.e., the superior of the Franciscan friary of Aracoeli where Bernardino was most likely residing], *e dissemi: — Voi non sapete? Elli va a fuoco ciò che ci è! — Io domando: — Come? che ci è? che è? — Elli sono stati accusati una grande quantità d'uomini e di femine. — Infine, veduto come la cosa passava, elli ne fu fatto consiglio col papa, e diterminossi che fusse prese le maggiori, cioè quelle che peggio avessero fatto* (R.1007).

[10] In his "Seraphim" Lenten sermon on witchcraft (Padua, 1423), using a similar expression, Bernardino admits: "*Nonnulli credunt quod ego somniem iste, et quod dicam de capite meo...*" (Some believe that I am dreaming up these things and that I make them up in my own head. Sermon 9, "*De amore vigoroso*," OOH.III.179b). Ginzburg characterizes the Roman audience's response as "astonishment," whereas I see it as indifference or feigned puzzlement, for as Ginzburg himself admits, by what did the audience have to be astonished? They had already heard all these traditional stories before about both witches and heretics (*Ecstasies*, 298-99).

[11] See Kieckhefer, *European Witch Trials, passim,* but especially 75. This is not to say that there may not have been among the thousands of prosecuted cases, genuine instances of punishable witchcraft-related evil- doing.

[12] This same Todi 1428 trial is one in a series examined by Kieckhefer giving evidence of this "imposition of learned notions" upon those of the common masses: "Indeed, all valid and relevant evidence indicates that this pattern was typical"

(*European Witch Trials*, 75). However, Ginzburg contests this view, pointing, instead, to much data which suggests, in fact, that "the Sabbath (diabolism)" is "rooted in popular culture," and is not "an image elaborated exclusively or almost exclusively by the persecutors," as "the thesis, still commonly accepted" would have it (*Ecstasies*, 6, 7). Ginzburg may indeed be correct in suggesting that the distinction between "learned" and "popular" with respect to notions of witchcraft must be less clearly drawn than hitherto theorized. However, what appears inaccurate in Ginzburg's criticism is his equation of "diabolism" with the idea of the sabbath. Independently of the impositions of the learned, the popular imagination may well have come on its own to believe in nocturnal gatherings convoked by some central, variously identified, non-Christian figure of leadership — such as in the 1384 case of Sibillia the Milanese woman, disciple of the mysterious but non-demonic "Signora Oriente" (Kieckhefer, *European Witch Trials*, 20-21; and Russell, *Witchcraft in the Middle Ages*, 211-12). Sibillia may have attended sabbath-like gatherings; however, she saw and worshipped no devil there nor did she engage in any real form of evil there: it was, instead, her "learned" accusers who diabolized her activity.

[13] See n. 6 above.

[14] Russell, *Witchcraft in the Middle Ages*, 205.

[15] We might ask the same question with respect to Martin's successor, Eugene IV, another pontiff on familiar terms with Bernardino, who published two letters on the subject of witchcraft during his reign. English translations of the two documents, a 1434 letter to the Inquisitor Pontus Fougeyron and a 1437 letter to "All Inquisitors of Heretical Depravity," can be found in A. C. Kors and E. Peters, ed., *Witchcraft in Europe 1100- 1700: A Documentary History* (Philadelphia: University of Pennsylvania Press, 1972), 98-101. For Martin's letter, see Hansen, *Quellen und Untersuchungen*, 17 (see n. 2 above). For the rapport between Bernardino and the two popes, see Massimo Miglio, "Il pontificato e S. Bernardino" in *Atti del convegno storico bernardiniano in occasione del sesto centenario della nascita di S. Bernardino da Siena* (L'Aquila: Comitato aquilano del sesto centenario della nascita di S. Bernardino da Siena, 1982), 237-49. See Eugene IV's 1432 bull, "Sedis apostolicae" (*Bullarium franciscanum*, 3 vols., ed. U. Hüntemann [Quaracchi: Collegio San Bonaventura, 1929]: 1. 27, n. 40) which clears Bernardino of all lingering suspicion of heterodoxy and sings his praise "such as has seldom been awarded to a religious person during his lifetime" (Origo, World of San Bernardino, 128. See also Facchinetti, San Bernardino da Siena mistico sole del 400 (Milan: Casa Editrice Santa Lega Eucaristica, 1933), 372-73).

[16] *Ecstasies*, 23. Ginzburg labels what Bernardino uncovered in Rome "a sect" even though Bernardino himself does not place any special emphasis here or elsewhere on the organized nature of the practitioners of witchcraft. As we shall later see, he does makes reference in the same sermon to a formal nocturnal gathering of "these enchanters" (*questi incantatori*). What he describes turns out to be a night-time dance in a field of mostly women and young people encountered by the servant of a Cardinal near Benevento. But that is as explicit as he gets in suggesting cooperation among themselves. As we shall later see, in his Latin treatise on witchcraft, Bernardino will also quote the famous canon Episcopi which refers to the Society of Diana (or Herodias, see n. 53 below), another indication of formal organization and regularly scheduled interaction among these so-called witches.

[17] Levack, *The Witch-hunt in Early Modern Europe*, 91 and 116.

[18] *[U]na grande quantità d'uomini e di femine ... diterminossi che fusse prese le maggiori, cioè quelle che peggio avessero fatto* (R.1007). In his 1443 version of this episode, Bernardino mentions that among these "worst cases" were three, not two, women. See n. 6 above.

[19] Rincagnato is a favorite among Bernardino's colloquial adjectives. Literally, it simply means "pug-nosed," a much too mild rendering in the present case. The word is, in fact, susceptible to a variety of disparate translations, according to the context. See Emilio Pasquini, "Costanti tematiche e varianti testuali nelle prediche bernardiniane" in *Atti del simposio internazionale cateriniano-bernardiniano* (*Siena*, 17-20 aprile 1980), ed. Domenico Maffei and Paolo Nardi (*Siena*: Accademia Senese degli Intronati, 1982), 704. The dark folklore surrounding the vetula, the old woman or crone, is ancient: see Jole Agrimi and Chiara Crisciani, "Immagini e ruoli della vetula tra sapere medico e antropologia religiosa (secoli XIII-XV)" in Poteri *carismatici e informali: chiesa e società medioevali*, ed. Agostino Paravicini Bagliani and André Vauchez (Palermo: Sellerio, 1992), 224-61. See also Barbara G. Walker, *The Crone: Woman of Age, Wisdom and Power* (San Francisco: Harper, 1985). Ovid was an important auctoritas in the medieval career of this figure: see Cohn, *Europe's Inner Demons*, 207. According to the medical teaching of Bernardino's day, all old women were thought to be "naturally toxic" because once they ceased menstruating, the poisons and infected humors naturally produced by the female body were no longer purged from them; hence their ability to bewitch or infect small babies with a mere glance (Agrimi- Crisciani, "*Immagini e ruoli*, "246-47). Even St. Anne, mother of the Virgin Mary, did not escape association with the realm of sorcery (Agrimi-Crisciani, "*Immagini e ruoli*," 243, n. 64).

[20] *Perché ella desiderasse d'essere incantatrice*, R.227. See also B.184: *El dimonio la prima arte ch'elli facessi mai fu quella dello indovinare ... così nel mondo [disse] a Madonna Eva: "Mangia di questo frutto e saprai el bene e 'l male, sarete iddii."* (The first art which the demon ever created was that of divination ... thus he said on earth to lady Eve: eat of this fruit and you will know good and evil and will be gods.) In explaining why the sin of sorcery occurs more among women than men, Alexander of Hales claims that this "doctrina" was first taught to woman (i.e., Eve) by the devil himself "seeing that she had lesser powers of discernment of spirits" (*quia ipse diabolus primo transfundit eam in mulierem, utpote quae minus habebat discretionem spiritus. Summa theologica* [Quaracchi: Collegio San Bonaventura, 1930]: 3.778, articulus VI). Peraldus and Antonino of Florence speak in similar fashion: see Agrimi-Crisciani, "*Immagini e ruoli*," 248. Jacopo Passavanti, instead, says that this was the sin of both Adam and Eve ("*questo fu il primo peccato de' nostri primi parenti*"), *Specchio di vera penitenza*, "*Trattato della Scienza*," reprinted in Sergio Abbiati, et. al., *La stregoneria. Diavoli, streghe, inquisitori dal Trecento al Settecento* (Milan: Mondadori, 1984), 36.

[21] *E fune presa una fra l'altre, la quale disse e confessò senza niuno martorio, che aveva uccisi da XXX fanciulli col succhiare il sangue loro; e anco disse che n'aveva liberati LX; e disse che ogni volta che ella ne liberava niuno, ogni volta si conveniva dare uno membro al diavolo per sagrificio, e davane uno membro di bestia; e a questo modo facendo, continuò gran tempo. E più anco confessò, che ella aveva morto el suo propio figliulo, e avevane fatto polvare, de la quale dava mangiare per tali faccende*

(R.1008). The same numbers, thirty and sixty, for respectively the murdered and the spared infants are given in the friar's 1443 account of this case (see n. 6 above). Hesitant to give credence to the woman's confession, the inquisitor obtained independent confirmation of the sudden deaths of these infants from the fathers of the victims, Bernardino assures us in the same paragraph.

[22] See, for example, the index to Russell's *Witchcraft in the Middle Ages* under "Blood-sucking" and "Children." As many scholars in the past have suspected, the infant deaths imputed to witches may have in fact been the result of the parents' or nurses' own neglect or, indeed, premeditated murder, or of inexplicable illness and trauma, such as what today is called "Sudden Infant Death Syndrome."

[23] See B.168 (Florence 1424) and G.279 (Siena 1425). Blood-sucking is mentioned also in one of the later Latin treatises, "*De mandato divinae dilectionis*" contained in the Lenten series, *De christiana religione (1430- 36)*; see OOQ.II.43. (For date of the treatise, see Pacetti, *De sancti Bernardini Senensis operibus ratio editionis critica* [Quaracchi: Collegio San Bonaventura, 1947]: 3-4.) In an earlier sermon in this same Siena 1427 cycle in which he tells of the Roman trial, Bernardino describes the gruesome preparation of a concoction made of the powdered remains of ritually murdered children on the part, not of witches but of the Piedmontese heretical sect "of the barilotto" (i.e., "the keg" from which they drink the potion), see R.793-94. See also Norman Cohn's discussion of Bernardino and this "sect of the barilotto" in *Europe's Inner Demons*, 49-54. The ultimate prototype of such secret nocturnal assemblies is the ancient lore of the "Society of Diana" (see n. 53 below): but "[h]ere the innocuously magical features of Diana's society have dissolved into the macabre and aggressive traits of the sect of the keg" (Ginzburg, *Ecstasies*, 299). Bernardino's description of the group also echoes the centuries-old calumnies traditionally used against dissident or other suspect minority groups — sexual orgy, infanticide, sodomy. For earlier examples, see Russell, *Witchcraft in the Middle Ages*, 88-95; and Cohn, *Europe's Inner Demons*, 19, 29-30. "These charges are all ancient," Russell reminds us, commenting on the persecution of the Cathars and Waldensians. "The Syrians brought them against the Jews, the Romans against the Christians, and the Christians against the Gnostics. Now they were being brought against the medieval heretics" (*A History of Witchchraft*, 59). As is well known, there was much cross-attribution between witches and heretics. In fact, Russell states: "Every one of [the constituent] elements [of European witchcraft] was either introduced into the tradition of witchcraft by heresy or at least heavily modified by it (*A History of Witchcraft*, 55).

[24] C.209-12. A greatly reduced version of the tale is found at G.196-97. In the Padua 1443 account of the witch trial, Bernardino reproduces the dialogue between the devil and the "witch" in direct discourse: see R.1008, n. 133. As Jacopo Passavanti explains, the pact could be either explicit or implicit (*Specchio di vera penitenza*, 34). For the Scriptural source of the idea of the pact with the worship-hungry devil, see Matthew 4: 8-9, the temptation of Christ in the desert ("All these I will give you, if you will fall down and worship me"). Also included in the devil-witch pact were sexual relations between the two parties, but here in 1427 Bernardino is silent on this detail, whereas in the "Godmother of Lucca" exemplum, he hints at it indirectly: the godmother-witch conjures up the devil in a state of complete nudity and with her hair unbound (C.210).

[25] R.1008, n. 132. See Kieckhefer, *European Witch Trials*, 55-56. See also Nancy G. Siraisi, *Medieval and Early Renaissance Medicine: An Introduction to Knowledge and Practice* (Chicago: University of Chicago Press, 1990), 27, 38, 44-46.

[26] Russell, *Witchcraft in the Middle Ages*, 260-61.

[27] *O medici, studuistis in gramatica, logica, philosophia, medicina, cum multis spensis, periculis et laboribus; e la vechi[a] rinchagnata n'à l'onore!* (OOQ.IX.369).

[28] See n. 6 above.

[29] Russell, *Witchcraft in the Middle Ages*, 257.

[30] Corrain and Zampini, "*Spunti etnografici nelle opere di S. Bernardino da Siena*" (see n. 3 above), provide a lengthy list of popular superstitions mentioned in the works of Bernardino (for the St. John's plant belief, see 898-99). A useful, concise primer on medieval magic and witchcraft is Kieckhefer's *Magic in the Middle Ages.*

[31] B.186 and OOH.III.179b. See also Russell, *Witchcraft in the Middle Ages*, 51, 61, and 201. Like Bernardino's Roman witch, the fourteenth- century French healer-sorcerers also gathered their herbs on Saint John's eve, to cite an example outside of Italy: see Pierrette Paravy, "*Streghe e stregoni nella società del Delfinato nel XV secolo*" in Poteri *carismatici e informali: chiesa e società medioevali*, ed. Agostino Paravicini Bagliani and André Vauchez (Palermo: Sellerio, 1992), 85-86.

[32] Russell, *Witchcraft in the Middle Ages*, 51.

[33] See Hilda Graef, *Mary: A History of Doctrine and Devotion* (London: Sheed and Ward, 1985) and Marina Warner, *Alone of All Her Sex: The Myth and the Cult of the Virgin Mary* (New York: Knopf, 1976). For the Society of Diana, see n. 53 below. It is no mere coincidence that the cult of Mary and the cult of Diana (Artemis) both have as their historic center the ancient city of Ephesus. The Artemisium, great temple of Artemis (the Greek counterpart to the Italic Diana) in Ephesus was one of the seven wonders of the ancient world. (For Paul's troubles with the statue-merchants of the Artemisium, see the *Acts of the Apostles*, 19: 23-40.) It was in Ephesus that Mary supposedly lived her final years and that popular devotion to Mary as theotokos, the "God-bearer" (in Latin, *Dei genitrix*) first developed. Amidst great controversy, the ecumenical Council of Ephesus ratified the orthodoxy of that title in 731.

[34] R.1008-09; see also G.278-79. Female shapeshifting and night-flight are ancient motifs as well, harkening back, among other things, to the Roman *strix* or *striga* (whence the Italian, *strega*, witch), "originally a screech-owl, then a night-spirit and vampire, finally a witch" (Russell, *Witchcraft in the Middle Ages*, 15). In a famous scene from *The Golden Ass* (3: 21, 24), to cite just one well-known example from antiquity, one evening, the young Lucius Apuleius spies on the sorcerer Pamphilë as she rubs an ointment on her naked body and is transformed into an owl. (Using the same ointment, he then is transformed into a jackass.) A similar story of shapeshifting comes to us from one of Bernardino's own contemporaries, the Sienese humanist, Mariano Sozzini the Elder, who relates in a 1462 letter to Antonio Tridentone of Parma the story of "the witch of Asciano" told to him as a boy in 1420 by an old

peasant, Nanni Ciancadiddio (or Cianchadeus), who swore vociferously that it was true episode from his own childhood: like Lucius, Nanni as a boy one night spied on a naked vetula (a nurse to whom he had been entrusted) as she smeared her body with magical ointment, turning into a goat in order to attend the witches' gathering at Benevento. (Again, like Lucius, Nanni too is transformed into an ass and is transported from the countryside to the Piazza del Campo in the center of Siena.) See Francesco Novati, "Una lettera ed un sonetto di Mariano Sozzini il vecchio," *Bullettino senese di storia patria* 2 (1895), 89-100. On Sozzini, see also Bonomo, *Caccia alle streghe*, 263-66. Sozzini's treatise, "*De sortilegiis*" (also called "*De divinatione*") provides us with much detailed information about fifteenth-century folklore and witch-related beliefs. For a summary of its contents, see Ludovico Zdekauer, "*Sullo scritto 'De sortilegiis' di M. Sozzini il Vecchio,*" Archivio per lo studio delle tradizioni popolari 15 (1896), 131-37.

[35] The canon *Episcopi* is reproduced in English in Alan C. Kors and Edward Peters, ed. *Witchcraft in Europe 1100-1700: A Documentary History* (Philadelphia: University of Pennsylvania Press, 1972), 29-30.

[36] See Franco Cardini, "*La predicazione popolare alle origini della caccia alle streghe*" (see n. 3 above).

[37] C.210 (see n. 25 above).

[38] Cardini, "*Magia e stregoneria nella Toscana del Trecento,*" 147 (see n. 3 above).

[39] R.1010. See also OOH.III.178a for further discussion by Bernardino of the same topic.

[40] *Elli so' stati già di quelli che hanno veduta la gatta quando va a fare queste cose; e tali so' stati tanto preveduti, che hanno auto qualche cosa in mano e arandellato a quella gatta, e talvolta l'hanno gionta. E di quelle so' state, che hanno riceuta tal percossa, che hanno rotta la gamba. E a chi credi che sia rimasa la percossa? Pure a la femina indiavolata, none al diavolo* (R.1010; see also G.278-79. Bernardino does not specify the color of the cat). This is, again, a traditional motif, that of the wound of the demonic animal which after the crime is found on the witch herself: see Russell, *Witchcraft in the Middle Ages, 53.*

[41] See n. 2 above.

[42] The entire passage reads: *Et constat, quod tempore Martini pape de anno 1420 quedam mulier strega residens trans Tiberim se transformaverat in cattum et actus humano ritui raros immo impossibiles et solis cattis applicabiles et pure cattivos exercuit. Et inter cetera pueros in cunabulis iacentes maleficiis infecit, quos ex post sanando, dum converteretur in hominem, mercedem usurpavit. Et hoc eius finale lucrum sibi coaptando reputavit, et de his et aliis publice confessa iudicialiter igne concremata vitam finivit.*

[43] *Ain groß zaichen von zaubrey. Erenreicher fürst, ich sag dir ain sach, die ich und manig man zu Rom gesehen und gehört haben. Es was in dem sechsten jar als bapst Martin gesetzt was, da stund uf zu Rom ain ungelaub, das etliche weib und man*

sich verwandelten in katzen und totten gar vil kinder zu Rom. Zu ainer zeit kam ain katz in ains burgers hus und paiß sein kind in der wiegen. Das kind schray, der vatter hub sich pald uff und nam ain messer und schlug die katzen, als sy zu ainem venster uß wolt, durch das haubt. Des morgens gar fru tett sich die fraw berichten mit den hailigen sacramentem; die nachpawrn clagten ir kranckhait, als da sitt ist. Der nachpawr clagt si auch; sy antwurt im: wär dir laid men krankhait, du hettest mir das nit getan. An dem dritten tag erschall, das die frawe ain wunden in dem haubt het. Der nachpawr gedacht an die katzen, auch an ir wort; er pracht das an den senat. Die fraw ward gefangen und verjach; sy sprach vor dem Capitoln überlaut, hett sy ir salb, sy wölt hinfarn. O wie gern hett ich und maniger curtisan gesehen, das man ir die salb geben hett. Da stund uff ain doctor und sprach, das ir die salb nit solt geben werden, wan der tüffel möcht mit gotz verhenknuss groß irrung machen. Die fraw ward verprennt, das hab ich gesehen. Item zu Rom was sag, das der leut gar vil. (My thanks to Professors David Gill, S.J. and Michael Resler for their assistance with this translation.)

[44] *Hujus temporibus murilegus sive cattus quidam Romae multos infantes in cunis jacentes, dum a nutricibus non bene custodiebantur, nacta oportunitate interficiebat. Tandem quidam vir senex sapiens, custodiens puerulum sibi comissum, simulans se cattum per fenestram ingredientem non videre, dum accessisset ad puerum suffocandum, ipse eundem cattum cum gladio usque ad effusionem sanguinis vulneravit. Ex tunc per vestigia sanguinis, et vulnus illatum, compertum fuit, illum cattum esse unam vetulam, de prope commorantem, quae a Cirologo in cura habebatur, et quando voluit in cattum mutabatur, sicque de interfectis parvulis, ut se diutius conservaret.*

[45] See n. 2 above.

[46] The entry reads:

> In quell'anno [1424] frate Bernardino fece ardere tavolieri, canti, brevi, sorti, capelli che fucavano le donne, et fu fatto uno talamo di legname in Campituoglio, et tutte queste cose ce foro appiccate et arse, et fu a 21 di iuglio [or July 11 or 25, or June 21 or 25, according to other mss.].
>
> Et dopo fu arsa Finicella strega, a dì 8 del ditto mese di iuglio [or June or July 28, according to other mss.] perchè essa diabolicamente occise de molte criature et affattucchiava di molte persone, et tutta Roma ce andò a vedere.
>
> Et fece frate Bernardino in Roma de molte paci, et de molti abbracciamenti, et benchè ce fusse stato homocidio.
>
> (In that year friar Bernardino had burnt gameboards, songsheets, talismans, fortune-telling paraphernalia and women's wigs, and a wooden chamber (?) was built on the Capitoline Hill and all of these things were placed in it and set fire, and this was on July 21. / And later the witch Finicella was burned, on the 8th day of the same month because she had diabolically killed many children and had put spells on many people, and all of Rome went to see the sight. / And friar Bernardino brought about much peace and reconciliation even between parties where there had been a murder.)

[47] *Item, quedam vetula Rome, nominata Funicella, interfecit 65 pueros et coxit brachium filii sui mortui pro incantionibus. Et dicebat sibi diabolus sic, quod non erat pèccatum interficere innocentes, quia salvabantur. Et hoc dixit mihi magister Nicolaus de Roma, ordinis nostri, tum inquisitor, et combusta est.* (Likewise, one old woman of Rome, named Funicella, killed 65 children and cooked the arm of her dead son for use in her spells. And it was the devil who told her [to do] so, that it was not a sin to kill the little ones, since they would be saved. And this was told to me by master Nicholas of Rome of our order, who was then inquisitor, and the woman was burnt at the stake.)

[48] Kieckhefer, *European Witch Trials*, 121.

[49] R.1011.

[50] For a complete list of the classic components of the witch scenario, see Russell, *Witchcraft in the Middle Ages*, 23-24.

[51] Russell, *Witchcraft in the Middle Ages*, 227.

[52] See Bonomo, *Caccia alle streghe*, 16-37; Russell, *Witchcraft in the Middle Ages*, 46-49 and passim; and Ginzburg, *Ecstasies, passim.* In place of Diana as the mistress of the assembly, Christians sometimes put Herodias, the murderous wife of Herod, responsible for the execution of John the Baptist.

[53] In the *Decameron*, Day 8, Novella 9. In Boccaccio, this same piece of folklore is called "*andare in corso*" (to go on a/the ride) and entails nocturnal gatherings in a secret place of sensual delights afforded to the members of a club of twenty-five men, under the direction of two disciples of the famous magician, Michael Scot (Michele Scoto). (For Michael Scot, see Kieckhefer, *Magic in the Middle Ages*, 123, 144, 165.) The men supposedly travel to the feasting place on the back of an obliging black, horned beast who must, however, not hear the mere mention of the name of God and the saints.

[54] B.169-70. *Tregenda* seems not to have be a common term among Bernardino's contemporaries or predecessors. The only medieval document, aside from Bernardino's sermon, in which I have thus far encountered it is Passavanti's already-mentioned *Specchio di vera penitenza* (see n. 21 above). The term does not appear in Ginzburg's *Ecstasies*, the longest treatment of the sabbath to date, nor in Russell's encyclopedic *Witchcraft in the Middle Ages*. As for Bernardino's use of the term in the sermon just cited (B.169-70), textual similarities lead me to suspect that Bernardino himself is either quoting, paraphrasing or unconsciously remembering Passavanti's *Specchio*.

[55] I have been able to identify neither "*Iobiana*" nor the source from which Bernardino might have taken the name. The similar term, "*zobianae*," as a synonym for witches occurs in a medical treatise on witchcraft written in Pavia by Antonio Guaineri (fl. 1410-40).

[56] *Inter has impiissimas feras sunt quaedam crudelissimae mulieres et etiam quandoque viri, credentes et profitentes cum Diana seu Iobiana vel Herodiade et innumera multitudine mulierum equitare super quasdam bestias et multa terrarum*

spatia intempestae noctis silentio pertransire eiusque iussionibus obedire velut dominae et certis noctibus sicut nocte Iovis et nocte post dominicam diem, ad eius servitium evocari. Asserunt etiam ab illis aliquas creaturas, maxime parvulos pueros, posse in deterius vel in melius permutare, aut in aliam speciem et similitudinem transformare. (OOQ.I.117) The italicized sections represent Bernardino's additions to or modifications of the canon. For the canon, see Russell, *Witchcraft in the Middle Ages*, 75-80, 291-93 et al. For the "society of Diana," see n. 53 above. See also the two Milan cases of Sibillia (1384) and Pierina de' Bugatis (1390), who confessed to having participated in the "game" (*ludum*) of "Madonna Oriente," nocturnal assemblies clearly ressembling those of Diana. However, nothing diabolical and nothing particularly criminal occurred under the guidance of "Madonna Oriente:" no night flight on the backs of animals, no metamorphoses, no renunciation of the faith, no homage to Satan (he is completely absent from the women's accounts) and no orgies. For these two trials, see Russell, *Witchcraft in the Middle Ages*, 211-14; Ginzburg, *Ecstasies*, 91-102; Bonomo, *Caccia alle streghe*,16-17; and Cohn, *Europe's Inner Demons*, 217-18.

[57] Doh, sai che intervenne di questi incantatori, eh? Intriamo in practica. Elli fu a Roma uno famiglio d'uno cardinale, el quale andando a Benivento [*sic] di notte, vidde in su una aia ballare molta gente, donne e fanciulli e giovani; e così mirando elli ebbe grande paura. Pure essendo stato un poco a vedere, elli s'assicurò e andò dove costoro ballavano, pure con paura, e a poco a poco s'accostò a costoro, che elli vidde che erano giovanissimi; così stando a vedere, elli s'assicurò tanto, che elli si pose a ballare con loro. E ballando tutta questa brigata, elli venne a sonare mattino. Come mattino toccò, tutte costoro in un subito si partirono, salvo che una, cioè quella che costui teneva per mano lui, che ella volendosi partire coll'altre, costui la teneva; ella tirava, e elli tirava. Elli la tenne tanto a questo modo, che elli si fece dì chiaro. Vedendola costui sì giovana, elli se ne la menò a casa sua. E odi quello che intervenne, che elli la tenne tre anni seco, che mai non parlò una parola. E fu trovato che costei era di Schiavonia. Pensa ora tu come questo sia ben fatto, che elli sia tolta una fanciulla al padre e a la madre in quel modo.* (R.1012-13)

[58] R. 1013. Bernardino's original Italian terms are *incantatrice, maliarda, incantatori, and streghe.* Though the list embraces both male and female, in his next utterance, the friar uses only feminine forms: "fate che tutte sieno messe in esterminio" (see to it that all of these women are exterminated). Furthermore, we may also note here that these and the other various witch-related labels, though technically referring to separate categories of practitioners, are used indiscriminately and interchangeably by the friar, nor does he ever stop to define them for his audience. (Technically, what separated the witch from the other categories of persons was that the former not only invoked but also worshipped the Devil. See Russell, *Witchcraft in the Middle Ages,* 214.) The lack of lexical discrimination is characteristic of witch-related literature in general, both historical and modern, as Kieckhefer points out (*European Witch Trials,* 7-8). For witch-related terminology and lexical distinctions, see Russell, *Witchcraft in the Middle Ages*, 3-18; Levack, *The Witch-hunt in Early Modern Europe*, 4-11; Kieckhefer, *Magic in the Middle Ages*, 8-16.

[59] See R.1012, n. 172 and Bonomo, *Caccia alle streghe*, 309. As we shall later see, Matteuccia of Todi, the "witch" brought to justice thanks to Bernrdino's preaching, confessed to attending regular witch assemblies at the "walnut tree of Benevento."

Sozzini's witch of Asciano was also going to the same destination and, applying the magic ointment to her body, recited a formula very similar to that used by Matteuccia: "*Sopra acqua et sopra vento menami a la noce di Benevento*" (Above water and above wind, lead me to the walnut tree of Benevento), in *Novati,* "Una lettera," 97 (see n. 35 above).

[60] For the association of "Slavonia" (in Italian, Schiavonia), that is, the Balkans, with the Bogomils, see Ginzburg, *Ecstasies*, 76-77. "Slavonia" was also home of many of the slaves ("domestic enemies" like witches and heretics) employed in Italian households. See Iris Origo, "The Domestic Enemy: Eastern Slaves in Tuscany in the Fourteenth and Fifteenth Centuries," *Speculum* 30 (1955), 321-66; Russell, *Witchcraft in the Middle Ages*, 120-22; and Malcolm D. Lambert, *Medieval Heresy: Popular Movements From the Gregorian Reform to the Reformation*, 2nd. ed. (Oxford: Blackwell, 1992), 55-61.

[61] See n. 24 above on the contemporary sect of the *barilotto*, described by Bernardino at R.793-94. See as well Vern L. Bullough, "Postscript: Heresy, Witchcraft and Sexuality" in *Sexual Practices and the Medieval Church*, ed. Vern L. Bullough and James Brundage (Buffalo: Prometheus Books, 1982), 206-17.

[62] The quote is from Origo, *The World of San Bernardino*, 44. Freedom is a dangerous thing in and for a woman, Bernardino says; too much freedom, for example, led Mary Magdalene to her initial ruination, as it will any woman (B.145 and E.183). On the other hand, the Virgin Mary was preserved in her virginity and moral respectability (as again will be any woman) because she was ever accompanied by twelve "mystical" (i.e., symbolic) handmaidens, the foremost of whom was Madonna Clausura, "Lady Cloister" (OOQ.IV.473-75 and R.861-62).

[63] See Delcorno, "*L'exemplum nella predicazione di San Bernardino*" in *Bernardino predicatore nella società del suo tempo* (Todi: Centro di Studi sulla Spiritualità Medievale, 1976), 73-107.

[64] Russell, *Witchcraft in the Middle Ages*, 116. I cite the 1983 bilingual edition: Walter Map, *De nugis curialium, Courtiers' Trifles*, ed. and trans. M. R. James, rev. by C. N. L. Brooke and R. A. B. Mynors (Oxford: Clarendon Press, 1983), 155-57, Dist. ii, c. 12, "Again of Such [Illusory] Apparitions." This is not the place to enter into a lengthy comparative analysis of the two tales, but the number of evident similarities between Bernardino's exemplum and Map's story make it reasonable to conjecture that the former is a re-working, perhaps entirely unconscious, of either the latter or of its many avatars in medieval literature. Both stories involve the figure of the page (though in different roles), a remote country setting, the nocturnal dance of "unusual" ladies, a protagonist who after initial fear draws courage and penetrates the group, then takes a fancy to one of the ladies whom he seizes, a struggle between the two resulting in his kidnapping of her, and a "three-unit" period of complete silence on her part (three years in Bernardino, three days in Map).

[65] The similarity is pointed out by the editors of *De nugis*,149, n.3. For the Swan Maiden, see Stith Thompson, *Motif-Index of Folk-literature: A Classification of Narrative Elements in Folk-tales, Ballads, Myths, Fables,* rev. ed. (Bloomington: Indiana University Press, 1989), D.361.1 (see also B 652.1), and Barbara Fass Leavy,

In Search of the Swan Maiden: A Narrataive on Folklore and Gender (New York: New York University Press, 1994).

[66] *De nugis*,159.

[67] Domenico Mammoli, *The Record of the Trial and Condemnation of a Witch, Matteuccia di Francesco at Todi,* 20 March 1428. Res Tudertinae 14 (Rome: n.p., 1972), 39. Mammoli gives the original Latin text of the trial with an English translation. The Latin text with commentary has also been published by Candida Peruzzi, "Un processo di stregoneria a Todi nel '400," *Lares* 21 (1955), 1-17. For further discussion of the trial, see Claudio Bondì, *Strix. Medichesse, streghe e fattucchiere nell'Italia del Rinascimento* (Rome: Lucarini, 1989), 25-42; and, in more summary fashion, *Bonomo, Caccia alle streghe*, 119-20; Kieckhefer, *Magic in the Middle Ages*, 59-60, and *European Witch Trials*, 73; and Ginzburg, *Ecstasies*, 299.

[68] I quote Peruzzi, "*Un processo di stregoneria*," 2. The trial is also briefly discussed in Bonomo, *Caccia alle streghe*, 119-20; Kieckhefer, *Magic in the Middle Ages*, 59-60 and *European Witch Trials*, 73; and Ginzburg, *Ecstasies*, 299.

[69] Mammoli, *Record of the Trial*, 31.

[70] Marino Bigaroni, "S. Bernardino a Todi," *Studi francescani* 73 (1976), 110-17. On the basis of compelling new evidence, Bigaroni corrects certain entries in the chronology of the friar's activities for the period March-April, 1426 previously established by Pacetti in his "*La predicazione di S. Bernardino in Toscana*" and "*Cronologia bernardiniana*" (see n. 78 below).

[71] Bigaroni, "*S. Bernardino a Todi*," 117.

[72] Mammoli, *Record of the Trial*, 29.

[73] Bigaroni, "*S. Bernardino a Todi*," 116-17. The entire text reads: *Item decreverunt ordinaverunt et reformaverunt, quod nullus debeat incantare demones seu facere aut fieri facere aliquas facturas seu malias. Et qui contrafecerit in predictis igne comburatur. Et possit potestas et quilibet alius officialis precedentibus in legitimis inditiis dictos incantatores, maliarios sive facturarios torquere secundum facti qualitatem et personarum conditionem.*

[74] "*Item decreverunt ... quod nullus debeat incantare demones seu facere aut fieri facere aliquas facturas seu malias.*" Bigaroni, "S. Bernardino a Todi," 123.

[75] "'To the fire, to the fire! Let us burn a little incense to God': Bernardino, Preaching Friars and *Maleficio* in Late Medieval Siena" in *No Gods Except Me: Orthodoxy and Religious Practice in Europe, 1200-1600*, ed. Charles Zika (Melbourne: History Department, University of Melbourne, 1991), 9. See also Chapter 7, "The Supernatural World," of her book, *Preaching Friars and the Civic Ethos: Siena, 1380-1480* (London: Centre for Medieval Studies, Queen Mary and Westfield College, University of London, 1992).

[76] Paton, "To the Fire," 26; see also 23-27 and her *Preaching Friars,* 295-303. We are left with the compelling question: why, when most of his peers were only mildly

disturbed by the phenomenon of witches, did Bernardino decide to wage such a fierce, relentless campaign against them? Paton sees it as an extension of the general "purging mentality" of this tenacious, not to say, fanatical reformer of Church and society. She also sees a degree of "personal paranoia" in Bernardino who himself had suffered persecution as heresiarch for his "idolatrous" cult of the Holy Name of Jesus ("To the fire,"28-29). But, what makes a man a fanatical reformer to begin with? The answer, I believe, in Bernardino's case is fear, fear of the utter dissolution of society and the wrath of an avenging God. As he himself describes in a sermon on the coming "end times" (OOH.III.355b) and as we well know, the landscape of early fifteenth-century Europe was one of upheaval, confusion, and apprehension on a massive scale affecting all realms of society, due to both natural disaster and moral decay. It was a time of catastrophic warfare between nations, towns, political factions, and rival families, repeated traumatizing outbreaks of the unconquerable "Black Death," widespread economic depression, and chronic famine. Added to this, the Church had to endure the continuance of what was to be nearly forty years of the "Great Western Schism," a major disruption of temporal and spiritual governance at all levels throughout Europe which itself had followed an even longer and likewise disruptive exile of the papacy in Avignon. Having himself experienced the utter precariousness of life in earliest childhood (Bernardino was orphaned of his mother at three years of age, of his father at six), the friar responded to all that he saw with great alarm and set out to save society from destruction from its own hand and from the wrath of God. This meant purging society of all he considered to be its depraved, dangerous elements, among them, the witches.

[77] In Arezzo in 1428, Bernardino orchestrated the dramatic destruction of an ancient pagan well, the *Fontetecta*, the site of much superstitious practice and witch-related activity. See F. van Ortroy, ed., "Vie inédite de S. Bernardin de Sienne par un frère mineur, son contemporain." *Analecta bollandiana* 25 (1906), 304-38. This anonymous biography known as the Vita S. Bernardini edita per quemdam fratrem was also published in the same year by Ferdinand-Marie d'Araules (Delorme), Vie de Saint Bernardin de Sienne. Texte latin inédit du XVe siècle. (Rome: n.p., 1906). In the Van Ortroy edition, the Fontetecta episode is found on 331-35; in d'Araules, on 34-39. There is some debate over the number of times and the precise years in which Bernardino preached in Arezzo; for a well-argued chronology, see Pacetti, "La predicazione di S. Bernardino in Toscana. Con documenti inediti estratti dagli Atti del Processo di Canonizzazione," *Archivum franciscanum historicum* 33 (1940), 268-318; 34 (1941), 261-83; for Fontetecta, see 34: 261-63.

[78] Giovanni da Capistrano, one of Bernardino's closest followers, tells us that after Bernardino's death, copies of his works were requested by all parts of the wide-flung Franciscan family, including those in the "Holy Land, Cyprus, Asia" and "even ... barbarian nations;" *Vita sancti Bernardini senensis*, OOH.I.xxxviii.b. See also John Moorman, *A History of the Franciscan Order* (Oxford: Clarendon Press, 1968), chap. 39 ("Great Was the Company of the Preachers"). Witchcraft — together with its allied topics such as superstition, heresy, and demonology — is one of the most recurrent themes among the hundreds of sermons and treatises collected in the twenty or so volumes of Bernardino's extant opera omnia. The friar appears to have preached on the topic wherever he traveled. Moreover, in many towns, as an appendix to his preaching, Bernardino also arranged for the staging of dramatic "bonfires of vanities;" these "bonfires" involved the public burning, not only of cosmetics, wigs, clothes, playing cards, dice, and other gambling items, but also magical books,

amulets, scapulars, and other instruments of magic, sorcery, and superstition. The anonymous scribe responsible for preserving of Bernardino's 1424 Florentine sermon cycle has left us a vivid account of one such conflagration: see B.87-88.

[79] Russell, *Witchcraft in the Middle Ages*, 200, 225-28; Levack, *The Witch-hunt in Early Modern Europe*, 185-86; and Kieckhefer, *Magic in the Middle Ages*, 194-95.

[80] Kieckhefer, *Magic in the Middle Ages*, 195.

[81] Levack, *The Witch-hunt in Early Modern Europe*, 185.

[82] The most recent and most scrupulous chronology is that assembled by Martino Bertagna, a member of the Quaracchi committee which published the critical edition of Bernardino's *opera omnia* and prepared the Vatican documentation for the preacher's nomination as official "doctor" of the Roman Catholic Church. See his *Chronologia bernardiniana hucusque nota* (Rome: Tipografia Guerra e Belli, 1960), also published as part of the Vatican document, *Sacra Rituum Congregatione Concessionis tituli doctoris in honorem S. Bernardini Senensis, confessoris ex ordine Fratrum Minorum...* (Città del Vaticano: n.p., 1966), 1-18. I have not been able to consult either one of these two editions of Bertagna's chronology. However, it was later reprinted in a revised version, which I cite in this study, in the *Enciclopedia bernardiniana*, 4 vols., ed. Enrico D'Angelo, et al. (L'Aquila: Centro Promotore Generale delle Celebrazioni del VI Centenario della Nascita di San Bernardino da Siena, 1980-85), 4. xi-xxiii, shorn, unfortunately, of its scholarly apparatus. Since, however, the 1960 original on which this 1980 "perfected" version is based (according to Delcorno, R.61) was done with "scholarly rigor" and with "an abundance of documentation" (Teodosio Lombardi, *Presenza e culto di San Bernardino da Siena nel ducato Estense* [Ferrara: Centro Culturale Città di Ferrara, 1981]: 88-89), I have used it with confidence. For Bernardino's curriculum vitae, see also Raoul Manselli, "*Bernardino da Siena*" in *Dizionario biografico degli italiani* (Rome: Istituto della *Enciclopedia Italiana*, 1967), 9: 215-26, as well as the older but well-documented and still indispensible essays by Dionisio Pacetti (director of the Quaracchi Opera Omnia commission): "*Cronologia bernardiniana*" in *S. Bernardino da Siena: Saggi e ricerche pubblicati nel quinto centenario della morte (1444-1944)* (Milano: Vita e Pensiero, 1945), 445-63 and "*La predicazione di S. Bernardino in Toscana*" (see n. 78 above), especially, for the trial date, 33: 299-301.

[83] As Bernardino himself tells us: see R.850. The most exhaustive investigation of Bernardino's heresy trial remains Ephrem Longpré, "S. Bernardin de Sienne et le nom de Jésus," *Archivum franciscanum historicum: 28* (1935), 443-76; 29 (1936), 142-68, 443-77; 30 (1937), 170-92. See also Iris Origo, *The World of San Bernardino* (New York: Harcourt, Brace and World, 1962), 117-30; A. G. Ferrers Howell, S. *Bernardino of Siena* (London: Methuen, 1913), 146-63; and Vittorio Facchinetti, *San Bernardino da Siena mistico sole del 400* (Milan: Casa Editrice Santa Lega Eucaristica, 1933), 364-70.

[84] I accept Pacetti's and Bulletti's ultimate argument as the most plausible, namely, the trial had to be in the spring of 1426 because from March to August of the following year, Bernardino was the prime candidate for the episcopal see of Siena, and nowhere in the ample correspondence between the pope, various cardinals, and other members of the papal curia, on the one hand, and the "Magnifica Signoria" of

Bernardino's hometown, on the other, throughout those many months of negotiation involving such an important appointment do we find the least mention of the trial or the suspicion of heresy. See Pacetti, "La predicazione di S. Bernardino in Toscana," *Archivum franciscanum historicum 33* (1940), 300-01, n. 5, citing the research of Enrico Bulletti, "Per la nomina di S. Bernardino a Vescovo di Siena," *Bullettino di studi bernardiniani*, 5 (1939), 27-48. Celestino Piana also seems to favor the 1426 date, pointing to the Benvoglienti canonization testimony which shall be discussed shortly. He offers as well further possible confirmation of this date based on a 1427 remark of Bernardino's ("dissivi come essendo io a Roma, mi diie il papa che io venissi qua [i.e., Siena]; et anco il vostro vescovo, che è ora cardinale, anco mel disse," R.663) and on the itinerary of Antonio Casini, bishop of Siena elevated to the cardinalate on May 24, 1426. See Piana, "I processi di canonizzazione su la [sic] vita di San Bernardino da Siena," *Archivum franciscanum historicum 44* (1951), 420, n. 2.

[85] Benvoglienti's testimony is found in Piana, "*I processi di canonizzazione*," 387. The original Latin reads: *Leonardus Bartholomei de Benvolientibus dixit et interfuisse Senis in anno praedicto* [1425] *ac etiam in anno Domini 1427 et Romae in anno Domini 1426, quibus temporibus beatus Bernardinus verbum Dei annuntiavit, addens quod Romae ac etiam Perusii in detestationem peccati sortilegi comburi fecit nonnullas sortilegas. Interrogatus quomodo scit, dixit audivisse.*

[86] This is due both to Infessura's faulty memory and disagreements among the manuscripts of the diary. See Tommasini's introduction to his edition of the diary (see n. 2 above). Infessura makes no mention of Bernardino's own heresy trial. Furthermore, as we have seen, the connection between Finicella and Bernardino is made in the diary by mere juxtaposition of chronicle items (see n. 47 above). Again, none of the other fifteenth-century sources (including, strangely enough, Bernardino's own friend and disciple, Giacomo della Marca) referring to this Roman witch trial mentions the friar's name in connection with it. A possible reason for this omission is that Bernardino's role in this affair seems to have been limited simply to his preaching on the topic, having had no active, official role in the Inquisitional trial and execution themselves. Bernardino seems also not even to have been present as a spectator at the trial and the execution (though he describes the latter in some detail), because in the 1443 version of the story he adds the phrase "according to what was recounted by the inquisitor of our order" (*prout retulit nostri ordinis inquisitor*, R.1007, n. 123; see n. 6 above).

[87] Carlo Ginzburg, the latest scholar to address this labyrinthine question of chronology, gives 1427 as the date of the witch trial, accepting Longpré's reconstruction of the sequence of events and assuming that this trial occurred during the same Roman sojourn in which Bernardino himself was put on trial for heresy (*Ecstasies*, 309). The latter assumption rests on the further assumption that by September 1427 Bernardino had preached publicly in Rome only on one occasion (see discussion below). The unannotated chronology offered by Delcorno in his edition of *Bernardino's Siena* 1427 sermons places both the heresy trial and the burning of Finicella under 1426, while omitting any mention of a Rome trip in 1424 (R.55-56), and later in a footnote says, "There is some uncertainty as to the date [of the trial], but the episode seems to have occurred in the spring of 1426," citing Manselli, Origo, and Bertagna (R.183). Yet, at R.1006, n. 123, he says "the facts [of

the witch trial recounted here by Bernardino] date back to 1424," citing Infessura to that effect.

[88] Hartlieb: *ich sag dir ain sach, die ich und manig man zu Rom gesehen und gehört habn. Es was in dem sechsten jar als bapst Martin gesetzt was* ... (Hansen, *Quellen und Untersuchungen*, 131). Hemmerlin: *Et constat, quod tempore Martini pape de anno 1420* ... (Hansen, Quellen und Untersuchungen, 110).

[89] We do not know when Bernardino left Rome, but according to Pacetti's chronology, he spent the months of August and September, 1426 in Siena (Pacetti, "*Cronologia bernardiniana*," 453).

[90] Bertagna, "*Cronologia di S. Bernardino*," xviii. On June 27, he was still in Urbino writing a letter to the pope about the episcopal nomination, while by August 15, he had arrived in Siena, beginning his famous course of sermons in the Piazza del Campo.

Charles D'Orleans: the Challenge of the Printed Text

Rouben C. Cholakian

The fifteenth century marked a crucial turning point in the struggle between oral and written expression. With the invention of the printing press, the written text would ultimately remove the creator from the physical presence of a live audience.[1] In this essay I should like to examine the ways in which this competition for verbalizing authority expressed itself in the work of one poet, Charles d'Orléans.

Charles was certainly aware of the fundamental distinction between oral and written discourse. At one point we find him saying: "*Plus que ne sçay raconter ou escrire*" (S 498);[2] but in any initial reading of the poetic language, he seems to see himself more often than not speaking rather than writing. At the most elementary level of analysis, one is immediately conscious that the text barely hides the arresting fact of a talking person. Conversation was an important part of the poet prince's daily existence and his verses often function as transcriptions of dialogue still ringing in his ear: "*pour dire voir,*" (B 7), "*je ne sçay que dye*" (B 10) "*Se je vous dy bonne nouvelle*" (B 33), "*se dire l'osoye*" (B 36), "*Je parle trop*" (B 100), "*Je vous dy*" (C 60), "*comme j'ay dit*" (R 47). "*Je vous suppli*" (B 1), "*je vous en prie*" (B 25), and "*conteray*" (R 59), the poet-dialoguist says everywhere. On occasion, he even chastises himself for talking too much:" *Trop mieux vaulsist me taire que parler*" (B 10), "*a brief parler*" (B 88), "*Je parle trop*" (B 100), "*Je me taiz*" (B 110).

This habit of speech pursued him into his solitariness when, for lack of a live audience, he was quite capable of talking to himself. Waking one morning to the sound of drums, he tells himself: "*il est trop matin,/Ung peu je me rendormiray*" (R 38). On another occasion he invents a lively internal dialogue wh ich begins:

> Mort de moy! vous y joueuz vous?
> — En quoy? — Es fais de tromperie.
> — Ce n'est que coustume jolie
> Dont un peu ont toutez et tous! (R 198)

Sometimes dialogue is so much a part of the textual manner that in the rapid-fire give and take it is no longer clear who is doing the talking or if the poet has simply fragmented himself to assume all the parts of his mini-drama:

> D'Espoir? Il n'en nouvelles.
> — Qui le dit? — Merencolie.
> — Elle ment. — Je le vous nye.
> — A! a! vous tenez ses querelles! (R 351)

In Ballade LV, he appears to be addressing a servant:

Helas! helas! qui a laissi, entrer
Devers mon cueur Doloreuse Nouvelle?
Cont, lui a plainement, sans celer,
Que sa Dame. Est a present en griefve maladie

In Rondeau 220 the other person seems but a vague phantome figure:

"Que pens,-je? dictes le moy/ Adevinez, je vous en prye."

Charles's poetry is noted for its allegorical style, so it should come as no surprise when his personifications engage in dialogue with him. For example, in one rondeau he creates a lively exchange with "Merencolye:"

"Qu'est cela? — C'est Merencolye.
— Vous n'entrerez ja. — Pourquoy? — Pour ce
Que vostre compaignie acourse
Mes jours, dont je foys grant folie. (R 287)
In Ballade 31, he carries on with Bonne Nouvelle:
Ven,s vers moy, Bonne Nouvelle,
Pour mon las cueur reconforter,
Contez moy comment fait la belle
L'avez vous point oy parler
De moy, et amy me nommer?

These invented poetic dialogues are emotional loci where the persona frequently defines the fluctuations of his volatile feelings. At one moment he says: "*Vous, soiés la tresbien venue/ Vers mon cueur, Joyeuse Nouvelle*" (B 47). Elsewhere, upon hearing the news of his wife's death, he tells Death: "*Las! Mort qui t'a fait si hardie,/ De prendre la noble Princesse*" (B 57). It is as if he cannot separate self-analysis from conversation.

Charles's most celebrated theatrical creation is his frequent pseudo-partner in dialogue, "*coeur.*" Ballade 6 begins by actually setting the scene for his internalized conversation: "*N'a pas long temps qu'alay parler/A mon cueur, tout secrettement.*" Amusingly enough, this invented alter ego himself can be identified by his own highly conversational style, interjecting phrases like "*Se m'aist Dieux*", "*Nennil* dya." In one curious moment self reprimands self, as "*coeur*" is made to say to his creator: "*Taisiez vous.*" All of us at one time or another have engaged in fantasized private conversations; it is something else again, however, when our imagined listener tells us to keep still.

Orality achieves its ultimate realization when Charles sets up his poetic text on the page much like a playwright's script. In Ballade 33, for example, the performers are named L'amant and Le coeur, and in Rondeau 243, the principal dialoguists are Le Coeur and Soussy. Like the playwright, Charles re-creates speech because, it seems, talking is more authentic than writing.

On the other hand, years of incarceration actually turned the poem into an important form of communication for the captured Charles who very effectively re-worked the epistolary form first popularized by classical poets.[3] To his beloved second wife Bonne d'Armagnac he writes:

> Pour ce que veoir ne vous puis,
> Mon cueur se complaint jours et nuis,
> Belle, nompareille de France,
> Et m'a chargi, de vous escrire (B 27).

Though we do not have her answer, we know she responded, because he later notes in another epistolary ballade:

> Je ne vou puis ne sçay amer,
> Ma Dame, tant que je vouldroye;
> Car escript m'avez pour m'oster
> Ennuy qui trop fort me guerroye (B 36).

Was her response poetically composed, one wonders?

In the case of his cousin the Duke of Burgundy, with whom Charles exchanged a series of poetic letters, both sides of the correspondance have been happily preserved (B 87-94). At the close of one of these ballads, Charles instructs his poem: "*Va, ma balade, prestement/A Saint Omer*" (B 87). It is as if he poetically added the address to the envelope of his letter.

It appears, moreover, that long after his return to France, Charles continued the practice of the epistolary poem with a certain Fredet (Complaintes IV, IVa,IVb). He begins one of these poems much the way one might start a prose letter today: "*Fredet, j'ay receu votre lectre*" (Complainte IVa).

The inevitable question here is whether these epistolary poems functioned more as communication or more as poetry. In short, were they recited?[4] There is considerable evidence that Charles intended his poetry to be read aloud for the best effectiveness. Aside from the Chansons which were probably meant to be put to music, he writes to his beloved, for example: "*s'il vous plaist escouter/Comment j'ay gard, en chiert,/Vostre cueur*" (B 32). Sending an epistolary poem from England to his Burgundian cousin, he again places emphasis on listening: "*Des nouvelles d'Albion, / S'il vous en plaist escouter*" (B 89).

In any case, if, during his long capture in England, the Duke of Orleans transformed the ballade into an epistle, he understood by this gesture that correspondance could serve as a substitute for conversation prohibited by distance. But near or far, there seems little doubt that Charles thought of his poems as barely removed from the speech act;

poetry for him functioned like a tape recorder which registered everything in verse form, whether people actually spoke that way or not.

Nonetheless, Charles is also very self-conscious about ,criture.[5] He sees himself as a "*faiseur*," a maker of "*Rymes en françoys ou latin*" (R 248), and that meant not only singing or declaiming, but putting words onto a readable page. Ballade 21 begins with the remark: "*Lou, sout cellui qui trouva/Premier la maniere d'escrire*."

Though he might prefer to speak personally to the woman he loves, he easily acquiesces when she asks "*d'une balade faire*" (B 19). Inversely, he urges, when contacting her: "*De m'escrire ne vous vueilliez lasser*." (B 38) He acknowledges that the written word can bring comfort: "*Pour m'oster de merencolie,/M'escrivy amoureusement*" (B 47). It gives permanence to one's thought: "*Doulx Souvenir*", Charles says in Ballade 42, "*chierement je vous pry,/Escrivez tost ceste balade cy*."

Although speech during most of the Middle Ages superseded writing as a reliable source of truth-telling, biblical scholarship was slowly bringing a different kind of authenticity to the written text. When in Ballade 30 Charles wants to give authority to his amorous intentions, when he seeks to define his love relationship, Amour's go-between is the "secretaire, Bonne Foy" who has composed "*la lectre du traicti,/ Et puis la seella Loyaut*." One recalls, in this regard, that the "*Requete*," included as part of the long sequel "*Songe en complainte*," and sent to "*Dieu Cupido et Venus la deesse*," functions like a formal written certificate. The closing lines read like an official document:

> Escript ce jour troisiesme, vers le soir,
> En novembre, ou lieu de Nonchaloir.
> Le bien vostre, Charles, duc d'Orlians,
> Qui jadis fut l'un de vos vrais servans" (547-50).

Charles not only is very aware of himself as one who puts words to paper, the concept of the text as a completed entity often appears in his poetry. Restless in bed at night he thinks of his "*rommant de Plaisant Penser*" (B 8). Similarly he refers to his "Livre de Joye" (R 26; B 95) and "Livre de Pensee" (R 33). When he ruminates on the allegorical figure of "Espoir," he promises to write "*ung grant livre*" about him (R 322); again when he muses on his martyrdom in love, he says: "*J'en sauroye, sur ma foy,/De ma main ung livre escripre*" (C 78). In much the same mood, when he asks "cuer" to tell of his dealings with love, the latter says he must first consult "*ses papiers*" (B 97). As time passes and Vieillesse becomes his more frequent escort, Charles speaks of looking into her "*hostel de noir de Tristesse*" and reading therein "*l'istoire de Destress/Qui me fait changer mon maintien/Quant la ly*" (B 121).

What makes these references in Charles d'Orléans' poetry interesting is the fact that his dates coincide with an important moment in the history of writing and book production. Moreover, because Charles was of royalty, his relations with the world of book creation are very well documented. Not only do we have information about his various purchases of writing materials, but his personal library was also carefully inventoried on two separate occasions, once in 1417 when he was a prisoner in England and again in 1442, shortly after his liberation.[6]

Charles came to his love of books naturally. He inherited the bibliophile's passion from his grandfather Charles V who was a well-known lover of manuscripts. Already by the end of the fourteenth century this king's own collection had been catalogued for him.[7] Both Charles's mother and father collected books. So by the time Charles was old enough to read, it seemed perfectly natural to him to have his own set of manuscripts and eventually a staff of scribes to make new copies as well.[8] I note, in passing, that the combined collections of grandfather, parents and son made up the beginnings of France's famous *Bibliothêque nationale*.[9]

One must not, however, jump to hasty conclusions about the impact of the early printed book or incunabula on our poet, and a review of some essential history is in order here. It was sometime in the decade between 1440 and 1450 that movable type was invented, probably by Gutenberg. It would be a good century, however, before printed books and publishers would actually render manuscripts, scriptoria and scribes obsolete. In the same way that the Church made possible the considerable number of manuscripts created throughout most of the medieval period, it was the sixteenth-century religious wars between Catholics and Protestants which inspired the need for inexpensive book production and therefore the rapid rise of printed materials.[10]

In Charles's library there are no incunabula to be found. When he speaks of books, he envisions not the printed words born of movable type, but hand-produced letters created by scribes. It is thus entirely inappropriate to think of Charles as an early devotee of the new invention; but quite to the contrary, as I wish to argue.

Firstly, Charles was very much a part of the medieval oral tradition of recitation, and as my investigation plainly points out, spoken language haunts the pages of this poetry where time and again he uses words like "*parler*", "*dire*", "*ouir*", "*raconter*", and "*couter*." Charles gives abundant proof throughout of being very skeptical about choosing writing over speaking and resorts to the former only when the latter is absolutely not available to him, for example, during his long years of imprisonment on foreign soil. It is a matter of some speculation whether his detention abroad turned him into a poet.[11]

What in fact makes Charles interesting is the way he fits into, or rather does not fit into the evolution from a "memorial culture" to one increasingly dependent upon printed matter. For centuries it was a sign of education to carry one's learning about in one's mind. The brain served as the first real book or container of the "text,"[12] and it is to that endangered habit that Charles desperately continues to cling.

Nonetheless, not only the act of writing but its results are a part of the poetic language here. Charles refers to "*le livre*" in several significant contexts.[13] What does he mean by this? How do we explain the apparent contradiction? When the Duke of Orleans speaks of "*le livre*," he speaks metaphorically; metaphor and its ally, allegory, make up much of the Duke's poetic discourse. Books, or more accurately manuscripts, were in and of themselves a sign of wealth and power. It is altogether in keeping with Charles's aristocratic prejudices to think of books as emblems of prestige and permanence.[14] The stability of the word fixed onto the page, like those important theological works which gave authority to the church, stood for mastery, strength and control. They marked important events in the restricted universe of those who count: the politically noteworthy of the late Middle Ages.

To that, I should like to add another metaphorical dimension of understanding. If the act of writing and its product may on the one hand represent domination, they also reveal a penchant for the intellectual life. If for some these manuscripts functioned as status symbols, for Charles they were also very definitely companions in solitude. This is true in two important senses. First, Charles found comfort in reading.[15] His love of the private, as distinguished from the public act of reading, his desire for the content or "text" as his own exclusive and subjective absorption without any negotiating agent to re-create the written symbols, define an important intermediary stage in the move from the communal to the unshared text.[16]

Second, because Charles became more and more introverted and valued the learning incorporated in the works of others, he himself sought to fix onto paper his own thoughts, to turn "pensée" into "livre." In that larger sense, the initial binary opposition is not manuscript/print but memory/script. If at first the written text inspired the reciter's memory, the phenomenon of words on paper came to represent a surer way of securing what Homer called the "winged word," volatile and impermanent.[17] It may well be that in time Charles would have gone the route of the printed word, but he was certainly sensitive to what it meant to put words to paper. As poet and political figure he understood the powerful authority attributed to the written word.[18]

Charles's inventories make specific reference to his "*livre de balades ...*" composed for the most part during his twenty- five years in England, because he deemed these poems a crucial part of his identity. History had made him an unwilling actor in the events of his country; but artistic temperament shaped him into a lover of verbal invention, a "faiseur" who transformed the ephemeral into the enduring. We, of course, are eternally grateful. Charles has not only provided historians with interesting documentation on the rise of print culture, he has given modern readers the memorable delights of his own "*livre de Joie*."

NOTES

[1] Though his analysis only goes up to the fourteenth century, M. T. Clanchy's text is very worthwhile reading in this regard: *From Memory to Written Record* (London: Edward Arnold, 1979).

[2] S=Songe, B=Ballade, C=Chanson, R=Rondeau. My basic text is the edition by Pierre Champion, *Charles d'Orléans: Poésies* (Paris: Champion, 1956). I have also consulted the new edition prepared by Jean-Claude Mühlethaler, *Charles d'Orléans: Ballades et rondeaux* (Paris: Livres de Poches "Lettres gothiques", 1992).

[3] The classical tradition of the epistolary verse form persevered into the poetry of the *langue d'oc*. See Donald A. Monson, *Les ensenhamens* (Paris: Klincksieck, 1981).

[4] Not only can one agree with Zumthor that "le MS est récréation", but one can also reasonably add that it frequently returned to its original orality. Paul Zumthor, *La lettre et la voix* (Paris:Seuil, 1987), 115.

[5] In another context it might be said that *écriture* also functions as one of several techniques used by the poetic persona to escape the pains of daily reality. See Rouben Cholakian, *Deflection/Reflection in the Lyric Poetry of Charles d'Orléans* (Potomac, Maryland: Scripta humanistica, 1983), 52-58.

[6] Pierre Champion, *La librairie de Charles d'Orléans* (Paris: Champion, 1910).

[7] It was Gilles Mallet who first catalogued the king's library for him in 1373. Champion, *La librarie de Charles d'Orléans*, V.

[8] The practice was quite widespread among aristocrats, especially those with an intellectual bent. Duke Frederic of Urbino, for example, had no less than forty copyists in his hire. See William D. Orcutt, *Master Makers of the Book* (New York: Doubleday, 1928), 18.

[9] Anthony Hobson, *Great Libraries* (New York: Putnam, 1970), 121-31.

[10] Douglas McMurtrie, *The Book: The Story of Printing and Bookmaking* (Oxford: University Press, 1943), 125-26.

[11] "After his capture at Agincourt, the composition of verse became for Charles a pastime that helped him endure the long years of imprisonment." John Fox, *The Lyric Poetry of Charles d'Orléans* (Oxford, Clarendon Press, 1969), 32.

[12] See Mary Carruthers. *The Book of Memory: A Study of Memory in Medieval Culture* (Cambridge: University Press, 1990).

[13] See especially *Ballades* 8, 95, 97, *Chanson* 78 and *Rondeaux* 33, 322. Poirion's useful *Le lexique de Charles d'Orléans dans les ballades*, (Geneva: Droz, 1967) has been recently complemented by Claudio Galderis, *Le lexique de Charles d'Orléans dans les "rondeaux"* (Geneva: Droz, 1993).

[14] "Wealthy and cultured princes of the fifteenth century [considered MSS] as something which belonged exclusively to them." Orcutt, *Master Makers of the Book*, 17.

[15] In contrast with some others, however, as Champion notes, "ce bibliophile lisait ses livres." *La librairie de Charles d'Orléans*, XXXVI.

[16] As in western classical antiquity which assumed that a worthy scripted message "deserved to be read aloud," so throughout most of the Middle Ages, "text" meant to be assimilated through the speech act. Walter Ong *Orality and Literacy: The Technologizing of the Word* (New York: Methuen, 1982), 115. See also on this aspect of the issue Roger Chartier. *The Culture of Print: Power and the Uses of Print in Early Modern Europe*. Tr. Lydia Cochrane (Princeton: University Press, 1987/89).

[17] Of course, as Sausserian lingustics has taught us, the "signifier" is always arbitrary and difficult to pin down to a single "signified."

[18] Alongside the sacred script was a growing body of written materials for the emerging bureaucracy of the Late Middle Ages. See Clanchy, *From Memory to Written Record*, 263.

Ein Schlüsselwort der Poesie des französischen XV. Jahrhunderts: passetemps *

Georg Roellenbleck

In der Literatur erscheinen das Wort *passetemps* [PDR1]1 (wie auch verwandte Begriffe, z.B. déduit) im Umkreis der Kurzerzählung, z.B. im Vorwort zu den *Cent nouvelles nouvelles* (Redaktion wohl zwischen 1456 und 1467), und zwar als Element der Eingangstopik, vor allem als Legitimationsargument für das Erzählen von Geschichten, die der bloßen Unterhaltung dienen sollen. So weist der anonyme Erzähler der CNN zu Beginn seines Widmungsbriefs darauf hin,

> qu'entre les bons et prouffitables passe temps, le tresgracieux exercice de lecture d'estude (est) de grande et somptueuse recommendation ...[2]

Spiel, Unterhaltung und Entspannung sind nach der Tradition legitim, ja in einem medizinischen Sinne sogar notwendig, um dem geistig Tätigen seine intellektuelle Spannkraft zu erhalten und zu erneuern[3]. Der spezifisch literarische Sinn und Gebrauch ist Teil eines größeren Feldes, in dem *passetemps* z.B. adligen "Zeitvertreib" wie die Jagd, Turniere, Bankette, das Schachspiel bezeichnet. Auch dieser Gebrauch spielt in der Literatur eine Rolle; als Beleg sei etwa Guillaume Cretins *Debat de deux dames sur le passetemps des chiens et des oyseaulx* genannt, ein Gedicht von fast 1300 Versen in der Tradition von Gace de la Buignes *Roman des deduis* (beendet zwischen 1373 und 1377). Unserem Thema näher stehen wieder die Belege, die Rolf Sprandel unter dem Titel "Kurzweil durch Geschichte" besprochen hat.[4]

Hier soll aber nur von einem Wortgebrauch des französischen XV. Jhdts. die Rede sein, der die Doppeldeutigkeit des Begriffs entdeckt und in einer Reihe von Dichtungen zum Ausdruck der "philosophie mélancolique" des XV. Jhdts. gebraucht[5]. In der Tat verbinden sich in dem hier gemeinten Gebrauch von *passetemps* emblematisch zwei der zentralen Gedankentendenzen der Literatur des ausgehenden Spätmittelalters, die Zeit- und Todesmeditation auf der einen Seite, und auf der anderen die Ausarbeitung der Perspektive eines *Ich*, das der Referentialität der Autor-Autobiographie sehr nahe kommt.

Die "Doppeldeutigkeit" des Begriffs, den eine Reihe von Dichtungen des XV. Jhdts. entdeckt und ausnutzt, besteht darin, daß *passetemps,* die leichte, angenehme, intellektuell nicht schwergewichtige Tätigkeit — etwa des Erzählens — darin besteht oder dazu gebraucht wird, den Zeitverlauf, den Ablauf des eigenen Lebens — *le temps qui passe, le temps passé* — zu betrachten und darzustellen. Das Gedicht kann sich den Titel *passetemps* geben und den Ablauf des eigenen Lebens zum Gegenstand machen, oder es kann sich *Passetemps* als allegorische Gestalt integrieren, die im Kräftespiel des psychischen Lebens, von dem das Gedicht in Form einer allegorischen Szene einen Ausschnitt darstellt, die Betrachtung des Verfließens der Lebenszeit vertritt.

Wenn ich jetzt die Autoren und Texte vorstelle, bin ich in der mißlichen Lage, zugeben zu müssen, daß zwei von ihnen weniger bekannt (und auch poetisch nicht von bedeutender Statur) sind, sodaß sich die Behauptung, sie stifteten für unser Verständnis der Literatur ihres Jahrhunderts ein Schlüsselwort, weniger auf ihren Erfolg bei den Zeitgenossen gründen kann[6], als darauf, daß sie in großer Konzentration ein Thema gestalten, daß in weiten Teilen der zeitgenössischen Poesie erscheint, und darauf, daß sie — in dem wortspielerischen

Stil, der bald herrschend werden sollte — eine ungemein glückliche Formel gefunden haben, um gleichzeitig das Werk (den Titel), seinen Gegenstand und die Position des Autor-Ichs im Gedicht zu bezeichnen.

Der dritte in der hier zu betrachtenden Reihe ist Charles d'Orléans, einer der großen Schöpfer, Mäzene und Anreger der Dichtung des Jahrhunderts; er ist der Älteste (geb. 1394) und könnte den Anstoß zu der hier betrachteten *passetemps*-Dichtung gegeben haben[7]. Die beiden anderen — Michault Taillevent und Pierre Chastellain[8] — hängen insofern eng mit ihm und untereinander zusammen, als Michault Taillevent von Charles die Anregung zu seinem Thema bekommen haben könnte, während die Gedichte Pierre Chastellains eine ausdrückliche Replik auf Michaults Gedicht mit vielfachen intertextuellen Bezügen darstellen.

Als Charles d'Orléans im Jahr 1440 nach einer Gefangenschaft von einem Vierteljahrhundert zurückkehrt, werden seine in England geschriebenen Dichtungen in Frankreich bekannt. Es sind fast durchweg Balladen, die Liebessituationen, aber auch Gefühle und Erfahrungen der Gefangenschaft in sehr persönlichem Ton behandeln. Diese Innenschau des Ichs wird in kleinen allegorischen Szenen entfaltet, deren Personal teilweise noch Gestalten des Rosenromans wie *Amour, Dangier* oder *Fortune* bilden, daneben aber auch Figuren, die Facetten der inneren Befindlichkeit darstellen und "dramatisieren", wie *Nonchaloir, Mélancolie, Désir, Souci*.

In den Jahren nach seiner Rückkehr nach Frankreich nimmt Charles' Dichtung unter dem Eindruck des Scheiterns seiner politischen Hoffnungen und Pläne und im Gefolge seines Rückzugs in die — fast möchte man sagen — Privatheit seines Hofs eine Wendung, bei der Melancholie und Resignation des Blicks auf das eigene Leben immer stärker hervortreten; die Szenerie, übrigens jetzt nicht mehr in der Form der Ballade dargestellt, sondern in der noch knapperen des Rondeau, bevölkert sich mit neuen Figuren, unter ihnen *Passetemps*. Wenn man von seiner Dichtung insgesamt sagen kann, sie stehe unter dem Zeichen der dahinschwindenden Zeit[9], so tritt jetzt, im Alter, diese Thematik endgültig in den Vordergrund.

Passetemps als Allegorie erscheint zuerst gegen Ende des *Songe en complainte* (Ball. VII, Vers 464, 484, dann wieder 507)[10]; Gegenstand des Gedichts ist der durch den Eintritt des Alters erzwungene Rückzug von der Liebe. Der Redende zieht sich in das Haus seiner Kindheit, *Nonchaloir*, zurück (Ball. VI, Refr.), dessen "gouverneur" *Passetemps* ist, und erklärt (im Refrain von Ball. VII), mit ihm wolle er gern den Rest seiner Tage verbringen:

> Le gouverneur de la maison
> Qui Passe Temps se fait nommer,
> Me dist: "Amy, ceste saison
> Vous plaist il ceans sejourner?
> Je respondy qu'a brief parler
> Se lui plaisoit ma compaignie
> Content estoie de passer
> Avecques lui toute ma vie. (*Songe en compl.*, Ball. VII, V.1-8)

In einer ein wenig anderen Beleuchtung erscheint *Passetemps* als Allegorie noch einmal in den Rondeaux (Nr. 339 Mühleth./428 Champ.): hier wird die Hoffnung (*Espoir*) beschworen als Gegengewicht zu *Fortune* und dem mit ihr verbündeten *Passetemps*: was die unvorhersehbare und unbeherrschbare Zukunft bringt, läßt sich mit *Espoir* bestehen.

Einen ähnlichen Gedanken behandelt die Jagdszene von Chanson 75, in der *cuer* die Beute in der *Gibessiere, de Passe Temps ouvrée* (V.9) unterbringt. Was gejagt wird, sind Gedanken, gefangen mit Hilfe des Jagdfalken (*aquilote*) *Souvenance*; der Festbraten besteht dann aus *un faisant d'Esperance Celée*: hier wird deutlich, so Alice Planche[11], wie *Passetemps* den Blick auf die gesamte Erstreckung von Zeit in Vergangenheit / Gegenwart / Zukunft öffnet, das Leben also als ganzes betrachtet und beeinflußt.

Daneben kommt das Wort auch, nicht als allegorische Gestalt, in seinem normalen Gebrauch als "Zeitvertreib" vor, so z.B. in der Ball. 58 Mühleth./58 Ch., oder in Rondeau 329 Mühleth./406 Ch., Verse 1-4:

> Il n'est nul si beau passetemps
> Que se jouer a sa pensee,
> Mais qu'elle soit bien despensee
> Par Raison; ainsi je l'entens.

Der ganz eigene Ton, den diese wenigen Stellen dem Reigen der Allegorien wie *Ennuy, Melancolie, Nonchaloir* (die ihrerseits ungleich häufiger vertreten sind) verleihen, ist deutlich: mit *Passetemps* als Allegorie wird die Ursache des Leidens benannt (das Verfließen der Lebenszeit, das Kommen des Alters); und dieselbe Wendung bezeichnet auch das Heilmittel: das gelassene Sichfügen in den Gang der Dinge.

Es ist natürlich die durchgängige Temporalisierung eines psychodramatischen Personenbestandes, der ohne Umschweife und ohne weitere Einkleidung Bilder des eigenen Ichs geben will, und nicht das Erscheinen der Allegorie *Passetemps* allein, die hier das Neue bedeutet, und diese veränderte Perspektive impliziert eine ganz neue Rolle des literarischen Ich, das den Zeitablauf als die wesentliche Dimension der eigenen Existenz erfährt und darstellt[12]. Die Allegorie wird noch unmittelbarer als im Rosenroman in den Dienst der *Selbstdarstellung* des Individuums genommen.

Etwa zur Zeit der Rückkehr von Charles d'Orléans aus der Gefangenschaft, also nach 1440[13], und, wie vermutet wird, unter dem Eindruck seiner Dichtung, entsteht Michault Taillevents Gedicht *Le Passetemps Michault Taillevent*. Michel Le Caron, gen. Michault Taillevent, gegen 1400 geboren, gestorben zwischen 1448 und 1458, *valet de chambre* und *joueur de farces* des Herzogs von Burgund, ist Autor eines nur schmalen Bandes von Dichtungen[14], darunter von einem witzigen Bericht, wie er bei Pont-Saint-Maxence von Räubern ausgeplündert worden ist, *Destrousse Michault Taillevent*[15]. Der *Passetemps* in 93 Siebenzeilern[16] mit regelmäßigem Sprichwortschluß setzt ohne Vorbereitung mit dem Ich ein, das im Monolog über sein Leben nachdenkt:

> Je pensoye n'a pas sept ans[17]
> Ainsy qu'on pense a son affaire
> Par maniere de passe temps (I, 1-3),

und in der zweiten Strophe heißt es:

> Et quant j'euz bien partout pensé
> Il m'alla aprez souvenir
> De la joye du temps passé
> Et de la dolleur advenir
> Ou il me convendra venir
> Car ainsy va qu'ainsy s'atourne:
> Temps passé jamais ne retourne (8-14).

Der Gedankengang des Gedichts, einer durchlaufenden Betrachtung ohne Erzählungen, läßt sich etwa so beschreiben: das Ich an der Schwelle des Alters blickt auf die unbedacht vertane Jugend zurück und faßt die Leiden des kommenden Alters ins Auge. Dieses Alter sieht der Redende ganz und gar unter dem Zeichen der Armut kommen, die es ihm bitter schwer macht, sich zu fügen, obwohl er von dem Gang der Natur, wie er ihm in der Abfolge der Jahreszeiten deutlich ist, weiß, daß nichts dauert und daß nur ein Narr sich auf die Dauer verläßt. Weise ist der, der seine Zeit zu nutzen versteht; indes, die Bitterkeit des Alterns bleibt.

Zwei Aspekte sind es, die diese schlichte pessimistische Lebensphilosophie für uns bemerkenswert machen. Sie wird in jedem Augenblick von dem Ich des Gedichts als seine persönliche Sicht geäußert, tritt also in *seiner* Perspektive vor uns; und wenn das auch als ein didaktisches Verfahren gesehen werden kann, das Dargelegte eindringlicher zu machen, so bleibt doch der Zuwachs an Freiheit der unvermittelten Ich-Rede und Ich-Perspektivierung für den Autor des XV. Jhdts. bestehen.

Der zweite Aspekt betrifft unser Thema: in fast jeder der 93 Strophen erscheint der Begriff "Zeit", oder es erscheinen Wendungen, die das Verbringen, das Vergehen, die Kürze oder die Dauer der Zeit besprechen, Jugend und Alter, Einst und Jetzt gegeneinanderstellen, Zeitrelationen bezeichnen oder die Idee von Wechsel und Wandel evozieren. Das geschieht in einer sicher nicht eleganten Sprache, aber in knapper, konzentrierter Wortkunst, voller Klang- und Reimspiele, voller Wortketten aus Parallelen, Spiegelungen, Oppositionen. Das hört sich etwa so an:

M'esperance diverse ment
Puis que de Viellesse ay un rain;
Je suis changie diversement,
Lyet au premier, tristre au derrain.
Se je fus d'or, je suis d'airain,
Onques ne passay pire pas:
Qui bien change n'empire pas. (XXVI, 176-182)

Kurz nach dem Bekanntwerden dieses Gedichts, und tief von ihm beeindruckt, hat ein Autor und Harfenspieler, von dessen Lebensumständen wir wenig mehr wissen, als was er selbst uns mitteilt, Pierre Chastellain, eine Replik verfaßt, die Michaults Siebenzeilerstrophe aufgreift, die Akzente aber anders setzt und vor allem die Seite des "äußeren" Lebensberichts so viel stärker hervortreten läßt, daß man zumindest von Stücken einer poetischen Autobiographie sprechen kann. Er nennt sein Gedicht *Le temps perdu* und läßt ihm einige Jahre später ein fast viermal so langes zweites, immer in derselben Strophenform, folgen, dem er den Titel *Le temps recouvré* gab; eine proustische Begrifflichkeit, die Daniel Poirion zum Anlaß genommen hat, der Genese unseres Themas in einem kurzen, auch grundsätzlich sehr instruktiven Aufsatz nachzugehen[18].

Zwischen beide Werke fällt ein bedeutsamer biographischer Einschnitt im Leben des vermutlich 1407 geborenen Verfassers, eine Reise nach Rom zum Jubiläum des Jahres 1450. Vor allem diese Reise, die Pierre Chastellain ein dramatisches Auf und Ab seiner finanziellen Umstände und persönlichen und beruflichen Erfahrungen bescherte, die ihn eine weitere Reise, dieses Mal ins Heilige Land, planen ließ (die er aber abbrechen mußte) und die ihn danach noch mehrere Jahre in Italien festhielt, hat Pierre Champion zu der Bemerkung veranlaßt, der Autor hätte einen Platz neben Villon verdient, entspräche seine Kunst der Darstellung nur der Abenteuerlichkeit seines "pikaresken" Lebens[19].

Der Bericht über diese Lebensstationen — Jugend, Musikertätigkeit, Liebe und Eheschließung, alchemistische Versuche, Romaufenthalt, die mißglückte Reise ins Heilige Land, verschiedene Dienstverhältnisse — ist, wie gesagt, eingebettet in die Auseinandersetzung mit Michault Taillevents Gedicht, und das "Diptychon" der beiden Temps-Gedichte ist zunächst einmal als moralistisch-didaktische Darlegung gemeint und gehalten[20]. Die autobiographische Perspektive bildet jedoch wie bei Michault Taillevent das Organisationsprinzip, und die autobiographischen Einzelheiten erscheinen in solcher Breite und Dichte, daß sie einen wichtigen eigenen Text im Text darstellen.

Hier ein Ausschnitt aus den römischen Erinnerungen des *Temps recouvré*; ich zitiere nur Ausschnitte, weil Pierre Chastellains Sprache in ihrer Suche nach wortspielerischer Kürze im allgemeinen schwer verständlich ist:

> En l'ostel d'un bourgeoys de Sene
> Enfin je m'alay herberger... (XXI, 141/142);
> Ce bourgeois moult bien escoutoit
> Mes gracieux mots et courtoys... (XXII, 148/149).

Pierre Chastellain, der fahrende Spielmann, unterhält seinen Gastgeber also mit dem Erzählen von — offenbar witzigen — Geschichten und verdient sich so Kost und Logis.

> Un sire de moult grant renom
> Estoit malade en sa maison... (XXIV, 162/163);

diesen angesehenen, reichen Mann, dem bisher niemand hatte helfen können, heilt Pierre Chastellain mit einem "buvraige" (180), und er wird dafür reich entlohnt. Der weitere Gang der Ereignisse muß jetzt nicht weiter verfolgt werden; es wurde schon gesagt, daß der Lebensbericht sozusagen den roten Faden bildet, der die Darlegungen und Reflexionen auch des zweiten Gedichts durchzieht und in ihrem Charakter kennzeichnet.

Der volle Sinn des Werkpaars erschließt sich aber erst, wenn man die beiden Zeit-Titel und, von ihnen ausgehend, das Verhältnis der beiden Gedichte zueinander betrachtet.

Ganz offenbar soll mit dem ersten Gedicht die Negativ-Bilanz einer vertanen Jugend, einer unerfreulichen Ehe, gescheiterter Berufsversuche, überhaupt einer verfehlten Lebensplanung aufgestellt werden:

> Tant que jeunesse m'a duré
> Temps perdu n'est de moy sailly
> Car jamais ne l'eusse enduré... (TP XXXI, 211-213);

Mühlethaler bezeichnet die zweite Hälfte des ersten Gedichts denn auch als "confession exemplaire" (zit. Aufs., S.162).

Demgegenüber macht schon der Titel des zweiten Gedichts deutlich, daß hier Bericht von einem Lebensabschnitt gegeben werden soll, in dem die Zeit *sinnvoll* genutzt wurde. Insofern führt die Proustähnlichkeit der beiden Titel in die Irre: es geht nicht um ein Wiederfinden und Gestalten der eigenen Vergangenheit — es gibt hier natürlich kein Identitätsproblem, und in dieser Hinsicht unterscheiden sich beide Teile nicht voneinander; es geht vielmehr darum, zu zeigen, daß die Zeit zwar nicht angehalten werden kann, daß aber der Schrecken ihres Verrinnens gebannt wird, wenn man sie nutzt, um das Rechte zu tun; und das heißt: Einsicht, Weisheit zu gewinnen.

Mühlethaler hat Pierre Chastellains christliches Denken den hoffnungslosen Klagen von Michault Taillevents Gedicht gegenübergestellt[21]. Aber dieses christliche Denken kommt bei unserem Autor erst im zweiten Gedicht voll zum Tragen. Mühlethaler zeigt das an der Behandlung der Alchemie, die im ersten Gedicht einen der Versuche des jungen Mannes meint, zu Geld zu kommen, und damit nur das nutzlose Streben nach vergänglichem Reichtum darstellt, während die Alchemie im zweiten Gedicht über weite Strecken im Zentrum des Interesses steht, jetzt aber um der Suche nach Wahrheit und Weisheit willen unternommen wird oder diese Suche selbst bedeuten und Wahrheit und Poesie vielleicht sogar identifizieren soll[22]:

> Richesse et pouvreté se monstrent
> Par tout le monde en habondance
> Mais de cent deux ne se demonstrent
> Entendre comme le bon dance.
> Mais est memoire qu'a la dance
> Macabre fault que chescun balle
> Que des truans a la triballe.
>
> Jamais richesse ne regarde
> Ne science ou elle se boute
> Et s'aucun sa richesse garde
> Autre la dissipe et deboute.
> En science ne voy je goute:
> S'a l'un est pure, necte et monde
> L'autre en quiert abuser le monde.
>
> Je ne me vy oncques mais rien
> Par vouloir venir a science
> En maison faire de mesrien
> Que desiroit ma conscience.
> Se tard y viens j'ay pacience,
> Entrer n'y cuidasse ja mais
> Encor mieulx vaut tard que jamais. (*Temps recouvré*, Str. CCLXXII ff.)

Welches sind die Voraussetzungen einer derartigen Poesie? Zum Teil bildet sie das alte Thema des *contemptus mundi weiter,* aus dem sich die Motive des *Ubi sunt*, des Totentanzes, der realistischen Darstellung des

Sterbens und des verwesenden Körpers entwickelt haben. Erst um die Wende des XIV. zum XV. Jhdt. treten solche Themen, einzeln oder in Kombination miteinander, in den Vordergrund, um weite Partien der poetischen Literatur zu bestimmen[23].

Das *motif macabre* wird autonom: es verliert weitgehend seine theologische Stoßrichtung und wird zum Element einer innerweltlichen Zustandsbeschreibung. Verschränkt mit der Obsession durch die unaufhörlich verfließende Lebenszeit, verliert die Todesthematik im XV. Jhdt. das Punktförmige, Plötzliche: insistiert der *Totentanz* auf dem jähen, unvorhersehbaren Zupacken des Todes, rückt der alte Gebrauch des *Ubi sunt*-Motivs die Gewesenen in die ungreifbare Ferne des Gewesen-, des Verschwundenseins, so verschiebt sich die Sicht jetzt auf die Erstreckung der Zeit, auf das Verfließen des Lebens selbst ("passe-temps")[24].

Damit trifft es auf die Autobiographie-Tendenz des XIV./XV. Jhdts.[25]: die Todesverfallenheit des Menschen wird nicht mehr moralistisch-allgemein am Bild der Stände und ihrer Gleichheit vor dem Sterben dargestellt, sondern von der Erfahrung des Einzelnen im Licht der *regrets* des Autor-Ichs an der Schwelle des Alters her gesehen.

Dabei nimmt es eine unerwartete Richtung: indem alles Geschehen in seiner Zeit-Erstreckung gesehen wird, wird der Gedanke vom Leben als Weg zum Tod zum Impuls (und zur Legitimation) der Autobiographie, einer Selbstbetrachtung (meist des alten oder sich als Alten gebenden Menschen), die die Stufen des Lebensgangs kritisch für sich selbst und zum Nutzen anderer durchmustert. Es versteht sich, daß hier von dem *contemptus mundi* nicht viel übrig bleibt: das Ursprungsmotiv hat sich in sein Gegenteil verkehrt oder ist, besser gesagt, abgelöst worden von einem Gefühl für die Kostbarkeit der irdischen Existenz; einem Gefühl, das dadurch verschärft wird, daß das hinter dem Betrachter liegende Leben nicht als Folge gleichwertiger Entwicklungsstufen gesehen wird, sondern immer noch wesentlich in der traditionellen Opposition von alt und jung (gern kombiniert mit der Opposition von arm und reich)[26].

An dieser Stelle wird der Zusammenhang unserer *passetemps*-Dichtung mit den Ursprüngen der poetischen Autobiographie des Mittelalters deutlich. Neben die Ich-Rede der hohen Lyrik tritt früh, wohl unter lateinischem Einfluß, die moralisierende, oft stark mit komischen Mitteln arbeitende Selbstdarstellung eines Ich von geringem sozialen Stand, das seine bedrängten Lebensumstände mit (schein-)realistischer Präzision (und immer in Versform) ausbreitet.

Es ist für die ganze Entwickungslinie bezeichnend, daß einer ihrer frühesten Texte gern als Vaganten*beichte* bezeichnet wird: *passetemps* und *regrets* verdanken ihre eigentümliche Tonart neben der Todesmeditation der Gewissenserforschung und fassen ihren Gegenstand daher meist mit moralischen (moralistischen) Kategorien. Von der (scheinbar) zerknirschten Beichte bis zu der Betrachtung zentraler Lebensstationen unter dem Gesichtspunkt von Gelingen und Mißlingen sind alle Register anzutreffen, und insistenter als die theologische Reflexion ist es die volkstümliche Weisheit, die der Darstellung ihre innere Ordnung gibt. Michault Taillevent wie auch Pierre Chastellain bedienen sich der Form des Siebenzeilers mit regelmäßigem Sprichwortschluß, einer von den Rhétoriqueurs sehr geschätzten Form[27]. *Passetemps* will also nicht nur den Verlauf der Zeit spürbar machen und ihr unaufhörliches Verrinnen beklagen; *passetemps* will auch beleuchten und erklären, wie die Lebenszeit verbracht worden ist, ob sie genutzt oder vergeudet wurde.

Hier schließt sich ein weiterer Kreis, denn das Wort *passetemps* tritt nie, welche Bedeutung es auch gerade hat — einfache Zerstreuung, frivoles Vergnügen, oder ernste Betrachtung — ohne wertende Bestimmung auf. Als “Unterhaltung, Entspannung” steht es ja von vorneherein in der Spannung zu dem ernsten, dem eigentlich wichtigen Tun; und so bedarf es stets der genauen Prüfung seiner relativen Seriosität.

Eine Standardverbindung, in der es in ganz verschiedenen Textsorten auftritt, lautet: “um Müßiggang zu vermeiden”. *Passetemps* nimmt also eigentlich eine Mittelstellung ein zwischen den Polen der ernsten Arbeit und des (immer verwerflichen) Müßiggangs. Mit dieser Mittelstellung verbindet sich wie selbstverständlich die Vorstellung des Leichten, des Angenehmen, wenig Anspruchsvollen; und so hat der Begriff seinen Weg in die Exordialtopik auch außerhalb der Novellistik gefunden, nämlich etwa in die der Historiographie[28], wo er in “affektierter Bescheidenheit” auf die geringen Gaben des Verfassers verweisen soll, der nicht müßig gehen will, mehr als das Vorgelegte aber auch nicht zu bieten hat. Andernorts werden in der noch immer beliebten Form des *débat* die relativen Vorzüge einzelner *passetemps* gegeneinandergestellt und abgewogen.

Jetzt wird, so scheint es, der volle Doppelsinn unseres Wortes deutlich. Das Leben einer so unbedeutenden Person — und dazu noch das eigene — im Detail mehr oder weniger unstilisiert darzustellen, die individuelle Erfahrung des Lebensflusses zum Thema zu nehmen, ist, wenn es auch kaum mehr *sur le mode comique* geschieht, doch nur unter dem Zeichen des beiläufigen, wenig erhabenen Tuns zu vertreten. Vielleicht soll auch der eigenartig “stolpernde” Siebenzeiler, eine von keiner hohen Tradition getragenen Form, deren sich Michault Taillevent und Pierre Chastellain bedienen, das Register verdeutlichen; ebenso vielleicht die Wahl des volkstümlichen Wertesystem der Sprichwörter, die den Gedanken an eine hohe, gewichtige Auseinandersetzung gar nicht erst aufkommen lassen, zugleich aber auch, besonders bei Michault Taillevent, die Klagen des todverfallenen Ichs mit ihrer zeitlosen Weisheit aufzufangen und zu stillen vermögen.

Wie weit die hier in Rede stehenden Gedichte wiederum von dem Wortgebrauch von *passetemps* im Umkreis der Novelle entfernt sind, sieht man daran, daß sie keineswegs die Kürze der Anekdote oder auch nur der Novelle suchen und nur hin und wieder *erzählen*; eine Lektüre leichter Unterhaltung stellen sie auf keinen Fall dar.

Unmittelbare Vorbilder für die von Michault Taillevent und Pierre Chastellain praktizierte "offene Form" kenne ich nicht. Natürlich kommt sie, wie die meiste französische Literatur des Spätmittelalters, vom Rosenroman her, und sie ist sicher nicht ohne den Vorgang von Guillaume de Machauts *Voir dit*, ohne die Tradition der Ich-Rede bei Jean Froissart, Eustache Deschamps und Christine de Pizan denkbar. Wenn man sie dem *dit* zuordnet, so sagt man nicht mehr, als daß unsere Autoren eine neue Variante dieses proteischen Formenkomplexes geschaffen haben, eines Formenkomplexes, der sich in dem artikuliert, was man mangels eines eingeführten Begriffs als die "Großform" bezeichnen müßte, wie sie die sog. Grands Rhétoriqueurs pflegen. Zu den stets verfügbaren Bauelementen dieser "Großform" gehören auch Mitteilungen über den eigenen Lebensgang des Verfassers; nirgends sonst aber werden diese Mitteilungen, soviel ich sehe, zum alleinigen Gegenstand eines Werks von einigem Umfang.

Ich fasse zusammen.

In den 40er Jahren des XV. Jhdts. — nähere Kausalitätszusammenhänge sollen hier nicht mehr erörtert werden — entstehen zum ersten Mal Formen einer selbständigen poetischen Autobiographie, die natürlich noch nicht mit "Entwicklungs"kategorien arbeitet, die aber den Zeitverlauf des Lebensgang prinzipiell ganz überblicken und als Erstreckung begreifen will. Die Grundfigur ist der *Rückblick*, das Grundschema ist der unaufhaltsame Gang von der Jugend zum Alter; als Ordnungsidee (und als Hinweis auf einen Naturprozeß, dem es sich zu fügen gilt) stehen die Jahreszeiten zu Verfügung.

Das Schema ist also alter- und todgerichtet und verrät damit seine Herkunft von der geistlichen Betrachtungsliteratur der Sterbebücher und des Totenzanzes. Es darf aber nicht übersehen werden — und Pierre Chastellain durchbricht das Schema klar und als ausdrückliche Korrektur von Michault Taillevents Vorgehen — daß eine Fülle von Motiven und Darstellungsweisen ausgebildet bereitstanden, die dem empirischen Ich des Autors[29] Konsistenz und eine Dichte der Realitätsanbindung geben, die in Verbindung mit dem seit dem Rosenroman immer feiner ausgebildeten Mitteln der Seelenanalyse und den vielfältigen Formen des poetischen Erlebnisberichts eine innere Weite des Zeitüberlicks ermöglichen, die den pessimistischen Drang zum Ende immer wieder suspendiert und den ruhigen Blick auf eine Reihe von Einzelheiten eigenen Rechts möglich macht. Diese Formen zu resümieren, ist hier wohl nicht nötig; es würde auch bedeuten, eine ganze Reihe der Entwicklungslinien der französischen Literatur seit dem Rosenroman zu besprechen.

Ein Punkt ist abschließend noch zu nennen. Die Nabelschnur, die die Ich-Texte mit der Tradition verbindet, der Boden, auf dem allein sie vorläufig noch wachsen, ist die *Versdichtung*. In der Versdichtung spricht sich das Ich zuerst aus; hier ist seine Darstellung aber auch immer noch mit einer letzten Fiktions-Aura umgeben, die das Wagnis einer unverstellten Ich-Rede gerechtfertigt erscheinen läßt. (Vielleicht ist Christine de Pizan die erste und in ihrer Zeit eine Ausnahme, wenn sie Stücke ihres Lebengangs *in Prosa* nachzeichnet.)

Was Michault Taillevent und Pierre Chastellain tun, ist schießlich nur auf dem Boden der Poetik der Grands Rhétoriqueurs denkbar. Deren Drang, die Gattungsgrenzen in sog. "Großformen " aufzulösen, geht die Komplizierung und Potenzierung der sprachlichen Mittel von Lexikon, Reim und Vers parallel, die sie lange Zeit von der Aufmerksamkeit der Literaturgeschichte ausgeschlossen haben. Die äußerste Bewußtheit, mit der die Rhétoriqueurs ihre poetischen Mittel handhaben, gibt ihren Dichtungen nicht nur ihre Künstlichkeit und ihre Intellektualität; in dem Ersatz der Metapher durch die allgegenwärtigen lexikalischen Tropen scheinen sie (man denke auch an ihre Vorliebe für das Prosimetrum) auch die Grenzen von Poesie und Prosa auflösen zu wollen.

Wenn also *Passetemps* als ein Schlüsselwort eines XV. Jhts. bezeichnet werden soll, in dem die hier besprochene Thematik ganz ohne Frage in Villons *Testament* ihren konzentriertesten und künstlerisch großartigsten Ausdruck findet — d.h. also *nicht* im Umkreis der Rhétoriqueur-Ästhetik — so zeigt das ohne Frage die poetischen Grenzen der *passetemps*-Literatur auf. Aber eine solche Feststellung setzt die Rhétoriqueurs nicht ins Unrecht — falls so etwas überhaupt möglich wäre: ihre Experimente an den Grenzen der poetischen Sprache und der Gattungen lassen Möglichkeiten der Literatur erkennen, die erst viel später und unter anderen Voraussetzungen — und dann mit mehr Kraft und Sicherheit — in großem Stil begriffen worden sind; und sie sichern ihnen, meine ich, ein Interesse, das sich nicht auf die Inventarisierung des poetischen XV. Jhdts. beschränken dürfte[30].

NOTES

* Der folgende Text, als Vortrag konzipiert, skizziert eine Thematik, die als Teil einer größeren Arbeit zur Dichtung des XV. Jahrhunderts in ihren Zusammenhängen näher ausgeführt werden soll.

[1] *Les Cent Nouvelles Nouvelles*, p.p. Pierre Champion (Genève: Slatkine Reprints, 1977), 13.

[2] Eine Studie zum Wort scheint nicht vorzuliegen. Übersichten geben Jean-Claude Mühlethaler, *Poétiques du Quinzième Siècle. Situation de François Villon et Michault Taillevent* (Paris: Nizet, 1983), 26-32, und Alice Planche, *Charles d'Orléans ou la recherche d'un langage* (Paris: Champion, 1975), 357-360.

[3] Vgl. etwa Laurent de Premierfaits *Prologue* zu seiner Übersetzung des *Decameron* (1414):

> Car les maistres et docteurs ou milieu de leurs leçons racomptent aux escoliers aucunes fables ou nouvelles joyeuses afin que par interposees paroles de honneste soulaz et esbatement les liseurs et escouteurs resveillent et rafreschissent leurs sens et entendements...

(zit. nach Attilio Hortis, *Studj sulle Opere latine del Boccaccio* [Trieste: Dase, 1879], 746.)

Die Weiterentwicklung dieser Topik z.B. in Boccaccios *Proemio* (Erzählen als Trost und Unterhaltung, besonders für Frauen) kann hier außer Betracht bleiben. Zu dem Themenkomplex "Literatur als Unterhaltung" s. Glending Olson, *Literature as Recreation in the Later Middle Ages* (Ithaca-London: Cornell University Press, 1982).

[4] In: *Studien zur spätmittelalterlichen Geschichtsschreibung in Deutschland. Mittelalterbilder aus neuer Perspektive*. Hsg. v. Ernstpeter Ruhe und Rudolf Behrens (München: Fink, 1980).

[5] "C'est en effet la méditation sur le temps qui permet d'opposer la philosophie mélancolique du XVe siècle à la philosophie ardente du XIVe siècle." (Daniel Poirion, *Le Poète et le Prince.* [Paris: Presses Universitaires de France, 1965], 537.) — Emile Mâle läßt mit dem Ende der Regierungszeit von Charles V (1364-1380) "le nouveau moyen âge" beginnen und begründet diese Periodisierung mit dem Einsetzen der leidenschaftlichen Todesmeditation (*L'Art religieux à la fin du moyen âge.* 4e éd. [Paris: Armand Colin, 1931], 354.) — Henri Guy hat in unseren Gedichten offenbar nichts gesehen, was sie als bedeutungsvoll aus den anderen Werken der Rhétoriqueurs heraushöbe: "Les poèmes que les Rhétoriqueurs intitulent Passetemps ne semblent pas — car cette dénomination s'applique aux choses les plus diverses — constituer un genre à part." (*L'Ecole des Rhétoriqueurs* [Paris:Champion, 1910], § 209.) Dementsprechend faßt er die Texte auch nicht bibliographisch zusammen. Ich darf bei dieser Gelegenheit bemerken, daß ich auf Werke des Titels *Passetemps*, die sich nicht mit Zeitbetrachtungen beschäftigen, hier nicht eingehen werde.

[6] Ein Einfluß Michault Taillevents auf die Dichtung des XV. Jhdts. wird aber immer wieder postuliert; so von Pierre Champion, der von der *déplorable influence, dans le jeu des rimes*, spricht, die er *sur toute l'Ecole bouguignonne, et par là sur tous les Rhétoriqueurs* ausgeübt habe (*Histoire poétique du XVe s.*, I 339), oder von Daniel Poirion, der *contexte et prétexte* der Dichtung Villons in dem Erbe Alain Chartiers und Michault Taillevents sieht: "L'Enfance d'un poète: François Villon et son personnage". In *Mélanges de littérature du Moyen Âge au XXe siècle offerts à Mademoiselle Jeanne Lods* (Paris: Coll. de l'Ecole Normale Supérieure de Jeunes Filles, 1978, 2 Bde.), I 517. — Es ist auch nicht recht vorstellbar, daß Pierre Chastellain das Vorbild des *Passetemps Michault Taillevent* so intensiv und grundsätzlich aufgegriffen hätte, wäre ihm das Gedicht nicht neuartig und wegweisend erschienen.

[7] Daniel Poirion, "Le temps perdu et retrouvé... au XVe siècle". In: *Revue des Sciences Humaines* 1981, 77/78, stellt einen solchen Einfluß ausdrücklich fest. Eine derartige Annahme setzt natürlich die Datierung von M.T.s Gedicht auf ca. 1448 voraus, die unten in Anm. 13 besprochen wird.

[8] Seine Identifikation mit dem Dichter Vaillant ist inzwischen aufgegeben worden. Vgl. die Daten zu dieser Frage in *Les Oeuvres de Pierre Chastellain et de Vaillant, poètes du XVe siècle*. Ed. crit. de Robert Deschaux (Genf: Droz, 1982), 11-13.

[9] Jean-Claude Mühlethaler in der Einleitung zu seiner Ausgabe *Charles d'Orléans. Ballades et Rondeaux* (Paris:Livre de Poche/Coll. Lettres Gothiques, 1992), 15. In dem oben, Anm. 2, zitierten Buch von Alice Planche findet sich auf S. 355 (Anm.) eine Zusammenstellung von etwa 90 Stellen aus dem Werk von Charles d'Orléans, an denen von *temps* die Rede ist. Die Bedeutung von *passetemps* bei Charles d'Orléans wird im selben Band auf S. 358 mit sehr überzeugenden Überlegungen besprochen.

[10] Siehe auch den *Index des Personnifications* in Mühlethalers Ausgabe (s. Anm. 9), 775-782.

[11] Alice Planche (wie in Anm. 2), 357.

[12] Den Zusammenhang zwischen dem Erscheinen eines individuell gefaßten, seine Lebensgeschichte thematisierenden Ich und der Markierung des Zeitverlaufs analysiert Paul Zumthor: "Le *je* de la chançon et le *moi* du poète" in *Langue, texte, énigme* (Paris: Seuil, 1975), 181. Zu dem *je* gehören *ici* und *maintenant* als "axe référentiel du discours dans le grand chant courtois"; das Gegenteil — eine Differenzierung der Zeit- und Raumbehandlung — hat also zu gelten, sobald sich, etwa bei Rutebeuf, das *moi* einer "poésie personnelle" (der Begriff erscheint nicht bei Zumthor) meldet.

[13] Die Datierung hängt — vgl. R. Deschaux' Ausgabe (s.u., Anm. 14), 43; wesentlich an der Datierung des im Folgenden noch zu besprechenden Gedichts von Pierre Chastellain, *Le Temps perdu*, einer direkten Replik auf Michault Taillevents Gedicht. Wenn man in P.Ch.s zweitem Gedicht (*Le Temps recouvré*) in Str. XIII, wo von dem ersten Werk die Rede ist, in V. 85 statt "*dix* ans davant ce temps de grace" (gemeint ist das Jubeljahr 1450) gegen die Hss. "*deux* ans" liest (eine Korrekur, die schon A. Piaget vorgeschlagen hatte: Champion, *Hist. poétique*, I 345, Anm. 2), wäre für die Vollendung von Michault Taillevents Gedicht ein Datum nahe an 1448 anzusetzen. Das wäre vielleicht nicht weiter erwähnenswert, gewänne damit nicht die Annahme mehr Plausibilität, Charles' d'Orléans Balladen hätten den Anstoß für die *passetemps*-Dichtung gegeben (s.o., Anm. 7): in diesem Fall hätten ja für das Bekanntwerden der Balladen nach Charles' Rückkehr 1440 einige Jahre zur Verfügung gestanden.

[14] Die Ausgabe von Robert Deschaux, *Un Poète bourguignon du XVe siècle: Michault Taillevent. Edition et étude* (Genf: Droz, 1975), enthält sämtliche Dichtungen sowie eine umfangreiche Studie zu Person und Werk.

[15] Dieses Gedicht ist ein Beispiel für die anekdotische Erlebnisschilderung, wie sie von Froissart (*Dit dou Florin*, 1389) und von Eustache Deschamps in zahlreichen Balladen gepflegt worden ist. Man mag dgl. auch im Zusammenhang mit Jean Regnier sehen, der seiner Gefangenschaft in Beauvais von der Gefangennahme bis zu den Bemühungen um das Lösegeld ein ganzes Buch gewidmet hat: *Livre de la prison* (verfaßt ca. 1432/33); Ausgabe in dem Sammelband seiner Dichtungen *Les Fortunes et adversitez* von E. Droz, Paris 1923 (SATF).

[16] Siebenzeiler-Strophen finden in dieser Zeit häufig Verwendung, vielfach auch mit dem bei Michault Taillevent erscheinenden Reimschema *ababbcc*, z.B. bei Charles d'Orléans: Ball. 75 Mühleth./100 Champion., 94 M./120 Ch., 98 M./75 Ch., 118 M./95 Ch. Siehe hierzu auch Paul Zumthor, *Le masque et la lumière* (Paris: Seuil, 1978), 154/55.

[17] Diese seltsame Distanzierung gibt wohl nur einen — möglichen — Sinn, wenn man sie als Reverenz vor dem Rosenroman versteht, in dem der Erzähler den Traum, der den Gegenstand des Gedichts ausmacht, gleichfalls bereits vor Jahren geträumt haben will:

> Avis m'estoit qu'il estoit maiz,
> Il a ja bien cinq ans ou maiz... (V. 45/46).

[18] Poirion, "Le Temps perdu et retrouvé..." (s. Anm. 7), 71-84. Der Herausgeber von Pierre Chastellains Dichtungen, R. Deschaux, zitiert auf S. 110 seiner Ausgabe (s. Anm. 8) eine Stelle aus Alain Chartiers *Breviaire des Nobles* ("Ballade de diligence", Ausg. Laidlaw, S. 404, V. 280-285), an der das Begriffspaar *perdre-recouvrir* in einem Zusammenhang erscheint, der an Gewinn und Verlust *in der Zeit* denken läßt und der damit die Grundfigur von Pierre Chastellains Dichtungen zu entwerfen scheint:

> Que vault homme qui muse et se pourmaine
> Et veult avoir mol lit et pance plaine
> Et demourer en repos a couvert?
> Et passe temps sepmaine aprés sepmaine
> Et ne lui chault en quel point tout se meine
> Qui soit perdu ne qui soit recouvert...

[19] "(L'oeuvre poétique de Pierre Chastellain) est aussi diverse, aussi mystérieuse qu'a pu l'être la vie picaresque de son auteur: un vrai roman où l'on devine beaucoup de choses cyniques, terribles peut-être, où se voit une fin brillante que l'on a de la peine à admettre tout d'abord. Si la qualité littéraire des vers de Chastellain répondait à l'imprévu de cette vie, il aurait droit à une place bien singulière et rare dans la littérature du quinzième siècle, à côté de Villon." (Pierre Champion, *Histoire poétique du quinzième siècle*, I 339).

[20] Jean-Claude Mühlethaler hat das Werk, ausgehend vom ersten Gedicht, in diesem Sinn interpretiert und dabei dem Thema der *Alchemie* besondere Aufmerksamkeit gewidmet: "Introduction à la poétique de Pierre Chastellain: lecture du *Temps Perdu*". In: *Vox Romanica* 42, 1983, 157-169. In den autobiographischen Mitteilungen — wenn sie denn immer echt seien und nicht nur traditionelle Motive aufnähmen — sieht er mehr *exempla,* als Angaben mit der Absicht der Selbstdarstellung. Auf die beiden Zeit-Titel, auf Einzelheiten im Verhältnis beider Werke zueinander, und auf die hier untersuchte "Verzeitlichung" der poetischen Rede geht er — an dieser Stelle — merkwürdigerweise überhaupt nicht ein.

[21] Mühlethaler (vgl. Anm. 20), 161. Wenn Pierre Chastellains erstes Gedicht in einigen Hss. also als "Contrepassetemps (Michault)" bezeichnet wird (vgl. die Ausgabe Deschaux, S. 19), dann könnte diese Wendung über die bloße Bezeichnung des Verhältnisses beider Texte zueinander auf diesen tieferen Gegensatz in der Zeitauffassung beider Autoren hinweisen.

[22] Mühlethaler (s. Anm. 20), besonders S. 166-168. Über die traditionelle Deutung der alchemistischen Praktiken als Erkenntnissuche hinaus hat die Deutung der Alchemie als Metapher starke Plausibilität in einer Zeit, in der die aus dem Bezirk "Geld" stammende Bildlichkeit insistent auftritt. Vgl. den Gebrauch von Wörtern wie *rente* bei Charles d'Orléans, und siehe dazu Poirion, "Le Temps perdu..." (s. Anm.7), 76/77.

[23] Hier zeigt sich eine Dimension des passetemps-Themas, die weder nach ihren Facetten, noch nach den Texten oder den Titeln der kritischen Literatur in diesem Rahmen auch nur angedeutet werden kann. Hier und im folgenden sollen daher nur einige Hinweise gegeben werden; so auf Bruno Roy, "La Danse des trois aveugles" in *Le Sentiment de la Mort au Moyen Âge. Etudes présentées au Cinquième Colloque de l'Institut d'études médiévales de l'Université de Montréal,* p.p. Claude Sutto (Montréal: "L'Aurore". Les Editions Univers, 1979).

[24] Auf diesem Gesichtspunkt, daß die "Kunst des Sterbens" im XV. Jhdt. das ganze Leben, also die Zeit einbezieht und zum Ziel hat, das Leben selbst als Vorbereitung auf den Tod verstehen zu lassen, insistiert Adèle Chené-Williams, "Vivre sa mort et mourir sa vie" in *Le Sentiment de la Mort...* (vgl. Anm. 21), 169 ff. In einem sehr instruktiven Aufsatz: "Les 'Danses macabré': Une image en négatif du fonctionnalisme social" in Jane M. H. Taylor (ed.), *Dies illa. Death in the Middle Ages. Proceedings of the 1983 Manchester Colloquium* (Liverpool: Francis Cairns, 1984), 15-27, weist Jean Batany auf eine fundamentale Verschiebung den Denkens der Epoche von Heils- auf Glücks-Kategorien hin.

[25] Ihre Genese ist hier nicht zu entwickeln. Es soll nur auf einige — wohlbekannte — Arbeiten hingewiesen werden, die für die hier entwickelten Überlegungen wesentlich gewesen sind: P. Zumthor, "Le *je* de la chanson..." (s. Anm. 12); J.-Ch. Payen, *Le motif du repentir dans la littérature française médiévale des origines à 1200* (Genf: Droz, 1967); Friedrich Wolfzettel, "La poésie lyrique en France comme mode d'appréhension de la réalité" in *Mélanges de langue et de littérature françaises du Moyen Âge et de la Renaissance offerts à Charles Foulon* (Rennes: Institut de Français. Université de Haute-Bretagne, 1980, 2 Bde.), I 409 ff.

[26] Vgl. dazu Poirion, "Le Temps perdu et retrouvé..." (s. Anm. 7), wo die Traditionslinie in ihren großen Zügen dargestellt ist.

[27] Vgl. Zumthor wie in Anm. 16.

[28] Vgl. den Nachweis in Anm. 4.

[29] Das empirische Ich des Autors bemächtigt sich, wie schon bemerkt, der *persona* des lyrischen Ich so unübersehbar nachdrücklich, daß dessen Darstellungsformen fast bedenken- und schrankenlos in den Dienst unstillisierter Ich-Rede eines Dichters genommen werden, der dadurch, daß er auf alle traditionelle Rollenstilisierung und ihre (komische) Inszenierung verzichtet, nur noch von einer minimalen Fiktionsdistanz in seiner unbedeutenden Menschlichkeit geschützt wird.

[30] In Pierre Chastellains Zeitbehandlung und in seiner Sicht der Alchemie den Ausdruck eines frühen *Humanismus* zu sehen, wie Robert Deschaux will ("L'humanisme de Pierre Chastellain, poète du XVe siècle", in *Recherches et Travaux*, Université de Grenoble, UER des Lettres, 28: *Humanismes. Hommage à Charles Bené*, 1985, 39 ff), scheint mir kein Anlaß zu bestehen. Abgesehen davon, daß

ein literarischer Humanismus mit so geringem Bezug auf antike Texte und Denkweisen und deren Studium schwer vorstellbar ist, gehört die Selbst- oder Fremdbetrachtung des von seiner "Gruppe" isolierten Einzelnen zu den Standardthemen der Epoche. Und ich finde keine Spur von "carpe diem", von "juvat vivere" bei ihm, also der Grundhaltungen des Optimismus und einer Weltbewältigung durch Wissen, die den Humanismus prägen, auch nicht in den Hoffnungen, die Pierre Chastellain auf eine moderne Wissenschaft setzt.

Les Voyages au Purgatoire de Saint Patrice: Illusion de la Réalité, Réalité de l'Illusoire

Peter M. De Wilde

Introduction

L'existence réelle d'un lieu où l'on peut être confronté aux peines des damnés et aux joies des bienheureux doit avoir à la fois terrifié et rendu curieux l'homme du moyen âge constamment à la recherche d'authentification et de confirmation de la réponse à la grande question: quel est le sort de l'âme après la mort? S'il existe un lieu réservé aux morts en continuité avec le monde des vivants, où est-ce qu'il se trouve, est-ce qu'il se visite et est-ce qu'il offre la possibilité de se purger des péchés commis? Le *Tractatus de Purgatorio sancti Patricii* par le frère H. de Saltrey (ca. 1185) a répondu à ces questions par l'affirmative. Toujours est-il que le genre des voyages dans l'Au-delà est nettement plus vieux que le texte auquel nous allons consacrer notre attention.

En effet, les fondements du genre sont essentiellement théologiques: saint Augustin[1] ouvre la voie à la temporalité après la mort, Grégoire de Tours exploite franchement ce qui n'était encore qu'hypothèse avancée avec hésitation. Le christianisme des premiers siècles ne s'est intéressé au voyage dans l'Au-delà qu'à propos du Christ et de saint Paul; dans ces deux cas, on pouvait se baser, plus ou moins solidement, sur une allusion scripturaire.[2] Dans l'*Apocalypse de Paul*, l'auteur affirme que Paul a atteint le troisième ciel dans son corps et il fait parcourir à son héros tout le séjour des morts. Ce texte, qui pourrait remonter au IIe siècle, semble avoir été le prototype pour toutes les visions médiévales.[3] La véritable origine du genre semble se situer au VIIe siècle, avec les grandes visions de *Barontus* et de *saint Fursy*.[4] On y retrouve le thème de la mort apparente et du ravissement de l'âme; chez Barontus surtout, on voit un panorama complet de l'Au-delà.[5] Le voyage de l'âme dans l'Au-delà devient un genre littéraire particulier caractérisé par le récit d'un homme (il n'y a presque pas de femmes parmi les voyageurs), apparemment mort et revenu à lui, et dont l'âme, détachée du corps, a parcouru (souvent sous la conduite d'un guide) les lieux où résident les morts. Ce genre change véritablement lorsqu'il n'est plus question d'une séparation de l'âme et que la personne pénètre "corporaliter" dans l'Au-delà. Le *Purgatoire de saint Patrice* en est le premier et le plus important exemple.

L'évolution des premiers siècles après les visions de Fursy et de Barontus se caractérise surtout par une précision croissante du mode de transfert de l'âme dans l'au-delà et par la présence toujours plus fréquente et plus intense d'un ou de plusieurs critères de véracité. C'est, en bref, l'installation du schéma de base auquel se conformeront la plupart des relateurs ultérieurs; on assiste aussi à la suppression de l'interdit paulinien sur la révélation des *caelestia* ineffables.

La *Vision de Fursy* se fonde sur un schéma initiatique double: la vieille typologie baptismale de l'*Apocalypse de Paul* d'une part, d'autre part une croyance ancestrale dans les vertus du feu. Le langage qui résulte de la superposition de ces deux schémas est neuf à l'usage des populations insuffisament christianisées. En signe d'adoption, il est inclus dans la prédication missionnaire. Mais le fait que cette innovation se produise justement dans un milieu irlandais nous suggère que l'influence de la littérature celte (païenne et non-latine) sur cette étape importante de l'évolution du genre ait été plus grande que l'on ne croit à l'heure actuelle. La *Révélation de Barontus* introduit le genre littéraire du voyage dans l'Au-delà bien mieux que la *Vision de Fursy*. Cette révélation témoigne de la continuité des conceptions antiques par le biais du christianisme (la théologie inspirée par la philosophie néoplaticienne). L'auteur de la *Révélation de Barontus* fait une lecture encore plus exploitrice de l'oeuvre de Grégoire le Grand que ce dernier avait fait de la lecture de saint Augustin.

Une cosmologie bien corporelle de l'au-delà se crée aux VIIe et VIIIe siècles, sous l'impulsion probable des moines irlandais: vu l'influence de la littérature celte, ce n'est pas le fait du hasard. L'importance de la notion de voyage et les aspects terrestres de l'au-delà celte (ressemblant parfois à un véritable pays de cocagne) sont caractéristiques de la littérature celto-irlandaise.

Grâce à Bède, la prière pour les morts s'intègre dans le processus pénitentiel et se fait dès lors le pont permanent entre l'ici-bas et l'au-delà, créant la solidarité entre les vivants et les morts. Le destin n'est donc plus scellé définitivement au moment de la mort: les vivants sont capables d'aider l'âme des trépassés à progresser sur la voie du paradis. Les deux lieux intermédiaires entre l'enfer définitif et le royaume des cieux, ce sont l'Enfer purgatoire, destiné à devenir purgatoire tout court, et le Paradis. Tous deux ont des caractéristiques terrestres et entraînent les deux lieux extrêmes dans leur évolution.

Quand débute sur le continent la renaissance carolingienne, le genre du voyage de l'âme est solidement installé dans le monde anglo-saxon: en témoignent les oeuvres d'Alcuin et d'Aethelwulf.[6] La discussion, ouverte par saint Augustin, sur le sort de l'âme après la mort, se poursuit. On a abouti à la situation que saint Augustin avait voulu éviter: le monde de l'après-mort est devenu connaissable (mais surtout visitable), et les vieux mythes sur la purification de l'âme ont repris droit de cité. A la fin de cette période, la conception néoplatonicienne de l'âme a laissé place à l'idée d'une âme, double parfait de l'homme, et de ce fait visible comme en témoignent les visiteurs de l'Au-delà, tels que les visionnaires carolingiens. Pourtant, on constate que les textes se font rares pendant le Xe et le début du XIe siècle. Pour retrouver des documents se rattachant directement au genre du Voyage de l'âme, il faut attendre le début du XIIe siècle.

Au XIIe siècle, on est entré dans une période où certains commencent à douter de la véracité des grandes visions de l'Au-delà. D'où, nous croyons, une réaction de la part du clergé -irlandais, une fois de plus- qui créera une visite corporelle en rédigeant le *Purgatoire de saint Patrice*. C'est surtout le départ de l'âme qui fait problème; on va donc insister davantage sur les circonstances qui entraînent et entourent ce départ. Pour renforcer la véracité du récit, en fait, il n'y a que deux solutions véritables: ou bien insister sur l'aspect pathologique du phénomène, et le présenter comme un processus de désincarnation de l'âme, ou bien mettre en évidence le caractère exceptionnel de l'événement, en faire un miracle. L'une et l'autre écartent la solution plus simple du rêve, objet de scepticisme depuis longtemps, et qui, plus tard, sera parfois tenu comme explication véritable de la visite de l'Au-delà (nous citerons plus bas l'exemple célèbre du seigneur de Lille rapporté par Froissart). Si le succès du genre du voyage dans l'Au-delà s'affaiblit à la fin du Moyen Age, ce n'est pas à cause du doute ou par manque de matière mais plutôt en raison d'un trop plein. D'ailleurs, au XIIe siècle aussi, *in tempore non suspecto*, il n'y a pas que le doute; le système pénitentiel lui aussi a évolué. L'aveu, immédiatement suivi par l'absolution et la pénitence, sont passés au premier plan du processus de purification de l'âme.

La scission entre vision et visite corporelle de l'Autre Monde est moins rigide que l'on ne doit croire. Mais la différence entre le voyage fait "en vision" (ou même en songe) et le voyage corporel n'est pas uniquement une question de vocabulaire; c'est aussi, nous croyons, une question de perception et de valeur narratologique. C'est ce que nous montre la tradition littéraire des voyages au Purgatoire de saint Patrice en Irlande.

Le "puits" de Patrice

Le récit du moine de Saltrey répond par l'affirmative à la question de savoir si l'Au-delà se visite corporellement; il va donc attirer pendant des siècles des milliers de pèlerins en Irlande, puisque c'est là, dans l'Ulster, que se situe le fameux "Puits" dit "Purgatoire de Saint Patrice".

La légende du Purgatoire de saint Patrice est un jalon important dans la lente création de l'imagerie de l'Autre Monde; elle recueille de manière éclectique la plupart des éléments traditionnels depuis l'Apocalypse de Paul et semble annoncer ceux des visions ultérieures. Elle est donc à la fois point de repère et point de départ. Cette histoire est conservée dans un très grand nombre de manuscrits, éparpillés à travers l'Europe entière.[7] Le grand succès du *Tractatus de Purgatorio sancti Patricii* par le frère H. de Saltrey (ca. 1185)[8] et de ses versions vernaculaires est dû au fait qu'il s'agit, pour la première fois au moyen âge, d'un voyage réellement corporel dans ce qui semble être l'Autre Monde. En effet, les aventures du chevalier

Owein au purgatoire et aux portes du paradis et les choses qu'il y vit (en 1153, selon les *Flores Historiarum* de Roger de Wendover), doivent avoir fait une impression inoubliable au public médiéval ayant l'habitude des visions qui, de par leur caractère, en fait n'impliquent que la participation directe du visionnaire et qui laissent donc une distance rassurante entre le lecteur/auditeur et les révélations.

Aux années '80 du XIIe siècle, il existait un vrai culte de saint Patrice. En 1185, on avait "retrouvé" les reliques du saint qui s'étaient perdues au cours des siècles. Avec l'autorisation du pape, elles furent enterrées en grande pompe le 9 juin 1186, avec celles de saint Colomban et de sainte Brigida dans la crypte de la cathédrale de Down par Malachie III, évêque de Down (1176-1201). L'église de saint Patrice à Dublin fut élevée à cette occasion au rang de cathédrale.[9] Ces événements furent accompagnés de grandes festivités et d'un intérêt renouvelé pour la personne du saint et pour les mythes relatant sa vie qui doivent avoir circulé depuis des années sous forme de tradition orale. Nous croyons qu'il faut situer dans cette ambiance l'origine du *Tractatus* tel qu'il a été écrit par H. de Saltrey; les reliques de Patrice sont d'ailleurs mentionnées dans le texte. Ce serait aussi le commencement des pèlerinages qui, à l'exemple du voyage d'Owein, mènent le pèlerin au Lac Rouge (Lough Derg) où, arrivé dans l'île (Station Island), il est enfermé pendant vingt-quatre heures dans ce que les textes appellent un *puteus, antrum, spelunca rotunda, fovea, scrobis,* ou encore *fosse, puits, cellier* etc.

Les pèlerins-visionnaires

Depuis son origine[10], le pèlerinage pénitentiel, qui persiste à nos jours, a attiré des participants de toute l'Europe. Certains de ces pénitents nous ont laissé le témoignage de ce qu'ils prétendent avoir vécu dans le "puits de saint Patrice".[11] La plupart d'entre eux s'inspirent directement du récit du moine de Saltrey.

Ainsi, en 1397, un noble français, Raymon de Perelhos, obtient un sauf-conduit jusqu'au Lough Derg et la permission d'entrer dans le Purgatoire. A son retour, le voyageur écrit en dialecte languedocien le récit de ses aventures.[12] Il a inséré partiellement, en se l'attribuant, l'histoire du chevalier Owein dans celui d'un voyage qui l'aurait conduit d'Avignon, sa résidence ordinaire, en Irlande. Dès qu'il met le pied en Irlande, la relation du voyageur devient assez fantaisiste. Toujours est-il que l'élément d'authentification est présent, tout comme dans le *Tractatus*: il s'agit du cadre et des personnages historiques, qui rendent au récit une certaine vraisemblance.[13] Car si l'auteur réussit à faire de sa prose un texte à valeur documentaire, l'impression de véracité en sera encore plus grande aux yeux du lecteur. De cette façon, l'ancien but d'édifier et de terrifier doit être atteint. Au moyen âge, on l'avait compris de cette façon et très souvent, on a compilé, consciemment ou non, le *Tractatus* avec des textes historiographiques.[14] Le texte de Raymon ajoute un élément personnel à ce procédé: le héros fait mention de personnes, récemment décédées à son insu, mais qu'il a connues dans le monde et qu'il aurait rencontrées à sa surprise au Purgatoire. La raison principale de son voyage de 1397 est d'ailleurs le vif désir de connaître le sort de son maître, Jean Ier d'Aragon, mort en 1395. Apparemment, le pénitent s'est transformé en curieux ou même en touriste; à son tour, c'est la relation qui doit satisfaire à la curiosité du public.

En 1409, le vendredi après la fête de l'Exaltation de la croix, au moment de la moisson (on remarque la double authentification temporelle), William Staunton, natif du diocèse de Durham en Angleterre, a séjourné dans la cave de saint Patrice. Il nous a laissé le récit des révélations extraordinaires qui lui furent octroyées.[15] Elles sont d'une grande originalité et plus développées que toutes celles qui précèdent; elles diffèrent encore plus de la légende du moine de Saltrey, surtout par le caractère de plus en plus subjectif de la narration.

Après lui avoir enseigné la prière qu'il devait répéter au cas où il rencontrerait de bons ou de mauvais esprits (c'est encore un élément repris à la légende), le prieur Mathieu le fit entrer dans le Purgatoire, à quatre heures du matin. Après avoir dormi un moment, William aperçut une petite lumière semblable à celle du jour qui se lève; il crut distinguer un homme et une femme, tous deux en vêtements blancs comme des religieux. C'étaient saint Jean de Bridlington et sainte Ive de Quitike.[16]

Ils souhaitèrent la bienvenue au pèlerin et lui donnèrent des indications sur le chemin qu'il devait prendre. Lorsqu'ils l'eurent quitté, William se mit en route. Il ne tarda pas à rencontrer des diables déguisés en hommes, qui firent tout ce qu'ils purent pour l'empêcher de poursuivre son voyage. Mais il ne les écouta point et continua. Alors lui apparurent beaucoup de terribles esprits par lesquels il fut fort effrayé. Certains avaient quatre visages ou cinq cornes; d'autres un visage sur chaque coude; et encore d'autres un visage sur chaque genou.[17] Ils firent autour de lui un bruit épouvantable et lui tirèrent leurs langues brûlantes. William était tellement effrayé qu'il ne pensait plus ni à Dieu ni à sa prière. Heureusement, saint Ive résurgit et lui rappela la Passion du Christ et l'oraison écrite sur son front; immédiatement, tous les esprits malins s'évanouirent.

William marcha encore l'espace d'un mille et retrouva saint Jean, sainte Ive et l'une de ses soeurs morte jadis en temps de peste. Cette dernière l'accusa de ne pas l'avoir laissée épouser l'homme qu'elle aimait. Saint Jean réprimanda sévèrement William et le conduisit auprès d'un feu immense, qui répandait une odeur fétide:

> J'y vis un grand nombre d'hommes et de femmes dont quelques-uns m'étaient connus. Plusieurs portaient des colliers d'or et d'argent ou de brillantes ceintures. D'autres avaient des vêtements garnis de clochettes et des longues poches à leurs manches. Les femmes étaient habillées de robes

> à traîne. On voyait sur leurs cheveux de pimpantes guirlandes d'or, de joyaux et de perles.[18]

Mais tous ces bijoux brûlaient comme du feu. Les étoffes étaient pleines de vipères, de crapauds et d'horribles bêtes qui torturaient sans relâche les malheureux. Les couronnes précieuses se transformaient en clous, que les démons enfonçaient à coups de marteau dans les têtes. Saint Jean lui dit: "Ces hommes là-bas sont ceux qui déshonorent Dieu par l'orgueil de leur coeur et de leur parure. Puisqu'ils n'ont point expié leurs fautes de leur vivant, ils souffriront ces peines jusqu'au jour du Jugement."

William fut conduit devant un autre feu plein de métaux en fusion. Au milieu des flammes, les démons coupaient les membres des pécheurs, leur arrachaient les ongles, la langue, le coeur ou les yeux. Ils bouchaient les blessures avec du métal bouillant et reformaient ensuite les corps mutilés. "Ce sont, dit saint Jean, ceux qui ont démembré Dieu par leurs terribles jurons, et ainsi ils seront torturés tant que l'Eternel voudra." Le troisième feu sentait abominablement mauvais; les diables y bourraient les âmes de boue brûlante comme on entasse dans un sac les flocons de laine. Ceux qui subissaient ce supplice étaient les profanateurs des jours saints. Au lieu d'aller à l'église et d'offrir à Dieu leurs prières, ils s'étaient attablés dans les tavernes et livrés à l'ivrognerie. La longue série des châtiments se continue par les parents qui n'ont pas enseigné à leurs enfants à les respecter, par les voleurs, les receleurs, les exécuteurs testamentaires infidèles, les faux témoins, les meurtriers, les débauchés, les parents trop indulgents et les calomniateurs.

Le pèlerin assista encore aux tourments des ecclésiastiques, curés, vicaires et prêtres qui avaient négligé leur devoir et préféré à la dévotion les plaisirs mondains.[19] William reconnut parmi eux un oncle mort depuis seize ans. Il voit aussi ceux qui n'avaient pas enseigné la bonne doctrine au peuple, ou qui avaient laissé tomber en ruine les églises.[20] Enfin, saint Jean l'emmena au bord d'une eau noire et sale; dans cette eau, il y avait beaucoup de démons hurlant et faisant un bruit horrible. William vit un pont grand et large sur lequel s'avançait un évêque suivi de clercs et de dignitaires; les diables arrachèrent les piliers du pont et tous furent précipités dans le bourbier. Saint Jean expliqua que l'évêque avait construit jadis ce pont pour le bien du commun peuple; mais il avait employé à sa construction de l'argent mal acquis. Aussi Dieu avait-il permis qu'il fût renversé.[21] Ici finit la révélation des châtiments du purgatoire.[22]

Quand saint Jean eut montré tous ces tourments, il dit à William que les âmes pouvaient être aidées par les bonnes oeuvres, les psaumes, les messes, les aumônes, les prières et les pèlerinages des vivants. Saint Jean disparut; il laissa William près d'une eau très profonde qui s'étendait au pied de rochers escarpés. De l'autre côté du fleuve se trouvait une haute tour. A son sommet, il vit une belle femme debout qui le regardait. William en fut content: il se mit à genoux et récita avec le plus de ferveur qu'il put ses prières. Il aperçut alors une échelle qui descendait du haut de la tour et atteignait la rive sur laquelle il s'était agenouillé. Mais elle était si petite qu'il paraissait impossible qu'elle pût supporter quelque chose; le premier échelon, à une telle hauteur qu'il le toucha à peine du bout des doigts, lui sembla plus tranchant qu'un rasoir. Ceci me semble être la nouvelle forme du pont de l'épreuve, le "Jenseitsbrücke". Heureusement, une corde fut jetée à William. La femme lui ordonna de se l'attacher autour de la ceinture. Il parvint ainsi sur le premier échelon qui ne le blessa nullement, puis sur la plate-forme supérieure. Lorsqu'il eut remercié le Seigneur de son assistance, la belle femme lui dit: "Cette corde est celle que tu as donnée jadis à un marchand qui avait été dépouillé par des voleurs[23], et qui te suppliait de l'aider pour l'amour de Dieu."

Il arriva ensuite dans une contrée où la terre était aussi brillante que du cristal. Des arbres magnifiques l'ombrageaient et l'embaumaient de parfums plus suaves que tous ceux de toutes les boutiques d'épices du monde entier.[24] Des oiseaux merveilleux l'égayaient de leurs chants. Ce pays était si beau que William aurait voulu l'habiter toujours; il s'étonna presque qu'il eût pu le quitter. Plus il allait, plus il l'aimait. William rencontra une procession de moines, de chanoines et de prêtres, vêtus de blanc, qui l'accueillirent avec douceur et le remercièrent de toutes ses bonnes oeuvres. Un évêque le bénit et loua Dieu de la protection qu'Il avait accordée à son serviteur. Il se lamenta ensuite sur la corruption des gens du monde, qui oublient trop souvent la grâce du Seigneur et négligent de se confesser et de faire pénitence. L'évêque lui ordonna de retourner dans son pays et d'être un homme de bien. S'il fuit le péché, il reviendra parmi eux; mais s'il succombe, il lui faudra repasser par les tourments auxquels il vient d'échapper. William insista pour demeurer plus longtemps dans ce lieu de délices; mais l'évêque lui enjoignit de ne pas demander l'impossible. "Pourtant, ajoute-t-il, tu vas encore assister au jugement de la supérieure d'un couvent..."

William suivit donc la procession sur la colline où cette âme venait d'arriver. Une foule de démons se tenaient autour d'elle. Aussitôt, l'un des moines venus avec l'évêque ouvrit un livre, qui contenait la règle d'après laquelle elle aurait dû vivre. Il l'interrogea sur sa conduite et sur la manière dont elle avait dirigé ses soeurs. La religieuse se défendit piètrement. Les esprits malins l'accusèrent, disant qu'elle était entrée dans les ordres non par dévotion, mais par amour du faste, par orgueil, et pour jouir abondamment des richesses mondaines. L'énumération des péchés qui suit est un reflet trop fidèle du passage célèbre des *Canterbury Tales* de Chaucer pour ne pas y chercher la source probable de Staunton. A l'imitation de l'abbesse mondaine des *Tales*, la religieuse de Staunton s'adonnait au luxe: elle portait des fourrures, des ceintures d'or et d'argent, des bagues aux doigts, des boucles précieuses à ses souliers. La nuit, elle se couchait mollement "comme une reine ou une impératrice" et ne daignait pas se lever pour le service divin. Les mets dont elle se nourrissait étaient toujours délicats, et de même sa boisson. La religieuse, en pleurant, déclarait qu'elle s'était confessée et repentie de toutes ses fautes, mais elle se reconnut coupable d'avoir mal gouverné son couvent. L'évêque lui enjoignit de supporter des tourments jusqu'au jour du jugement pour expier les péchés qu'elle avait commis durant sa vie. Puis, il commanda à William de reprendre le chemin de sa maison et de ne rien craindre, car il ne verrait pas un seul mauvais esprit. William prit congé et arriva aussitôt à la porte par laquelle il était entré. Pour finir, il demande au lecteur de prier pour son âme.[25]

Procédés d'authentification

Le long de son récit, William se présente comme recevant une certaine formation morale par une espèce de guide (saint Jean). C'est un topos assez fréquent dans le genre de la vision et celui du voyage: pensons par exemple à la Vision de Tondale, à la Divine Comédie ou à un très grand nombre d'histoires relatant une visite de l'Au-delà. Ceci est encore un moyen d'authentification, nous dirions même un procédé stylistique qui permet à l'auteur de rapprocher le héros du lecteur, qui, au cours du récit, va s'identifier au voyageur souvent intrépide mais ignorant (et donc innocent). C'est d'ailleurs, aux yeux du lecteur, cette ignorance qui doit faire pardonner un bon nombre de fautes commises. Par l'intermédiaire du guide, l'auteur peut habilement transmettre un message non seulement au héros, mais surtout à son public, c'est-à-dire "al cristen men that heryn or redyn this".

Cette compilation d'éléments repris à la légende ancienne et de procédés d'authentification ajoutés par la suite va atteindre son apogée avec le pèlerinage de Laurent de Pászthó. En 1408, Laurent, seigneur de Pászthó, baron hongrois, entreprend le long pèlerinage. Sa visite à l'île du Lac Rouge est racontée en latin dans un ouvrage manuscrit du XVe siècle par un certain Jacques Yonge, "notarius imperialis" à Dublin.[26] Après une introduction sur la fondation du Purgatoire de saint Patrice, l'auteur annonce son intention de parler de quelqu'un qui y est entré lui-même, au temps de Henry IV d'Angleterre, la douzième année de son règne. On voit que l'authentification historique n'est pas loin. A l'appui de celle-ci, l'auteur se sert d'une indication astronomique: la visite se faisait en l'an du Seigneur 1411, alors que le soleil était dans le signe du scorpion et la lune dans celui de la balance. Le douzième chapitre reproduit un certificat de John Fleming, archevêque d'Armagh, attestant qu'il a reçu du prieur du Purgatoire une lettre qui confirme la visite de Laurent. Grâce à ce témoignage et à deux autres lettres (qui en fait appartenaient simplement à la procédure d'entrée), l'histoire de Laurent gagne en authenticité aux yeux du lecteur. Ces documents rendent crédible ce que Laurent prétend avoir vu au Purgatoire: la ruse du diable et les peines réellement corporelles des damnés.

Yonge précise qu'il a écrit ce que Laurent lui a raconté (ce qui dispense Yonge bien sûr de toute responsabilité). Laurent a vérifié le récit et y a ajouté une déclaration (cha XIII) dans laquelle il affirme que ses expériences étaient bien corporelles. Afin de prouver la réalité de ce qu'il a vécu -preuve assez curieuse à notre avis- Laurent mentionne qu'en sortant du Purgatoire, il a brûlé l'un après l'autre les neuf bouts d'une chandelle rompue. Il fait aussi l'inventaire de ses capacités: il connaît le grec, l'hébreu, le latin et d'autres matières du *trivium* et du *quadrivium*, il est donc digne de foi. Toutefois, pour ne pas trop contrarier les lecteurs sceptiques, les choses vues ont été modifiées afin d'être plus acceptables: il n'y a plus de vision du paradis terrestre. On s'aperçoit du reste que Yonge s'est inspiré partiellement du *Tractatus*, mais aussi de la relation de Raymon de Perelhos.

A partir de ces trois récits de voyage — et nous pourrions multiplier les exemples — on constate que les auteurs disposent d'un certain outillage permettant de rehausser la valeur de réalité de leurs récits. C'est surtout la précision de l'espace et du temps qui doivent accorder à l'histoire son caractère de vraisemblance. Pour cette même raison, il nous semble, ces récits de voyage dans l'Au-delà ont été compilés par la suite avec des textes historiographiques ou du moins relevant de la science.

Ainsi, Van der Zanden signale[27] que la version du *Tractatus* qui se trouve dans le manuscrit 173 I.H. 17 de la Bibliothèque de l'Université d'Utrecht présente au début une addition curieuse; c'est, sans mention de provenance, la copie textuelle de la Distinctio II, Ca V de la Topographia Hibernica de Giraud de Cambrie (nous traduisons):

> Il y a dans l'Ulster un lac qui contient une île divisée en deux parties [...]. Ce lieu est appelé par les gens du pays le Purgatoire de saint Patrice. Le saint, jadis, s'était efforcé de faire admettre aux païens la réalité des peines de l'enfer et l'éternelle durée de la gloire des élus. Pour mieux imprimer dans leurs rudes intelligences ces choses qui leur semblaient si nouvelles et qui étaient si opposées à leurs préjugés, il obtint par ses prières qu'elles fussent réalisées sur terre et sous leurs yeux.

Est-ce le copiste hollandais du XVe siècle qui l'a ajoutée ou bien l'un de ses prédécesseurs? Meinsma ne signale pas l'existence d'un manuscrit de l'oeuvre de Giraud aux Pays-Bas.[28] Toujours est-il qu'un scribe, peu satisfait de la description sommaire de l'endroit où se trouve le Purgatoire et désirant donner à son texte une authentification géographique, a fait précéder l'histoire édifiante qu'il avait à copier de certains détails trouvés ailleurs. Ce qui prouve que certaines analogies du *Tractatus* et de la *Topographia* se présentaient déjà à l'esprit de ce copiste médiéval.

Les pèlerinages mentionnés ne sont sans doute qu'une parcelle de la totalité des pèlerinages exécutés au cours du XVe siècle. Caxton, dans sa version de la *Légende Dorée*, fait mention sous l'année 1483 de la grande popularité du Purgatoire de saint Patrice.[29] Néanmoins, au début du XVIe siècle, la gloire du purgatoire était passée. D'un côté, le zèle des fidèles peut avoir diminué; de l'autre, le purgatoire était devenu un spectacle tenant de la foire, destiné à augmenter les revenus du monastère chargé de son entretien. Richard Stanihurst, traducteur de Virgile, affirme que les visions ont cessé de se produire; les visiteurs ne semblent plus ressentir qu'un irrésistible besoin de sommeil.[30] Le déclin des anciennes croyances explique sans doute la première destruction du Purgatoire ordonnée par le pape en 1497[31] entraînant la fin définitive des grands pèlerinages littéraires. Mais le sanctuaire se releva bientôt de ses ruines. Pendant deux siècles encore, sa renommée ne fit que grandir, surtout en Irlande. On s'ingénia à trouver des explications à l'ordre du pape; certains prétendirent qu'il s'appliquait uniquement à l'une des caves, parce qu'elle n'occupait pas la place décrite dans les documents les plus anciens.[32]

Néanmoins, la réputation du Purgatoire n'était plus ce qu'elle avait été. Les critiques, formulées par Stanihurst et le moine d'Eymstadt, se multipliaient les années suivantes. Dans ses *Britannicae Historiae*, Ponticus Virumnius cite un certain Blasius Biragus qui lors de sa visite au Purgatoire aurait déclaré: "est enim insula, ubi puteus per sex gradus in saxo descendit, non ut mythici canunt in foro; ego ingressus vidi omnia".[33] Erasme, discutant dans ses *Adages* le proverbe "in antro Trophonii vaticinatus est", tourne le Purgatoire en dérision. Dans son *Dialogue de Menedemus et Ogygius*, Erasme exprime son scepticisme par la bouche de Menedemus: il ne croit pas aux soi-disant miracles du Purgatoire.[34]

Ce scepticisme, contrairement à ce que les Humanistes auraient bien voulu croire, n'est pas le produit de la soi-disant Renaissance. Froissart, dans ses *Chroniques*, cite l'histoire de Guillaume de Lille.[35] Celui-ci avait fait le pèlerinage du Purgatoire, qu'il appelle le "trou Saint-Patris", et il était descendu, accompagné d'un chevalier anglais, dans la cave (appelée "celier") après s'être soumis aux rites d'entrée. Sur quoi

> chalour nous prist ens ès testes, et nous asseismes sur les pas qui sont de pierre, et, nous illec assis, très-grant voulenté nous vint de dormir, et dormismes toute la nuit [...]. Et quant au matin nous feusmes eveilliés, on ouvry l'uys, car ainsi le avions-nous ordonné, et yssismes hors, et ne nous souvint de chose que euissions veu, et tenions et tenons encoires que ce soit toute fantosme.

Il faut dire que les auteurs des relations de pèlerinage ont laissé eux-mêmes la porte entre-ouverte au scepticisme de certains contemporains et des Humanistes. Ils permettent (consciemment ou non) à leurs lecteurs d'échapper à la réalité du surnaturel: c'est ce que je qualifierais d'élément d'apaisement, une espèce de serrure de sûreté qui empêche la "réalité" de l'aventure de percer dans notre monde. Ainsi, Raimon de Perelhos très habilement s'évanouit au moment même où il est enfermé dans la cave; le moment avant sa sortie, il s'est endormi.[36] Laurent de Pászthó, après avoir pris toutes les mesures possibles de la cave où il est enfermé, se perd dans ses prières comme en trance; immédiatement après, il sent deux diables invisibles. William Staunton "somewhat slumbered and slept".[37] Ces éléments remettent en doute, malgré tous les procédés de vérification, la réalité de l'aventure. Car qui croirait à ce que les voyageurs ont vu comme à travers les portes du sommeil?

Pourtant, le Purgatoire de saint Patrice ne cessa pas d'inspirer les auteurs; il devint au XVIe siècle un sujet fertile pour les romans d'aventures, pour le théâtre et pour les légendes populaires.[38]

Université d'Anvers, Belgique

NOTES

[1] Saint Augustin évoque au treizième livre de la *Cité de Dieu* l'instant de la mort. Il introduit la notion de "temps intermédiaire", c'est à dire le temps entre la mort et la résurrection, où l'âme vit de façon autonome après avoir quitté son corps. Dans ses *Sermons*, Augustin précisera cette conception générale qui va mener à l'élaboration de tout un système d'intermédiaires, exploité par Grégoire de Tours.

[2] L'allusion est nette dans le cas de Paul: II Cor 12/1-4; elle l'est un peu moins pour le Christ: II Pierre 3/18-20 et 4/6.

[3] C'est du moins ce que prétend Claude Carozzi, *Le voyage de l'âme dans l'Au-delà d'après la littérature latine*, Rome, Collection de l'Ecole française de Rome 189, 1994, 4. La littérature apocalyptique juive et judéo-chrétienne était déjà abondamment développée à cette époque. Mais ces écrits s'intéressent très peu au sort des âmes après la mort; ils forment un genre littéraire à part centré sur des révélations concernant le sort futur d'Israël, la venue du Christ ou le Jugement dernier. Saint Augustin semble avoir eu connaissance de l'existence du texte de l'*Apocalypse de Paul*; il y fait allusion dans le *Tractatus* 98 sur l'*Evangile de Jean*. Il en traite le contenu avec dédain.

[4] B. Krusch a édité la Vita de saint Fursy dans les *Monumenta Germaniae Historica, Scriptores rerum merovingicarum* IV, 423-440, mais il a omis le texte de la vision. Carozzi, o.c., 677-692, en donne une édition.

[5] La Vision de Barontus a été éditée par W. Levison in *Monumenta Germaniae Historica, Scriptores rerum merovingicarum* V, 368-394; voir aussi M. P. Ciccarese, "La visio Baronti", in *Romanobarbarica* 6 (1981-1982), 25-52.

[6] Ed. E. Dümmler, *Aethelwulf, De Abbatibus*, XXII, *Monumenta Germaniae Historica, Poetae latini medii aevi* I, 601-603.

[7] Yolande de Pontfarcy estime qu'il existe au moins 150 manuscrits du texte latin et autant en langue vernaculaire (voir Michael Haren et Yolande De Pontfarcy, *The Medieval Pilgrimage to St. Patrick's Purgatory. Lough Derh and the European Tradition*, Enniskillen, Clogher Historical Society, 1988, 48-49). Nous croyons qu'une recherche plus poussée (p.ex. dans les bibliothèques monastiques) permettrait encore une augmentation sensible de ce nombre.

[8] Il circule à propos de ce moine cistercien bon nombre de mauvaises informations. Le nom de l'auteur est indiqué dans certains manuscrits par la majuscule "H"; Mathieu Paris en fait au XIIIe siècle "Henricus" (dès lors, cette solution a été reprise par la plupart des critiques), Thomas Tanner en 1748 l'appelle "Hugues" et il n'y pas trop longtemps, un historien de la littérature confond même "Saltrey" avec "Salisbury" (Urban T. Holmes, *A History of Old French Literature*, New York, Crofts, 1948, 45). Sur l'identité du moine et la datation incertaine de son oeuvre, voir Eduard Mall, "Zur Geschichte der Legende vom Purgatorium des heiligen Patricius", in *Romanische Forschungen* VI (1891), 139-197; F. W. Locke, "A New Date for the Composition of the *Tractatus de Purgatorio sancti Patricii*", in *Speculum* XL (1965), p 641-646; Robert Easting, "The date and dedication of the *Tractatus de Purgatorio Sancti Patricii*", in *Speculum* LIII (1978), p 778-783; Yolande de Pontfarcy, "Le Tractatus de Purgatorio Sancti Patricii de H. of Saltrey, sa date et ses sources", in *Peritia* III (1984), p 460-480.

[9] Voir James Carney, *The Problem of St. Patrick*, Dublin, 1961; Philippe De Félice, *L'Autre Monde, mythes et légendes. Le Purgatoire de saint Patrice*, Paris, 1911, 31.

[10] L'origine du sanctuaire appelé Purgatoire de saint Patrice reste mystérieuse. La légende fait remonter sa fondation à saint Patrice; nous croyons que le sanctuaire est d'une haute antiquité et qu'il pourrait être un héritage du monachisme primitif en Irlande; en plus, le texte du *Tractatus* semble avoir été influencé par de vieux exemples irlandais, notamment par l'immram, genre du voyage.

[11] Sur ces "pèlerinages littéraires", voir Peter De Wilde, "Les pèlerinages au Purgatoire de saint Patrice en Irlande", in *Serta Devota in memoriam Guillelmi Lourdaux*, Mediaevalia Lovaniensa, Louvain, Universitaire Pers, 1995, vol. 2 p 401-440; Eileen Gardiner, *Medieval Visions of Heaven and Hell. A Sourcebook*, Garland Medieval Bibliographies vol. 11, New York, Garland, 1993, 151-178.

[12] Nous employons l'édition de texte de Jeanroy et Vignaux, *Voyage au Purgatoire de saint Patrice; Visions de Tindal et de saint Paul, textes languedociens du quinzième siècle (Toulouse Bibl. Municipale ms. 894)*, Toulouse, 1903, accompagnée d'une bonne introduction. Voir également D. D. R. Owen, *The Vision of Hell: Infernal Journeys in Medieval French Literature*, New York, Barnes, 1971.

[13] La plupart des personnages mentionnés dans le *Tractatus* sont historiques, tout comme les couvents et les autres lieux; le texte spécifie qu' Owein a visité le purgatoire sous le règne du roi Etienne (1135-1154) et qu'il fonctionnait d'interprète pour les Cisterciens qui avaient discrètement commencé leur "conquête" de l'Irlande. Il est vrai que le *Tractatus* a été un bon moyen de propagande. Né de la conjonction de l'expansion cistercienne et normande (invasion de 1169) et de la fascination que l'Irlande exerça sur les nouveaux-venus, le *Tractatus* charrie dans certaines versions les "messages" politiques de son époque: "Mult dei, dist il, bien servir ceaus / E tuz de l'ordre de Cysteaus; / Ausi les devez volentiers / En vostre reaume aver mult chiers. / Ne vi genz, bien vus dis pur veir, / En repoos si grant glorie aveir / Cum cez de l'ordre de Cysteaus. / Pur ceo, honurer deit l'um plus ceaus" (Brit. Lib. Cotton Domit. A IV, *Purgatorium Sancti Patricii Gallico carmine, a Monacho Saltriensis Monasterii*, fol. 264 d, vers 1329-1336). Sur l'origine du sanctuaire, la naissance du pèlerinage et les sources historiques du *Tractatus*, voir Haren et Pontfarcy, *o.c.*, 7-34.

[14] C'est le cas pour Brit. Lib. Cotton Domit. A IV, qui contient des chroniques (*Cronicon Angliae a tempore Brittonum ad tempora H.6*, fol. 1-57a; *Cronicon ab orbe condito ad annum 1469*, fol. 247-256b), et pour un grand nombre d'autres versions du *Tractatus*.

[15] Il y a deux manuscrits du récit de William Staunton: le ms. du Brit. Libr. Royal 17 B XLIII (décrit par WARD, *o.c.*, II, 484), et le ms. Brit. Libr. Add. 34.193 (Ward, o.c., II 487). On trouve une édition critique du premier de ces manuscrits chez George Ph. KRAPP, *The Legend of Saint Patrick's Purgatory. Its later Literary History*, Baltimore, 1900, 54-77. Robert Easting a édité les deux versions: S*t. Patrick's Purgatory. Two versions of Owayne Miles and The Vision of William of Stranton together with the long text of the Tractatus de Purgatorio sancti Patricii*, The Early English Text Society 298, Oxford University Press, 1991. Le manuscrit Royal 17 B XLIII, dont nous nous sommes servi puisqu'il nous paraît plus proche de l'original, commence ainsi: "Here begynneth the revelacion the which William Staunton saw in Patrik is purgatorie the friday next after the fest of the exaltacion of the crosse in the yere of owre lord MCCCCIX. Y William Staunton born in the bisshoprycke of Dereham of Englond, bi goddes grace entred in to the purgatorie of seint Patrik in the bisshopriche of Cleghire in Irlande the VIII owre bi fore the none of the friday next after holyrode day in harvest. I was put in by the prior of seint Mathew of the same purgatorie with precession and devougte prayers of the same priour; and the Covent toke me on orison to blesse me with and to write the first worde in forehede, the which prayer is this: 'Ihesu Christe fili dei vivi misereri michi peccatori' "(fol 133 v°). Voir Easting, *o.c.*, 78. Easting estime que la leçon "Stranton" dans le ms. Additional est la bonne, en s'appuyant sur le fait que dans l'évêché de Durham il y avait un village nommé Stranton. Pourtant, il admet qu'en 1380 et plus tard, une famille appelée "Staunton" est attestée dans le comté de Meath, donc tout près du Purgatoire. Il me semble que ce fait ne peut relever de la coïncidence: William semble fort bien connaître l'Irlande et la région de Station Island. "Staunton" serait ainsi la lectio difficilior dans le ms. Royal qui, nous croyons, est plus proche de l'original pour un grand nombre de raisons (qu'Easting énumère d'ailleurs lui-même en introduisant son édition de texte).

[16] Saint Jean de Bridlington, saint populaire dans le Yorkshire à la fin du XIVe et au début du XVe siècle. Il mourut prieur de Bridlington le 10 octobre 1379. Sainte Ive (ordinairement Ia, Ye ou Ya) est probablement une des missionnaires qui accompagnèrent saint Patrice en Irlande, et dont la popularité eut son apogée en 1410-1426. Quitike = Quethiock. Voir Krapp, *o.c.*, 57-58; De Félice,o.c., 61.

[17] "And than y went forthe that way and sone ther appered to me many fereful and horrible spirites of the which y was moche afered and dred. And summe of tho spirites had IIII visages, summe with VII hornes and summe with V; summe had a visage in every elbowe, summe on every kne. And thei maden to me an hudious noyse..." (fol. 134-135).

[18] Cette traduction, que nous avons corrigée par endroits, est de De Félice, *o.c.*, 62-63.

[19] Nous retrouvons ici un élément qui va à l'encontre de ce que prétend Jacques Le Goff: c'est l'existence du *refrigerium*, qui, selon Le Goff, disparaît à partir de la fin du XIIe siècle: "Le feu qui a représenté au XIIe siècle le lieu même de la purgation en

a chassé le froid. La naissance du Purgatoire donne le coup de grâce au *refrigerium* [...]" (Le Goff, *La Naissance du Purgatoire*, Paris, Gallimard, 1981, 266).

[20] Saint Jean montre deux tours à William: l'une était pleine de feu, l'autre de glace et de neige. Chauffées à blanc dans la première, les âmes étaient ensuite jetées dans la seconde. Des serpents, des crapauds, des vers horribles les mordaient cruellement: les bêtes venimeuses étaient les dentelles et les armes des mauvais évêques. Ceux qui brûlaient dans le feu suivant étaient aussi gonflés que des tonneaux. Des reptiles les suçaient jusqu'au moment où leur corps avait repris sa forme normale; ensuite, ils les piquaient de nouveau pour les faire enfler. Des voix criaient: "Jésus-Christ, Fils du Dieu du Ciel, juge juste, vengez nous." C'étaient des religieux, moines, chanoines ou autres, qui auraient dû vivre d'abstinence. Ceux qui demandaient vengeance étaient les malheureux qui auraient pu être aidés avec ce que les premiers avaient dépensé en folles prodigalités.

[21] On constate ce changement curieux du pont de l'épreuve, par lequel ne peut passer que le vrai pénitent. Le soi-disant "Jenseitsbrücke", un élément que l'on retrouve déjà dans la littérature classique de l'Orient, est donc devenu la punition éternelle d'un seul pécheur et non plus l'épreuve par laquelle toutes les âmes sont forcées de passer. Voir l'excellente étude de Peter Dinzelbacher, *Die Jenseitsbrücke im Mittelalter*, Diss. Univ. de Vienne (104), 1973.

[22] "Finis revelacionum penalium" (fol. 144 r°).

[23] Dans le manuscrit Royal 17 B XLIII, on trouve "dépouillé par des Juifs". Le ms. Add. 34.193 porte "dépouillé par des voleurs" (fol. 146 r°). Voir Krapp, o.c., 73 et Easting, o.c., 232-233. La présence d'une corde à cet endroit surprend quelque peu et ne s'explique point.

[24] Mise à part l'imitation apparente du récit d' H. de Saltrey, on remarque de nombreuses ressemblances avec des visions précédentes, surtout avec le système descriptif de la *Visio Pauli*.

[25] "Wherfore al cristen men that heryn or redyn this, I beseche yow for the love of God that ye have me in yowre praier, and ye shul be yn myne. Explicit." (Royal 17 B XLIII fol. 148 v°). La fin d'Add. 34.193 semble manquer.

[26] Brit. Libr. Royal 10 B IX fol. 36b-44b (papier, fin XVe), édité par H. Delehaye, "Le Pèlerinage de Laurent de Pászthó", in *Analecta Bollandiana* XXVII (1908), 35-60. Voir également H. L. D. Ward, *A Catalogue of Romances in the Departement of Manuscripts in the British Museum*, Londres, 1893, II 489; G. Krapp, *o.c.*, 33; De Félice, *o.c.*, 59.

[27] Voir C. M. VAN DER ZANDEN, "Un chapitre intéressant de la *Topographia Hibernica* et le *Tractatus de Purgatorio sancti Patricii*", in *Neophilologus* XII, 1927, 132-137.

[28] K. O. Meinsma, *Middeleeuwsche bibliotheken*, Amsterdam, 1902. Van der Zanden suppose quant à lui que Giraud, frère H. et Jocelin (biographe de saint Patrice) ont puisé à une même source une inspiration commune, mais l'ont utilisée différemment; si Van der Zanden a raison, cette source doit être une tradition orale

similaire à celle que rapporte le *Tractatus* et qui circulait en Angleterre avant d'être fixée par des auteurs comme le moine de Saltrey. Chose curieuse: le ms. Royal 13 B VIII de la British Library, datant de la fin du XIIe siècle, renferme entre autres une copie de la *Topographia* et un *Tractatus* arrivé au terme de son évolution.

[29] W. Caxton, *Golden Legend*, réédité par William Morris, 422: "As touchyng this pytte or hole, whyche is named saynt Patrykes purgatorye, somme holde opynyon that the second patryke whiche was an abbot and no bysshop, that God shewed to hym this place of purgatorye, but certeynly suche a place there is in Yrelonde wherein many men have been, and yet dayly goon in and come ageyn, and somme have had there mervayllous vysions and seen grysly and horryble paynes, of whome there been bookes maad as of Tundale and other".

[30] *De vita s. Patricii.* Lib. II. Auctore Richardo Stanihursto Dubliniensi. Anvers, MDLXXXVII, 65-66: "Verum qui nostra memoria in hunc sese locum compingunt, nullum sibi terrorem injici sentiunt, nisi forte eos arctior somnus complectatur."

[31] Un moine du monastère d'Eymstadt, en Hollande, faisait le pèlerinage au Purgatoire. Comme il était sans argent, on lui refusait longtemps l'entrée du sanctuaire. Finalement, le moine réussit à triompher des obstacles et obtint la permission d'entrée; il se soumit au jeûne et fut enfermé dans la cave. Pendant une nuit entière, il y resta accroupi, tremblant de peur (ou de froid?) et s'attendant à voir apparaître l'armée des démons. Le lendemain matin, lorsqu'on lui ouvrit la porte, il n'avait eu la moindre vision. Le moine se rendit à Rome et se plaignit au pape Alexandre VI; celui-ci, convaincu que ce purgatoire n'était qu'une imposture, ordonna la destruction du sanctuaire. Elle fut exécutée en grande pompe le jour même de la fête de saint Patrice, en 1497. Voir *Acta Sanctorum Boll. Mart.*, vol. II, le 17 mars, paragraphes 48 à 50. Le fait est rapporté aussi dans les *Annales de l'Ulster*, à la date de 1497, et par James Ware, *Gesta Hibernorum. The Antiquities and history of Ireland*, Londres, 1705. Voir aussi De Félice, *o.c.*, 71-72; Krapp, *o.c.*, 41-42.

[32] "The people understanding out of the History of the Knight, and other ancient Bookes, that this was not the Purgatory which Patricke had from God, although the people resorted from it". Voir *Annales de l'Ulster*, chez Jones, *Treatise of saint Patrick's Purgatory, containing the Description, Originall, Progresse and Demolition of that superstitious place*, Londres, 1647, 121.

[33] *Pontici Virunii viri doctissimi Britannicae Historiae Libri VI.* [Col.] Augustae Cindelicorum, Anno a Christo nato 1534. Cité d'après Krapp, *o.c.*, p 42-43.

[34] "Quae quidem Trophonii fabula mihi adeo videtur similis ei quae de Patricii antro, quod est in Hybernia fertur, ut altera ex altera nata credi possit. Tametsi non desunt etiam hodie permulti qui descendunt, sed prius triduano enecti ieiunio, ne capite sane ingrediantur. Qui descendunt, aiunt sibi ridendi libidinem in omni vita ademptam." Voir *Erasmi Roterdami Adagiorum Chiliades tres ac centuriae fere totidem.* [Col.] Venetiis in Aedibus Aldi mense sept. MDVIII. Cité d'après Krapp, o.c., 43. Pendant l'Antiquité, l'antre de Trophonius à Lebedaea était très connu (ex. chez Pausanias, IX, 39, 4-14); selon une tradition populaire, celui qui y entrait pouvait voir les choses de l'Autre Monde.

[35] FROISSART, *Oeuvres complètes*, éd. Kervyn de Lettenhove, tome XV (Bruxelles, 1871), 145-154.

[36] "Ieu me condormi [...]; ieu caziey, ayssi coma si cazes del cel". Bibl. Munic. de Toulouse, ms. 894 fol 17 r°-17v°. "E ayssi totz assegutz per lo lassec e per lo trebalh que aviam passat am la engoyssessa que cascun se pot pessar nos adormim [...]". Fol. 38 v°.

[37] Pászthó: "statem iacens procliuus in terram cum letanie recitatione iterata [...] usque ad noctis crepusculum subsequentis iugiter persistebat. Milite vero sic oracionibus persistente, duo maligni spiritus invisibiliter advenerunt". Voir Delehaye, *o.c.*, 50. Staunton: "and there y abode and sumwhat slumbered and slepte". Royal 17 B XLIII folio 133 v°, cité d'après Easting, *o.c.*, 78.

[38] L'étendue de la matière ne permet pas d'entrer dans les détails. Krapp, *o.c.*, *passim*, parle longuement du sujet, tout comme Verdeyen et Endepols, *Tondalus' visoen en St. Patricius' vagevuur*, Gand, 1914-17, t. I, 223-252. Les derniers donnent une liste des traductions ou des adaptations manuscrites et imprimées de la légende en français, néerlandais, breton, espagnol, portugais, catalan, italien, anglais, allemand, suédois, polonais, tchèque et hongrois. Les ouvrages les plus importants qui s'inspirent de la légende sont J. Perez de Montalvan, *Vida y Purgatorio de S. Patricio*, Madrid, 1628 (traduit en français, néerlandais et italien); cette histoire, dont le héros s'appelle Luis Ennius, a servi de source au drame religieux de P. Calderon de la Barca, *El Purgatorio de S. Patricio*, éd. J. E. Hartzenbusch, *Comedias de Don Pedro Calderon de la Barca*, Madrid, 1848, vol. I, 150-166. Ces deux adaptations espagnoles ont été très populaires. Il existe un roman anonyme italien qui, selon Krapp, *o.c.*, 44, appartient à "the picaresque type", ce qui serait remarquable vu sa date d'apparition (1477); ce roman s'intitule *In questo Libro vulgarmente se trata alchuna ystoria breve del re Karlo Imperatore. Poi del nascimento e opere di quelo magnifico cavalier nominato Guerino et prenominato Meschino.* In Venexia, A. Di. XXII de Novembre MCCCCLXXVII. Le Lib. VI, cap. CLXII relate la visite du héros au Purgatoire de saint Patrice; le tout semble être, selon Krapp, une adaptation fantastique de la légende, mais nous n'avons pas vu l'oeuvre même. Un autre ouvrage anonyme remarquable s'intitule *The delightfull History of the Life and Death of that Renowned and Famous St. Patrick, Champion of Ireland*, Londres, 1685. Saint Patrice y serait le héros d'un roman chevaleresque.

Humanism and Good Government: A Burgundian Rendering of the Romuleon *by Roberto Della Porta*

Christiane Raynaud

> "Ne prennoit plaisir quen histoires romaines et es faictz de Jule Cesar, de Pompee, de Hannibal, d'Alexandre le Grand et de telz aultres grandz et haultz hommes, lesquels il vouloit ensuyre et contrefaire".
>
> — Philippe Wielant, Antiquités de Flandres, p. 56

Romuleon is a brief history of Rome written in Latin by the young Benvenuto da Imola, and attributed to Roberto della Porta[1], who worked at the behest of a Spanish chevalier, Gomez d'Albornoz[2], governor of Bologna (1361-1362). A hundred years later, Jean Mielot[3] translated the work into French for Philip the Good. There are six remaining copies[4] of this translation. One of the most richly illustrated[5] is produced for Antoine de Bourgogne[6]. The 322 sheets of parchment were transcribed by David Aubert[7] and the grisailles[8] done by Jean le Tavernier d'Audenarde[9] amongst others. Tavernier d'Audenarde was one of the most original artists at the Court of Burgundy. The iconographic references used in part repeat themes already established in illustrations to the "*Faits des Romains*[10], *l'Histoire ancienne jusqu'à César*[11], and, above all, in Livy's *l'Histoire Romaine*[12]. But they also include a number of new scenes. Faithful to the text, these raised issues from the period in which they were drawn. Thus we discover a coherent, and very Burgundian[13] reflection on the exercise of power and the basis of its legitimacy: the countryside and the architecture are that of the north of France, and the clothes of the fifteenth century. But is this anachronism a traditional formula intended to be didactic? Is it a conscious, deliberate approach to make abstract notions more accessible, and examples from Antiquity more alive to the public, or is it just a profound ignorance of a long-submerged past? While the text, in spite of its limits (Latinism, misinterpretations, etc.), is part of the Humanist current, can this be said of the images as well? Are they not in contradiction with the Humanist approach of a return to the past. To attempt to answer these questions, we need to examine the main lines of the iconographic program: they show the Prince[14] as blessed by the gods (section I), his legitimacy based on a series of military victories (section II), and on good government (section III) based on close consultation with wise counselors.

I. A Prince Blessed by the Gods

The Gods approval gives him a legitimacy which is independent of the sacred[15] elements in his accession to the throne. This very French ritual is evoked in coronation in a somewhat tendentious manner. Respect for the original text and a misinterpretation of Roman institutions does not alone justify the choices made by the artist, which suggest antagonism to the Kingdom of France.

The first representation occurs in Figure 1 as part of a description of the long conflict between Rome and Veii[16]. Wars between Veii and Rome for Fidenes go on during the 5th century. At its very end begins the 10 year long siege, ended by the capitulation of the Etrurian city in 395, by the dictator Camillus. The text evokes the political changes that the lengthy war provoked on both sides. The rubric specifies:

> "comment il y eut une longue et griesve guerre entre les veyetains et les rommains pourquoy fut accomply le nombre des tribuns des chevalliers a toute puissance consulaire. Et les Veyetains a celle cause creerent pour eulz ung roy chascun an". It adds "les rommains amplierent le nombre des tribuns des chevalliers car on en crea huit a tout puissance consulaire. Les veyetains creerent pour eulz ung roy chascun an par le centurion des dignitez".

In the foreground, the picture shows different stages of a violent battle[17]. The banner of the Veii, azure, dotted and bordered with gold recalls the arms of France, and gives the key to the scene taking place in the middle ground.

Rome is seen on the right and a Veian palace to the left in Figure 1. In this mansion[18] a figure is being crowned. He is already seated and dressed in royal robe. The chosen moment is when the open crown, with gold fleurons, is being placed[19] on his head: he is not being given the sacrament. In the text, the coronation happens just prior to the final defeat in order to remedy an already difficult situation. The illustration conveys the same idea, as there are two possible interpretations. The coronation happens after the defeat (*behind)*. However, as in the Middle Ages, the picture reads from the backround[20]. The association with the subsequent defeat of the Veii invalidates or at least questions the legitimacy of the new king. The second coronation is in a picture showing four scenes tracing the life of Hadrian (Figure 5)[21]. It stresses, very simply, that Hadrian succeeded to power in the normal way (that is to say, by adoption)[22] The illustration transposes this rule and shows a coronation by a cleric and a layman before three witnesses.

By contrast, two examples show the privileged relationship that prestigious leaders had with the gods, and in a spectacular way. From this divine relationship they gain an exceptional aura and an incomparable legitimacy.

Folio 156 illustrates the "miracle" that showed the gods approval for Lucius Marcius as he harangues his men, his head surrounded by a halo of flames[23]. After a brief recital of his many exploits, the text quickly describes the incident, perhaps with a hint of scepticism, "It is said that ...". The image, however, adds to the text. Two enemy "logis"[24] are seen about to be surprised by the Romans, show the wood in which part of the Roman Army is hiding. Two groups of six and four "knights" listen to the "inn-keeper", who is the army's elected general and supreme commander. The prodigy is needed because of the election of the general by the army. This procedure is rare, though it is not contrary to the spirit of institutions, as the army is still made of citizens[25]. While he explains his point to his second-in-command, his mouth is wide open, his eyes stick out and his beard is forked. The attention he is attracting by his speech and the flames[26] surrounding his head, give him the appearance of one possessed, in both the ancient and the Christian sense of the word. The miracle provokes astonishment and comments from his soldiers. To the right, one of the knights is leaving, and another puts his hand on his sword, showing he intends following and obeying the signs given by the gods.

The role played by the sacred in Figure 2[27] is very different, because it is Christian. Before his return to Rome, where he becomes emperor, the young Octavius[28] comes to consult Sibyl of Tibur[29]. The Virgin and Child appear, showing their benevolence towards this new dynasty.

Under a blue sky, with the pure and translucent air, the Virgin and Child stand to one side, surrounded by rays of light at the center of a golden mandorla[30]. The Sibyl acknowledges the holy pair and reveals the mystery of the Incarnation to Octavius and his cortege. The prophets take part in the veneration of Christ and his mother. Followed by a companion, she has the air of a young noblewoman. It is more accurate to consider this maid as Sybil's friend than as Octavius's mother *"fille de Julie suer de Jule César"*. Augustus, without his crown, and seen three-quarters from behind, looks surprised. Octavius is not distinguishable from his companions by means of a crown yet. He has only a sheathed scimitar on his left side and his name is written in gold letters on his back. His seven companions share his interest, but the lack of any respect or devotion on their part prove they have remained pagan[31]. The emperor is not adoring the Virgin and the Child in contradiction with the text, and does not understand this special sign of approval.

The piety of a prince is normally sufficient to establish his privileged relationship with the divine. The prince is the intercessor of his people. His devotion has some similarity with ancestor worship (Figure 3)[32]. The rubric summarizes the chapter:

> "comment Jule Cesar entra seurement en alexandrie faignant qu'il vouloit visiter les temples des dieux et les autres beaulx lieux de la cité. En la parfin il descendy en ung temple ou estoit le sepulcre de alexandre le grant filz du roy phelippe de macedonne homme eureux".

As he feels the Egyptian hostility towards his entering Alexandria after his lictors, Caesar acts as if he was visiting the city.

> "Cesar doncques non sourprins par quelque doulceur des choses ne pour or ne pour argent ne pour aornemens des dieux ne aussi pour les murs de la dite ains pour simulee cremeur descendy ou sacraire dun temple ou il y avoit plusieurs sepulcres de roys. Et entre les autres y estoit le sepulcre de alexandre le grant quy fut filz du roy phelippe homme furieux et eureux duquel les os repus en ung lieu sacre se devoient plus tost espardre par tout le monde ainsi qu'il avoit este contraire a tout le monde. Certes il fut ung mal predestine et ung fouldre quy sembloit frapper tous pueples".

Sacraire (*sacrarium*): an ancient Roman shrine or sanctuary in a temple or a home holding sacred objects. The picture brings together the two great conquerors of Antiquity in a dramatic moment; Caesar's visit to Alexander's tomb. It evokes the passing from one Empire to another, and suggests that the gods have deified them both. To develop the idea, the recumbent Alexander, dressed in his armor, is not pictured in full. His head and the upper part of his bust are not visible. The miniaturist thus avoids the problem raised by the needs to decide whether to represent the two princes as equals. His presentation is predominantly symbolic: Caesar is taking the place of the great Captain, but only to join him later in his tomb. For the moment he is climbing the steps leading to the sepulcher. He is already part of the sacred[33]. Seven men at the foot of the steps watch the strange scene with astonishment[34]

In a way, this scene is foreshadowed by the visit of Cato of Utica to the Temple of Jupiter Amon (Alexander claimed to be Amon's son):[35] "*comment Caton et les siens parvindrent a ung temple de Jupiter dit Amon le plus venerable et le plus renomme de tous les autres devant la porte de ce temple se tenoient plusieurs orientaulz quy estoient venuz pour avoir response de Jupiter des choses advenir*". The miniaturist gives the building the same general shape[36] as the tomb, and gives Jupiter's altar and Alexander's sarcophagus the same niches. Cato is kneeling on the ground before the god, in front of the Temple. Caesar is standing in the mausoleum. Their different ways of behaving illustrate their differences in character linked to the difference of their regimes. Cato's attitude, showing respect for a false god, is a premonition of his defeat. He is shown to the left of the picture, on the same side as several people from the East who, on their way to the oracle[38], have given way to him out of respect for his wisdom. To the right, his supporters wait without getting off their horses. They do not take part in this homage. While Cato wears a seemingly eastern costume, has a beard etc., his first man has a burgundian armor, a sallet with the vizor down, and he is holding a spear.

Unless there is some supernatural intervention or divine grace from the Sacrament when feudal homage is paid to the Church, the only real basis of legitimate power is success in battle.

II. A Victorious Prince

Being a successful leader in battle is so important that it leads to the prince, defender of the city usurping the place of the prince who built the city. The presentation of the episode of the founding of Rome[39] is revealing in this respect. The long standing inconographic tradition usually shows Romulus directing the works, or the murder of Remus. In France in the fifteenth Century, this aspect of the story was considered significant, as the French claimed Remus was among their ancestors[40]. The Burgundian Court was aware of the claim, and the version offered here is in some ways its reply. Romulus has his back to the city walls under construction. His clothing contrasts favorably with that of his brother, and his behavior leaves no doubt as to his intentions. Seen three quarters from behind, he is hiding[41] the scepter he holds in his right hand behind his back. He has come to take possession of the town, and he justifies Remus's murder in advance. Remus's duplicity, justifies or at least explains, his murder. The thesis of a preventive tyrannicide has been a familiar one in the Burgundian Court since 1407. The miniaturist shows a double silhouette[42] to remind the spectator that Romulus and Remus are twins, and that this double-headed power is monstrous in character.

As defender of the city, the Prince is first of all a conqueror, in the comparison between the four scenes contrasting Nero's life (Figure 4)[43]. The picture is before the rubric in red at the bottom of the first column:

> "Comment neron parricide commença ses occisions a claudius empereur en mengant les champeignons venimeux. Il occist aussi par venin britannicus son frere. Et fist occire sa mere puis ala veoir le corps mort blasmant ou loant ses membres. Le chap. XVIIIe Suetonius".

Hadrian's life (Figure 5)[44] underlines this idea:

> "Cy commence le dixieme et dernier livre de ce traittie nomme Romuleon parlant des fais des empereurs cesares depuis lempereur Adryen jusques a Constantin le grant empereur. Et contient en soy XXXVII Chapitres".

The two princes are opposite by the way they came to power (Nero tried to drown his mother[45], Hadrian was crowned in the normal way) and then by the way they left it (Nero consulted astrologers on his future which could only be bad as a result of his crimes[46], Hadrian, after a full life, having chosen his successor, put an end to his sufferings by poisoning himself, and was then deified)[47]. Seneca's suicide and the burning of Rome under Nero's rule contrast with Hadrian's exploits: armed with a club, pictured here as a new Hercules, he gallops off on his horse to conquer vast territories before climbing the slopes of Mount Etna[48], while his men make their way towards a strongly defended town. In neither instances does the enemy appear. The emphasis is on the land which is the object of the conquest, and on the wild character of the mountain. Nero's murderous madness, as he faces his friends[49] and the city[50], thus appears event more scandalous.

A victory in war was traditionally[51] followed by the surrender of the conquered town (history books and chronicles often recall the moment when city inhabitants come together to give the keys to the victor and ask for mercy) or by the victor's triumphal entry into Rome on his return. As concerns Ardea[52], the rubric states:

> "comment Marcus giganeus desconfy les ennemis assiegans la cite de ardee et les mist soubz le joug de servitude a leur grant vitupere. Et luy triumphant sen revint a romme menant devant son charriot triumphal curillus duc des volsques".

The miniaturist appears to have gone directly to Livy. Thus, in the middle ground, the nine foot-soldiers who come out of the town of Ardea and pass in front of the cross marking the limits of its territory, represent the rebellious crowd who will pillage the property of the aristocracy in the surrounding countryside. In the foreground, seven inhabitants in long shirts, their heads bare, are on their knees rendering the keys of the town to the consul Marcus Geganius. At the head of the Roman cavalry, Geganius holds out his right hand to take them. With his clenched left fist he shows his hostility to the Ardei. Beside him is a rider turning his saddle and holding a white banner with a gold cross. He is one of the nobles from the town who called on the Romans to help them. The main character in the scene, however remains the consul.

The scene of the triumph[53]—"*Comment la famine grevoit lost des romains et la pestilence traveilloit les françois qui furent tous desconfis et occis par le dictateur camillus quy sen revint triumphant a romme. Et fut appele romulus pere du païs et de la chose publique*"—following Camillus's campaign against the "French," posed a problem for the miniaturist. It is neither shown as a civil[54] entry of a king, nor as an entry under arms, a variant of the former, sanctioning the town and its inhabitants[55]. To show the specificity of this Roman triumph, the inhabitants of the town are not shown, and the army crosses the city by the shortest route, going from gate to gate, in good order, without occupying it. The dictator's rear guard, in the foreground, consists of foot-soldiers who have an exotic, Eastern look to avoid any confusion with the events occurring in Burgundy at the time. The main body of the troops on horseback and on the lower ground, seen three-quarters from behind in Burgundian military equipment rush through a gate. Camillus and the Roman banner close the procession. Although victorious, the dictator does not abuse his power. "Ainsi comme Camillus saulva le païs en guerre samblablement le saulva il en paix. Et se fust tantost despouille de sa dictature".

Thus, a prince must show personal leadership in military operations, but to govern well, must also surround himself with wise counselors.

III. The Prince and his Council

Rather than comparing the different forms of government (monarchy, republic or empire), the iconographic program presents an opposition between good government and bad government the latter of which is represented by tyranny.

The juxtaposition of Caesar giving ear to the deliberating Senate is not done to compare the relative merits of monarchy and parliamentary government (Figure 6)[56]. The Senate is not shown as a possible alternative. The republican heritage is only represented by its first magistrates, the consuls, or one of the dictators. The large painting at the beginning of Book VIII, while not illustrating a specific passage, is, for half of it, given over to debate between fifteen senators divided into three groups. The subject under discussion is being presented by one of the four speakers, the oldest and most dignified, who holds a scepter in his right hand. Two others are stating the case of a more numerous left-hand group of eight. The first of them is speaking. To the right, five senators are in disagreement with those in Caesar's party. The Senate is questioning the soundness of restoring the monarchy, without reconsidering the power of the prince. The audience to the left allows one to sense the unease felt by Caesar's adversaries. In the foreground, the two dogs fighting are symbolic. At the back of the hall, there is a small group of men talking or plotting. A young nobleman, with a falcon on his right wrist[57] and a cane in his left hand and three witnesses, are assisting the homage being rendered by a person kneeling, his right hand in that of the prince. At the request of a counselor to the right of the prince, the man is taking off his hat. Special attention is given to this mark of deference and to Caesar's attitude, his left hand is on his waist asserting his power, suggesting that the accusations against him[58] are not entirely without substance. The luxury of his clothing is pejorative.

Corruption and intrigue[59] to win the favors of the prince at any price, as intrinsic aspects of tyranny, are severely judged. Caesar, (Figure 7)[60] with his closed crown, his regal collar, his robes and his central position, is set off from the courtiers, shown in a circle around him. In the middle ground, one of them lowers his head sadly[61], while in the foreground, two compete in showing off their authority. Their elbows partly hide the prince's arm; a way of showing the struggle for influence between rival factions, each striving to win his favor. Caesar is apparently supporting the more arrogant, seen three-quarters from behind, with his mouth open, making his point to the officer on his right. He is the only one wearing a helmet and has his left arm on the guard of his sword (a large one to be held with two hands). The image (Figure 8)[62] shows that, with Caligula, much ground has been covered going from Principate to Empire, although tyranny has also progressed. The courtiers are now at a respectful distance from the Prince, either behind or beside him. To the left, the two courtiers moving away are Cassius Chaerea and Cornelius Sabinus[63]. The fact that the hands of the others are not visible or are hidden and the hat of one of them is peculiar and pointed, shows that they act "*non mie sans le sceu daucuns tres puissans affranchis et des prevosts du pretoire*". Caligula's attitude explains and justifies the implications of the picture. He has a scepter in his right hand, and is fascinated by his own image in a richly decorated mirror. The limner is denouncing the excesses of absolute power, which lead to madness[64] and an inordinate desire for wealth.

The contrast is made with the exceptional personality of Emperor and philosopher Marcus Aurelius (161-180). Already on Tertullian's account (*Apol. V*) he is "Marcus Aurelius the wise", model of virtue[65], in spite of his remaining pagan.

The text frequently shows the wisdom of the Emperor Hadrian, given over to the study of philosophy[66], showing respect to the Senate "*Nul prince ne honnoura le senat oncques plus quil fist*", choosing new senators from amongst "*les pauvres sans vices*", and above all surrounding himself with wise counselors, "*Il eut tous iours en sa compaignie docteur en loiie et en decret et especialement scevola homme tres escellent*".

In Folio 304 verso, Marcus Aurelius, wearing a crown and the robes of a philosopher, is seated on a richly decorated cruciform dais throne. He is consulting an enormous book on the lectern in front of him. His left hand is giving approval (after having referred to the text), to the jurist who is developing a second argument with great care. Marcus Aurelius is pictured taller than him and the others in the scene. He makes his decisions on his own. He listens to the jurists before deciding, but the placing of the book in the picture shows that what is written plays a considerable part in what he decides. His accepting the authority of the written texts, and his role as a lawgiver, are aspects that are emphasized by the limner, that Marcus Aurelius shared with Charles the Bold, Duke of Burgundy.

Taken as a whole the iconographic program used in the grisailles illustrating Roberto della Porta's *Romuleon* appears to illustrate the realities of Burgundian political life in the XVth C, rather than that evoked in the text. This anachronism, aimed at helping the reader understand the way institutions that are foreign to his way of thinking really function, is not always intentional, and illustrates a genuine ignorance. Certainly, this desire to use examples from classical Antiquity as propaganda can lead to the illuminators deforming the images to better fit what is required by the polemic. The illustration thus takes up the main lines of Charles the Bold's aristocratic program, when, at the start of his reign and at the head of the League of the Public Weal, he was involved in a terrible struggle with Louis XI, and even raised doubts about the way the Valois exercised power. But the illustration is not limited to this program, and the illuminators did not cut all links with the text. Thus, with the text in mind they joined hands with the theoreticians, and those in power in Burgundy, and, as advocated by the Duke himself, promoted the image of strong leadership, which was inspired by the antique model but far removed from the tyranny which had led to the capricious princes and obsequious manoeuvres of the Res Publica. To effectively counter the French model, the Burgundian Court tried, in effect, to create a founded alternative, amongst other things, of the prestige of the Roman institutions, if not by applying them in exactly the same way.

NOTES

[1] Gomez d'Albornoz (dead in 1377) is the nephew of Cardinal Gil Alvarez Carillo of Albornoz (1310-1367), legate in Bologna in 1356. He is the founder of the University College for young Spanish named after him.

[2] P. Perdrizet, "Jean Miélot, l'un des traducteurs de Philipe le Bon," *Revue d'Histoire littéraire,* 1907, t XIV, 472-482; *Manuscrits datés et conservés en Belgique,* tome IV, 1461-1480, notices établies sous la direction de F. Massaï et de M. Withek, éd. scientifiques E. Story-Scientia, Bruxelles, Gand, 1982, 43, n° 467

[3] J. Montfrin "Le goût des lettres antiques à la cour de Bourgogne au Xve siècle", *Bulletin de la Société nationale des antiquaires de France,* 1967, 286-287; C. Willard, "Isabel of Portugal patroness of humanism", *Miscellanea di studi e ricerche sul quattrocento francese a cura di F. Simone,* Turin, 1966, 538

[4] To the list suggested by B. Woledge, *Bibliographie des romans et nouvelles en prose française antérieurs à 1500* Genève (Droz), Lille (Giard) 1954, 2e édition 1975 (Société des publications romanes et françaises, XLII, 113) may be added Arsenal's manuscript: *Romuleon, soixante figures en 410 planches reproduisant les miniatures initiales du ms.677* de la Bibliothèque de l'Arsenal, Paris, Les joyaux de l'Arsenal, Imprimerie Berthaud, France, 1910.

[5] G. Doutrepont, *La littérature française à la cour des ducs de Bourgogne Philippe le Hardi, Jean sans Peur, Philippe le Bon, Charles le Téméraire,* Paris, Champion, 1909, 141, notes 4 et 5, 142, notes 3 et 4, 143, note 1; J. Van den Gheyn, *Catalogue des manuscrits de la Bibliothèque royale de Belgique,* Bruxelles, 1901-1948; F. Lyna, *Les principaux manuscrits à peintures de la Bibliothèque royale de Belgique,* t.III, 2e partie éditée par Mme P. Pantens, Bruxelles, Bibliothèque royale Albert 1er, 1989, Notice 311, 456-458.

[6] P. Lauer, *Déchiffrement de l'ex-libris du grand bâtard de Bourgogne* Paris, Nogent-le-Rotrou, Imprimerie de Daupeley gouverneur 1923, *Bibliothèque de l'Ecole des Chartes,* 1923, t. LXXXIV.

[7] G. Samaran et R. Marchal, *Catalogue des manuscrits en écriture latine portant des indications de date, de lieu ou de copistes,* Paris, CNRS 1959, t.II, 129. A. Pinchart, *Miniaturistes enlumineurs et calligraphes employés par Philippe le Bon et Charles le Téméraire et leurs oeuvres,* Bruxelles, Imp. Bols, Wittouck, 1865; P. d'Ancona, E. Aeschlimann, *Dictionnaire des miniaturistes du Moyen Age et de la Renaissance dans les différentes contrées de l'Europe",* 2e édition, Milan, U. Hoepli, 1949; J. W. Bradley, *"A dictionary of miniaturists, illuminators, calligraphers and copyists with references to their works and notices of their patrons from the establishment of christianity to the 18th century",* London, B. Quaritch, 1887-1889; F. de Mely, *Signature de primitifs, les miniaturistes,* s.l.n.d. in folio.

[8] *Miniatures en grisailles,* Catalogue par P. Cockshaw, Bruxelles, Bibliothèque royale Albert 1er, 1986, notice 17, 34.

[9] On Jean Le Tavernier and the context: J. P. Lecat *Le siècle de la Toison d'Or,* Paris, Flammarion, 1986; W. Prevenier, *The Burgundian Netherlands,* W. Prevenier et W. Blockmans picture research by a Blockmans Delva foreword by Richard Waughan, Cambridge, New York, Cambridge University Press, 1986. F. Winkler, *Die flämische Buchmalerei des 15 und 16 Jahrhunderts Künstler und Werke von den Brüdern Van Eyck bis zu Simon Bening,* mit 91 Lichtdrucktafeln, Leipzig, 1925; K. Winkler, "Studien zur Geschichte der niederländischen Miniaturmalerei des 15. und 16. Jahrhunderts", *Jahrbuch der Kunsthistorischen Sammlungen des Allerhöchsten Kaiserhauses* 32, 1915. "What role did Jean Miélot play?" H. Focillon, *Le peintre des miracles de Notre Dame",* Paris, 1950; *Miracles de Notre Dame,* collected by Jean Miélot, secretary to Philip the Good, duke of Burgundy, reproduced in facs. from Douce ms. 374 in the Bodleian library for John Malcolm of Poltalloch with text, introduction, and annotated analysis by George F. Warner, Westminster Nichols and sons, 1885, Publication of Roxburghe Club. *Les miracles de Notre Dame* compilés par Jehan Miélot, Etude concernant trois manuscrits du XVe s. ornés de grisailles par le comte A. de Laborde, Paris, Société française de reproductions de manuscrits à peintures, 1929; Christine de Pisan, *Epître d'Othéa, déesse de la prudence, à Hector, chef des Troyens,* reproductions de cent miniatures du ms. 9392 de Jean Miélot par J. Van den Gheyn, Bruxelles, Vroment (s.d.); *Speculum Humanae Salvationis,* texte critique, trad. inédite de Jean Miélot (1448). Les sources et l'influence iconographique principalement sur l'art alsacien du XVe siècle, avec la reproduction en 140 pl. du ms. de Sélestat, de la série complète des vitraux de Mulhouse, des vitraux de Colmar, de Wissembourg, éd. par J. Lutz et P. Perdrizet, Mulhouse, Imprimerie de E. Meininger, 1902-1907

[10] On *Faits des Romains*: R. L. Wyss *Die Caesarteppiche und ihr ikonographisches Verhältnis zur Illustration des "Faits des Romains" im 14 und 15 Jahrhunderts,* Bern, K. J. Wyss, 1957; L. F. Flutre, *Les manuscrits des "Faits des Romains",* Paris, Hachette, 1932; L. F. Flutre, *Li "Fait des Romains" dans les littératures française et italienne du XIIIe au XVIe siècles,* Paris, Hachette, 1932

[11] On *l'Histoire ancienne jusqu'à César:* Doris Oltrogge, *Die Illustrations Zyklen zur Histoire ancienne jusqu'à César,* 1250-1400, Frankfurt am Main, Paris, P. Lang, 1989, Europäische Hochschulschriften 28 Kunstgeschichte 94.

[12] On *l'Histoire romaine* by Tite Live: H. Omont, Bibliothèque Nationale, Département des Manuscrits, *Histoire Romaine* de Tite Live, traduction française de

Pierre Bersuire, reproduction des 63 miniatures des mss. fr. 273 et 274 de la B.N., Paris, Imprimerie de Catala (1922). *Catalogue of the Livy of the Bâtard de Bourgogne*, London, Sotheby, 1931. P. Durrieu, "Le Tite Live de la Sorbonne et le forum romain", Paris E. Leroux, 1915, *Extraits des Monuments Piot,* t. XXI, — B. Gagnebin *Le Tite Live du duc de Berry*, Genève, s.n. 1959, p. 193-214, *Geneva*, n.s. VII, 1959. A. de la Mare, "Florentine manuscripts of Livy in the fifteenth century", London Routledge and Kegan Paul, Toronto, University of Toronto Press, 1971, 177-199, extrait de Livy, ed. by T. A. Dorey. I Zacker, *Die Livius Illustration in der Pariser Buchmalerei* (1370-1420), Berlin Zentrale Universitäts druckerei, 1971 Inaug-Diss. Philosophie des Fachbereichs Kunstwissenschaften Berlin Freien Universität 1971, Bibl. 1-6.

[13] E. Gaucher, "La confrontation de l'idéal chevaleresque et de l'idéologie politique en Bourgogne au XVe siècle: l'exemple de Jacques de Lalaing, Presses Universitaires de Reims, *Rencontres Médiévales en Bourgogne (XIV-XVe siècles)*, 1992, 2, 3-27. Y. Lacaze, "Le rôle des traditions dans la genèse d'un sentiment national au XVe s.", *Bibliothèque de l'Ecole des Chartes*, t. XXIX, 1971, Paris, 1972, 303-380. J. Lemaire, "La conception de l'histoire chez les chroniqueurs bourguignons d'après les prologues de leurs oeuvres", Göppingen, Künmerle, 1991, p. 235-249, extrait de *l'Histoire et littérature du Moyen Age*, Actes du colloque du Centre d'Etudes Médiévales de l'Université de Picardie, Amiens, 24 mars 1985. A. J. Vanderjagt, "Burgundian Political Ideas between Laurentius Pignon and Guillaume Hugonet", *Fifteenth-Century Studies*, 1984, 197-213.

[14] Consul, propretor, dictator, king, emperor, whatever their titles, they first get their legitimacy from God or gods. Poor knowledge of antique institutions (Roman, Greek or Carthaginian) and transpositions for didactic purpose combine in different proportions in different cases. J. Gaudemet, *Les institutions de l'Antiquité,* 3e édition, Montchrestien, 1991, M. Humbert, *Institutions politiques et sociales de l'Antiquité*, Dalloz, 1984 Transposition consists of the operation by which the form or the content are changed by passing from one domain to another, from a language, that of the text, to another, that of the image. Thus the consuls are evoked in the images of a person crowned like a king or emperor, or put forth as a military leader.

[15] Translator and illuminators tend to turn anointing benediction into a royal unction equivalent.

[16] M. Le Glay, J. L. Voisin, Y. Le Bohec, *Histoire romaine*, Paris, PUF, 1991

[17] In a battle, warriors use their spears first (foreground) then they fight hand to hand with sword (second line) with on the Roman side, a preparation by archers.

[18] In the manuscript, walls of castles, of palaces, of temples have wide openings through which we can see scenes happening inside.

[19] When anointing ritual is evoked in "*Grandes Chroniques de France*", most often the scene chosen is that when 12 pairs of France, 6 clerics and 6 laymen perform a highly symbolic gesture. cf. P. Contamine, "Les pairs de France au sacre des rois (XVe siècle), nature et portée d'un programme iconographique" in *De Jeanne d'Arc aux guerres d'Italie. Figures, images et problèmes du XVe siècle* (Orléans,

Paradigme, 1994, 111-138), *Bulletin de la Société nationale des antiquaires de France*, 1988.

[20] M. Pastoureau, *L'étoffe du diable, une histoire des rayures et des tissus rayés*, La Librairie du XXe siècle (Paris, Seuil, 1991 12-13), in fact, it happens before. The battle on the foreground has one battle only, two different stages in the conflict between Rome and Veii.

[21] Folio 301 verso, the picture recapitulates and conveys the main stages of his life evoked in chapters I, II and III of the 10th book of *Romuleon*.

[22] In the Empire, the normal succession proceeds via the adoption of a successor by the emperor.

[23] The prodigy is related by Valerius Maximus (1.6.2) and Pline (2,241) who is referring to Valerius Antias. The mystic theme is already given by Iule Lavinia (en 2 880.686; 7, 71-77) and Servius Tullius (Liv. I 39; 1-3). R. Bloch, *Les prodiges dans l'Antiquité classique* (*Grèce, Etrurie, Rome*), Paris, PUF, 1963, 164., Mythes et Religions (2). M. G. Grossel, "Démons et merveilles... et raison. La peinture de la religion antique" dans *Li Fet des Romains, in Fées, dieux et déesses au Moyen Age*, Centre d'Etudes médiévales et dialectales de Lille III, Colloque des 24 et 25 septembre 1993, to be published in *Bien dire et bien apprandre*. A. Neyton, *Le merveilleux religieux dans l'Antiquité. Aspects choisis* (Paris, Letouzey et Ané, 1991).

[24] After the failure of the Carthaginian attack against camp of the Roman Army in Spain, and when Maricus has been elected chief, he decides to attack. Two Carthaginian camp are seized (211 B.C.) (Tite Live 25-38, 23 et 39; 1 à 18): "*ainsi en une nuit et ung jour deux logis furent ruez jus*". The Romans made an attack by surprise: "*Il y avoit ou mylieu une vallee avec plante d'arbres une cohorte des rommains sestoit muchie ou mylieu de la forest et les autres furent menez en silence devers les ennemis voisins*".

[25] C. Nicolet, *Le métier de citoyen dans la Rome républicaine* (Paris, Gallimard, 1976, 144). Tite Live does not call him *Imperator* but *Dux* (26. 2-1-2) and this procedure has been forbidden by plebeian tribunes. Marcius has been held against him to have unduly taken the title of propretor. cf. M. Bonnefond-Coudry, *Le sénat de la République romaine de la guerre d'Hannibal à Auguste: pratiques délibératives et prises de décision* (Bibliothèque des Ecoles Françaises d'Athènes et de Rome, fascicule 272, Ecole française de Rome, Palais Farnèse, 1989, 447-455).

[26] The open mouth is pejorative. Flames may be a reminder of winged helmets. F. Garnier, *Le langage de l'image au Moyen Age*, t. II Grammaire des gestes, Paris, Le Léopard d'Or, 81-83.

[27] Folio 279. "*comment gayus octavius (...) auquel la sebille tiburtine monstra l'air estant pur et cler ung cercle empres le soleil ou estoit une vierge et son enffant qu'il aoura*".

[28] Caesar's grand nephew, adopted as his son by testament, is coming back from Appolonie in Illyria where he had studied.

[29] The Sybill of Tibur was honoured almost as a goddess by the Romans. A little temple was built for her close to her cave. Antoine de la Salle in *Le Paradis de la reine Sybille* (Préface D. Poirion, Stock/Moyen Age, 1983, 51) states that she was the tenth Sybill. Martin de Troppau, in the *Chronique des Empereurs*, says she was the author of the verses *Judcii signum*. Sainte Augustine denies it in *La cité de Dieu,* chapter XXVI. However the Church Father agrees with Lactance about Christian prophecies of most Sybilles.

[30] The Illuminator illustrates the rubric and not the text corpus, evoking a mere physical and meteorological phenomenom: "*quant il entra a romme environe leure de tierce lair estant pur et cler ung cercle a la samblance de l'arc ou ciel (chaingny) soudaniement le corps du soleil comme sil demoustrat ainsi que dist orose quil estoit ung seul et tres grant ou monde en qui temps devoit venir celluy quy avoit fait le soleil meismes*".

[31] Octavius's seven companions are in three or four ranks behind him. The further they are standing from him, the more they accumulate pejorative signs: headbands, turned-up noses, mantel tied at the shoulder, excessive luxury of their clothing, turbans, seen in profile or three-quarter behind. Bias stripes or black decorations on the hem discretely show that they are from the same family.

[32] Folio 265.

[33] The word must be understood in its modern meaning as well: *Dictionnaire de la langue française* de Paul Robert:

1. *qui appartient à un domaine interdit et inviolable et fait l'objet d'une vénération religieuse.*

2. *qui est digne d'un respect absolu, qui a un caractère de valeur absolue*. In the Roman religion, *devotio* (a promise to get a significant favour) and *consecratio capitis* (religious condemnation leading to a civil condemnation exile, or death together with confiscation of possessions) are meant to declare somebody *sacer* i.e. to doom him to infernal gods.

[34] Seven men, one of whom seems surprised, are looking at him. They are probably Egyptians. None of them holds the *fasces*, insignia of the right of death or life of Roman lictors.

[35] Folio 261.

[36] Two thin columns support a heavy sloped roof with an indented ridge in gold (folio 265) or silver (261).

[38] Alexandre, who had consulted the oracle, said he was Amon's son, which strengthens the link with the illustration of folio 265, and helps the reader to understand reactions to Cato's death.

[39] Together with the myth of the founding of Rome.

[40] Cf. C. Beaune, "*Naissance de la nation française*", Paris, Gallimard, 1985, 52.

[41] His clothing is short with slit sleeves, sown with black, reversed crescent, a golden star on his hoses. cf. M. Beaulieu, J. Bayle, *Le costume en Bourgogne de Philippe le Hardi à la mort de Charles le Téméraire (1364-1477)*, Paris, PUF, 1956. F. Piponnier, *Costume et vie sociale, La cour d'Anjou, XIVe-XVe siècles*, Paris, Mouton, 1970, Ecole pratique des Hautes Etudes, Sorbonne VI e section

[42] F. Garnier, *Le language de l'image*, t. II, op. *cit., 67-72.*

[43] Folio 292 verso.

[44] Folio 301 verso. Three of them are about Hadrian. *Le premier chapitre comment lempereur adrien filz de Helius adrien cousin de lemperaur Trajan et de pauline sa mere nee en espaigne fut orphelin le Ve an de son eage mais par la faveur de plotine femme dudit traian il fut adopte de luy. Et depuis le laissa successeur de lempire Helius sparcianus.* The second chapter evokes Hadrian's travels and conquests. The third, after a description of his character, tells of his last moments.

[45] A ship whose hull has two hollows, in the stern, close to the bulwarks, with seven men and a woman who is tearing off her clothing. All this evokes the theme of murder prior to the murder of Agrippina.

[46] The bottom part of the picture shows Rome in flames. Nero in royal robe, with seven courtiers around him, is looking at the fire. On his right, an astrologer reads a book whose contents we cannot know. The picture suggests that Nero is afraid of the fire (and not of a comet passing by, as the text says) because he sees in it his death and his everlasting punishment.

[47] Deification is suggested by a gold decor (shining ring) above his head. Hadrian with a white beard (age) holds a poisonous cup and drinks while two candidates to his succession are present (possibly M. Annius Verus, future Marcus Aurelius and T. Aurelius Fulvus Boionius Arrius Antonius, Antonius).

[48] He climbs alone, probably because of the mountains and steep cliffs.

[49] Thus Seneca must commit suicide. In a bathtub Seneca is about to drink poison; the text states that he cut his veins. The illustration does not show the constraints on him, but gives the reason: his wealth (the sumptuous house that shelters him is a measure of it).

[50] The attempt to kill his mother together with Seneca's suicide may be a sign that Nero is, at least morally, responsible for Rome's fire, which is a sanction to his crimes.

[51] This ceremony from Roman Antiquity began in Italy and spread to France in the second half of the XV century. It followed the wars in Italy. Its disposition is inspired by classical texts and sculptures, of which there are many.

[52] Folio 70 verso, F. Lyna, *Les principaux manuscrits à peintures,* op. cit., 456-458, wrongly considers that it is Marcus Giganeus Macerinus triumphant on his return to Rome. P. R. S. Broughton, M. L. Patterson, *the magistrates of the Roman Republic,* published by the American Philological Association, NY 1951, volume 1, 509 BC-100 B.C., 53. M. Giganeus Macerinus was consul in 443 B.C.

[53] Folio 81 verso

[54] B. Guenée, F. Lehoux, *Les entrées royales françaises de 1328 à 1515* (Paris, CNRS, 1968). N. Coulet, "Les entrées solennelles en Provence au XIVe s. Aperçus nouveaux sur les entrées royales françaises au bas Moyen Age", *Ethnologie française*, 1977, VII, 63-82. *Le journal d'un Bourgeois de Paris*, année 1429, dirigée par M. Zinck. See Le Livre de Poche 1989 for an ordinary solemn entry.

[55] F. Autrand, "*Charles VI*", Paris, Fayard, 98-99 pour Rouen.

[56] Folio 234. The picture illustrates the VIIIth book of *Romuleon* in its whole: "*Cy commence le VIIIe livre de ce traittie nomme Romuleon duquel se traitte des fais de Jule Cesar premier empereur des rommains*".

[57] This bird of prey is shown in other manuscripts in the Burgundian Court, in miniatures, or in scenes of court life. (Cf. B van Den Abeele, "*La fauconnerie au Moyen Age, connaissance, affaitage et médecine des oiseaux de chasse d'après les traités latins*" Paris, Klincksieck, coll. Sapience, 1994). It is held by a member of the court or of the assistance (Bruxelles, B.R. 9066, folio 11, *Chroniques et conquêtes de Charlemagne*; Bruxelles, B.R. 9243 folio 1, *Chroniques de Hainaut*; Bruxelles, B.R. 9967, Jean Wauquelin. *Histoire de sainte Hélène,* folio 39; Florence, B.N. Med. Palat. 155 Quinte Curce, *Histoire d'Alexandre le Grand*, folio 13; Paris, B.N., ms. fr. 201, Jean Bouteiller, *La somme rurale*, folio 9 verso: Paris, B.N. ms. fr. 562, Aristote, *Le livre des secrets*, folio7; Paris, B.N., ms. fr. 22457, folio 1, *Les Faiz du Grant Alexandre*, folio 1, etc...

[58] "*Luy tout seul administra a son plaisir la chose publique.*" Precocious accusation. The text quotes oppositions that Caesar could not prevent from being raised, thus when it speaks about his clemency to Cornelius "*de quy les agaits de nuyt il avoit a paynes eschappe*", when he asks for the Egyptian province: "*ne il ne la obtint point par une partie des nobles le contredisant*". "*Il demanda ung tres grant pontificat non mie sans grande contradiction*" and further we read "*mais pour ce que plusieurs le contredisoient il fut constraint de demander le tryumphe a celle fin quil ne fust forcloz du consulat*".

[59] This accusation is not specific to the duke's counselors; it is also in the argument of the members of parliament (cf. F. Autrand, *Naissance d'un grand corps de l'Etat. Les gens du Parlement de Paris* (1345-1454), Thèse de doctorat d'Etat, Paris, 1981, Publications de la Sorbonnne), baillis and sénéchaux (A. Demuger, Guerre Civile et changement du personnel administratif dans le royaume de France de 1400 à 1418: l'exemple des baillis et des sénéchaux, *Francia*, 1978, 151-298).

[60] Folio 273. The picture illustrates a physical and moral description of Caesar.

[61] Like his neighbors, he does not approve the scene happening before him. Are his "masked" adversaries Sextus Pompée, Brutus or Cassius?

[62] Folio 288 verso: " *Comment gayus gallicula fut de haulte estature. Il ot le corps grant et pale couleur le col et les cuisses maigres les yeulx et les temples cavez le fron large (...)*".

[63] After two successive conspiracies have failed, the third one succeeded. It also was hatched in the Senate. Pretorian prefects and two tribunes of pretorian cohorts take part in the conspiracy, Cassius Chaerea and Cornelius Sabinus, and the most powerful liberated people (for example, Calliste).

[64] M. Laharie, *La folle au Moyen Age XI-XIIIe siècles*, Préface de J. Le Goff, Paris, Le Léopard d'Or, 1991.

[65] A. J. Vanderjagt, "*Laurens Pignon O.P. confessor of Philip the Good*" Groningen, Jean Miélot and Cie, 1985.

[66] "*Estudia en philosophie tellement que a son VIIe an il print habit de philosophe*".

"*Marcus se delita en combatre en venerie a prendre oiseaulx et juat tres bien a la pamme mais lestude de philosogphie le revoqua de toutes ces choses et le rendy grave*".

Figure 1 (folio 73 verso)
Veii defeated by the Romans; Coronation of a king in Veii

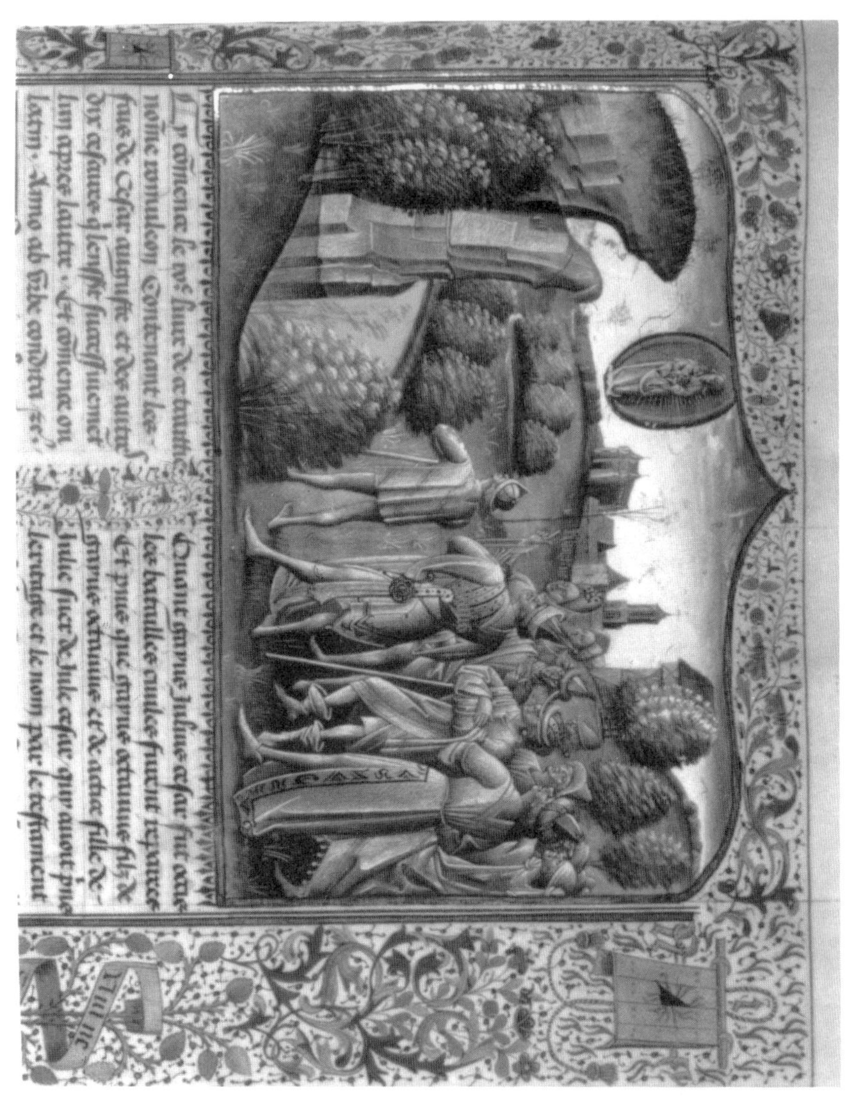

Figure 2 (folio 279)
Augustus and the Sybile of Tibur

Figure 3 (folio 265)
Julius Caesar in front of the tomb of Alexander the Great

tu point quil mest necessaire or fut sorle a celle fin que nul nait riens. Au dernier il osta les biens de plusieurs temples.

Comment neron par triacle commenca ses occisions a claudius empereur en mengant les champeignons venimeux Il occist aussi par venin britannicus son frere. Et fist occire sa mere puis ala veoir le corps mort blasmant ou loant ses membres. Le chap. xviii.

Suetonius.

Figure 4 (folio 292 verso)

Nero tries to drown his mother; Seneca commits suicide in his bath; Nero with the astrologers while Rome burns

Figure 5 (folio 301 verso)
Hadrian's coronation; Hadrian in Africa; Hadrian in Sicily about to climb Mount Etna; Hadrian drinking poison observed by Antonin and Marcus Aurelius

Figure 6 (folio 234)
Caesar and the Senate

Figure 7
Caesar among his courtiers

Figure 8 (folio 288 verso)
Emperor Caligula among his courtiers

The Significance of the Insignificant: Reading Reception in the Burgundian Erec *and* Cligès

Jane H. M. Taylor

When it comes to reception, Walter Benjamin is brisk: "In the appreciation of a work of art or an art form," he says, "consideration of the receiver never proves helpful."[1] He is of course — in context and out — perfectly right: not only are readerly and other responses no guide to authorial meaning or "correct" interpretation (which is what he himself is talking about), but the responses of translators and illustrators and rubricators and *remanieurs* tell us only about how *they* read; they do not help us to interpret the original, and, as Norris Lacy warns us in a pertinent footnote to an earlier article about the Burgundian *Erec*,[2] we should be "very skeptical" of using such evidence, especially evidence from three centuries after the original, as a basis for authoritative, "archeological," interpretations of our own.

This does not, however, mean that it is uninteresting to look at these responses in their own right, as evidence of shifting hermeneutic attitudes and policies, and it was my original intention to analyze precisely in this light the interpretative responses of the Burgundian *mises en prose* to some of the larger and more contentious ethical questions raised for us by Chrétien's romances: what *did* a Burgundian jobbing *prosateur* make of Erec's furious flight into the forest with Enide? What *did* he understand by the *Joie de la Cort*? How *did* he understand the intertextual counterpoint created by *Cligès* read against the *Tristan* romances? But even before I realized how far Martha Wallen[3] and Norris Lacy[4] and Betty Lou Bakelaar[5] had in any case pre-empted me, I had become interested less in the way in which the *prosateurs* resolved the narrative conundrums that Chrétien sets us than in something rather broader: a particular process of intralingual translation[6] which allows us privileged insights into socio-cultural and ideological phenomena not in the source but in the target culture, and for which I shall borrow a term from anthropology — *acculturation*. It has, of course, a number of senses, linguistic and anthropological;[7] as a provisional definition (because this paper will, I hope, progressively clarify my meaning), I offer: a process whereby the socio-culturally unfamiliar is recast in familiar terms, so that the reader can understand systems and phenomena in a source text as corresponding to his own ideologies, preconceptions, and behavior patterns. In this endeavor, "significant" variations, curiously enough, are in some ways less rewarding than "insignificant" ones — and hence, playing on Martha Wallen's title, my focus on the *insignificant*. I propose ultimately to concentrate on two particular episodes (pending a fuller study of *acculturation* which I hope to carry out at a later date and to extend to other of the *mises en prose*): Cligès's tour of Jehan's tower in *Cligès*, and Arthur's proclamation of the Hunt of the White Stag in *Erec et Enide*. The ways in which the *prosateur*[8] treats these two episodes argue, I shall suggest, for hermeneutic and acculturating, not merely linguistic, interests and skills. I do not wish, of course, to imply that he (or she)[9] had systematized in any conscious way the procedures and techniques that (s)he was using: the grammar of *mise en prose*[10] is probably largely internalized.[11] Nevertheless, I think that we can detect in the *modus operandi* a systematic concern not just with diction but with reinterpretation,[12] which makes the words *hermeneutic* and *acculturating* not inappropriate even for a *remanieur* who has usually been accused — at best — of mediocrity.[13]

Let me start, then, with an episode whose editorial moves will, I hope, begin to show precisely how complex are the acculturating processes, cultural and ideological, deployed by the *remanieur*: Jehan's tower in *Cligès*. I have italicized two major sections which are the *remanieur*'s independent invention — and in passing, I shall point out that even when he is doing no more than translating,[14] our *remanieur*, unlike many others,[15] tends to engage in wholesale rejuvenation of the lexis and syntagma of the source-text, retaining no more than the barest lexical "skeleton" or "invariant core" of the original;[16] he will also suppress, adjoin, substitute, permute:

"Et s'est si aeisiez cist leus
Con vos veroiz jusqu'a n'a gaires.
Ci vuel que soit vostre repaires
Et vostre amie i soit reposte.
Tex ostex est boens a tel oste,
Qu'il i a chanbres et estuves
Et l'eve chaude par les cuves,
Qui vient par conduit desoz terre.
Qui voldroit leu aeisié querre
Por s'amie metre et celer,
Molt li covandroit loing aler
Einz qu'il trovast si covenable.
Molt le tanroiz a delitable
Quant vos avroiz par tot esté."
Lors li a Jehanz tot mostré,
Beles chanbres et vostes paintes,

Et quant ilz furent entres dedens ilz trouuerent belles fontaines doulcez et cleres comme argent machonnees de porfire a manierez de pipez . entailliez de plus de cent facons de diuerses bestez et oizeaux . qui par leurz gueulez rendoient l'eaue de cez fontainez et d'illeuc venoit une petite riuere qui par dessoubz terre s'en alloit rendre a vne aultre. Apres ilz trouuerent baingz estuues piscines chambres vaultees clerez et plaisanz garnies de lis encortines et de mestierz a ouurer de soye ou il ne falloit quelque estoffe du monde . car ilz en estoient garnis. Et qui ja me demanderoit comment cest homme auoit peu faire ce lieu si plaisant tout seul . sans ayde de personne . voire et l'auoit tant ricement orne que nul plus beau ne pourroit estre fait . respond l'istoire que l'ouurier qui estoit soubtil auoit trouue en ceste maison vne miniere d'argent par la vendicion de laquelle il s'estoit gouuerne bien. viii. ans sans entendre se non a son ouurage (et auoit pou

Et si li a mostrees maintes De ses oevres, qui molt li plorent. Qant tote la tor veüe orent, Lors dist Cligès: "Jehan amis, Vos et trestoz voz oirs franchis."	d'aultre chose et) auec ce auoit il trouve ce lieu vaulte de prime face . si n'auoit en [sic; read eu?] a faire si non a agencyr et a y faire besongnes soubtillez pour soi racheter vne fois du seruage ou il estoit . ce a quoy il est maintenant paruvenu . car son intencion est tournee a bon effect. Cliges est moult joieux d'auoir trouue ce plaisant lieu manoire et habitacle. Il affrancist Jehan et lui ottroie tout ce qu'il lui demandera.
Cligès, 5602-22[17]	Prose *Cligès*, pp. 327-28.[18]

We remember, of course, that Cligès has in his service an *ovrier* — "Jehanz a non et s'est mes sers" (*Cligès*, 5363) — whose skills are such that he is sought out and emulated by the most masterly of architects and craftsmen in Antioch and Rome. Jehan agrees to provide Cligès and Fénice with the fake coffin and tomb that allows Fénice to escape her marriage; he also offers them the refuge of his marvelous tower. Cligès is delighted, and Jehan invites him to visit it: this is a part of the description of the underground *estaige voultiz* which is the finest example of Jehan's art. The *remanieur*, of course, has taken considerable liberties — in the first place, considerably developing the bare, if admittedly piquant, couplet of the source text: "... estuves / Et l'eve chaude par les cuves, / Qui vient par conduit desoz terre" (*Cligès*, 5607-09).

In the Burgundian prose *remaniement*, *estuves* are the merest detail: Jehan's tower is a riot of sophisticated plumbing, with porphyry fountains, birds and beasts gushing water from their beaks and mouths, little streams, tubs and baths and pools. Now, this in itself constitutes a minor example of acculturation, in the sense that a writer patronized by the Dukes of Burgundy could not but be aware of their fascination with water and hydraulics: the highly complex installations at their estate at Hesdin,[19] which had been carefully repaired under Philip the Bold (he employed his master artist, Melchior Broederlam, to oversee the renovations),[20] and which notably included hydraulically controlled automata like an enthroned figure which could be made to move while surrounded by mechanical twittering birds, and then finally restored to their full glory and ingenuity under Philip the Good in the 1430s;[21] the water-borne *entremets* at the Dukes' feasts (like the Feast of the Pheasant in 1454 where among the chief attractions were fountains, a carrack floating on a lake, and a fountain with a Mélusine[22]), not to mention great artifacts like the Moses Fountain created to commission for Philip the Bold in 1395.[23] Are the *prosateur*'s embellishments, then, a subtly flattering tribute from one of Philip the Good's literary craftsmen to the Duke's battalion of plastic artists?[24] I find it at the least interesting that a *prosateur* should choose just this aspect of Jehan's tower especially to develop — that he should express artistic perfection, the aesthetically sublime, in terms that the Burgundian court was for cultural reasons particularly apt to appreciate.

But it is not that which is my principal concern; rather, I am interested in the ideological thrust of the *remaniement*, and specifically in what it is that the *prosateur* makes of Jehan himself — and by *ideology*, here, I mean those modes of discourse which enable a society, consciously or unconsciously, to represent its own power relations and to set out 'the imaginary relationship of individuals to their real conditions of existence.'[25] The *remaniement* here, I suggest, allows us to explore with particular clarity changing presuppositions specifically about power.[26] Chrétien's Jehan is, of course, both a *maistre*, a man of some means as befitting a master-craftsman or *magister*, and — as Cligès points out with some force — a *serf*:[27]

> Tu es mes sers, je sui tes sire,
> Et je te puis doner ou vandre
> Et ton cors et ton avoir prandre
> Come la chose qui est moie. (*Cligès*, 5472-75)

Stiennon has adduced a number of parallels to this curious — and to us equivocal — status:[28] *ministeriales* who built up fortunes and even used their artistic endeavors to accede to the nobility. Even so, the astonishing opulence of Jehan's tower (and the source of his wealth is never made explicit), described with such lingering satisfaction by Chrétien, does invite comment and suggests, as Haidu says, that it is a *locus magicus*, "not entirely a real place."[29]

Our *prosateur* clearly shares the modern reader's faint perplexity — indeed he projects precisely that perplexity with that characteristic hypothetical relative clause "qui ja me demanderoit ...." His answer to the conundrum covers two fields: the economic and the teleological. Jehan, it turns out, is no longer the oddly ambivalent, slightly mysterious figure that Chrétien had devised; rather, he had stumbled by accident on an underground chamber already *vaulté* — and above all, he had had the good fortune in the course of his excavations to discover *une miniere d'argent* which has financed labor and raw materials for some eight years. Now, it is easy to make political capital out of suggesting that a joylessly mercantile spirit has replaced the glad and aristocratic world of Chrétien where joy is creation — but this is unfair; rather, I think we should read this along with the Burgundian elaboration of plumbing matters as a prime example of acculturation. This is a writer who, like all those surely at the Burgundian court, understands the cost of artistic and architectural excellence and the financial implications of patronage. I referred above to the major renovations that Philip the Good made to his estate at Hesdin; by great good fortune, the *devise* for the building work, submitted by his *maître d'oeuvre* Colard le Voleur, survives. Everything is costed, everything specified — the *best available materials, good quality oil colors* — all of which cost, in 1432, the staggering sum of 1000 *livres*.[30] But this is merely one small example among hundreds: the surviving ducal accounts[31] are peppered with references — and carefully accounted and itemized payments — to the Dukes' artists and writers and architects and sculptors and musicians and furnishers.[32] At the lavish Burgundian court, the aesthetic is costed — and our *prosateur* has, as it were, written the costings into what seemed, no doubt, a puzzlingly incomplete account of artistic endeavor, partly no doubt for mimetic reasons, but partly, perhaps, because in the environment for which he was writing artistic and aesthetic excellence *is* a matter also of costings. Just as he also writes in — another example of acculturation — a purpose for Jehan. Again, in Chrétien's carefully-constructed, non-mimetic universe, artistic skill and endeavor are, it seems, gratuitous: has Jehan constructed his marvelous tower out of sheer joy in artistic creation, as a place apart where the "oevre et point et taille" (*Cligès*, l. 5528)?[33] But the system of values operating in the Burgundian universe is not one of art for art's sake; rather, the Jehan of the prose *Cligès* has constructed his tower with the express intention of achieving his manumission: "pour soi racheter une fois du seruage ou il estoit." How this was to work is unspecified: Chrétien's romance had made Jehan's freedom conditional only on the latters successfully constructing Fénice's fake tomb. But here again, it seems, spontaneous artistic excellence, art for art's sake, is not something that is easily compatible with the extensive system of patronage operating in Burgundian circles: by what I would see as a process of acculturation, our *remanieur*, operating as he must in a specific temporal schema and within a specific economic, ideological, and socio-political framework, has divested his source of what must have seemed its obsolete disguise and articulated its core of meaning within a new, different socio-cultural background.[34] He has, in other words, applied what Juliane House calls a "cultural filter"[35] to his raw material and accommodated it to a more economically wary and informed readership.

A similar "cultural filter," this time in the broadest sense political, seems to me to have been applied by the *remanieur* to the acculturation of the *premerains vers* of *Erec et Enide* — and I concentrate on two short segments in which, once again, I italicize the *prosateur*'s contributions. The first is the opening of the narrative proper:

Au jor de Pasque, au tans novel, a Quaradigan, son chastel, ot li rois Artus cort tenue; einz si riche ne fu veüe,	Le roy artus *duquel la glorieuse renommee s'espandoit par tout le monde*, tinst par ung jour de pasques sa court au chasteau de Karadigan . dieux scet a belle baronnie. Car de roys ducs princes contes seigneurs cheualiers avoit il lors plus avec

que molt i ot boens chevaliers,
hardiz et conbatanz et fiers,
et riches dames et puceles,
filles de rois, gentes et beles;
mes einçois que la corz fausist,
li rois a ses chevaliers dist
qu'il voloit le blanc cerf chacier
por la costume ressaucier.
Mon seignor Gauvain ne plot
mie ....

Erec et Enide, 27-39

lui que james il nauoit eu pour ung jour. De dames et damoiselles de hault et de noble lignage demander ne fault pas. Il en y auoit plus de .v. cens et deues sauoir que c'estoit noble chose de voir leur estat. *Nostre comple ne s'arrestera pour a parler des dances joustes et aultres esbatemens mais trop bien pour entrer en matere vendra a dire qu'en ce temps que le roi Artus se tenoit a Karadigan, en la forest auentureuse scituee assez pres d'icelle part auoit ung cerf impareil aux autres, car il estoit tout blanc. Par pluseurs fois il auoit este chassie et auoit le roi fait ung edit pour esmouuoir son barnage que quiconques prendroit ce cerf, sans preiudice nul il pourroit a son chois auoir vng baiser de la plus belle dame ou damoiselle de sa court.* Aduint doncques que le roy Artus ains que sa feste fu passee pour ce qu'il auoit plente de cheualiers voult aler en la forest aduentureuse chasser le cerf.

(Prose *Erec et Enide*, p. 253)

It is Spring (the *tans novel*), and we discover Arthur's court at its zenith, thronging with the valiant knights and beautiful damsels. With two pragmatically significant definite articles, Chrétien explains that Arthur wants to hunt *the* white stag, in pursuit of *the* custom. This, it seems, displeases Gauvain — and we shall, of course, find out that he is nervous of the jealousies and rivalries that the custom is likely to provoke. The second segment is taken from the *dénouement* of that same adventure:

"Raison doi garder et droiture.
Ce apartient a leal roi
Que il doit maintenir la loi,
Verité et foi et justise.
Je ne voudroie en nule guise
Feire desleauté ne tor,
Ne plus au foible que au fort.
N'est droiz que nus de moi se
plaigne
Ne je ne vuel pas que remaigne
La costume ne li usages
Que siaut maintenir mes lignages.
De ce vos devroit il peser,
Se je vos voloie alever
Autres costumes, autres lois,

Tantost que Enide a prins vne ferme contenance de soir. la reyne prent a dire au roy que s'il veult choisir la plus belle de sa court qu'il n'a gueres a faire pour prendre le baisier qui lui est deu a cause du cerf. A ceste ramenteuance le roi *mande ses plus priues* et dist que en la pucelle d'estrange terre a plus de beaulte qu'en nulle aultre. Il en demande a chascun l'oppinion. Mais *comme faire le poeuent par leur sentence* il est *briefment adjugie* qu'elle doit auoir l'honneur du cerf et que *lic-*

Que ne tint mes pere, li rois.
L'usage Pandragon, mon pere,
Qui fut droiz rois et enperere,
Doi je garder et maintenir,
Que que il m'an doie avenir.
Or me dites toz voz talanz!
De voir dire ne soit nus lanz ...."

Erec et Enide, 1796-816

itement il en puet prendre le baisier sans nul preiudice pour garder son honneur son droit et entretenir sa parolle roiale. A chief de conclusion toux debas venus en vne arestee concordance ....

Prose *Erec*, p. 264.

Erec has brought Enide back to court, where Guinevere, impressed by the girl's beauty, tells Arthur that he has now found the young woman to whom the kiss is due. At this point, of course, in Chrétien's romance, Arthur makes a long speech to the assembled court — to whom Chrétien simply calls the *chevaliers* (l. 1736). He praises Enide's unique beauty, declares her worthy of the kiss of the white stag, inquires if any of them will *contredire* his choice or appose a *desfanse* (ll. 1746-47), and then gives a disquisition on the duties and principles of kingship that is, as Donald Maddox points out,[36] the fullest statement of the kind which Chrétien ever lends to Arthur. The central point of this statement harks back insistently to the lexemes and the pragmatics of the first passage to which I briefly drew attention, *the* white stag, *the* custom:

Et je ne voel pas que remaigne
la costume ne li usages
que siaut maintenir mes lignages.
De ce vos devroit il peser,
se ge vos voloie alever
autre costume et autres lois
que ne tint mes peres li rois.
L'usage Pandragon, mon pere,
qui rois estoit et emperere,
voel je garder et maintenir. (*Erec et Enide*, 1756-69)

As many commentators, most recently and most notably Donald Maddox, have pointed out, the whole of this episode is based on the sense that there exists in the Arthurian world an *anterior order*[37] which is now under (social) threat: Arthur remains the representative of a more primitive, socially cohesive court in which custom held sway, but operates uneasily in the world of which Gauvain is the spokesman, and where a "chivalric class" now prefers to "exalt prowess and individual nobility."[38]

Now, what does the Burgundian *prosateur* make of this? The opening of the adventure is, I think, significant — and particularly for its transformation of the pragmatics of the adventure. No longer is this *le blanc cerf;* rather, this is *ung cerf* — remarkable because by some unspecified freak it is pure white, *impareil aux autres*. This is not, it seems, the first time that it will have been hunted, but there is no suggestion of a *costume*: rather, the king himself has instituted an *edit* in order to inspire his *barnage*. And finally, the nature of the *edit* is carefully ambiguous; someone (*il*; the successful hunter? the king?) will have as a prize *a son chois ... ung baiser de la plus belle dame ou damoiselle de sa court*.

Then, looking now to the *dénouement* of the *premerains vers*: in the Burgundian prose version, Arthur turns for advice not to the court as a whole but rather to his "*plus priues*" to whom, it seems, is accredited the power of judgment (*comme faire le poeuvent par leur sentence*). Arthur, they opine, can safely offer the kiss without prejudice to his royal power, in order to *entretenir sa parolle roiale*. Now, two things are lost here, and one gained; all three crucially alter the dynamics of the romance. First, of course, the *remanieur* loses the consciousness of an anterior order; and second, closely bound with it, the delicate depiction of a balance of authority and custom. That fundamental — indispensable — political irony which, in Chrétien's *Erec*, makes Arthur insist on subservience to time-honored social custom at the risk of creating social mayhem is entirely foreign to the Burgundian world where Arthur's insistence is purely autocratic: he has proclaimed a hunt and must maintain his *parole et conuenance*.

But is this a question of incomprehension, of incompetence, or of strategy? Before attempting a provisional answer, let me look briefly at another, apparently minor, point in this *premerains vers*: participation in the hunt. In Chrétien's *Erec*, we remember, Erec, elegantly dressed for a day at court and not a day's sport, has (for inscrutable reasons) elected not to obey Arthur's summons to the hunt.[39] The prose version is quite different: here, it seems, Erec is escorting Guinevere, and both of them are hastening towards the hunt in order to take part when Arthur and his huntsmen, impatient for sport, prematurely flush the stag in a thicket — and the two "ne sceurent si tost venir en la forest que le cerf ne fust leue." Ideologically, this minor point seems to suggest not a consensual but rather a highly centralized court, in which all do — must — participate. Decisions are, very largely, the responsibility of the king, aided at most by a small coterie of advisers: it is the king who chooses, and imposes, the diversions of his courtiers, it is the king who pronounces judgment.

I shall resist the temptation to argue that the system of government presented so embryonically in the prose version of *Erec* is somehow a calque of the Burgundian system: in any case, the concise, not to say terse, information given by the *remanieur* would not be enough to substantiate any such claim. What one can say, however, is that by a process of acculturation the prose text assimilates the mysterious or the ironic political systems of Arthur's court to a model that would have been comfortably comprehensible to a Burgundian audience — a model in which the ruler's choices, the ruler's edicts, are primary and incontrovertible. As everyone knows, the Burgundian court was fascinated by matters of precedence and etiquette, precisely because all status and every action was measured against the dukes themselves. In a society of rigid and codified systems, of positively Byzantine complexity,[40] could it have seemed even conceivable that customs inaugurated in a pre-ducal world might be binding on the Dukes, that anyone would knowingly decline to take part in a ducally-ordained hunt or fail to be present for any of the *fastes* of the court? At most, the dukes consulted with an "aulic" council, that is to say, a council "made up of any officers, relatives or friends of the duke who happened to be with him at the time,"[41] like Philip the Good's *grand conseil* or *groote raade*, which was quorate at just four or five.[42] But by its very nature, this aleatory council was staffed at the duke's whim or favor with "*ses* plus privés." By a process of *acculturation*, in other words, the *prosateur* has assimilated a puzzling and disturbing model of Arthur's Britain to a more familiar Burgundian — or indeed general — model of government: he looks in incomprehension at the idea of a *truly* consultative monarchy, thereby, of course, losing precisely that sense of a court "poised on the brink of anarchy" which is so fundamental to Chrétien's *Erec*.[43] On the other hand, of course — and no doubt for the Burgundian *prosateur* this was a gain — the loss of that sense of threatening crisis does return Arthur to the center of his own court, creating a court which, like that of Burgundy, is a centripetal organization where all acts focus on the person of the ruler.

It is this deletion of the alterity[44] of Chrétien's Arthurian kingdom which has made me use the term *acculturation*: this scribe is not just an editor, but — to borrow a term this time from Karen Stetting — a conscientious[45] *transeditor*[46] who refracts the cultural and ideological *présupposés* of his source text to keep it alive and functioning in the receptor culture. True, it is axiomatically the case that cross-cultural translation must be a matter of imposition, since how can we understand anyone except in terms of categories that make sense to us or are extensions of some that do?[47] True also, the *remanieur* is not, as far as we can tell, transgressing appropriateness conditions and intersubjectively mediated rules and norms dominant in the field of *mise en prose* in his own culture and time: after all, if *mise en prose* is assimilable to translation, then Quintilian himself is an advocate of interventionist *conversio*, or paraphrase.[48] But the *opérations ré-énonciatives*[49] that I have isolated show, I think, an analytical, rather than a slavish, translator invoking Burgundian ideologies, Burgundian sociocultural systems, to shape his view of causality. I am reminded of the poet Edward Fitzgerald, in *The Rubaiyat of Omar Khayam*: "It is an amusement for me to take what Liberties I like with these Persians who (as I think) are not Poets enough to frighten one from such excursions, and who really do want a little Art to shape them."[50] Fitzgerald's may have been an act of "creative treason"[51] — but it was also a celebration and a revival.[52] The much-reviled Burgundian *prosateurs* may indeed have been committing an act of creative treason — but they were also celebrating and reviving an exciting literature which their patrons had lost the art of understanding;

their acculturating parameters and criteria are things that we should learn to read and understand.

NOTES

[1] "The Task of the Translator," in *Illuminations*, trans. H. Zohn (London: Fontana, 1982), 69. The German reads: "Nirgends erweist sich einem Kunstwerk oder einer Kunstform gegenüber die Rücksicht auf den Aufnehmenden für deren Erkenntnis fruchtbar": "Die Aufgabe des Übersetzungers," in *Gesammelte Schriften*, ed. Tillman Rexroth, 7 vols. (Frankfurt a. M.: Suhrkamp, 1972), IV/1, 9.

[2] "Motivation and Method in the Burgundian *Erec*," in *Conjunctures: Medieval Studies in Honor of Douglas Kelly*, ed. Keith Busby and Norris J. Lacy (Amsterdam: Rodopi, 1994), 271-80.

[3] Martha Wallen, "Significant Variations in the Burgundian Prose Version of *Erec et Enide*," *Medium Aevum* 51 (1982), 187-96.

[4] Lacy, "Motivation and Method."

[5] "From Verse to Prose: A Study of the Fifteenth-Century Versions of Chréstien's *Erec and Cligès*" (Diss. Ohio State University, 1973).

[6] The term is Jakobson's: see Roman Jakobson, "On Linguistic Aspects of Translation," in *Selected Writings*, 5 vols. (The Hague/Paris: Mouton, 1971), II, 261.

[7] For a useful summary, see Keith H. Basso, "Semantic Aspects of Linguistic Acculturation," *American Anthropologist* 69 (1967), 471-77.

[8] Opinion is divided as to whether we have one or two *prosateurs*; this is a question which Maria Colombo Timelli's approach in a companion paper in this volume should go far to answer.

[9] I am anxious not to assume *a priori* that the translator was a man — apart from the fact that "anon" may often be a woman, we know of at least two famous French medieval women translators (Christine de Pizan and Marie de France) as well as other, less well-known translators such as Eleanor Hull (see Alexandra Barratt's interesting article "Dame Eleanor Hull: a Fifteenth-Century Translator," in *The Medieval Translator: The Theory and Practice of Translation in the Middle Ages. Papers Read at a Conference Held 20-23 August 1987 at the University of Wales Conference Centre, Gregynog Hall*, ed. Roger Ellis (Cambridge: D. S. Brewer, 1989), 87-101.

[10] That there is such a thing as a *grammar* of *mise en prose* seems, empirically, to be clear — but of course the *mises en prose* are still a largely unexploited source, in spite of Georges Doutrepont's pioneering *Les Mises en prose des épopées et des romans chevaleresques du XIVe au XVIe siècle*, Académie Royale de Belgique, Classe des lettres, Mémoires 40 (Brussels: Palais des Académies, 1939), to the careful scholarship of which we owe a great deal.

[11] Most historians of translation are sceptical of translation theory as applied to the everyday translator; see for instance Frederick M. Rener, *Interpretatio: Language and Translation from Cicero to Tytler* (Amsterdam: Rodopi, 1989), 279.

[12] In the 1520s, Luis Vives distinguished three sorts of translation: the first concentrates on sense alone; the second concerns itself only with diction ("sola phrasis et dictio"); the third is the happy mean ("et res et verba"); see Rener, *Interpretatio*, 185.

[13] See Gaston Paris on the subject: "une très médiocre rédaction en prose," *Romania* 13 (1884), 446.

[14] I would agree with Roman Jakobson in seeing *mise en prose* as intralingual translation: see his "On Linguistic Aspects," 261.

[15] Compare for instance Maurice Delbouille's remarks on the more slavish methods of the *prosateur* who produced the prose version of the *Roman du Châtelain de Coucy*: "Scrupuleusement fidèle au modèle qu'il translatait, le prosateur suit le texte de Jakemes vers par vers, se contentant le plus souvent de briser le rythme de l'octosyllabe et d'effacer la rime par le choix de mots nouveaux, de constructions différentes ou de tournures plus jeunes. Moins concis dans sa phrase, il lui arrive peut-être d'atteindre à plus de clarté que le texte ancien, mais il est rare qu'il cherche à se libérer de la pensée du poète. C'est à peine s'il introduit ça et là quelque détail qu'il espère plus naturel ou plus vraisemblable, s'il commente ou explique brièvement certaines attitudes et certains gestes de ses personnages." (See his introduction to Jakemes, *Le Roman du Castelain de Couci et de la Dame de Fayel*, SATF [Paris: J. E. Matzke, 1936]: xc; the prose version has now been edited by Aimé Petit and François Suard [Lille: Presses Universitaires de Lille, 1994]).

[16] Again, the *remanieur*'s translational techniques would merit a study, and particularly a study of the way in which he juggles what Popovic calls the "invariant core" of "stable, basic and constant semantic elements" against his own *remaniements*; see on this topic Anton Popovic, *Dictionary for the Analysis of Literary Translation* (Edmonton, Alberta: University of Alberta, 1976), 11.

[17] I use the new edition by Stewart Gregory and Claude Luttrell (Cambridge: D. S. Brewer, 1993).

[18] I use the only available editions, those which Wendelin Foerster appends to his edition of Chrétien de Troyes's *Sämtliche Werke*: *Cligès* in vol. I (Halle: Niemeyer, 1884), 283-338, *Erec et Enide* in vol. III (Halle: Niemeyer, 1890), 253-94.

[19] On Hesdin, see J.-M. Richard, "Notes sur quelques peintres des premières années du XIVe siècle," *Bulletin archéologique du comité des travaux historiques*, 1885, 273-320; Chrétien Dehaisnes, *Documents et extraits divers concernant l'histoire de l'art dans la Flandre, l'Artois et le Hainaut avant le XVe siècle*, 2 vols. (Lille: L. Danel, 1886), I, 204-05, 216, II, 566, 580; Marguerite Charageat, "Le parc d'Hesdin, création monumentale du XIIIe siècle," *Bulletin de la Société de l'histoire de l'art français*, 1950, 94-106. It may be interesting, in connection with Jehan, to note that Charageat (98-102) attaches the Hesdin *joyeusetés*, and particularly those of the hydraulic type, to Arab influences. Most recently, Lambertus Okken has set Hesdin in the context of descriptions of artificial paradises, and examined its hydraulic devices; see *Das*

Goldene Haus und die Goldene Laube: Wie die Poesie ihren Herren das Paradies einrichtete, Amsterdamer Publikationen zur Sprache und Literatur 72 (Amsterdam: Rodopi, 1987), 171-78. I am grateful to my colleague Dr. Karen Pratt for this reference.

[20] See Richard Vaughan, *Philip the Bold: The Formation of the Burgundian State* (London: Longmans, 1962), 205-06.

[21] In an extremely expensive operation for which we have the itemized account, *devise*, drawn up 21 February 1432, the sum of £1000 was paid to a certain Colard le Voleur, "valet de chambre and painter of my lord the duke." (See Richard Vaughan, *Philip the Good: The Apogee of Burgundy* [London: Longmans, 1970], 137-39, and see also, briefly, Luc Hommel, *Marie de Bourgogne ou le grand héritage* [Brussels: Ad. Goemaere/Paris: Presses Universitaires de France, 1951], 127-78).

[22] On the *entremets*, see Olivier de la Marche, *Mémoires*, ed. H. Beaune and J. d'Arbaumont, 4 vols (Paris: Renouard, 1884), II, 340-80, and Mathieu d'Escouchy, *Chronique*, ed. G. du Fresne de Beaucourt, 3 vols. (Paris: Jules Renouard, 1863), II, 130-39. See also Otto Cartellieri, *The Court of Burgundy: Studies in the History of Civilization* (New York: Haskell House, 1970), 142-50, and Vaughan, *Philip the Good*, 143-45, who points out that Colard le Voleur — a specialist precisely in water effects and in the *engins d'esbattement* there — was especially called from Hesdin to help with the extravagances for the banquet.

[23] See Kathleen Morand, *Claus Sluter: Artist at the Court of Burgundy* (London: Harvey Miller, 1991), 91-120.

[24] See Jonathan Beck, "Formalism and Virtuosity: Franco-Burgundian Poetry, Music, and Visual Art, 1470-1520," *Critical Enquiry* 10 (1984), 644-67. Beck suggests — interestingly, although far too briefly — correlations across the whole aesthetic system of the Burgundian court. I am not attempting anything so ambitious.

[25] See Louis Althusser, "A Letter on Art in Reply to André Daspre," in *Lenin and Philosophy and Other Essays*, trans. Ben Brewster (London: New Left Books/New York: Monthly Review Press, 1971), 223.

[26] Althusser, "A Letter on Art," 222: art "makes us *see* ... the ideology from which it is born, in which it bathes, from which it detaches itself as art, and to which it *alludes*."

[27] A combination which has excited comment among a number of modern critics, notably J. Stiennon, "Histoire de l'art et fiction poétique dans un épisode du *Cligès* de Chrétien de Troyes," in *Mélanges offerts à Rita Lejeune* (Gembloux: Duculot, 1969), 695-708; Robert W. Hanning, "Poetic Emblems in Medieval Literary Texts," in *Vernacular Poetics in the Middle Ages*, ed. Lois Ebin, Studies in Medieval Culture 16 (Kalamazoo, MI: Medieval Institute Publications, 1984), 1-32; Michelle A. Freeman, *The Poetics of* Translation Studii *and* Conjointure*: Chrétien de Troyes's* Cligès, French Forum Monographs 12 (Lexington, KY: French Forum, 1979), 164-67, and Peter Haidu, *Aesthetic Distance in Chrétien de Troyes: Irony and Comedy in* Cligès *and* Perceval (Geneva: Droz, 1968), 100-04.

[28] "Histoire de l'art," 698-99.

[29] Haidu, *Aesthetic Distance*, 100-03.

[30] Quoted in full in translation by Vaughan, *Philip the Good*, 138-39; for the original text, see L. de Laborde, *Les Ducs de Bourgogne: Etudes sur les lettres, les arts et l'industrie pendant le XVe siècle*, 3 vols (Paris: Plon, 1849-52), I, 268-71.

[31] Fortunately, as Vaughan, *Philip the Good*, 139, points out, nearly a quarter of Philip's *escroes* or daily accounts survives at Lille.

[32] The fullest source for Philippe le Hardi as patron of the arts is Patrick M. de Winter, "The Patronage of Philippe le Hardi, Duke of Burgundy (1364-1404)" (Diss. New York University, 1976). On Philip the Good in this role, see among others Cartellieri, *The Court of Burgundy*, 52-74, and Vaughan, *Philip the Good*, 127-63.

[33] Several critics — notably Hanning — have built on the gratuitousness of Jehan's artistic endeavours to suggest parallels between the craftsman and the Chrétien "who can, by his art, endow beautiful, courtly narratives with higher, metaphorical significance" (Hanning, "Poetic Emblems," 13).

[34] André Lefevere, "The Translation of Literature: An Approach," *Babel* 16 (1970), 75-79, makes some interesting remarks, 77, on translation in this connection, as does Richard Jacquemond, "Translation and Cultural Hegemony: The Case of French-Arabic Translation," in *Rethinking Translation: Discourse, Subjectivity, Ideology*, ed. Lawrence Venuti (London: Routledge, 1992),139-58.

[35] Juliane House uses it to designate a series of strategic moves which accommodate the originals to a target culture group's different "presuppositions about the social relationship, social attitude and participation of the addresser vis-à-vis the addressee"; see her "A Model for Assessing Translation Quality," *Meta*, 22 (1977), 107, and see also her *A Model for Translation Quality Assessment* (Tübingen: Gunter Narr, 1977), 37-50, where, although she does not use the term, she describes some of the parameters which this "cultural filter" will need to address.

[36] Maddox, *The Arthurian Romances of Chrétien de Troyes: Once and Future Fictions* (Cambridge: Cambridge University Press, 1991), 26-31.

[37] Maddox, *The Arthurian Romances*, 14-34, and, more particularly his *Structure and Sacring: The Systematic Kingdom in Chrétien's Erec et Enide* (Lexington KY: French Forum, 1978), 73-119.

[38] Maddox, *Structure and Sacring*, 103.

[39] For some tentative explanations of the point, however, see Reto Bezzola, *Le Sens de l'aventure et de l'amour* (Paris: La Jeune Parque, 1947), 96-97; Norris J. Lacy, "Thematic Analogues in *Erec*," *L'Esprit créateur* 9 (1969), 273.

[40] See Olivier de La Marche, *L'estat de la maison du duc Charles de Bourgogne*, in *Mémoires*, IV, 1-94 (summarised at length by Cartellieri, *Court of Burgundy*, 65-70); Aliénor de Poitiers, *Les honneurs de la cour*, ed. La Curne de Sainte-Palaye, *Mémoires sur l'ancienne chevalerie*, 4 vols (Paris: Girard, 1826), II, 143-219 (composed between 1484 and 1491; her account of matters of etiquette and

precedence under Philip the Good and his son is also discussed by Cartellieri, *Court of Burgundy*, 70-72); *Ordonnance touchant la conduite du premier escuier d'escuerie* (see catalogue item 4004 in Th. Frimmel, "Urkunden, Regesten und artistisches Quellenmaterial aus der Bibliothek der kunsthistorischen Sammlungen des allerhöchsten Kaiserhauses," *Jahrbuch der kunsthistorischen Sammlungen des allerhöchsten Kaiserhauses* 5/2 [1887]: v-vi). See also Luc Hommel, *Marie de Bourgogne*, 116-21.

[41] See Richard Vaughan, *Philip the Bold*, 140, and cf. his remarks on the same subject in *Philip the Good*, 164 ff.

[42] See Wavrin's *Chroniques*, iv, 127-31, for details of which see Vaughan, *Philip the Good*, 171; J. Richard, "Les institutions ducales en Bourgogne," in *Histoire des institutions françaises au moyen âge*, ed. F. Lot and R. Fawtier, 3 vols. (Paris: Presses Universitaires de France, 1957), I, 209-47; Marie Thérèse Caron, *La Noblesse dans le duché de Bourgogne, 1315-1477* (Lille: Presses Universitaires, 1987), 133 ff.; for the *Grand Conseil*, which, as the writer says (133), was "too amorphous, too indefinite, too personal to be regulated into a strict existence," see P. S. Lewis, *Later Medieval France: The Polity* (London etc.: Macmillan, 1968), 126-32.

[43] Maddox, *The Arthurian Romances*, 30; Sara Sturm-Maddox, "The *Joie de la cort*: Thematic Unity in Chrétien's *Erec et Enide*," *Romania* 103 (1982), 513-28, and Dominique Boutet, "Carrefours idéologiques de la royauté arthurienne," *Cahiers de civilisation médiévale* 28 (1985), 3-17.

[44] Barbara Folkart, talking in a modern context of the same process of assimilation, talks of "une acculturation factice qui nie ... l'altérité de l'unité culturelle, au terme d'une assimilation qui est le refus de toute distance"; see her *Le conflit des énonciations: Traduction et discours rapporté*, Coll. L'Univers des discours (Candiac, Québec: Les Editions Balzac, 1991), 160.

[45] We should be wary of thinking of the *prosateur* as lacking in imagination or empathy; I would see him as attempting, dutifully, to take measures to counter a legitimate sense of incomprehension shared, if we are honest, by the modern critic. See, for instance, Haidu's pertinent remark: "After we have learned to parse the odd and seemingly awkward languages, after we have dutifully appended the historical footnotes to guide our literal interpretation of the text, we find outselves still far from being able to read, in any meaningful sense, the world of literary forms before our eyes" ("Making it (new) in the Middle Ages," *Diacritics* 4 [1974], 217-36).

[46] "Transediting — a New Term for Coping with the Grey Area between Editing and Translating," in *Nordic Conference for English Studies* 4, ed. Graham Caie et al. (Copenhagen: Department of English, University of Copenhagen, 1990), 371-82; I am also, of course, thinking of Elspeth Kennedy's article "The Scribe as Editor," in *Mélanges Jean Frappier*, 2 vols. (Geneva: Droz, 1970), I, 523-31.

[47] See the interesting discussion in *Current Anthropology*: Robert Feleppa, "Emics, Etics and Social Objectivity," *Current Anthropology* 27 (1986), 243-55; Thomas J. Scheff, "Is Accurate Cross-Cultural Translation Possible?" *Current Anthropology* 28 (1987), 365; Tamara Nazarova and Velta Zadornova, "On Cross-Cultural Translation," *Current Anthropology* 30 (1989), 209-10.

[48] *Institution oratoire*, Book X, ch. 5, 5 (I use the bilingual edition by Jean Cousin [Paris: Les Belles Lettres, 1979], VI, 127): the "interpreter" or translator should not translate but rather explain the text by paraphrasing it — and preferably, by outdoing it ("circa eosdem sensus certamen atque aemulationem").

[49] Folkart, op. cit., p. 216.

[50] Edward Fitzgerald, *The Variorum and Definitive Edition of the Poetical and Prose Writings*, 7 vols. (New York: Doubleday, 1972), VI, xvi.

[51] I borrow the term from Robert Escarpit, "'Creative Treason' as a Key to Literature," *Yearbook of Comparative and General Literature* 10 (1961), 16-21.

[52] For some stirring thoughts on this theme, see Danielle Quéruel's interesting article "Des mises en prose aux romans de chevalerie dans les collections bourguignonnes," in *Rhétorique et mise en prose au XVe siècle: Actes du VIe Colloque International sur le Moyen Français, Milan, 4-6 mai 1988, II*, ed. S. Cigada and Anna Slerca (Milan: Vita e Pensiero, 1991), 172-93.

St Hilda's College, Oxford

Adaptation as Reception: The Burgundian Cligès

Norris J. Lacy

Around the middle of the fifteenth century, an anonymous author, acknowledging the "bon usage de lirre et escouter rommans et histoirez," prepared a prose adaptation of Chrétien de Troyes's *Cligès* for the Burgundian court. In its unique manuscript, it is entitled *Le Liure de Alixandre empereur de Constentinoble et de Cligès son filz*.[1] The redactor does not credit Chrétien with authorship, noting only that he is following the current practice "de transmuer de ryme en prose les fais d'aulcuns nobles anchians" [283].

And in the same prologue, he speaks also of himself, announcing that his skill ("*engin*") is inadequate, his ignorance excessive, and his language rough and plain ("*dur et mal aorne*"). This is nothing more than the traditional modesty topos, of course, but not all modesty is false: in this case the redactor offers, in my view, a reasonably accurate appraisal of his aptitudes and accomplishments. Nonetheless, the product of his efforts may well offer a revealing and important insight (only a small part of which can be traced here) into techniques of adaptation, into the tastes that prevailed at that time and place, and conceivably into the reception of the text.

Martha Wallen, in a 1972 dissertation that treats both this text and a contemporary version of Chrétien's *Erec et Enide*,[2] argues that the purpose of the adaptation was the transmittal of chivalric ideals to "later courtly and bourgeois society" [6]. Wallen provides a very thorough and systematic analysis of the modifications made by the redactor. My esthetic evaluation of the result is less charitable than hers,[3] and I also tend to be less confident than she that we can with assurance identify the reasons for most alterations. That, however, does not detract from the value of her work, which is capably done and, of course, far more extensive than my own can be here.

Wallen is indisputably right to argue [9] that the *Cligès* is far more than a translation or prosification into which unfortunate modifications have been introduced by a uncomprehending or misguided writer. As she notes, that author was obviously making changes in order to adjust the text to a fifteenth-century audience at the Burgundian court. Specifically, she contends that the purpose was "... not so much to resurrect old ideals of heroism or primitive models of love and passion, but rather to present modern attitudes through a pre-existing intrigue" [280].

She suggests [301] that many of the alterations and emphases (such as the focus on genealogy) can be explained as the glorification of the Burgundian duke (Philip the Good), his son Charles, and "all persons of the ducal succession," who are taken as "latter-day Alexanders." The adaptation, she concludes, is "a document of political flattery" (302) in which both Alexandre and Arthur are seen as precursors of the dukes.

The prose text is thus, if we accept Wallen's view, a kind of late conduct book. It is a mirror for princes, in which the Duke can see himself as the reflection of his illustrious predecessors.[4] And that understanding of the text enables us to explain many of the alterations — specifically the glorification of the heroes and the perfection of the love that exists between Cligès and Fénice.

Even a cursory reading of the text reveals the Burgundian redactor's preference for tourneys, battles, and wars, as opposed to more peaceable pursuits. Many of the battle scenes, though considerably modified and modernized, maintain roughly the length and detail they had in Chrétien's original. It is clear that such a practice was in accord with the tastes prevalent at the late Burgundian court: that court's culture was primarily a military culture. Yet, for most modern readers and for our present purposes, those scenes are less engaging and, in particular, less revealing than are others. And it is the latter kind — the scenes involving love, intrigues, monologues, and analyses — that will most occupy our attention here.

Permitting ourselves some oversimplification, we can divide many or most of the innovations into two classes: those that rationalize Chrétien's text and those that redefine his vision of love and the court. A few examples will prove instructive, after which I will turn to the discussion of two major passages that illustrate in dramatic fashion the methodologies of the redactor.

Wallen emphasizes the redactor's concern for motivation or rationalization, noting that he frequently introduces alterations in order to explain what might otherwise be less than credible [Wallen 229-32].[5] That category includes the most prominent addition made by the Burgundian author. It is an episode, absent from Chrétien's text, that explains why Cligès, after an extended absence, suddenly misses Fénice — or understands her grief at his absence — and wants to return to her [cf. Chrétien's *Cligès*, 5056]. The redactor simply invents a lovelorn maiden, weeping for her absent lover; hearing her words, Cligès thinks of his own lady and of the sadness that his absence has caused them both [323].

A second example: when Chrétien's Cligès asks his servant Jehan to prepare a tomb for Fénice (who had taken a potion to make her appear dead), he learns that Jehan has already completed just such a tomb: richly decorated, magnificent, fit for a saint and thus suitable for the "saintly" Fénice. (Indeed, Jehan calls Fénice a *molt sainte chose*, 6074).[6] In the Burgundian text [327], Cligès asks Jehan to make a tomb for Fénice's body, and the servant agrees; but when Cligès divulges his plan to take Fénice from the tomb and leave that land, Jehan replies that there is no need to do so, that they can stay in the house. Now, it happens that Jehan has made some additions, and in the house is a secret door leading to a marvelous place where there are splendid fountains, baths, pools, and chambers.

At this point, though, the incongruity of a *serf* who has both the time and money to prepare all this appears to have occurred to the redactor, and so he explains the source of Jehan's independent wealth: he had found a silver mine in the house [327], enabling him to spend all his time working on this place and making plans eventually to purchase his freedom. Only in the fifteenth-century text — certainly not in the twelfth — would there be a need to offer such an explanation.

Although rationalizations offer dramatic evidence of the evolution of literary psychology over three centuries, they fundamentally alter the character of the text far less than does the redactor's treatment of love and, especially, of Chrétien's ironic view of it. Three examples will have to suffice.

As all readers of Chrétien's text recall, Soredamors was insistently scornful of the notion of love, and she would not lower herself to love any man, no matter how noble or valiant or handsome. The source of this attitude toward love was obvious: arrogance and haughtiness [*orguel* and *dangier*, 458; *orguel* and *desdaing*, 469].

The Burgundian text makes a few simple but important alterations in the passage: the redactor, like Chrétien, notes that she would not deign to love any man, but then he adds that "*elle cuidoit nul homme estre suffisant pour paruenir a sa bonne grace*" [287]. This too surely qualifies as an expression of pride or arrogance, but it seriously attenuates her resistance, which now appears less an unwillingness to love in general than a simple determination merely to wait for the right man. But then the author departs further from Chrétien's premise by noting that, at the same time, she really did *want* to love, that she was in fact so eager to love that she would be happy if even a squire gave her his affection. (Indeed, this modification makes her loveless situation sound like desperation or defensiveness, that is, like the fury of a woman scorned or ignored, rather than a principled resistance to love.)

Following Chrétien's allusion to Soredamors's disdain for love, he has her engage in the kind of interior monologue dear to the author's heart. In it, her eyes vie with her heart and betray it [475-523]; she debates how it is that what she sees (that is, Alexandre) can torment her when it also pleases her. The Burgundian equivalent of these fifty or so lines is a simple statement, a single sentence, concerning the *batailles* fought within her by pride and love [287]. It would be inaccurate to suggest that the Burgundian redactor was unconcerned with love, but he is obviously more interested in focusing on the external obstacles to love than to dramatizing inner conflicts about it.

This alteration and a good many related ones can tell us something useful about the redactor's method and purpose. Specifically, such alterations amount to a simplification of textual motivation. That is to say that the redactor reduces internal tensions and effaces the psychological or amorous conflicts that might complicate a relationship. Perhaps ironically, the result is to focus the text more sharply — not more effectively, just more sharply — than had Chrétien. In the Burgundian text, conflicts will pit the court's knights and lovers alike against their external obstacles and foes, but never against one another and certainly never seriously against the notion of love itself. The court is largely unified and harmonious, a conception that may well have pleased the Duke of Burgundy.

My final two examples are dramatic responses to Chrétien's ironic vision of his story and characters, and the first of those examples also involves the redactor's remarkable rehandling of his predecessor's rhetorical virtuosity. The passages in question are the long and complex "Love's arrow" monologue (pronounced by Alexandre) and the conclusion of the romance.

In regard to these episodes, and indeed to most related passages, let it be said immediately that the Burgundian text most often appears to be a solid exercise in subtlety reduction. But before we condemn the redactor for literary incompetence, we should acknowledge our difficulty in determining whether he missed the subtleties of Chrétien's refined (and sometimes contorted) rhetorical demonstrations — not a hard thing to do when we are dealing with rhetorical elaborations of such complexity — or whether he grasped them but assumed, no doubt correctly, that they would not be appreciated at court.

In the Burgundian composition, most monologues are seriously truncated, though in interesting ways. That is true, necessarily, of Soredamors's debate concerning her newfound love: large components of the monologue are extraneous if her resistance to love is fundamentally redefined. More complex is the case of Alexandre's famous monologue about Love's arrow, an extended and complex passage (some 250 lines in all in Chrétien's work, 626-872) that is reduced to less than a page of the prose [289]. The best analysis of the passage in Chrétien is still, to my mind, that of Peter Haidu,[7] who points out that Alexandre's tortured logic and rhetorical distortions mirror his courtly unsophistication.

There are three divisions of the monologue in Chrétien. The first is the discussion of love as a malady afflicting the lover. This is kept with only nominal alterations in the Burgundian text. Second is the discussion of the way the arrow shot by love can enter through the eye without harming it.[8] The redactor keeps this as well, but reduces it significantly and negates both its subtlety and its force. He asks if love could have entered that way ("par l'eul," 289) and responds "nennil certez, car il seroit creue" [crevé]. Then, we are told, there comes to Alexandre "un entendement," an inspiration or a clarification of this enigma. That solution is a traditional explanation — Love's arrow entered his thought the way "the sun passes through a glass without breaking it" [290] — but it is also both perfunctory and dismissive: the *entendement* instructs Alexandre, now that he understands the principle, not to waste any more of his time on it ["*ad ce propolz ne te fault ja arrester ne occuper ton temps*," 290].

This conclusion, it must be said, also sounds suspiciously like the view of the narrator, who appears to see little point in silly debates, monologues, and rhetorical disquisitions; he simply dismisses the numerous lines that Chrétien's Alexandre devotes to this monologue. In the prose, Alexandre is accordingly told to worry less about whether and how he loves Soredamors than about how to please her; he should stop thinking and start acting.

The third division of the monologue in Chrétien's text is both revealing and (at least for patient readers) extraordinarily fascinating [770-872]. It involves Alexandre's description of Love's arrow, a meditation that transforms the arrow into a highly sensuous evocation of the lady. He begins to describe and analyze the arrow's symbolism — the feathers, for example, represent her beautiful hair — but quickly forgets it in his rapturous praise for her brow, eyes, nose, lips, teeth, throat, and shoulders. He returns to the arrow metaphor only to point out how it has failed him: although he has seen enough of her body (down to her *piz nu*, 844) to recognize its beauty, he cannot continue the description, because the "shaft" of the arrow is hidden in the quiver — the woman's clothes. (There also appears to be here another quiver, which is of sexual excitement as Alexandre thinks of what he cannot see.) I have summarized this section of the monologue, familiar as it is to all readers of Chrétien, in order to dramatize the change made by the redactor: he eliminates it all. And that is that.

Moreover, the conclusion of the work confirms the Burgundian author's reconceptualization of his source. In both texts, the emperor Alis (Alix in the prose) learns how he was deceived by the potion that protected his wife from his intended sexual advances. He orders his army to seek Cligès everywhere. Arthur summons his barons in order to do battle with Alis's, but before he can set out, messengers come to announce that Alis has conveniently died and that all his subjects want Cligès as emperor. Cligès and Fénice are crowned and married and live happily ever after.

In Chrétien, however, those assurances are immediately followed by authorial commentary that qualifies the passage considerably and transforms it into a complex and highly ambiguous ending (which I have discussed elsewhere).[9] The narrator, speaking of Fénice's happiness, notes that she was never kept confined, as many empresses have been since her time. It turns out that this practice of confining wives can be traced directly to Cligès and Fénice, for since their time,

> ... n'i ot empereor
> N'eüst de sa fame peor
> Qu'ele nel deüst decevoir
> ...

> Por ce einsi com an prison
> Est gardee an Costantinoble,
> Ja n'iert tant haute ne tant noble
> L'empererriz, quex qu'ele soit,
> Que l'empereres ne la croit
> Tant con de cesti li remanbre.
> Toz jorz la fet garder en chanbre ...
> (6743-45, 6750-56)

And Chrétien's concluding words remark that only eunuchs are safe from Love's snares [6760-61].

The conclusion of the verse romance thus informs us that the two lovers live on in bliss, but it is in a sense blissful ignorance, for they are unaware that their actions, while bringing them happiness, have condemned their female descendants to captivity and their male descendants to perpetual fear and doubt.

The Burgundian romance lacks all these qualifications, as the narrator appears eager to provide the happiest ending possible — and in the shortest time possible. He thus tells us, in the last few hundred words [338], of Alix's discovery of the truth, his intent to kill the lovers, Arthur's response, Alix's death, and Cligès's and Fénice's marriage and coronation. At this point, where Chrétien begins to cast ironic doubt on the happy ending, the Burgundian author simply tells us that the two of them were greatly loved by their people. They founded chapels and were so generous that God loved them greatly; He gave them several children, the oldest of whom ruled after them. Thereupon, the redactor announces that he will conclude the story that has been *transmuee de rime en prose* in March 1454. And he says no more.

The explanation — or at least a justification — for this alteration is provided by the author's view of the love that unites his characters. He is explicit about that view: Amour, he says, "veult que leur [Cligès's and Fénice's] entreprise soit celleement parfaite" [333]. Love, indeed, will brook no opposition, and the happy state of the lovers at the end is inevitable and predetermined. And that conception of the power of love is clearly incompatible with the involuted and highly ambiguous conclusion that, in Chrétien, leads us to question the efficacy of the course of action chosen by Cligès and Fénice. Chrétien's cynical conclusion concerning Love's snares is simply foreign to the spirit and conception of the Burgundian composition: love — or at least the attempt to accommodate it — may be destructive in Chrétien, but never in the later text.

And those observations about love retrospectively clarify a number of other alterations in the text, including some involving the connections with the Tristan story. It has been recognized[10] that Chrétien's Fénice loudly and frequently insists, not so much that she does not want to be like Iseut, but rather that she does not want people to be able to say that she is [see, for example, 3125-29]. The result, once again, is that the reader of

Chrétien understands something about the lovers and their love of which they themselves seem oblivious.

In the adaptation, however, the concern for public opinion is simply dropped.[11] As a result (of this and a great many other modifications),[12] the distance separating our point of view from the lovers' is diminished or entirely effaced. They have no doubts about their love, and the redactor excises or alters the passages that might use irony to compromise their happiness or the propriety of their actions. What remains is far simpler and more direct — or, as I said, more focused — than Chrétien's text, and their love is uncompromised by irony.

The redactor underlines this conception of their love by relating it to fortune. The text offers frequent references to "fortune," and in a number of them, it refers not to the kind of rise and fall exemplified by the Wheel of Fortune in many Arthurian texts, but rather to a different kind of "fate," specifically the fate that ties Cligès to Fénice. Here, "fortune" is the functional equivalent of love, and, as I noted, it is love that is ordained and indomitable.[13] The Burgundian romance is in fact less a *drama* of love than an illustration, almost a parable, of the inevitable and natural triumph of love over all obstacles and oppositions. Just as the hero is the consummate knight in the adaptation, he and Fénice are bound by a perfect and inexorable love. And in love there is no room for chance, choice, irony, or doubt.

Literary judgments are not simple in regard to this adaptation. Although we can identify and intellectually appreciate the structure and context within which the readactor was working, and the probable purpose that guided him (that is, to present to the Duke of Burgundy an ideal prefiguration of himself), we have still to deal with the critical question, which is really double: is his composition a good romance? and was it considered successful in its day?

My brief discussions of these passages may leave the impression that the redactor has cut the artistic heart from Chrétien's romance. And that notion, in my view, is not entirely without foundation.[14] I am not by any means arguing that Chrétien's vision or his text should be retained intact. Yet the fact remains that the adaptation, with irony excised, style homogenized, and dialogue reduced to a minimum, is flat and unengaging, sounding less like a story than like the detailed summary of a story. Even judgment tempered by charity produces only scant esthetic appreciation. The fifteenth-century *Cligès* is, in other words, an enormously fascinating creation, but not a very good one.

If it is not by our criteria a literary masterpiece, can we conclude that its reception was more positive and enthusiastic in 1454 than today? The question is even more difficult than the preceding one, and like Chrétien's romance, this essay must be left with an ambiguous ending, necessitated by the difficulty of assessing reception in the absence of explicit corroboration.

Whereas Wallen concludes that the adaptation "must have satisfied the intended public" [306], Charity Cannon Willard, noting that the *Cligès* is extant in a unique manuscript, infers from that fact that the adaptation was considerably less than successful.[15] Both of these contentions invite caveats: first, in response to Wallen, we have no real evidence that the adaptation was well received; second, to Willard, we must be exceedingly cautious, when evaluating literary success, not to rely too heavily on the number of extant manuscripts.

So where does this leave us? Given what we know about both the quality of the work and the tastes of the Burgundian court, we might well speculate that what was rejected was neither the redactor's project nor his vision, but his execution: he did precisely what he set out to do and presumably what he should have done to please his readership — but what he brought to the task was more earnestness than literary talent.

If that is true, we may have to content ourselves with taking the adaptation as a confirmation of the tastes prevalent at the end of the Middle Ages. Such an approach will permit us to conclude the following: first and unsurprisingly, that detailed accounts of adventure and war appealed far more strongly to the audience than did stories of love; second, that when love was treated at all, it was appropriate to emphasize its inevitability and its power, rather than introduce qualifications and quibbles; and finally, that literary tastes (or the personal preferences of those at the court) imposed the reduction or elimination of ironic formulations that threw into question the very premises the narrator appeared to be endorsing. In catering to those tastes, the redactor was in fact a reasonably capable reader of his audience and perhaps even of his text. But clearly he will not be mistaken for Chrétien de Troyes.

NOTES

[1] Christian von Troyes, *Sämtliche Werke*, vol. I, ed. Wendelin Foerster (Halle: Niemeyer, 1884); the Burgundian Prose *Cligès* is presented on pp. 281-353. References to Chrétien's verse text are to Chrétien de Troyes, *Cligès*, ed. Stewart Gregory and Claude Luttrell (Cambridge: D. S. Brewer, 1993). I cite Chrétien's romance by line number, the prose by page number.

[2] "The Art of Adaptation in the Fifteenth-Century *Erec et Enide* and *Cliges*" (diss. U of Wisconsin, 1972). I previously published a brief study of the *Erec* adaptation: "Motivation and Method in the Burgundian *Erec*," in *Conjunctures: Medieval Studies in Honor of Douglas Kelly*, ed. Keith Busby and Norris J. Lacy (Amsterdam: Rodopi, 1994), 271-80. It is possible but by no means certain that the two adaptations were made by the same author.

[3] Wallen states, concerning anachronisms, for example, that "... in this modernized Arthurian romance [they] need not be taken too seriously, because the adaptation does not really concern Arthur's court, but the court and leaders of

Burgundy in 1454" (306). True, but understanding its intended audience does not excuse its flaws.

[4] I find that suggestion reasonable and persuasive, and it reflects the customary practice in literary adaptations. It must be admitted, though, that we have no objective confirmation that such was the redactor's purpose. In part it is a self-confirming hypothesis; if we assume that purpose, many of the alterations make perfect sense.

[5] It must be noted that, in a good many passages, motivation is altered for reasons that are not easy (and sometimes not possible) to deduce. For example, in Chrétien, Soredamors's weaving of a strand of her hair into a shirt was a test to see if anyone could distinguish it from the gold of the threads (ll. 1163-68); the Burgundian composition, on the other hand, modifies the test, telling us that she wanted merely to learn which one — her hair or the gold — would last longer (292). This is a small and perhaps insignificant alteration, but it is an interesting and curious one. Perhaps we might conclude that a fifteenth-century public (or author) would find Chrétien's explanation — concerning a test of ability to distinguish real gold from her golden hair — trivial or far-fetched, but that is entirely speculative, and in any case it would require far more speculation to justify Soredamors's concern with the longevity of her hair.

[6] An example of Chrétien's irony, since Fénice is using deceit to escape her husband and live in sin with Cligès.

[7] *Aesthetic Distance in Chrétien de Troyes: Irony and Comedy in "Cligès" and "Perceval"* (Geneva: Droz, 1968).

[8] An excellent discussion of this image is offered by Claude Luttrell, "The Heart's Mirror in *Cligès*," in *Arthurian Literature*, XIII, ed. James P. Carley and Felicity Riddy (Cambridge: D. S. Brewer, 1995), 1-18.

[9] See *The Craft of Chrétien de Troyes* (Leiden: Brill, 1980), esp. 49-50.

[10] By a number of critics. For my observations on the subject, see *The Craft of Chrétien de Troyes*, 49.

[11] There is one small exception to this statement: when Cligès suggests that they flee openly (325), Fénice does express concern for her reputation.

[12] Wallen (313-16) suggests that the redactor further exonerates the lovers by emphasizing the notion of natural succession; that is, he points out that Cligès is, from the moment Alexandre dies, the proper and true emperor. Thus, Fénice, who was to marry the emperor, by rights belonged to Cligès.

[13] See for example 289 and 317, references to fortune tormenting and testing lovers; the passages leave no doubt that fortune is the equivalent of love. On one occasion the redactor refers to love as an "accident" (309), but in the context that implies that it is the work of fortune — love is destiny — rather than a matter of human emotion.

[14] But lest we condemn the redactor too hastily, let us admit that there are modern readers and students who find Chrétien's meandering monologues as tedious, and his irony as elusive, as the Burgundian author (or his audience) apparently did.

[15] See Willard's entry "Chrétien de Troyes, Burgundian Adaptations of," in *The New Arthurian Encyclopedia*, ed. Norris J. Lacy, et al. (New York: Garland, 1991), 91-92.

Washington University in St. Louis

Syntaxe et Technique Narrative: Titres et Attaques de Chapitre dans l' Erec *Bourguignon*

Maria Colombo Timelli

Les romans en prose du XVe siècle se définissent entre autres par une segmentation prononcée par rapport au continuum narratif qu'offraient les anciens romans en vers, cette partition textuelle se structurant essentiellement sur deux lieux que je définirais "névralgiques": titres et attaques de chapitre.[1] Lieux de la rupture les premiers, lieux de la reprise les secondes, ils dénoncent l'autonomie du prosateur vis-à-vis du texte-source, sa physionomie d'auteur plutôt que de simple "translateur" d'un contenu donné dans une langue et une forme renouvelées.

A partir de l'étude fondatrice de Georges Doutrepont sur les "mises en prose",[2] l'accent a été mis tout spécialement sur les procédés de ré-écriture affectant le contenu (en gros: abréviation, suppression d'une part, et d'-autre part allongement voire introduction de nouveaux épisodes),[3] les aspects plus strictement linguistiques et structuraux ayant très rarement fait l'objet d'analyses; rares sont encore aujourd'hui les études portant sur les techniques mises en œuvre dans ce passage, si souvent pratiqué et tant goûté au XVe siècle, de l'ancienne langue à la langue "moderne" et du vers à la prose.[4]

Du point de vue de leur fonction narrative, titres et attaques de chapitre s'opposent en partie, tout en s'intégrant réciproquement: si les rubriques anticipent sur le contenu, le filtrent (par la mise en relief de quelques éléments et l'effacement de quelques autres), l'interprètent et, par là, orientent la lecture; les attaques de chapitre se rapportent nécessairement au "déjà dit" (en ignorant, ou presque, l'interruption qui les précède), renvoient au "déjà connu", tout en introduisant et en déclenchant une nouvelle phase du récit.

Cette analyse a donc pour objet titres et débuts de chapitre dans la mise en prose bourguignonne du *Conte d'Erec* de Chrétien de Troyes,[5] rédigée selon toute probabilité vers 1454 et en tout cas avant 1468.[6] Mon but est de montrer comment et dans quelle mesure les nouveautés introduites par le prosateur — nouvelle lecture de la crise du couple, de la quête, de la réconciliation[7] — trouvent leur collocation et leur expression en quelque sorte "minimale" dans les moments de rupture du dérimage par rapport au texte de Chrétien. Les chiffres et pourcentages proposés plus loin n'auront d'autre but que de montrer comment des données quantitatives peuvent aussi contribuer à la reconnaissance du rapport entre deux textes si semblables — au point que l'un a pu n'être considéré que la "traduction" de l'autre — et cependant si différents.

1. Texte-source et remaniement

L'anonyme prosateur bourguignon répartit sa matière en 42 chapitres[8] de longueur sensiblement différente: des 16 lignes du chapitre VI (Erec empêchant la demoiselle de prendre l'épervier) aux 82 du chapitre XXXIX (histoire de Mabonagrain, fête de la "Joie de la Cour"), la moyenne étant de 41 lignes.[9] Sans pouvoir toujours reconnaître la logique qui sous-tend le morcellement du récit et l'organisation de celui-ci en fragments plus ou moins étendus, on constate que les chapitres brefs isolent pour la plupart un épisode qu'il s'agit de mettre en relief et dont l'importance se perdrait au sein d'une narration plus ample. C'est le cas du chapitre VI, que l'on vient de rappeler, et des chapitres XII et XIII (Enide habillée par la reine et prenant place à côté du roi, épisodes qui marquent l'entrée et l'assimilation de la jeune fille dans la cour arthurienne).

Le rapport entre le nombre des vers du roman (6932 à l'exclusion du prologue, v. 1-26) et le nombre des lignes de la prose (1719 à l'exclusion du prologue et des titres) peut encore apporter des éléments utiles à l'appréciation du travail du remanieur. Bien que celui-ci s'éloigne parfois remarquablement de la "rime" de Chrétien (et ceci tout spécialement à la fin du roman: chapitres XL-XLII), nombre des vers de la source se reconnaissent dans la version bourguignonne,[10] ce qui permet de suivre l'une sous l'aspect formellement renouvelé de l'autre et de mettre ainsi en relation les chapitres de la prose et les vers correspondants du roman du XIIe siècle.[11]

Mon relevé a montré que:

a) la prose représente en moyenne 50% du texte en vers. Un pourcentage compris entre 41% et 60% se relève en effet pour 16 chapitres sur 39 (les trois derniers ne pouvant pas être pris en compte à ce propos), qui se distribuent assez régulièrement dans les deux premiers tiers du roman, jusqu'au chapitre XXXI (combat victorieux d'Erec contre les deux géants).

b) dans 12 chapitres sur 39, le rythme de la prose ralentit considérablement: les lignes représentent alors 61%-80% des vers dans six chapitres, 81%-100% dans six autres, ce phénomène se réalisant surtout au début et vers le milieu du récit.

c) dans 8 chapitres sur 39, en revanche, le rythme de la prose accélère sensiblement (entre 21% et 40% des vers), cinq de ces chapitres se situant vers la fin du roman, notamment à partir du chapitre XXXII (mort simulée d'Erec).

d) dans les trois chapitres qui restent, enfin, la proportion s'inverse: la prose amplifie, développe le texte de départ jusqu'à le dépasser (11%, 12% et 12% pour les chapitres XV, XXVII, et XXXIII respectivement). Le contenu de ces tranches de texte ne nous surprend pas: il s'agit d'une part du tournoi organisé après les noces d'Erec et Enide,[12] de la longue complainte d'Enide sur la mort / évanouissement de son mari.

Certes, ces données ne disent rien sur la technique de la version en prose, ni, d'ailleurs, sur les procédés utilisés; une proportion de 100% ne saurait impliquer que le *même contenu* est transposé du vers à la prose. Une telle analyse contribue pourtant à une meilleure connaissance du texte bourguignon en montrant que si, dans la partie la plus importante du récit, le prosateur s'en tient assez fidèlement à sa source. Vers la fin du roman il affirme sa liberté jusqu'à abandonner tout à fait le texte en vers pour introduire un long épisode entièrement nouveau (le dernier tournoi, où Erec se bat *incognito*) et pour élaborer une conclusion relativement autonome.

2. Titres de chapitre

Donner un titre à un fragment de texte — pas moins que le découpage lui-même — n'est pas un acte dépourvu de sens.[13] Dans l'*Erec* en prose, les titres de chapitre jouent trois fonctions: non seulement ils répartissent le texte en un certain nombre de fragments, mais ils assument d'une part une valeur informative, et, de l'autre, une valeur interprétative incontestable. Si le contenu du titre est censé couvrir en le synthétisant le même contenu que le morceau du récit qui va suivre, ceci ne se réalise pas toujours dans la réalité textuelle: une lecture suivie des rubriques, comme dans une "table des matières", le prouverait sans difficulté.[14] Non seulement un tri est opéré sur l'ensemble de la matière — ce qui est, bien entendu, inévitable — mais des épisodes sont ignorés, des personnages gommés, ce qui empêche de suivre le déroulement linéaire du récit. Quelques exemples parmi les plus frappants:[15]

— le titre du chapitre XIV ("Comment le roy baisa Enide") ignore tout à fait l'épisode capital du mariage des deux protagonistes;

— le titre du chapitre XVII ("Comment Erec se parti de la court du roy Artus et s'en ala en son pays") néglige quant à lui Enide et le charme qu'elle exerce sur son mari, source cependant du déséquilibre qui va provoquer la crise du couple et le début de la quête;

— le titre du chapitre XXXVII ("Comment le roy Evrain vint a l'encontre de Erec") ne fait aucune mention de l'aventure de la "Joie de la Cour" qui démarre pourtant juste après l'accueil du couple de la part du roi.

En somme, c'est souvent le non-dit (dont le lecteur est à même de se rendre compte seulement *a posteriori*, la lecture du chapitre une fois achevée) qui semble l'emporter. S'agit-il d'un choix conscient et voulu du prosateur, ou bien exagérons-nous la valeur interprétative des rubriques du roman? Sans vouloir forcer le texte, il me semble remarquable que ce non-dit concerne très souvent Enide, sa présence à côté du protagoniste, sa vie psychologique, les mouvements de son âme et de son coeur, qui constituent pourtant le véritable moteur de ses actions, et, par là, de celles d'Erec. Dans au moins cinq cas on ignore — délibérément? — l'héroïne:

Ch. V: "Comment Erec fu armé et comment il alla au lieu ou l'en devoit prendre l'esprevier"; toute la première partie du chapitre est consacrée aux pensées d'amour des deux protagonistes;

Ch. XVII: "Comment Erec se parti de la court du roy Artus et s'en ala en son pays"; le couple est accueilli à la cour du roi Lach, et Enide y est tout spécialement fêtée;

Ch. XXII: "Comment Erec vault faire coucier Enide en une forest, mais elle ne vault et lui dist qu'il en avoit milleur besoing qu'elle"; le chapitre est en grande partie occupé par le monologue de l'épouse;

Ch. XXIII: "Comment le seigneur d'un chasteau pria Enide d'amourz"; le titre se tait quant à la réaction de la jeune femme aux propositions malhonnêtes du chevalier;

Et surtout Ch. XXXV: "Comment Guivret abbati Erec a ung cours de lance dont aprés il fu bien marri"; aucune allusion n'est faite à la paix enfin rétablie entre les époux; pour ne rien dire des titres du type "Comment Erec..." qui seraient bien plus fidèles au texte sous la formule "Comment Erec et Enide..." (ch. XXXVI, XL, XLII).

Il n'est peut-être pas hasardé de voir dans la formulation même de ces intitulés une confirmation de la lecture de Martha Wallen:[16] la culpabilité d'Enide ne faisant pas de doute pour le prosateur, celui-ci "punirait" l'héroïne par son effacement presque systématique dans les lieux députés à la mise en relief des éléments essentiels du récit.

Par leur énonciation, ainsi que par l'ordre de présentation de leurs composants, les titres de chapitre établissent également une hiérarchie des signifiés (personnages, faits, circonstances).

Remarquons d'abord que nos rubriques ont *toutes* un sujet animé, dans la plupart des cas défini par un nom propre,[17] ce sujet trouvant toujours sa collocation juste après l'adverbe inaugurant *Comment*. Il n'est pas étonnant de relever la présence d'Erec en fonction de sujet dans 26 titres sur 42,[18] auxquels il faut ajouter 11 autres occurrences en fonction de complément, direct ou indirect.[19] Ceci revient à dire que le protagoniste est sur scène 35 fois sur 42.

Qu'en est-il de son épouse? Notre lecture anti-Enide trouve-t-elle une confirmation dans ce relevé? Les chiffres sont univoques. Enide est présente 17 fois dans les titres: 9 comme sujet,[20] 8 comme complément.[21] Le pourcentage est donc nettement inférieur à celui d'Erec.

Ce n'est pas tout: les deux époux apparaissent ensemble dans 11 intitulés, mais deux seules fois ils y constituent un couple grammatical (sujet du même verbe: ch. XI; objet direct: ch. XXX). Dans les autres cas ils sont chacun l'objet de l'action de l'autre, ils coexistent sans former unité. Est-ce trop d'affirmer que l'éclatement du couple se reflète dans la structure syntaxique des titres?

Une dernière remarque, enfin, pour le centre autour duquel, chez Chrétien, l'aventure prenait son sens: la cour du roi Artus. Celui-ci constitue le sujet de trois titres: le premier, où il est expressément nommé ("comment le roi Artus vouloit aler chassier le blanc cerf..."),[22] et deux autres (chapitres XIII et XIV), où il n'est indiqué que comme "le roy".[23] Dans les six autres cas où le nom d'Artus apparaît, il ne constitue que le complément du nom de "la cour", ce qui revient à dire qu'il n'incarne qu'une des circonstances (locative) de l'action.[24] Et, de fait, le rôle joué par le roi à l'intérieur de notre dérimage est plutôt celui d'un point de repère, qui n'agit presque pas — ou presque plus — mais qui représente les coordonnées spatio-temporelles d'un vague passé et d'une tout aussi vague géographie.

L'ordre des mots dans les intitulés relève plutôt du domaine de la syntaxe de phrase, mais il révèle tout aussi la hiérarchisation des informations telle que le prosateur la conçoit. Une lecture même rapide des rubriques de l'*Erec* montre que le seul procédé de mise en relief utilisé est le choix du sujet. La place du sujet étant toujours la deuxième, après l'adverbe *Comment* (qui joue simplement la fonction d'indicateur de titre), c'est la forme active ou passive du verbe qui permet le cas échéant de souligner l'importance d'un personnage. Ceci devient sans doute plus évident dans les cas de recours au verbe passif:

V. Comment Erec fu armé...

VIII. Comment le chevalier fu vaincu...

XI. Comment Erec et Enide s'amie furent rechupz...

XII. Comment Enide fu vestue....

Un peu moins de la moitié des titres (16 sur 42) présentent une structure simple, du type sujet-verbe-complément(s) direct et/ou indirect:

II. Comment une damoiselle et Erec furent ferus d'un naim.

XIV. Comment le roy baisa Enide.

XXI. Comment Erec occist V bringans chevalierz l'un aprez l'aultre.[25]

Dans les cas de titres "bicéphales",[26] formés de deux propositions coordonnées par la conjonction *et* (la seconde proposition pouvant ou non être précédée de *comment*), la structure reste la même, mais le sujet de la seconde proposition, conformément aux habitudes du français de l'époque,[27] n'est exprimé que lorsqu'il diffère du précédent:

XIII. Comment *Enide* entra en salle et *le roy* le fist soir d'enprés luy.

XVII. Comment *Erec* se parti de la court du roy Artus et s'en ala en son pays.

XXVII. Comment *Erec et Guivret* joustent ensamble et aprez se combatent a l'espee.[28]

Dix-huit intitulés présentent une structure complexe, avec deux subordonnées, et, parfois, des propositions coordonnées par *et* ou *mais*. Il s'agit bien entendu de rubriques longues et surtout plus proches que les précédentes de l'articulation de la prose du texte:

III. Comment Erec se loga sur ung hoste *qui* avoit une belle fille de noble lignage *mais* povre estoit.

XXII. Comment Erec vault *faire coucier* Enide en une forest, *mais* elle ne vault *et* lui dist *qu*'il en avoit milleur besoing qu'elle.

XXVI. Comment Guivret le Petit poursuivi Erec et comment Enide se doulousa *quant* elle le vit venir.

XL. Comment Erec s'en alla a la court du roy Artus *et* eust nouvelle *que* le roi son pere estoit mort.

Une brève remarque sur le titre du chapitre XXVII, qui se détache des autres par une particularité morphologique: c'est le seul où les verbes soient conjugués au présent de l'indicatif ("Comment Erec et Guivret *joustent* ensamble et aprés *se combatent* a l'espee").[29] Si l'on vérifie le contexte, on remarque qu'aussi bien la fin du chapitre précédent que le début du même chapitre XXVII actualisent l'action — il s'agit du combat d'Erec et de Guivret — par l'emploi systématique du présent de narration:

fin du ch. XXVI: se retourne / prent a dire / tance / a talent / congnoit / ayme / puet / craint / est / vainct.

début du chapitre XXVII: entend et sent / se retourne / semond / voyt / deffie / couchent / est / s'entrefierent / ont / s'entrenavrent / ont / se arrestent / pueent.

Le choix du prosateur semblerait donc déterminé par la volonté d'accorder la formulation du titre à la narration, en évitant toute rupture même grammaticale. Cette explication ne saurait toutefois s'appliquer à l'ensemble de l'*Erec*. Sans trop nous éloigner de cet exemple, entre la fin du même chapitre XXVII et le début du chapitre suivant, tous les deux rédigés au présent, s'insère un titre au passé:

fin du ch. XXVII: ardent / cessent / y a / ait / perdront / se rende.

titre: Comment Erec *rompi* l'espee de Guivret qui en *eut* grant duel.

début du ch. XXVIII: voit / s'entreessaient / scet / fault / chiet.

Des titres formulés au passé peuvent interrompre un récit rédigé en partie au présent, en partie au passé:

> fin du ch. XXV: s'en va / treuvent / osent / se mettent / emmeinent.
>
> titre: Comment Guivret le Petit *poursuivi* Erec et comment Enide *se doulousa* quant elle le *vit* venir.
>
> début du ch. XXVI: se delivra / eust cheminé / se trouva.

Force nous est de constater en somme que le temps grammatical du texte n'exerce aucune contrainte visible sur celui de la rubrique. De plus, si dans le récit on peut passer sans aucune gêne du passé simple au présent et l'inverse, la formulation des titres est en revanche beaucoup plus régulière: avec la seule exception que l'on vient de signaler (titre du ch. XXVII), les intitulés renvoient tous au passé, c'est-à-dire à une action révolue, à une histoire déjà connue, à un texte déjà écrit.

Les critiques s'accordent à affirmer que dans une mise en prose la composition des titres est faite *a posteriori*, une fois le travail de dérimage, remaniement et segmentation du texte achevé.[30] Il s'agirait en somme de la dernière touche donnée à un ouvrage complet. J'ai voulu vérifier comment les titres de l'*Erec* ont été assemblés, en recherchant une — éventuelle — correspondance entre les éléments de la rubrique et le texte lui-même: recherche tour à tour fructueuse et décevante. Tout au début du roman, le titre du chapitre Ier se retrouve deux fois dans le texte, une première fois fragmenté, une seconde fois en entier:

> comment le roi Artus vouloit aler chasser le blanc cerf en la forest adventureuse.
>
> le roi Artus... en la forest aventureuse... cerf... blanc... il avoit est chassi; (p. 253, l. 19-21)
>
> le roy Artus... voult aler en la forest adventureuse chassier le cerf. (p. 253, l. 24-26)

Il peut arriver que les éléments du titre figurent dans le texte à l'intérieur d'un discours direct:

> ch. X: Comment Erec conclud au souper d'enmener l'endemain Enide a la court du roy Artus.
>
> "J'emmaineray demain... Enide... a la court du roi Artus". (p. 261, l. 35-37)

Parfois encore, titre et texte utilisent soit des synonymes, soit des paraphrases renvoiant au même contenu:

> ch. XV: Comment ceulx de la court du roy Artus firent ung tournoy aprés lez nopces.

lez chevaliers de la Table Roonde entreprinrent ung tournoy... aprés lez nopcez. (p. 265, l. 38-39)

ch. XVIII: Comment Erec interroga Enide pour quoy elle plouroit et elle lui en dist la cause.

son mari... l'interroga pour savoir la cause de cez pleurs... Si lui dist:... (p. 268, l. 41-44; p. 269, l. 1)[31]

Etendue au total de la prose, cette petite fouille confirme à mon sens non seulement l'ordre hypothétique du travail du dérimeur (mise en prose du texte, *puis* rédaction des titres), mais aussi sa technique de construction des intitulés, qui peuvent ne pas respecter pleinement le contenu du récit qu'ils ouvrent, mais en tirent dans la plupart des cas leurs composants.

Dans l'ensemble, cette analyse sur les titres de chapitre nous éclaire, me semble-t-il, sur la fonction que le "metteur en prose" *se* confère: il s'agit pour lui d'exploiter toutes les possibilités pour réorganiser, voire pour réinterpréter, une matière dont il n'est pas le créateur, mais qu'il peut s'approprier pour en faire profiter un nouveau destinataire, de nouveaux lecteurs, une nouvelle époque.

3. Attaques de chapitre

Nous avons déjà remarqué que le découpage en chapitres de l'*Erec* ne coïncide pas (toujours) avec le découpage des épisodes ou des différentes phases du récit, ce qui revient à dire que normalement il n'y a pas de correspondance directe entre tranche de texte et tranche de récit. Les ruptures de l'histoire, c'est-à-dire les passages d'une séquence à l'autre, explicités par le prosateur, se situent plutôt, aussi bizarre que cela puisse paraître à nos yeux, à l'intérieur des chapitres:

Nostre compte ne s'arrestera point a parler... mais trop bien pour entrer en matere vendra a dire...; (p. 253, l. 17-18)

mais nostre compte atant laissera a parler... et maintenant vendra au fait de Erec...; (p. 261, l. 11-13)

Cy laira ung petit nostre compte a parler... et maintenant vendra a dire que Erec...; (p. 264, l. 21-22)[32]

Nous laisserons... pencer aux lisans... et pour parler des fais de Erec nostre histoire racompte que...; (p. 265, l. 36-38)

Du tournoy ne parlera non plus avant nostre present compte; (p. 267, l. 23)

Et atant revendrons nous a parler de Erec...; (p. 283, l.4)

> mais atant laisserons nous ung petit a parler de Erec et vendrons a racompter que.... (p. 285, l. 28-29)[33]

Il est nettement moins fréquent que cette transition se situe entre la fin d'un chapitre et le début d'un autre. Je n'en relève que trois exemples:

> atant vendrons nous a parler de Erec... (p. 255, l.15: fin du chapitre II)

> comme cy aprez sera dit. (p. 268, l. 26: fin du chapitre XVII)

> plorant et disant en ceste maniere. (p. 269, l. 16-17: fin du chapitre XVIII)

La structure des chapitres de l'*Erec* peut se schématiser comme suit: clôture d'un chapitre (non de l'épisode) // suspension (titre) // ouverture du nouveau chapitre (non d'un nouvel épisode).[34] Cette "ouverture" constitue donc plutôt la reprise d'un récit momentanément suspendu et se fait grâce à des éléments de liaison aussi bien "scéniques" (portant sur le décor, les personnages), que syntaxiques et linguistiques (connecteurs, déterminants etc.).

Du point de vue syntaxique, 17 chapitres sur 42 (40%) s'ouvrent par une attaque temporelle:[35]

compléments temporels	*propositions temporelles*
durant: XI	quant: IV, VII, XXIII, XXX, XXXIV, XXXV, XXXVII, XXXIX, XLII
aprés: XIII, XXXII	comme: IX, XLI
a: XXIX	tantost aprés que: XIV
	aprés ce que: XVII

En particulier, les propositions constituent sans aucun doute l'un des moules les plus constants qui aient servi à l'agencement des chapitres dans l'*Erec*. L'ordre chronologique linéaire des actions forme la charpente solide sur laquelle le récit tout entier se bâtit.

Groupe moins nombreux mais significatif, les attaques en sujet nominal (11 sur 42: 26%)[36] mettent en jeu, selon la définition de Jean Rychner, la "relation dramatique":[37] le passage d'une phase à l'autre du récit porte alors sur le sujet, sans recours à aucun élément hétérogène. La typologie en est différenciée: deux seuls sujets inanimés (I, XVI) contre neuf animés; parmi ceux-ci Erec revient trois fois (III, XXVII, XXXI), Enide trois fois également (XV, XXVIII, XXXIII); les trois attaques qui restent mettent en scène "la reyne Guenievre" (II), "le sire du chasteau" (VI: il s'agit du comte de Lalut), "les chevaliers du royaulme" (XVIII).

Quant aux attaques circonstancielles, on relève d'abord l'absence des propositions, à côté de cinq attaques en adverbe / locution adverbiale et une en complément: six attaques au total, correspondant à 14%.[38]

Trois relations fondamentales structurent donc l'*Erec* en prose, tout au moins en début de chapitre:[39] la relation temporelle, la relation dramatique, la relation circonstancielle. Comme le souligne Jean Rychner pour la *Mort Artu*,[40] les relations logiques (hypothèse, cause, concession, but) ne jouent ici aucun rôle.

On remarquera pour conclure que la présence sur scène d'Erec en ouverture de chapitre est bien plus massive que ne le feraient supposer les trois attaques en Erec-sujet nominal. De fait, le protagoniste constitue le sujet exprimé de six propositions temporelles (IV, XI, XXXV, XXXVII, XLI, XLII) contre une seule occurrence pour Enide (XIV); en outre, parmi les attaques en complément temporel, une fois sur trois Erec est le sujet de la proposition principale (XXXII); parmi les attaques circonstancielles, enfin, on relève: un sujet Erec (X), deux sujets Enide (V, XX), un sujet "double" (XXI: "Ainsi s'en vont Enide et Erec", avec un renversement inhabituel des deux termes du couple).

Il faut encore souligner que dans la grande majorité des cas le sujet exprimé en début de chapitre est déjà en scène dans la dernière phrase du chapitre précédent, quelle qu'y soit sa fonction syntaxique, ce qui renforce à la lecture la sensation de continuité d'un fragment de texte à l'autre. De plus, le prosateur a recours à de nombreux éléments de liaison (reprise de mots, synonymes, déterminants, connecteurs, mais aussi verbes exprimant la perception, ou la réaction, d'un personnage à la scène précédente). Il va de soi que le cumul éventuel de ces éléments dans une même attaque intensifie la cohérence du récit d'une séquence à l'autre par l'annulement de l'interruption que représente le titre. Quelques exemples parmi les plus frappants:

fin du ch. XV: [Saigramors et Gavain] *rompent lancez*, cassent escus et font tresbucier hommes et chevaulz...

[rubrique]

début du ch. XVI: *Les lancez* ne sont pas encores toutez *desbrisies* quant Erec...

(emploi de synonymes: *rompre*, *debriser*; reprise d'un substantif: *lancez*; introduction de l'article défini: *les* lancez)

fin du ch. XXXVI: [Guivret commence à révéler à Erec le mystère du jardin enchanté] illec a *ung vergier* ouquel jamaix yver ne esté n'a default de nouveau fruit ne de fleurz, et si ne est si hardi homme de soy y embatre ne d'i porter armez pour *une adventure* quy y est.

[rubrique]

début du chapitre XXXVII: Quant Erec *entend la façon du vergier* et qu'il y a *aulcune adventure*...

(reprise des deux mots-clés: *vergier*, *adventure*; passage de l'indéfini *ung* au défini *le* (*du*); résumé de la description du jardin: *la façon du vergier*; emploi du verbe de perception: *entendre*).[41]

Plutôt que de profiter de la valeur inaugurante des débuts de chapitre pour introduire de nouveaux personnages ou une nouvelle aventure, en somme, l'auteur de l'*Erec* en prose semble rechercher tous les moyens pour agencer le récit, pour reprendre le fil de son discours après une suspension momentanée qui n'affecte pas le déroulement de l'histoire.

4. En conclusion

Quel bilan, fort partiel évidemment, pouvons-nous tirer de cette analyse? Nous permet-elle éventuellement de porter un jugement sur la technique qui régit la mise en prose de l'*Erec* et d'en reconnaître les traits marquants?

Reprenons d'abord les propres mots du dérimeur, qui s'exprime en première personne dans le prologue du roman,[42] où, à partir d'une *sententia*, d'une affirmation de portée générale, conformément aux préceptes de la rhétorique médiévale, il réaffirme l'utilité de connaître les histoires des anciens:

> "Au continuel exercice du racomptement dez histoires contenans les fais des nobles anchians *l'en puelt assez proffiter* par divers moyens. Et pour ce que l'en m'a presentee le histoire de Erec le filz du roy Lach *en rime*, je, au plaisir de Dieu, occuperay mon estude ung petit de tamps a le *transmuer de rime en prose* selon la maniere qui s'ensuit, priant que ceulx qui cy aprés le lirront qu'ilz ayent mon ruide stille de parler pour excusé." (p. 253, l. 1-6; c'est moi qui souligne)

Si l'accent porte ici sur le passage du vers à la prose — et en second lieu sur le "ruide stille" du prosateur (véritable *topos* dans les prologues du XVe siècle) — aucune allusion n'est faite quant au rajeunissement linguistique, rendu nécessaire par l'évolution remarquable du français au cours des trois siècles qui séparent le roman de Chrétien du public bourguignon, évolution qui pouvait rendre, et rendait de fait, incompréhensibles les anciens textes, et qui est une des causes du mouvement littéraire des "mises en prose" selon G. Doutrepont.[43]

Rien non plus n'est dit quant aux procédés mis en œuvre dans ce passage "de rime en prose", ce qui n'implique d'ailleurs pas une technique approximative, ou inconsciente, chez le prosificateur. Ce que la critique moderne ne reconnaît normalement pas, et que ces artisans de la parole ne se reconnaissent eux non plus, ce sont des compétences précises, ayant trait notamment, d'une part, à la langue ancienne, et, d'autre part, aux techniques de modernisation nécessaires pour rendre un vieux texte à nouveau lisible et profitable. S'il s'agit en premier lieu de conserver une *histoire* (cf. le prologue ci-dessus), il faut d'un côté rénover la langue, et de l'autre agir sur le contenu pour qu'il soit agréable aux nouveaux destinataires. Comment notre dérimeur a-t-il agi sur le vieux récit? La lecture en détail des titres et des débuts de chapitre nous a réservé quelques surprises: si le roman de Chrétien se voulait bien "d'Erec, le fil Lac... le contes" (v. 19), le remanieur accentue le côté masculin de l'histoire; il s'agit de plus en plus de l'"histoire de Erec," où Enide, malgré son amour et sa fidélité, est mise à l'épreuve par son époux — et par le nouvel auteur — bien plus cruellement qu'elle ne l'avait été trois siècles auparavant, au point qu'elle a failli disparaître — tout au moins dans les lieux portants du nouveau roman.

NOTES

[1] Les interruptions éventuelles dans les textes en vers, marquées par l'aspect graphique des manuscrits, ne provoquent pas de véritable rupture dans le récit. Interruptions essentiellement visuelles, elles ne comportent pas de fait la reprise de la narration qu'exige l'introduction d'un titre de chapitre.

[2] Georges Doutrepont, *Les mises en prose des épopées et des romans chevaleresques du XIVe au XVIe siècle* (Bruxelles, 1939; Genève: Slatkine Reprints, 1969).

[3] Jean Frappier, "Sur le *Perceval en prose* de 1530", *Fin du Moyen Age et Renaissance — Mélanges de Philologie française offerts Robert Guiette* (Anvers: De nederlandsche Boekhandel, 1961), 233-47; Charity C. Willard, "A Fifteenth-Century Burgundian Version of the *Roman de Florimont*," *Medievalia et Humanistica* n.s., II (1971), 21-46; Martha Wallen, "Significant Variations in the Burgundian Prose Version of *Erec et Enide*," *Medium AEvum* 51 (1982), 187-96; Danielle Quéruel, "Des mises en prose aux romans de chevalerie dans les collections bourguignonnes," *Rhétorique et mise en prose au XVe siècle (Actes du VIe Colloque International sur le Moyen Français;* Milan: Vita e Pensiero, 1991), II, 173-93; Elina Suomela Härmä, "La mise en prose de *Renart le Nouvel*," *Rhétorique et mise en prose*, II, 229-43; Hans-Erich Keller, "La technique des mises en prose des chansons de geste," *Olifant* 17 (1992), 5-28; Norris J. Lacy, "Motivation and Method in the Burgundian *Erec*," *Conjunctures: Medieval Studies in Honor of Douglas Kelly*, ed. K. Busby and N. J. Lacy (Amsterdam: Rodopi, 1994), 271-80.

[4] François Suard, *Guillaume d'Orange. Etude du roman en prose* (Paris: Champion, 1979), notamment ch. III, "Les aspects caractéristiques du style": 195-272; Aimé Petit et François Suard (éds.), *Le livre des amours du Chastellain de Coucy et de la Dame de Fayel* (Lille: Presses Universitaires de Lille, 1994), 25-26; de brèves remarques aussi dans: C. J. Harvey, "Jean Wauquelin 'translateur' de *La Manekine*", communication au VIIIe Colloque International sur le Moyen Français, *Néologie et création verbale*, McGill, Montréal, 7-9 octobre 1996 (Actes sous presse). En dehors du rapport direct vers/prose, voir l'étude de Cedric E. Pickford, *L'évolution du roman arthurien en prose vers la fin du Moyen Age d'après le manuscrit 112 du fonds*

français de la Bibliothèque Nationale (Paris: Nizet, 1970), surtout 154-75; et les observations de Henry John Chaytor, *From Script to Print. An Introduction to Medieval Vernacular Literature* (Cambridge: Cambridge University Press, 1945), notamment 83-114, "Prose & Translation".

[5] C'est à dessein que j'utilise cet intitulé, le seul qui apparaisse dans le roman de Chrétien (v. 19), malgré le renvoi célèbre du premier vers de *Cligés* ("Cil qui fit d'Erec et d'Enide") qui s'est imposé par la suite. De manière tout fait cohérente, le remanieur du XVe siècle annonce dans son prologue "le histoire de Erec le filz du roy Lach" (éd. Wendelin Foerster, *Erec und Enide von Christian von Troyes* [Halle: Niemeyer, 1890]:253). La transcription de l'*Erec* en prose par W. Foerster (253-94; notes 334-36) est encore la seule "édition" disponible du texte bourguignon: je prépare actuellement l'édition critique. Toutes les citations qui suivent ont été vérifiées sur le manuscrit de Bruxelles, Bibliothèque Royale, fonds général n. 7235, avec les interventions habituelles: distinction u/v i/j, résolution des abréviations, séparation des mots, normalisation des majuscules, introduction de l'accent aigu sur 'e' tonique final, introduction de la cédille et de quelques signes de ponctuation. Je n'ai pas tenu compte ici de la version partielle du roman transmise dans le manuscrit fr. 363 de la B.N. de Paris (fo 193r°–222r°) ni d'ailleurs du fragment d'une feuille contenu dans le ms. douce 388 de la Bodleian Library d'Oxford. Pour une étude linguistique des deux rédactions d'*Erec* et de la mise en prose de *Cligès*, on se rapportera à: Bette Lou Bakelaar, "Certain Characteristics of the Syntax and Style in the Fifteenth-Century *mises en prose* of Chrestien's *Erec* and *Cligès*," *Semasia* 3 (1976), 61-73.

[6] Pour la datation, cf. Doutrepont, *Mises en prose*, 262-64. Le rapport avec la mise en prose de *Cligés* est traité par le même Doutrepont (261-64), ainsi que par Foerster (*Erec und Enide*, XVI). Les tables en annexe renvoient à l'édition Foerster, aussi bien pour la numérotation des vers que pour les lignes de la rédaction en prose.

[7] Cf. Wallen, "Significant Variations"; ainsi que Lacy, "Motivation and Method".

[8] Une ultérieure division semble être marquée par une lettre capitale occupant deux lignes (c'est la dimension normale des lettres indiquant le début des chapitres) au f. 35v° du manuscrit (Foerster, *Erec und Enide*, 272: "A grans regretz ..."). Cette disoit Enide cez parollez rupture, qui suivrait immédiatement un monologue d'Enide, est très vraisemblable: une rubrique pourrait avoir "sauté" au cours de la transcription. Sur la répartition de la "matière" en chapitres, voir l'analyse de François Suard, *Guillaume d'Orange*, 148-60.

[9] Cf. tables 1a et 1b en annexe. A remarquer que 12 chapitres sur 42 occupent de 35–45 lignes.

[10] Les renvois présents dans l'édition Foerster peuvent être complétés.

[11] La table 2 illustre la correspondance lignes / vers et le rapport proportionnel entre les deux: pour déterminer celui-ci, j'ai établi l'équivalence 1 ligne = 2 vers, sur la base du nombre moyen de mots compris dans une ligne de la prose de l'édition utilisée (12/14 mots) et dans un vers de Chrétien (6 mots). Malgré le taux d'approximation des pourcentages ainsi obtenus, ceux-ci gardent une valeur relative d'un certain intérêt.

[12] Plus besoin d'insister sur l'engouement pour les tournois et les jeux chevaleresques à la cour de Bourgogne. Pour un panoramique des réalisations littéraires de ce

motif dans quelques romans du XVe siècle, je me permets de renvoyer à ma thèse de doctorat (*Le motif littéraire du jeu chevaleresque dans les romans du cycle "Jehan d'Avennes" (XVe siècle)*, Università degli Studi di Milano, a.a. 1988-89) ainsi qu'à mon étude "Entre littérature et vie: le jeu chevaleresque dans la Bourgogne de Philippe le Bon," *Rencontres Médiévales en Bourgogne (XIV-XVe siècles)* 2 (1992), 27-45.

[13] Les observations qui suivent sont inspirées en partie à Pierre Demarolle, "De la narratologie à la syntaxe: les titres des chapitres de la mise en prose de Garrin le Lorrain par Philippe de Vigneulles," *Rhétorique et mise en prose*, II, 245-55. Sur la fonction des rubriques, voir aussi Pickford, *Evolution*, 163-70.

[14] Sur l'habitude de réunir les rubriques en tête ou en queue d'un volume dans le but de fournir une table analytique du roman concerné, cf. Pickford, *Evolution*, 171-72.

[15] Sur l'imprécision des rubriques, voir les remarques de François Suard, *Guillaume d'Orange*, 151. Les titres de chapitres de notre *Erec* sont groupés en annexe (table 3).

[16] "Significant Variations."

[17] Sujets non identifiés par un nom propre: II. Comment *une damoiselle* et Erec...; VII. Comment Erec et *le chevalier aux armez blancez*...; VIII. Comment *le chevalier*...; XIV. Comment *le roy*...; XV. Comment *ceulx de la court*...; XXIII. Comment *le seigneur d'un chasteau*...; XXXVIII. Comment Erec et *le chevalier*...; XXXIX. Comment *le champion de la damoiselle*... Les 42 titres sont groupés dans la table 3.

[18] Chapitres: II, III, IV, V, VI, VII, X, XI, XVI, XVII, XVIII, XX, XXI, XXII, XXV, XXVII, XXVIII, XXIX, XXXI, XXXII, XXXIV, XXXVI, XXXVIII, XL, XLI, XLII. Voir table 4.

[19] Chapitres: VIII, XVIII, XIX, XXII, XXIV, XXVI, XXX, XXXIII, XXXV, XXXVII, XXXIX. Dans deux cas (ch. XVIII et XXII), Erec apparaît aussi bien en fonction de sujet que comme complément: il est peu significatif que la seconde fois il le soit sous forme de renvoi pronominal.

[20] Chapitres: XI, XII, XIII, XVIII, XIX, XXII, XXIV, XXVI, XXXIII.

[21] Chapitres: III, X, XIV, XVIII, XXII, XXIII, XXX, XXXII. On remarque que dans l'intitulé du chapitre III Enide n'est évoquée que comme "une belle fille", sans nom. Dans les titres des chapitres XVIII et XXII (cf. Erec) elle est complément d'abord, sujet ensuite.

[22] Inutile de souligner que c'est à partir d'une décision du roi que l'action démarre et donc que l'écriture de cette action se justifie.

[23] Cette dénomination — non suivie de nom propre — est réservée au roi Artus; dans les autres cas, les rubriques spécifient "le roy Evrain" (ch. XXXVII), "le roy Erec" (ch. XLI), dans ce dernier cas pour relever le changement de statut du protagoniste après la mort de son père.

[24] Chapitres: X, XI, XV, XVII, XL, XLII.

[25] Voir aussi: I (à partir de: "comment le roi Artus..."), VII, XI, XII, XV, XVI, XX, XXIII, XXV, XXXI, XXXIV, XXXVII, XXXVIII.

[26] Demarolle, "De la narratologie à la syntaxe," 247-48.

[27] On remarque que la répétition de *comment* entraîne la reprise du sujet (cf. ch. V: "Comment Erec fu armé et comment *il alla*...").

[28] Autres titres "bicéphales": XXIX, XXX, XXXIX, XLI, XLII.

[29] Le seul autre recours au présent dans une rubrique se relève au début du texte ("Cy s'ensuit l'histoire... et *contient* ce premier chapitle..."), mais en dehors du véritable titre ("comment le roi Artus...").

[30] Cf. Demarolle, "De la narratologie à la syntaxe," 251. Voir aussi Pickford, *Evolution*, 163-9.

[31] Et encore:

> ch. XIII: Comment Enide entra en salle et le roy le fist soir d'enprés luy.
> Enide... s'en vient en celle salle ou est le roy... [Quant la belle fille] est entree en la salle... le roy... l'assiet delez luy... (p. 263, l. 32-35; p. 264, l. 2-6).
> ch. XVI: Comment Erec faisoit merveillez d'armes.
> [Erec] fait merveillez d'armez. (p. 266, l. 44).
> ch. XXXVII: Comment le roy Evrain vint a l'encontre de Erec.
> le roi Evrain... leur [= Erec et Enide] vint au devant (p. 287, l. 25-32).
> ch. XL: Comment Erec s'en alla a la court du roy Artus et eust nouvelle que le roi son pere estoit mort.
> Erec arriv[a]... ou estoit le roi Artus... nouvellez vindrent que le roy Lach pere de Erec estoit trespassé (p. 291, l. 35-41).
> ch. XLI: Comment le roy Erec entra ou tournoyement et fist pluseurs chevaleries.
> le roi Erec vint au tournoy... et commence a faire tant grans fais de chevalerie... (p.292, l.20-36).
> ch. XLII: Comment Erec se parti de la court du roi Artus et s'en ala en son roialme.
> le roi Erec et Enide la reyne prinrent congié du roy Artus... furent convoiez jusquez en leur roiaulme... (p. 293, l. 43; p. 294, l. 1-2).

[32] Cet exemple et le précédent ont leur source dans les vers de Chrétien: "Or redevons d'Erec parler" (v. 1244); "Ci fine li premerains vers" (v. 1844).

[33] Je néglige ici les formules diverses d'abréviation qui ponctuent tous les romans du XVe siècle (formules d'accélération: "fin de compte" p. 256, l. 3; p. 262, l. 32; p. 265, l. 18-19; "conclusions" p. 268, l. 39; catégories résiduelles: "et plenté d'aultres chevaliers" p. 262, l. 35-36; "et aultres pluseurs" p. 263, l. 43-p. 264-l. 1; "et pluseurs aultres" p. 267, l. 2; p. 267, l. 20; "et aultres choses" p.267, l.40; "et de pluseurs aultres façons" p. 268, l. 6; prétéritions: "Dez aultrez dont il y en vint plenté, pour la faire briefve, nostre compte se taira" p. 264, l. 42-43; "Des metz, entremetz, vin, ypocras, ne fera nulle mencion nostre compte, car ce seroit trop longue chose a des-

cripre" p. 265, l. 4-6; "Des chanteurz, harpeurz... ne ferons nous point long racomptement..." p. 265, l. 7-8; "Du surpluz se taist nostre descripcion" p. 265, l. 24; "lez esbatemens qui y furent fais ne sont pas a racompter ne descripre" p. 265, l. 35-36. Le dépouillement a été limité au 21 premieres chaptires), pour ne retenir que celles qui marquent un véritable changement de focalisation dans le récit. Sur la fonction de la formule "or dist li contes" (et analogues), voir les observations d'Emmanuèle Baumgartner, "Les techniques narratives dans le roman en prose" (*The Legacy of Chrétien de Troyes*, ed. by N. J. Lacy, D. Kelly, K. Busby [Amsterdam: Rodopi, 1987-1988]: I, 167-90 [175-77].

[34] La plupart des aventures du roman s'étendent au-delà des limites d'un ou de plusieurs chapitres: le combat d'Erec et Yder (VII, VIII, IX), l'accueil d'Enide à la cour d'Artus (épisode fortement morcelé: XI, XII, XIII, XIV), le tournoi après les noces (XV, XVI), le combat d'Erec et Guivret (XXVII, XXVIII), celui d'Erec et Kex (XXVIII, XXIX), la "Joie de la Cour" (XXXVII, XXXVIII, XXXIX), le tournoi final (XL, XLI, XLII). Cette structure, dépourvue de formules d'introduction aussi bien que de formules de conclusion, en début et en fin de chapitre, s'oppose en quelque sorte à celle que François Suard a constatée dans la prose du *Guillaume d'Orange* (*Guillaume d'Orange*, 151-55).

[35] Sous-classe des attaques de phrase, les attaques de chapitre reçoivent un accent rhétorique très marqué et transmettent une donnée (nominale, temporelle, circonstancielle) réputée fondamentale pour la phase narrative qu'elles ouvrent. Il y a plus: si la délimitation des phrases dans un texte en prose du XVe siècle est souvent affaire délicate, le chapitre se pose en revanche comme une unité clairement définie dans les manuscrits mêmes: par conséquent la valeur inaugurante de l'attaque de chapitre ne fait aucun doute. Pour une analyse systématique des attaques de phrase, cf. l'étude de Jean Rychner, *L'articulation des phrases narratives dans la Mort Artu* (Neuchâtel-Genève: Faculté des Lettres-Droz, 1970); pour une application à des romans bourguignons: Maria Colombo Timelli, "Les attaques de chapitre dans trois romans du XVe siècle: *Jehan d'Avennes*, *La fille du comte de Pontieu*, *Saladin*," *Rhétorique et mise en prose*, II, 105-35.

[36] Chapitres: I, II, III, VI, XV, XVI, XVIII, XXVII, XXVIII, XXXI, XXXIII.

[37] Rychner, *Articulation*, 17.

[38] Attaques en adverbe ou locution adverbiale: X, XII, XX, XXI, XL; en complément: V.

[39] Huit attaques n'ont pas été considérées ici pour des raisons diverses (attaques non "narratives", interventions de l'auteur, expédients rhétoriques peu représentés), vocatif (début d'un discours direct: ch. XXXVIII), exclamation (monologue / complainte: ch. XIX); exclamation de l'auteur ("Dieux!": ch. XXIV); appels aux lecteurs (ch. XXVI, XXXVI); structure *moult* + verbe *être* + attribut (ch. VIII, XXV); adjectif (ch. XXII).

[40] *Articulation*, 235.

[41] Autre expédient économique: le renvoi aux *parolles* (discours direct) par lesquelles s'achevait le chapitre précédent (ch. IV, X, XXIII, XXIX).

[42] Prologue tout à fait indépendant de celui de Chrétien (v. 1-26).

[43] *Mises en prose*, 380-413.

Università di Milano

Table 1a

longueur des chapitres en lignes (édition Foerster)

11-20 lignes: VI, XII, XIII, XXXVI	4
21-30 lignes: XI, XX, XXIV, XXVII, XXXI, XXXII, XL, XLII	8
31-40 lignes: IV, V, VIII, XV, XVIII, XXIX, XXXIV, XXXV, XXXVIII	9
41-50 lignes: I, II, III, VII, X, XVI, XIX, XXIII, XXV, XXVI	10
51-60 lignes: IX, XVII, XXI, XXXVII, XLI	5
61-70 lignes: XIV, XXII, XXVIII, XXX	4
71-80 lignes: —	
80 + lignes: XXXIII, XXXIX	2

Table 1b

longueur des chapitres en lignes (édition Foerster)

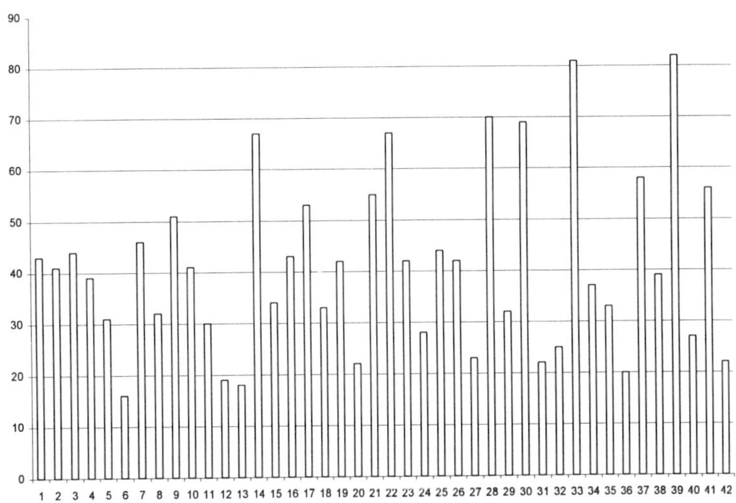

Table 2

Rapport texte en prose / texte en vers

chapitre	lignes	vers	nombre des vers	rapport lignes/vers
I.	43	26-148	123	70%
II.	41	149-341	193	42%
III.	44	342-546	205	43%
IV.	39	547-690	144	54%
V.	31	691-800	110	56%
VI.	16	801-836	36	89%
VII.	46	837-960	124	74%
VIII.	32	961-1080	120	53%
IX.	51	1081-1292	212	48%
X.	41	1293-1478	186	44%
XI.	30	1479-1586	108	56%
XII.	19	1587-1677	91	42%
XIII.	18	1678-1762	85	42%
XIV.	67	1763-2108	346	39%
XV.	34	2109-2170	62	110%
XVI.	43	2171-2272	102	84%
XVII.	53	2273-2442	170	62%
XVIII.	33	2443-2588	146	45%
XIX.	42	2589-2856	267	31%
XX.	22	2857-2924	68	65%
XXI.	55	2925-3085	161	68%
XXII.	67	3086-3247	162	83%
XXIII.	42	3248-3344	97	87%
XXIV.	28	3345-3485	141	40%
XXV.	44	3486-3661	176	50%
XXVI.	42	3662-3769	108	78%
XXVII.	23	3770-3806	137	34%
XXVIII.	70	3807-4039	232	60%
XXIX.	32	4040-4109	70	91%
XXX.	69	4110-4378	269	51%
XXXI.	22	4379-4475	97	45%
XXXII.	25	4476-4606	131	38%
XXXIII.	81	4607-4739	133	122%
XXXIV.	37	4740-5000	261	28%
XXXV.	33	5001-5259	259	25%
XXXVI.	20	5260-5446	187	21%
XXXVII.	58	5447-5918	471	25%
XXXVIII.	39	5919-6006	88	89%
XXXIX.	82	6007-6341	335	49%
XL.	27	6342-	—	— -
XLI.	56	—	—	— -
XLII.	22	—	—	— -

total 1719 lignes (X 2) / 6932 vers (+26 prologue) = 50%

Table 3: titres de chapitres

I. Cy s'ensuit l'istoire du noble et vaillant chevalier Erec, et contient ce premier chapitle comment le roi Artus vouloit aler chassier le blanc cerf en la forest adventureuse.

II. Comment une damoiselle et Erec furent ferus d'un naim.

III. Comment Erec se loga sur ung hoste qui avoit une belle fille de noble lignage mais povre estoit.

IV. Comment Erec requist son hoste d'avoir unes armeures.

V. Comment Erec fu armé et comment il alla au lieu ou l'en devoit prendre l'esprevier.

VI. Comment la damoiselle s'aproça pour prendre l'esprivier, mais Erec l'en destourba.

VII. Comment Erec et le chevalier aux armez blancez jousterent l'un contre l'aultre.

VIII. Comment le chevalier fu vaincu et se rendi a Erec en lui criant merci.

IX. Comment Yder se rendy a la reyne Guenievre qui le retinst de sa mesnie.

X. Comment Erec conclud au souper d'enmener l'endemain Enide a la court du roy Artus.

XI. Comment Erec et Enide s'amie furent rechupz a grant joye a la court du roy Artus.

XII. Comment Enide fu vestue de rices habillemens.

XIII. Comment Enide entra en salle et le roy le fist soir d'enprés luy.

XIV. Comment le roy baisa Enide.

XV. Comment ceulx de la court du roy Artus firent ung tournoy aprés lez nopces.

XVI. Comment Erec faisoit merveillez d'armes.

XVII. Comment Erec se parti de la court du roy Artus et s'en ala en son pays.

XVIII. Comment Erec interroga Enide pour quoy elle plouroit et elle lui en dist la cause.

XIX. Comment Enide se complaindi a par elle de ce qu'elle avoit dit a Erec.

XX. Comment Erec occist trois bringans.

XXI. Comment Erec occist V bringans chevalierz l'un aprez l'aultre.

XXII. Comment Erec vault faire coucier Enide en une forest, mais elle ne vault et lui dist qu'il en avoit milleur besoing qu'elle.

XXIII. Comment le seigneur d'un chasteau pria Enide d'amourz.

XXIV. Comment Enide admonnesta Erec du chevalier qui la vouloit avoir a force.

XXV. Comment Erec occist le dire du chasteau et son seneschal ausi.

XXVI. Comment Guivret le Petit poursuivi Erec et comment Enide se doulousa quant elle le vit venir.

XXVII. Comment Erec et Guivret joustent ensamble et aprez se combatent a l'espee.

XXVIII. Comment Erec rompi l'espee de Guivret qui en eut grant duel.

XXIX. Comment Erec jousta a Kex le seneschal et l'abati du premier coup.

XXX. Comment messire Gavain recongnut Erec et Enide et leur fist grant feste.

XXXI. Comment Erec occist deux gayanz en ung bois l'un aprés l'aultre.

XXXII. Comment Erec faindi d'estre mort quant il revint devers Enide.

XXXIII. Comment Enide se complaindy pour la mort d'Erec qu'elle vit choir soudainement.

XXXIV. Comment Erec occist le conte de Limors.

XXXV. Comment Guivret abbati Erec a ung cours de lance dont aprés il fu bien marri.

XXXVI. Comment Erec arriva en la ville de Brandigan et enquist du lieu et de la place a qui elle estoit.

XXXVII. Comment le roy Evrain vint a l'encontre de Erec.

XXXVIII. Comment Erec et le chevalier jousterent ensamble.

XXXIX. Comment le champion de la damoiselle congnut a Erec son fait et lui cria merci.

XL. Comment Erec s'en alla a la court du roy Artus et eust nouvelle que le roi son pere estoit mort.

XLI. Comment le roy Erec entra ou tournoyement et fist pluseurs chevaleries.

XLII. Conment Erec se parti de la court du roi Artus et s'en ala en son roialme.

Table 4: présence d'Erec et d'Enide dans les titres de chapitre.

Erec	Enide	Erec + Enide
II, IV, V, VI, VII, VIII, XVI, XVII, XX, XXI, XXV, XXVII, XXVIII, XXIX, XXXI, XXXIV, XXXV, XXXVI, XXXVII, XXXVIII, XXXIX, XL, XLI, XLII	XII, XIII, XIV, XXIII	(III), X, XI, XVIII, XIX, XXII, XXIV, XXVI, XXX, XXXII, XXXIII

Table 5: attaques de chapitre

I. Le commencement de nostre present compte est tel que...

II. La reyne Guenievre aiant aperceu le chevalier et la damoiselle, elle veult savoir qui ilz sont toux deux...

III. Erec doncques ne cesse de convoier a veue d'uel le chevalier...

IV. Quant Erec a entendu lez parolles de son hoste, il le prise et loe en son cuer...

V. De cest ottroy ne fait nul samblant la gente pucelle...

VI. Le sire du chasteau conte de Lalut vient veioir le fait dez deux chevaliers et lez damez pareillement.

VII. Quant le chevalier aux armes blancez a entendu que Erec se offre d'entrer en bataille, par grant desdaing il s'adresse vers luy...

VIII. Moult est terrible la bataille des deux chevaliers.

IX. Comme Yder eust fait bender sez plaiez, lui veullant tenir sa promesse, monta a cheval...

X. Atant finerent leurz parollez Erec et le sire du chasteau.

XI. Durant le chemin Erec le gentil chevalier tenir ne se poeult de regarder sa belle et doulce amie...

XII. Atant s'aproça la reyne de la belle damoiselle Enide.

XIII. Aprés l'acheminement de la gente damoiselle Enide, la reyne, qui bien le voit en point, oncques plus joieuse ne fu.

XIV. Tantost aprés que Enide a prins une ferme contenance de soir, la reyne prent a dire au roy que...

XV. Enide fu grandement honnoree et bien aymant son seigneur Erec...

XVI. Les lancez ne sont pas encores toutez debrisies quant Erec...

XVII. Aprés ce que chascun eust laissi le tournoier, chevaliers furent tost mis hors de leurz armes.

XVIII. Les chevaliers du royaulme voians Erec entierement delaissier le noble mestier d'armes pour l'entretenement de l'amour de sa femme, sans laquelle il ne pouoit vivre ne durer, ilz en furent moult desplaisans...

XIX. Hellas meschante chetive...

XX. Atant se retourne Enide et a grant paour se mest a chemin...

XXI. Ainsi s'en vont Enide et Erec jusquez environ VI heurez aprés midi...

XXII. Toute resconfortee fu Enide quant elle vit Erec revenir a chief de ces V bringans.

XXIII. Quant le sire du chasteau a entendu cez parollez, tout le cuer lui euvre de joie pour la belle dame.

XXIV. Dieux, comme est marri ce seigneur quant il ne puelt suborner ne attraire a son veul la belle et bonne dame!

XXV. Moult fu marri Erec quant il entendi le mal que le seigneur vouloit commettre envers sa tresamé dame.

XXVI. Comme vous avés oy se delivra Erec de sez ennemis...

XXVII. Erec entend et sent son enemi aprocer, si se retourne...

XXVIII. Enide la treslealle dame voit la bataille dez II chevaliers qui...

XXIX. A ces parollez s'est Kex eslongié de Erec...

XXX. Quant messire Gavain voit que par nulle maniere il ne puelt faire retourner Erec, il envoie ung de sez escuiers au roy...

XXXI. Erec s'en va grant oirre, suivant le train dez deux gayans...

XXXII. Aprés ces fais vient Erec au chevalier qui...

XXXIII. Enide le trescertaine dame en beault voiant que Erec estoit chut sans parler, elle acourt vers lui toute desesperee...

XXXIV. Quant ce conte se treuve arrivé, il fait machonner hastivement une tombe...

XXXV. Quant Erec a entendu Guivret, nonobstant qu'il soit lass d'avoir exercité les armes,... il mist main a l'espee...

XXXVI. Que vous diroi je plus?

XXXVII. Quant Erec entend la façon du vergier et qu'il y a aulcune adventure, il conjure Guivret de Dieu qu'il lui en die la verité.

XXXVIII. Chevalier, dist Erec, quant il vous plaira vous parlerez ung pou plus courtoisement...

XXXIX. Quant le chevalier se voit convaincu par le bien faire du trespreu en armes Erec, il lui requert qu'il aye piti de luy...

XL. Conclusions, a grant honneur la damoiselle de Lalut fust menee au chasteau de Guivret, et Erec...

XLI. Comme doncquez Erec sceut que le roi et lez dames fussent sur lez rens et que lez chevaliers avoient commencié le tournoy, il se parti...

XLII. Quant Erec voit que nul ne veult plus maintenir le tournoi, il se part secretement de la praerie...

Frulovisi, Humanist Writer: A Career Abandoned

Grady A. Smith

Titus Livius Frulovisi (c.1400-c.1464) began his career as a humanist writer in Venice by setting down what are today the oldest extant Latin school comedies in Italy and the first in the classical tradition that were actually performed. Frulovisi wrote the last two of his seven comedies while in the household of Humphrey Duke of Gloucester (1390-1447), and *Peregrinatio*, the sixth of these seven stage works, was the first humanist play written in England. Its more than one hundred dialogue parallels with Terence and Plautus illustrate the classical influence in Frulovisi's comedies.[1] Other works produced under the aegis of Humphrey include the *Panegyricos Humfroidos* and the *Vita Henrici Quinti*. In addition, Frulovisi's *De Re Publica*, written prior to his English sojourn, while unsuccessfully seeking employment from Leonello d'Este, is the first description of a Renaissance state by a humanist.

But although these latter three works of encomium, history and political philosophy marked Frulovisi as a promising journeyman humanist, his comic writing militated against success in his chosen profession. The five comedies of his Venetian period became magnets for controversy, while the two written during his stay in England were to varying degrees imprudent or impolitic. Moreover, there was a facet of Frulovisi's personality distinctly at odds with the image of a successful humanist, and time after time the response of critics to his comedies goaded that darker side into rash actions and words. This paper will examine Frulovisi's comedies and correspondence to determine how the critical reception of his stage works and the flaws in his own personality combined to foreclose his humanist career before its time and shift his life's work into another profession entirely.

Frulovisi began his playwriting efforts while operating his own school at the parish of Santo Basso[2] in Venice, and he no doubt expected a favorable reception from supportive parents and students. Though these expectations were met to an extent, he stimulated opposition as well. All of his adversaries attacked Frulovisi on a personal level, and, in addition, some included institutional pressure. Another playwright accused him of plagiarism; a group of antagonistic teachers wrote a play satirizing him; and a local priest, representing both scholasticism and ecclesiastical authority, denounced him from the pulpit. In the Terentian tradition, Frulovisi joined battle with these critics in his plays' prologues.

After his first comedy, *Corallaria*, was performed, Frulovisi was accused of plagiarism by Jacopo Langosco,[3] a potent adversary who had been a ducal secretary and a professor at the University of Padua. In the prologue of *Corallaria* Frulovisi had claimed the play was the product of his own invention:

> Non adducimus veteres fabulas ... veteres sunt ita tritae ... nova delectant, nova placent, vetera senium inducunt.
>
> We don't bring old plays ... old plays are trite ... new things delight, new things please, old things bring on senility. (6)[4]

But in the prologue to his second play, *Claudi Duo*, his defense against the charge of plagiarism was based on quite a different proposition:

> Hunc Langusci dedisse fabulam, non suam: furem appellant .... Qui quum Livium accusant, et Plautum accusant, quem hic noster autorem habet.[5]
>
> They charge this teacher with having given Langosco's play instead of his own: they call him a thief .... But when they accuse Livius [i.e., Frulovisi], they also accuse Plautus, whom this teacher of ours considers the author. (35)

The presentation of *Corallaria* resulted in more than charges of plagiarism. For Frulovisi's second play, his antagonists apparently were able to prevent him from using the professional actors and costumes he employed for his first play:

> Incipit *Claudi Duo*. Acta Venetiis sine mimis .... Vix impetravimus sine mimis istanc agere posse. Si desunt histriones, ornatus supplebit agentum industria et ingenium adulescentum nostrorum discipulorum.
>
> Here begins *Claudi Duo*. Presented at Venice without actors .... Without actors we barely succeeded in being able to present this comedy. But if performers are lacking, the industry of allies and the ingenuity of our young pupils will supply the costumes. (35)

Moreover, Frulovisi's detractors had learned beforehand that some of the characters in *Claudi Duo* were pagan deities:

> Nunc nova dedere: deis quod uti non liceat comoedis .... Hunc accusant nostro antistiti[6] superstitionis novae .... Veretur hic pontifices .... Non orabit Iovem coelesti pompa.
>
> Now you give new false charges: it is not permitted to use pagan deities in comedies .... They accuse this teacher of *nova superstitio* to our pastor .... But this man respects the hierarchy .... He will not pray to Jove in the pomp of his heaven. (35-6)

Frulovisi rebutted the charge of *nova superstitio* by asserting loyalty to church authorities and by carrying the accusations to their ridiculous logical conclusion, namely the possibility of his praying to an ancient pagan deity. But Frulovisi had reason to be concerned because, as Margaret L. King points out, Venice used the ecclesiastical apparatus as a means of governance.[7] In effect, he had been brought to the attention of both ecclesiastical and state authorities.

Meanwhile, a group of rival schoolmasters, in direct affront to Frulovisi, formed an *ad hoc* committee to write jointly and to produce a play called *Magistrea*, using professional actors. Frulovisi mentions the play in the prologue to his third comedy, *Emporia*, to pay it the insult of scant heed, but it must have rankled because he brought it up again in a later comedy.[8] Still, it is ironic that both Langosco's unnamed play and the jointly written *Magistrea* are no longer extant, and are known to history only through Frulovisi's mention of them in his prologues.[9] Whether these plays imitated classical models is not known, but it can be inferred that at least Langosco's play did, since it was similar to *Corallaria*, a play whose Plautine antecedents Frulovisi acknowledged. In any case, although Frulovisi was not able to employ professional actors for *Emporia*, costumes were reinstated.

In *Symmachus*, his fourth play, Frulovisi limited himself to attacks on a generalized "they":

> Haec ubi nova data est, statim comperiunt quod dicant male .... Ignavii vix aliorum qui dicta sentiant, detrectatione sua magnos se credunt viros factos!
>
> As soon as this new play is presented, they see it at once so that they might criticize it .... The ignorant, who scarcely grasp the things said by others, believe they make themselves great men by their disparagement! (107-8)

This citation also indirectly invokes the belief of many humanists that the entrenched scholastic tradition was incapable of deeper conceptual understandings.[10]

In *Oratoria*, the fifth and last play he wrote at Venice, Frulovisi returned to polemics with intensity and specificity, going so far as to name his primary antagonist from the stage. He also shows much more explicitly that a major aspect of the discord lies in the hostility between scholasticism and humanism. His particular target was a Dominican, one Fra Leone, for whom biographical details are lacking. In the prologue Frulovisi attacked him through pun and word play:

> Iam scholastici vincunt .... Nos impugnat leo .... Leo in altis blaterat tronis. Sancti qui sunt, prophanos poetas nominat .... Mulierculae et leo bestia pro scholasticis hominem impugnant.
>
> Now the scholastics conquer .... A lion attacks us .... A lion roars among the lofty thrones. They who are sacred in their calling he describes as irreligious poets .... Foolish women and the lion-beast attack the man on behalf of the scholastics. (154)

Frulovisi also used Fra Leone as a character, one Friar Leocyon, in *Oratoria*. In a subplot this Dominican attempts to seduce the beautiful young Hagna when she comes to him in the confessional. As a result she runs away in an uproar. Later Friar Leocyon disguises himself as a Roman noble and loudly announces his love outside her window. The bishop orders his arrest but at the end of the play he breaks out of prison and makes good his escape. The real Fra Leone could not have been much pleased.

Later Frulovisi would add an explanatory gloss to the manuscript of the work's fair copy:

> Leocyon vero nomen fratris cuiusdam qui praedicaverat me et omnes poetas esse excom[m]unicatos: quamvis solum vocaretur leo. Sed ad maius decus additur κύων quod est canis ad demonstrandum quod dupliciter erat bestia.
>
> Leocyon is in fact the name of a certain friar who had declared me and all poets to be excommunicated: in spite of the fact that only the lion should be so designated. But for a more complete distinction κύων is added to show that he is a jackal, that he was in two ways a beast. (158)

But at the same time that Frulovisi resorts to this slashing, personal attack in his last Venetian play, he also resigns the field:

> Quinta fuerit *Oratoria*, quam vobis dabit, et ultima. Heu, heu, ultima. Nos deo bestiae privant, virtute tanta. Flete, iuvenes, flete de ignavis crabronibus, leone, et bestiis impugnari bonos.
>
> *Oratoria* is the fifth comedy he will present to you, and the last. Alas, yes, the last. They deprive us of the beast's God, of so much virtue. Weep, young students, weep at the contemptible hornets, the lion, and the beasts assaulting good men. (154)

The contrast between the generalized polemics of *Symmachus* and the personal attacks of *Oratoria* is so sharp, and the commitment not to write again is so unequivocal, that Frulovisi seems to have been both deliberately burning his bridges and to have had a plan for the future. That plan must have centered around one of his major works, the *De Re Publica*. Coming, as it does, more than seventy-five years before Machiavelli set down *Il Principe,* it is undeniably a milestone, the first representation of a Renaissance state.[11]

Seeking employment, Frulovisi dedicated the *De Re Publica* to Leonello d'Este and presented him with a copy as a kind of writing sample. But the young duke of Ferrara declined to hire him, and he was left, as he says, *nulla opera*, without employment.

In the *De Re Publica* Frulovisi had stated:

> Non imitabor ciceronem, ad summum qui dignitatis fastigium ascendit, neque Virgilium vestrae patriae dictatorem. Paupertatem Plauti non erubescam, quum irrumpet in tectum meum; nec mea sola virtus pecuniis exilibus mecum stabit.

> I shall not imitate Cicero, who rose to the highest rank of honor, nor Virgil, a magistrate of your country. I will not blush at the poverty of Plautus, when it rushes in under my roof; nor with me will my sole worth depend upon slender wealth. (369)

Partly affected romantic idealism, partly a request for remunerative employment, the statement had taken on a grim reality. Frulovisi stood at a bleak crossroad.

Some critics hypothesize that at this point Frulovisi probably made a journey to the Mediterranean, to Crete and to Rhodes, which are prominent in his next comedy.[12] Either during or subsequent to this journey, Frulovisi received the offer of a position as poet and orator[13] to Humphrey. The job prospect probably began with Petrus Montanus (1405-1457), the papal collector of Peter's pence in England, as intermediary. A Venetian, he had studied Greek with Frulovisi under Guarino,[14] and through his humanist pursuits had fostered a friendship with Humphrey. If the good offices of Montanus did contribute to the employment of his classmate Frulovisi by Humphrey, the connection proves an early example of finding a position through networking. In any case, Frulovisi was probably already in residence in Humphrey's household when on March 7th, 1437 his denization was formally declared.[15]

Frulovisi remained in Humphrey's employ less than three years. On the one hand he accomplished the near-term political works requested of him by writing a panegyric on Humphrey,[16] followed by the *Vita Henrici Quinti*,[17] the first biography of the duke's brother, Henry V. But Humphrey had set longer-term humanist goals as well. Prominent among them was the translation of Greek works into Latin for the use of English scholars, but Frulovisi's Greek was too shallow. Perhaps Frulovisi hoped to make up for this lack through his playwriting, but Humphrey was apparently unimpressed.

The situation of Frulovisi the playwright was significantly different in England. Most prominent was the fact that the two plays he wrote there, *Peregrinatio* and *Eugenius*, received no production. In the unique copy of his plays,[18] the first page of each of his Venetian comedies has the details of performance in red at the top. The first page of each of his British comedies leaves room for these details, but both are blank. His patron Humphrey declined to have them staged, and as a result there were no running polemics. Still, although there were no impolitic denunciations by Frulovisi from the stage, he made other errors of judgment and miscalculations in the body of his plays, side by side with good sense and forthright flattery.

Problems exist in both of these comedies. In one scene between young Clerus and the courtesan Porna in *Peregrinatio*, dialogue ranges from unintended sexual innuendo on the part of the boy to graphic suggestiveness by the courtesan. Whether this scene would have been objectionable to Humphrey personally is problematic, but one wonders about the composition of the audience Frulovisi had hoped for. Surely a work produced by Humphrey would have had English clerics among its auditors.

Less problematic but more complex is a situation in his second British comedy, *Eugenius*, one of his most ambitious and least successful plays. In the prologue Frulovisi flatters the duke, promises him poetic immortality and informs him that when he reads the play "in alio quasi per speculum te videbis (you will see yourself in another as in a mirror)." (224) In fact Frulovisi uses the duke as the model for his title character, and associates the theme of divorce with Eugenius to echo earlier events in Humphrey's life.

Young Eugenius is completely dedicated to learning and eschews marriage even in the face of his father's determined insistence. In scene three, a long scene in a long play, Eugenius debates with his father and some other old men about the conflict between marriage and learning. Eugenius has just made the point that if he marries a woman whom he finds incompatible, he will be tied to her for life.

> MES. Immo repudium dices mulieri.
>
> EUG. Non licet.
>
> MES. At decet, et licet quoque sapientibus et magnis viris, non vulgaribus aut insipientibus, qui vel propter vinum vel levissimas causas coniugii iura violarent.
>
> PHR. Sic est.
>
> EUG. Iam istud plurimum me vicistis.

> MES. On the contrary, you could divorce the woman.
>
> EUG. But that's not lawful.
>
> MES. No, but it's sensible, and legal too for wise and influential men, though not for the common or foolish, who because of wine or quite frivolous reasons would tear up the marriage bond.
>
> PHR. It's true.
>
> EUG. You've conquered me most with that thought. (236)

Finally, acknowledging the inevitable, Eugenius marries the impoverished girl of his choice in his father's absence. When his socially ambitious father returns he is forced to divorce her and marry a wealthy girl. This second woman proves a virago not only to Eugenius but also to his father, and she too is divorced and replaced with the original wife, a veritable Griselda of patience.

Frulovisi's intent must have been to exercise Humphrey's sense of his own position in the upper nobility (at this time he was heir apparent to the English throne) and to present the duke as one who is worldly wise. But it must also have evoked some unpleasant memories for the Duke, for certain aspects of Humphrey's life show the design of Eugenius' fictional situation to be both relevant and imprudent.

A summary of the pertinent biographical details provides perspective on this issue. A decade and a half earlier, Humphrey had wed the already married Jacqueline of Hainault on the strength of an annulment from the antipope Benedict XIII, after the Roman pontiff Martin V let it be known informally that he could not dissolve her marriage. Jacqueline's territories were hers in her own right but she had fled them because of the brutishness of her earlier husband, John of Brabant, who governed in her absence. Humphrey, fourth son of a king, undoubtedly hoped to come into a rule of his own through Jacqueline, and he began raising troops to return her by force. England at this time, however, was at war with France, and the Duke of Burgundy, then an ally of England but also a cousin of Brabant, constituted the balance of power on the continent. Burgundy let it be known that if Humphrey invaded Hainault and made war on his cousin, he, Burgundy, would consider it a *casus belli*. Fully aware of this, Humphrey put his personal agenda ahead of England's national interests and took Hainault, and Burgundy began negotiations with the French. Intense pressure on Humphrey to withdraw built up at home. Then, after he suffered a few military casualties when a segment of Hainault's population rebelled, he returned to England, ostensibly to raise more troops, and left Jacqueline to her fate. Quite soon thereafter her earlier husband died. The Roman pontiff then affirmed the validity of her marriage to John of Brabant and declared that the wedding of Jacqueline and Humphrey would have to be repeated. The Duke declined.

Frulovisi, then, must have hoped with *Eugenius* to flatter the duke and fan his sense of self importance, thereby solidifying his own position under Humphrey and perhaps even obtaining the funds needed to produce his play. But surely the duke's memories of the tangled business with Jacqueline included the failure of his personal quest for a rule of his own, his rejection by the church when it refused the annulment, the jeopardy into which his personal goals threw England's continental strategy, and the callous abandonment of Jacqueline following the collapse of his own ambitions. The effect of *Eugenius* on Humphrey cannot have been what Frulovisi intended.

Besides these unpleasant private reminders for Humphrey, a performance of *Eugenius* or even its circulation to selected readers would have had a corrosive effect on the public persona of the duke, which he had been at such pains to cultivate in significant part through the writing skills of Frulovisi. The Italian's *Panegyricos Humfroidos* had resulted in a very favorable reception of the duke by parliament early in 1437, and Frulovisi's *Vita Henrici Quinti* sought to reinforce support for both the dead King's war policy on the continent and for Humphrey as its primary continuator.[19] That the author of these two documents apparently failed to grasp their deeper purpose, and how the *Eugenius* would militate against the duke's goals, comments upon Frulovisi's fundamental lack of understanding of the thoughts and intentions of his master. It is at about this time that Humphrey terminates Frulovisi's employment and leaves him once again *nulla opera.*

In this same period Frulovisi wrote to his old classmate, Petrus Montanus, seeking help. Perhaps Humphrey had discussed Frulovisi's plays with the churchman or had even asked him to read them. In any case, in his reply Montanus first describes their past friendship and his own efforts at maintaining it. Then he alludes to the fact that Frulovisi, notwithstanding the honors he has received, deeply distrusts Montanus. Yet despite this distrust Frulovisi persists in associating his own name with the papal collector's in conversation, and because of this fabricated closeness to Frulovisi, Montanus is treated by others as an outcast. Montanus pointedly suggests that Frulovisi makes himself a source of information for malicious people concerning Humphrey's household "aliter quam doctum ac sapientem virum deceat (in a way that is otherwise than seemly to wise and learned men)." Then Montanus, in an assault on the very idea of writing comedy, continues:

> Horum autem detrahentium commenta et fraudes quibus, ut apud comicum est: solent ex stultis insanos facere.
>
> To the wise, however, these slanderous comments and deceits are like what is found in the works of a writer of comedy, because such wise men are accustomed to dealing with the ravings of fools.[20]

After rounding on Frulovisi so fiercely, Montanus shifts to an hortatory mode. If Frulovisi wishes to be taken for a wise man, a learned man, an educated man, indeed for a philosopher, why then doesn't he produce works of philosophy? He should read the lives of illustrious men, admire their deeds and praise their character. Frulovisi should always have a book in his hand. If Frulovisi can amend his life along these lines, Montanus is prepared to offer him a position as subcollector.

This attitude of Montanus toward comedy calls to mind Umberto Eco's *The Name of the Rose*. The blind Friar Jorge considers the idea of an African alchemist that creation arose out of divine laughter to be folly. And concerning Aristotle's second book of the *Poetics*, notionally recreated by Eco and stating among other things that comedy inspires the pleasure of the ridiculous to purify us of that passion, Jorge declares the work to have the power of a thousand scorpions. Though less murderous than the fictional Jorge, Montanus is apparently sympathetic to his views. The churchman's attack did not focus on any plot or character flaws. Rather, he assumed that the very act of writing any comedy was in and of itself intellectually unworthy. Had Montanus read the plays? Perhaps, but not necessarily. His quarrel is with the concept of writing comedies at all, for him an activity clearly beneath contempt for a serious scholar.

Frulovisi, in desperate financial straits, must have submitted to Montanus' views. Perhaps his decision was a simple matter of economics, or perhaps, after the protracted polemics of Venice followed by dismissal from Humphrey's service, Montanus' scathing condemnation became the climactic blow for Frulovisi the humanist. In any case, the former playwright was given employment by the churchman until he was arrested following a fight with a local priest. At that point Montanus also dismissed him. Within a few years Frulovisi would obtain a medical degree from the University of Toulouse, abandoning the profession of humanist writer in the process.

On the threshold of the *quattrocento*, Coluccio Salutati and Giovanni Dominici engaged in an extended dispute which resulted in Salutati's writing some fundamental early documents of humanism and Dominici's setting down the clearest and most rational scholastic criticism of the new learning to come out of the early years of the new century. Moreover, theirs was a debate which garnered honor for them both and which was characterized by a mutual respect.

Frulovisi's polemics with Fra Leone in Venice were by contrast strident and personal, and he did not demonstrate anything like mutual respect in responding to Jacopo Langosco's charges of plagiarism, nor in addressing the joint authors of the satirical *Magistrea*. Nevertheless, one can say that in the Venetian arena Frulovisi more or less held his own, even though his responses to the early attacks revealed a dogged intemperateness of personality and a foolish tenacity in pursuing quarrels. Later the opposition of Montanus, coming at a moment of maximum vulnerability from a churchman who could rescue him with employment, proved climactic and decisive. Frulovisi subsequently changed professions, becoming a doctor. Once having taken up the profession of medicine Frulovisi, as far as is known, never wrote anything in a humanist strain again.[21]

His personal abrasiveness notwithstanding, Frulovisi's departure from the cause of humanism is to be regretted. He was comfortable in many of the major genres of the movement and was as often as not among the first to assay them: his comedies in the manner of Plautus and Terence are the earliest extant examples of the type actually to be performed; his humanist history of Henry V and the events surrounding his reign anticipated Polydore Vergil by a hundred years; and the political theory of the *De Re Publica* foreshadowed the work of Machiavelli in the next century. At perhaps forty years of age, Frulovisi was capable of giving much more to the movement and its works. That he did not is clearly a loss.

NOTES

[1] Margaret L. King, *Venetian Humanism in an Age of Patrician Dominance* (Princeton: Princeton University Press, 1986), 378. Charles W. Previté-Orton, ed., *Opera Hactenus Inedita T. Livii de Frulovisiis* (Cambridge: Typis Academicae, 1932), xvi. For a translation of *Peregrinatio*, with line citations of Terence and Plautus demonstrating Frulovisi's familiarity with, and use of these Roman comic writers, see Grady A. Smith, "Frulovisi's *Peregrinatio*: A Translation with a Life of the Playwright" (Diss. University of Maryland, College Park, 1994).

[2] Contemporary references to Frulovisi are rare outside of his own writings and exchanges of correspondence. In one such, April 12, 1429, he is listed ("Titus Livius Perlovisiis") as a notarial witness, and is further identified as the son of Domenico and *rector scholarum* in the parish of Santo Basso. Enrico Bertanza and Giuseppe Dalla Santa, *Documenti per la Storia della Cultura in Venezia*, Vol. 1, pt. 1, *Maestri, Scuole, e Scolari in Venezia fina al 1500* (Venezia: a Spese della Società, 1907), 315.

[3] Frulovisi details the charge and defends himself against it in the prologue to his second play, *Claudi Duo*, in *Hactenus Inedita*, 35-6.

[4] Page numbers for direct citations from Previté-Orton, *Hactenus Inedita*, will be indicated in the body of the text in parentheses. Translations are the author's unless noted otherwise.

[5] Compare Terence, *Eunuchus*, 23-4: Exclamat furem, non poetam fabulam / dedisse; and *Andros*, 18-19: Qui quom hunc accusant, Naevium, Plautum, Ennium / accusant, quos hic noster autores habet.

[6] *Antistes* can mean ecclesiastical superior, prior, rector of a school, chaplain, priest or bishop. In the *De Re Publica*, Frulovisi defined the term for himself in using it: "The bishop (*episcopus*) has pastors (*antistites*) who supervise each one of the churches, through whom he diligently inquires into the life of priests (*sacerdotum*) and who among them fall away from their obligations." (334)

[7] King, 219.

[8] Frulovisi, *Hactenus Inedita*, 67-8, 153-4.

[9] Antonio Stäuble, *La Commedia Umanistica del Quattrocento* (Florence: Nella Sede Dell'Istituto Palazzo Strozzi, 1968), 65-6.

[10] See, for example, Leonardo Bruni's *Dialogi ad Petrum Histrum* (1401): "The Philosopher [i.e., Aristotle] says this, they tell us. It is impious to contradict him, and for them *ipse dixit* has the force of truth, as if he had been the only philosopher .... Not that I say this to censure Aristotle; I have no war with that very wise man, only with the folly of these Aristotelians .... Not even in the least thing do I believe they rightly grasp what Aristotle thought." *The Humanism of Leonardo Bruni: Selected Texts,* tr. David Thompson (Binghamton: MRTS, 1987), 67-8.

[11] Previté-Orton, xxxvi.

[12] Previté-Orton, xiii; Remigio Sabbadini, "Tito Livio Frulovisio, Umanista del Secolo XV," *Giornale Storico della Letteratura Italiana*, CIII (1934), 58-9.

[13] Before the term "humanist" was coined in the late fifteenth century, "poet" and "orator" identified those who practiced this profession. Paul Oskar Kristeller, *Eight Philosophers of the Italian Renaissance* (Stanford: Stanford University Press, 1964), 153.

[14] Frulovisi's status as a student of Guarino is probable but not a certainty. To support such a claim Previté-Orton cites statements by the author of the *De Orthographia*, erroneously attributed to Frulovisi. But a letter of Montanus to Frulovisi alludes to their shared student days (*movet me hec litterarum ac studiorum communio quam mecum habes*), making the latter's attendance at Guarino's school a reasonable inference. Johannes Haller, *Piero da Monte* (Rome: W. Regenberg, 1941), severely abbreviates the lengthy letter, omitting the supporting quotation. The letter is printed in full by Sabbadini in "Tito Livio," 74-8; the quotation is on 76.

[15] Thomas Rymer, *Foedera* (London: A. & J. Churchill, 1704-35), 10:660-1.

[16] The *Panegyricos Humfroidos* survives uniquely in the Biblioteca Capitular y Columbina, MS 7.2.23.

[17] Published at Oxford, 1716, Thomas Hearne, ed. Helen Louise St. John, "The *Vita Henrici Quinti* of Tito Livio Frulovisi" (Master's Thesis, University of Notre Dame, 1974), provides the Latin text and an English translation. Her "A Critical Edition of the *Vita Henrici Quinti* of Tito Livio Frulovisi" (Diss. University of Toronto, 1982) satisfies a significant scholarly need in Frulovisi studies.

[18] Saint John's College, Cambridge library, MS 60.

[19] Ralph A. Griffiths, *The Reign of King Henry VI* (Berkeley: University of California Press, 1981), 202-5; Gerald L. Harriss, *Cardinal Beaufort* (Oxford: Clarendon Press, 1988), 262-3; Charles Oman, *The History of England from the Accession of Richard II to the Death of Richard III (1377-1485)* (rpt: New York: Greenwood Press Publishers, 1969), 326-7.

[20] Sabbadini, "Tito Livio," 74-5. The letter bears a July date but lacks a year. Sabbadini assigns it to 1439 based on the full dating of the letters immediately preceding and following it in codex Vat. Lat. 2694.

[21] John Koelhoff the Elder printed *De Orthographia* at Cologne in 1480, erroneously ascribing authorship to Frulovisi. Previte-Orton accepted this ascription, believing it to be the mature product of the Italian's later years. In fact, major parts of two separate works by other humanists make up the *De Orthographia*, one with the same title by Gasparino Barzizza, the other the *Ars Diphthongandi* by Guarino. On the issue of authorship, see for example Maximilian Lehnerdt's review of *Opera Hactenus Inedita* in *Gnomon* 10 (1934), 157-9.

University of Maryland, College Park

Form und Bedeutung. Zum Verhältnis von Historia *und Allegorie in Einigen Werken Mantegnas*

Kristine Patz

Mein Beitrag beschäftigt sich mit dem Buchstaben Y,[1] den anthropomorphen, vegetabilen sowie architektonischen Nachbildungen dieses Zeichens und mit seinen Bedeutungen im Werk des italienischen Malers Andrea Mantegna.[2]

Bis in das 17. Jahrhundert hinein war man der Ansicht, Pythagoras habe das Y in seiner Doppelfunktion als Buchstabe und Signum zugleich erfunden: *Y litteram Pythagoras Samius ad exemplum vitae humanae primus formavit.*[3] Das Y war folglich weder ausschließlich Buchstabe noch Chiffre, sondern die sichtbare Gestalt des Buchstabens ermöglichte in bedeutungsverschlüsselter Form das menschliche Leben abzubilden. Somit war die mit dem Namen des Pythagoras verbundene griechische Majuskel Y Zeichen für das menschliche Leben, das sich am Entscheidungspunkt gabelte zwischen *virtus* und *voluptas* für Herkules am Scheideweg[4] oder heilsgeschichtlich zwischen Erlösung und Verdammnis.[5] Das Y-Signum kam hierin der christlichen Rechts-Links-Symbolik[6] entgegen, da es wie diese die linke Seite als negative, die rechte als positive wertete.

Über die konkrete *bivium*-Bildlichkeit hinaus, die die emporweisenden Y-Teile als das Bild zweier Bergwege auffaßte, konnte das Y vegetabile Formen annehmen. Die zu erst bei Persius und den Aeneis-Kommentaren nachweisbar wirksamen und besonders von Isidor geförderten Vorstellungen vom Y-Signum als einem Baum, sind bereits im Mittelalter vielfältig belegbar.[7] In der Form des Baumes verband sich das Y mit dessen Bedeutungen als Baum der Erkenntnis[8] oder als Kreuzesstamm[9], und über die *cornua*[10] des Buchstabens wie des Kreuzes konnte das Y weiteren Formen Bedeutung geben.

Dementsprechend unterlag auch die Hornbildlichkeit gleichen Gesetzen und Affinitäten, da die beiden "Arme" des Y wie auch die Enden des Kreuzes als *cornua* bezeichnet wurden. Die Polysemie des Wortes *cornu* bzw. *cornua* ermöglichte eine Erweiterung dieser Hornbildlichkeit; als Folge konnten beispielsweise die gehörnten Tiere des alten Testamentes, wie der Widder des Isaak-Opfers und der gehörnte Stier des "Josephssegens" das Kreuz präfigurieren. Horn- und Pflanzenmetaphorik vereinigte schließlich David als sprießendes Horn.[11]

Das sind die Beziehungen zwischen Form und Bedeutung, deren Neuschöpfungen im Werk von Mantegna nachfolgend analysiert werden. Vorangestellt sei das allgemeine Resultat der Untersuchung, das angezeigt werden kann als Bestimmung der Relation zwischen *historia* und Allegorie: Die Handlung repräsentiert die *historia,*[12] während das Y meist als Baum die Aufforderung und die Materialien zum allegorischen

Verständnis[13] liefert. Diese Beziehung zwischen *historia* und Allegorie läßt sich im Sinne eines durch die bildliche Darstellung vorgebrachten Gegensatzes zwischen täuschender Repräsentation und Einsicht in die Täuschung[14] interpretieren, und dieser Gegensatz darf als zentral für Mantegnas Künstler- und Bildverständnis angenommen werden.

Beweis hierfür ist die griechische Künstlersignatur im *St. Sebastian*[15] von ca. 1458/59. Architektonische Realisation des Y-Signums in der Ruine und Signatur des Künstlers erhellen sich wechselseitig in diesem zeitlich frühesten der hier behandelten Werke. Im unbeschädigten Zustand der Architektur, in der die Signatur nicht in Erscheinung getreten wäre, hätten die sichtbaren Architekturteile die Form eines Y-Signums besessen. Im ursächlichen Zusammenhang mit dem Einsturz des Arkadenbogens, der die Entscheidung Sebastians für Gott bezeichnet, die zugleich eine Abkehr von der Möglichkeit ist, den linken Weg für sich zu wählen, steht die Abscherung der Arkadenpfeiler, die den Namen des Künstlers zum Vorschein gebracht hat. Mit dem pythagoreischen Y sind Vorstellungen des Aufstiegs, wie ihn die Viktoria andeutet, und Sturzes, der als Motiv die gesamte linke Bildhälfte beherrscht, verbunden. Kennzeichnend für die linke Bildseite der Darstellung ist ihr ungeordneter materieller Bestand. Nicht nur sind die Wolken als "Zufallsbilder"[16] besonders anfällig für ständige Veränderungen, sondern auch die aus dem architektonischen Zusammenhang herausgelösten skulpturalen Teile sind auf ihren materiellen Bestand reduziert dem Wirken fremder Kräfte offen ausgeliefert. Aufgabe der *ars*[17] ist es, die Entscheidung des Zufalls, auf den nur der Ungeübte hofft und mit dessen Entscheidung sein Werk gelingen soll, auf ein Minimum zu reduzieren. Sie tritt als notwendige Ergänzung der Natur, der stofflichen Substanz wie des Ingeniums auf. Der naturhaft entdeckende und entbergende Charakter des Ingeniums[18] tritt in der Freilegung der Künstlerinschrift auf dem linken Arkadenpfeiler unterhalb dem Ansatz der Arkadenbögen bzw. der Gabelung der *littera Pythagorae* zutage. Indem die Inschrift im Zuge der Entscheidung hervortritt, unterliegt das Ingenium bereits dem Korrektiv des *iudicium*[19] und ist so Metapher für die Herstellung eines Bildwerkes, in dem sich die *virtus* des Künstlers mitteilt.

In der *Beschneidung Christi*[20] bildet die architektonische Konstruktion das Gabelkreuz vor und ab, indem die zur Hälfte dargestellten Arkadenbögen mit der sie stützenden Säule die Form des Y annehmen, dessen Extremitäten wie die der Bögen und des Kreuzes ebenfalls als *cornua* bezeichnet wurden.[21] Das Hornmotiv ist auch den als *bronzi finti* (als fingierte Bronzereliefs) dargestellten und der *pietra di paragone* aufliegenden alttestamentarischen Historien inhärent (Abraham und Isaak mit dem Widder als Ersatzopfer[22] [links im Bild], der gehörnte Moses[23] mit den Gesetzestafeln [rechts im Bild]), die in dem "Gehörnten" ihre heilsgeschichtliche Steigerung und Erfüllung finden.[24] Als Stein prüfenden Vergleichs entspricht die *pietra di paragone*[25] der im Bild angelegten

Typologie, die zeitdifferenziert Ähnliches mit Hilfe von Architektur und fiktiven Reliefs simultan zusammenbringt. Indem die *bronzi finti* dem "Prüfstein" aufliegen, signalisieren diese, daß sie nicht täuschen können, vielmehr als Realprophetien wahr sind.[26]

Der in der *Anbetung der Hirten*[27] hervorgebrachte Gegensatz zwischen täuschender Repräsentation und Einsicht in die Täuschung kulminiert in der Figur des Joseph. Nur vordergründig nimmt sich die Bestimmung des Bildthemas als Anbetung der Hirten aus. Eine genauere Betrachtung zeigt, daß die Aufmerksamkeit der Hirten dem falschen Objekt, nämlich Joseph, gilt. Die Täuschung, der die Hirten unterliegen, trifft unter verkehrten Vorzeichen auch auf den Betrachter zu, dem die Reichweite der Inkarnation Christi hinreichend bekannt, die besondere Gewichtung von Joseph dagegen unverständlich ist. Allein dem theologisch gebildeten Betrachter ist und war es möglich, in der assoziativen Zusammenstellung von Stier (bzw. Ochse ohne Anwesenheit des Esels) und Joseph, nicht den Nährvater Christi, sondern den alttestamentarischen Namensvetter zu sehen, der aufgrund des Wortlautes der "Segnung des Moses" *tauri decor eius, cornua unicornis cornua eius* ein Typus Christi war.[28] Joseph stützt sich in der Astgabel des Baumes auf und ist so Abbild jener Wahlsituation, die dem Y-Signum inhärent ist.[29] Sein Kopf befindet sich oberhalb des abgesägten Astes und zeigt damit das Ende des jüdisch-alttestamentarischen Stranges an, das durch die große Zeitenwende eintrat. Über ein solches Urteilsvermögen verfügen die beiden Hirten nicht, denn anstelle des inkarnierten Gottes, der vor ihnen liegt, bekunden sie Joseph ihre Verehrung. Nur ihm, dem theologisch gebildeten Betrachter, war es möglich, die unmittelbare Abbildung der Erzählung als Täuschung zu erkennen, der der unwissende Betrachter erliegt.

Zusammen mit drei weiteren Tugend- und Lasterdarstellungen (von Perugino und Lorenzo Costa) bilden die beiden Gemälde Mantegnas *Minerva vertreibt die Laster aus dem Garten der Tugend* und *Parnaß* den Kernpunkt der im Kontext eines Paragone (Künstlerwettkampfes) konzipierten Innendekoration für das Studiolo von Isabella d'Este in Mantua.[30] Mantegna bestimmt die Funktion des Studiolo als einen Ort der Regeneration. Während er in dem *Minerva*-Bild jene Seele darstellt, die in sich zerrissen in Unstimmigkeit geraten ist und damit zugleich auf die Gefahr eines unmäßigen Gebrauchs von *otium*[31] als latente Gefahr der Nutzung dieses Raumes verweist, zeugt der *Parnaß* von dem Bemühen, die verschiedenen Seelenvermögen unter der Wirkung der Musenkunst in eine Form der Übereinstimmung zu bringen. Literarische Grundlage des *Minerva*-Bildes ist der von Ovid in den Metamorphosen beschriebene Wettkampf zwischen Musen und Pieriden.[32] Als wahre Dichtung im Wettkampf mit der Dichtung der Lüge singt die Muse bei Ovid ihr Lied. Sie nimmt das Thema des Liedes der Pieride den Kampf der Giganten gegen die olympischen Götter auf und kann die Gottlosigkeit der

Lügendichtung nicht wirkungsvoller zurückweisen, als an demselben Stoff verbunden mit der ausgedehnten Schilderung des Raubes der Proserpina die Größe der Götter zu zeigen. Was anderes aber bedeuten die Wolkenbilder bei Mantegna wenn nicht *phantasmata*, mit denen der Riese Typhon der Lüge zugewiesen wird.[33] In seiner wahren Gestalt zeigt sich Typhon hier als Vulkantätigkeit des Ätna; wahr in Bezug auf seine Niederlage, wahr aber auch hinsichtlich der Beschränkung auf seine physikalische Deutung. Mittels ihrer Überredungskunst hatte Venus die die nicht in ihre Absicht eingeweihten Göttinnen auf die Wiesen gelockt, an deren Pracht sie sich müßig erfreuen.[34] Auf eine auf Überredung beruhende Täuschung gibt sich *historia* hier zu erkennen. Dabei bezeichnet die *delectatio* bzw. die *voluptas* der *historia* im Sinne von Leon Battista Albertis *De pictura*[35] nicht nur das ästhetische Wohlgefallen am Bild, sondern als Mittel der Überzeugung trägt sie als *ornatus* zum Erfolg des *movere* bei. Indem die Göttinnen den Wirkungen von *delectare* und *movere* unterworfen sind, entsprechen sie darin dem Rezipienten. Venus hingegen stünde für die Lüge des sophistischen Malers, die das Paradox der Malerei selbst einschließen dürfte, nämlich den Anschein körperlicher Wirklichkeit auf der Bildfläche zu erwecken, indem sie die Dreidimensionalität mittels *rilievo* und *colore* auf der Bildfläche vortäuscht. Täuschung und Irrtum hingegen beruhen letztlich auf Unwissenheit. Indem die Täuschung der Göttinnen im Bild mit einer Ent-täuschung, einer Erkennung aus dem Umschwung der Handlung einhergeht, ist mit dem Moment des Erkennens ein kognitiver Prozeß verbunden. Ihr entgegengestellt ist Daphne, die als archaische Holzskulptur Wesen und Wahrheit impliziert.[36] Auf das pythagoreische Y reduziert,[37] ist ihr ein Unterscheidungsvermögen zwischen Gut und Schlecht, Richtig und Falsch, Wahrheit und Lüge inhärent. In der mittelalterlichen Auslegungstradition ist Daphne als immergrüner Lorbeerbaum mit dem Kreuz Christi[38] identifiziert worden. Als furca-förmiges Kruzifix trägt sie vegetative Formen.[39] Auf das Kreuz spielt auch das in den Sprachen Hebräisch, Griechisch und Latein abgefaßte Spruchband an, das sich um ihren Stamm windet. Als *lignum vitae aeternae* steht der Lorbeer für den Weg des Lebens und zugleich für den, der vor dem Tod bewahrt, wenn der Mensch sich für ihn entscheidet. Die *via mortis* hingegen vertritt Pluto, der als *ignorantia* gleichsam zu Grabe getragen wird.[40] So wie Ovid den "Raub der Proserpina" als wahre Dichtung im Wettkampf mit der Dichtung der Lüge schildert, so bestimmt Mantegna über den Daphne-Baum in Form eines Y moderne Malerei als ent-täuschende Erkenntnis.

Insbesondere den Grisaillen Mantegnas liegt eine typologische Geschichtskonzeption[41] zugrunde, die alttestamentarisches Geschehen als *historia* abbildet. Das pythagoreische Y wird hier sowohl zum Indikator von Tugend und Laster und der Entscheidungssituation, wie auch zum Auslöser einer heilsgeschichtlichen Reflexion. Verbindendes Element ist die Verdinglichung des Y zu einem Baum, der auf mehrfache Weise, aber stets unter Einbeziehung der Hornmetaphorik das Kreuz Christi präfiguriert.

So ist die Ulme in der moralischen Auslegung von *Samson und Dalila*[42] Abbild von Samsons Leben[43], während sie in der allegorischen Exegese das Gabelkreuz vordeutet, da Samson trotz seiner Verfehlung auch als Typus Christi gedeutet werden konnte.[44] In der *Opferung des Isaak*[45] ist der Baum Sabek, in welchem sich der Widder mit seinen Hörnern verfangen hatte, aufgrund der Polysemie des Wortes "Hörner" (*cornua*) baumförmige Präfiguration des "gehörnten" Kreuzes.[46] Die Entscheidungsmöglichkeit zwischen Laster und Tugend, Tod und Leben, zeigt der Y-förmigen Baum in *David mit dem Haupt Goliath*[47] mittels des dürren bzw. abgeschlagenen und grünen Astes an, der Pflanzen- und Hornmetaphorik in sich vereint, indem er David als "sprießendes" Horn bezeichnet,[48] das das Horn des Heils,[49] nämlich Christus, hervorbringt.

Als fiktive Reliefs verkörpern die Grisaillen geradezu begrifflich *rilievo*: lebensähnliche bildliche Präsenz, die nur Schein ist, im Gegensatz zur Bildhauerei, die Substanz sowohl in Hinblick auf ihre physische Ausdehnung wie im philosophischen Sinn von "Essenz" bildet.[50] Die der illusionistischen Malerei zugrundeliegende Dialektik von Täuschung und Enttäuschung findet in der Wahl der jeweiligen *historia* ihre Entsprechung. Einsicht in die Täuschung bietet sich dem Betrachter über das pythagoreische Y an, das entsprechend der moralisch-allegorischen Schriftauslegung der *historia* Wesen und Eigenwert des Mediums Malerei reflektiert, indem es wahre Malerei als ent-täuschende Erkenntnis festlegt.

NOTES

Der vorliegende Text ist ein um Anmerkungen ergänzter Vortrag, gehalten im Rahmen des Symposions: *Fifteenth Century/Le Quinzième Siècle/Das Fünfzehnte Jahrhundert*, Kaprun (Salzburg), July 2-7, 1995.

[1] Zur *littera Pythagorae* E. Panofsky, *Hercules am Scheideweg und andere antike Bildstoffe in der neueren Kunst* (Leipzig-Berlin 1930); ferner L. Volkmann, *Bilderschriften der Renaissance. Hieroglyphik und Emblematik in ihren Beziehungen und Fortwirkungen* (Leipzig 1923), hier 108; C. Pascal, "Il bivio della vita e la 'littera Pythagorae'," *Miscellanea Ceriani* (Mailand 1910), 57-67; A. Brinkmann, "Ein Denkmal des Neupythagoreismus," *Rhein. Museum f. Philologie* 66 (1911), 616-625; F. de Ruyt, "L'idée du 'bivium' et le symbole pythagoricien de la lettre Y," *Revue Belge de philologie et d'histoire* 10 (1931), 137-144; M.-A. Dimier, "La lettre de Pythagore et les hagiographes du moyen âge," *Le Moyen Âge* 60 (1954), 403-418; H. Silvestre, "Nouveaux témoignages médiévaux sur la 'Littera Pythagorae'," *Le Moyen Âge* 63 (1957), 55-57. Zuletzt in umfassender Form W. Harms, *Homo viator in bivio. Studien zur Bildlichkeit des Weges* (München 1970).

[2] Ein nahezu vollständiges Verzeichnis der Literatur zu Mantegna enthält R. Lightbown, *Mantegna: With a Complete Catalogue of the Paintings, Drawings, and Prints* (Oxford-Berkeley-Los Angeles 1986); Ergänzungen finden sich vor allem bei

Andrea Mantegna, ed. J. Martineau, Katalog der Ausstellung London, Royal Academy of Arts (New York, The Metropolitan Museum of Art, 1992).

[3] Isidor von Sevilla, *Etymologiarum sive originum libri XX*, ed. W. M. Lindsay (Oxford 1911, repr. 1962), I,3,7. So auch die Kommentare des Angelo Rocca und Mutio Pansa (Angelo Roccha [sic], *Bibliotheca Apostolica Vaticana a Sixto V. Pont. Max. in splendidiorem, commodioremque locum translata ...*, [Rom 1591], 126ff.; Mutio Pansa, *Della Libreria Vaticana ragionamenti*, [Rom 1590], 285ff.), die unmittelbar zum Auftrag der Ausmalung der Decke des sixtinischen Saals der vatikanischen Bibliothek mit den *inventores litterarum* gehören. Dazu P. J. J. van Thiel, "Litterarum inventores. Een uniek thema in de Sala Sistina van het Vaticaan," *Nederl. kunsthist. Jaarboek 15* (1964), 105-131. Kurzer Überblick auch bei W. Oechslin, "Architektur und Alphabet," *Architektur und Sprache. Gedenkschrift für Richard Zürcher*, ed. C. Braegger (München 1982), 216-254.

[4] Hierzu Näheres bei Panofsky (wie Anm. 1), bes. 65ff., und D. Wuttke, *Die Histori Herculis des Nürnberger Humanisten und Freundes der Gebrüder Vischer, Pangratz Bernhaubt gen. Schwenter* (Köln-Graz 1964), bes. 118ff. (mit ergiebiger Bibliographie).

[5] Für den weiteren Zusammenhang verweise ich auf Harms (wie Anm. 1), 158-199. Vgl. ebd. Abb. 1 u. 2, p. 37: Y-Signum mit Attributen aus Dantes *Divina Commedia* und Y-Signum mit Attributen des Lohnes und der Strafe, aus: Geofroy Tory, *Champ Fleury* (Paris 1529), 63^{v} und 63^{r}.

[6] O. Nussbaum, "Die Bewertung von rechts und links in der römischen Liturgie," *Jahrbuch für Antike und Christentum* 5 (1962), 158-171; U. Deitmaring, "Die Bedeutung von Rechts und Links in theologischen und literarischen Texten bis um 1200," *Zeitschrift für deutsches Altertum und deutsche Literatur* 98 (1969), 262-292.

[7] Die mittelalterliche Tradition zusammenfassend zitiert der Florentiner Humanist Coluccio Salutati im vierten Buch seiner Schrift *De laboribus Herculi*, ed. B. L. Ullman (Zürich s. a. Vorwort: 1947), hier 571,17-577,22, neben Bernardus Silvestris (*Arborem Pitagoras humanitatem appellavit quoniam in duos ramos i. e. in virtutem et vitium se dividit [*Comm. super sex libros Eneidos Virgilii, ed. W. Riedel, Greifswald 1924: 58, 23f.]) auch ausführlich Servius und über diesen ebenfalls Persius, als er Vergils Baum und das pythagoreische Signum miteinander in Beziehung setzt. Vgl. dazu Harms (wie Anm. 1), 57ff.

[8] Sowohl das Y als auch Vergils Baum und goldener Zweig sind mit der Thematik der Entscheidung in Zusammenhang gesehen worden. In besonderer Weise ist diese Thematik jedoch dem "Baum der Erkenntnis," dem "*lignum scientiae boni et mali*, " inhärent. Vgl. z.B. die mittelalterliche Predigt *Facilis est descensus Auerni* ... (*Aeneis* VI, 126. 128-129) von Alanus ab Insulis, teilweise abgedruckt in: P. F. Ganz, "*Archani Celestis Non Ignorans.* Ein unbekannter Ovid-Kommentar," *Verbum et Signum. Beiträge zur mediävistischen Bedeutungsforschung*, eds. H. Fromm, W. Harms, U. Ruberg, Bd. 1 (München 1975), 195-208, hier 202, Anm. 26: *Y littera tractum habet cui innititur, et a tertio procedens in duos ramos velud in duo brachia diuiditur. Alter sursum erigitur; unus descendit, alter ascendit; ad cuius similitudinem Y mistica, id est humani arbitrii natura in primi hominis corde designata libere*

voluntati tanquam trunco innitebatur, et in velle bonum et malum tanquam in duo brachia diuidebatur.

[9] Vgl. hierzu beispielsweise Giovanni Pisano, Kruzifix, Pistoia, S. Bartolomeo u. ders., Kruzifix aus Siena, Opera del Duomo, abgebildet bei M. Lisner, *Holzkruzifixe in Florenz und in der Toskana. Von der Zeit 1300 bis zum Cinquecento* (München 1970), Abb. 20 und 11. Zu den Ursprüngen der Gabelkreuzvorstellung siehe M. von Alemann-Schwartz, *Crucifixus Dolorosus. Beiträge zur Polychromie und Ikonographie der rheinischen Gabelkruzifixe* (Diss. Bonn 1976), 205-272. Zur Typologie vom Baum des Lebens und dem Kreuz Christi F. Kampers, *Mittelalterliche Sagen vom Paradiese und vom Holze des Kreuzes Christi in ihren vornehmsten Quellen und in ihren hervorstechendsten Typen* (Köln 1897), 87-92; R. Bauerreis, *Arbor vitae. Der "Lebensbaum" und seine Verwendung in Liturgie, Kunst und Brauchtum des Abendlandes* (München 1938); M. R. Bennet, "The Legend of the Green Tree and the Dry," *Archeological Journal* 83 (Ser. 2, 33, 1936), 1929: 21-32; E. S. Greenhill, "The Child in the Tree. A Study of the Cosmological Tree in Christian Tradition," *Traditio* 10 (1954), 323-371. Allgemein L. Stauch, Art. "Baum, A-B", *Reallexikon zur deutschen Kunstgeschichte*, Bd. 2 (Stuttgart 1948), Sp. 63-73; J. Flemming, Art. "Baum, Bäume", in: Kirschbaum u. a., *Lexikon der christlichen Ikonographie*, Bd. 1 (Freiburg 1968-1974), Sp. 258-268.

[10] Hierzu und zum Folgenden G. Q. Reijners O. S. C., *The Terminology of the Holy Cross in Early Christian Literature as Based upon Old Testament Typology* (Nijmegen 1965), 97-107. Die dort zu den Namen des Kreuzes gesammelten frühen Zeugnissen für *Horn(s) as a Name for a Cross* beziehen sich auf den Josephssegen (Deut. 33, 17), der eine ähnliche exegetische Relevanz besitzt wie die Hornstellen Gen. 22, 13; Hab. 3, 4 und Ps. 21, 22. Andere biblische Hornstellen gelten bei den Vätern nicht oder selten als *testimonia crucis* mit Ausnahme von Ps. 91, 11. Zur Hornmetaphorik des oberen Teils des Y vgl. den mit Mantegna befreundeten Felice Feliciano, *Alphabetum Romanum,* ed. G. Mardersteig (Verona 1960), fol. XII^{r}.

[11] Vgl. hierzu meine Ausführungen zu folgenden Gemälden Andrea Mantegnas: *Die Anbetung der Hirten* (New York, Metropolitan Museum); *Die Opferung des Isaak* (Wien, Kunsthistorisches Museum) und *David mit dem Haupte Goliaths* (Wien, Kunsthistorisches Museum).

[12] Näheres bei K. Heitmann, "Das Verhältnis von Dichtung und Geschichtsschreibung in älterer Theorie," *Archiv für Kulturgeschichte* 52 (1970), 244-279 (hier bes. 250-259); R. Landfester, *Historia magistra vitae. Untersuchungen zur humanistischen Geschichtstheorie des 14. bis 16. Jahrhundert* (Genf 1972), 80-94; E. Keßler, "Das rhetorische Modell der Geschichtsschreibung," in *Formen der Geschichtsschreibung. Theorie der Geschichte*, eds. R. Koselleck, H. Lutz, J. Rüsen, Bd. 4 (München 1982), 37-85; H.-W. Goetz, "Die 'Geschichte' im Wissenschaftssystem des Mittelalters," in: F.-J. Schmale, *Funktion und Formen mittelalterlicher Geschichtsschreibung* (Darmstadt 1985), 165-213. Im Zusammenhang mit der Kunsttheorie Kristine Patz, "Zum Begriff der 'Historia' in L. B. Albertis 'De Pictura'," *Zeitschrift für Kunstgeschichte* 49 (1986), 269-287.

[13] Überblick über die Allegorieforschung im typologischen Zusammenhang bei C. Meier, "Überlegungen zum gegenwärtigen Stand der Allegoriediskussion. Mit be-

sonderer Berücksichtigung der Mischformen," *Frühmittelalterliche Studien* 10 (1976), 1-69.

[14] Zum sophistischen *quello che non è, sia* vgl. D. Summer, *Michelangelo and the Language of Art* (Princeton 1981), bes. 41-55.

[15] Wien, Kunsthistorisches Museum, abgebildet bei Lightbown (wie Anm. 2), Cat.-no. 10, Abb. 43, p. 170. Die griechische Inschrift "To ergon tou Andreou" entspricht der lateinischen Signatur "opus Andreae (Mantegna)." Außer Lightbown vor allem M. Levi D'Ancona, "Il 'S. Sebastiano' di Vienna: Mantegna e Filarete," *Arte Lombarda* 18 (1973), 70-74; dies., "Il San Sebastiano di Vienna del Mantegna," *Commentari* 28 (1977), 73-91; dies., "An Image Not Made by Chance: The Vienna *St. Sebastian* by Mantegna," *Studies in Late Medieval and Renaissance Painting in Honor of Millard Meiss*, eds. I. Lavin and J. Plummer, Bd. 1 (New York 1977), 98-114; J. M. Greenstein, *Mantegna and Painting as Historical Narrative* (Chicago-London 1992), 71-85.

[16] Eine zufriedenstellende Erklärung des Wolkenbildes, wie etwa die des Typhon in Mantegnas *Minerva vertreibt die Laster aus dem Garten der Tugend,* ist bis jetzt nicht gefunden worden. Allgemein H. W. Janson, "The *Image Made by Chance* in Renaissance Thought," *De Artibus Opuscula XL.* Essays in Honor of Erwin Panofsky, ed. M. Meiss (New York 1961), 254-266; M. Kemp, "From Mimesis to Fantasia. The Quattrocento Vocabulary of Creation, Inspiration and Genius in the Visual Arts," *Viator* 8 (1977), 347-398.

[17] Zu den folgenden Ausführungen H. Lausberg, *Handbuch der literarischen Rhetorik. Eine Grundlegung der Literaturwissenschaft* (München 1960), §§ 1-3, p. 25f.

[18] Zum artistisch-topischen Modell von Invenieren und Beurteilen#Ordnen#Machen, das zwei Verfahren miteinander verbindet, vgl. W. Schmidt-Biggemann, *Topica universalis. Eine Modellgeschichte humanistischer und barocker Wissenschaft* (Hamburg 1983).

[19] Für den weiteren Zusammenhang D. Summers, *The Judgement of Sense. Renaissance Naturalism and the Rise of Aesthetics* (Cambridge, 1987).

[20] Triptychon, Florenz, Uffizien, abgebildet bei N. Garavaglia, *Das Gesamtwerk von Andrea Mantegna* (Mailand 1967), Tafel XXXV, no. 34c. Zum Gemälde Lightbown (wie Anm. 2), Cat. no. 13-16, 411-13; F. Saxl, "Heidnisches Opfer in der Italienischen Renaissance," *Journal of the Warburg and Courtauld Institutes* 2 (1938-9), 362, stellte zuerst die Identität des Themas als "Beschneidung" in Zweifel und schlug statt dessen die "Darbringung im Tempel" vor. Eine ausführliche Darlegung dieser Problematik bei Greenstein (wie Anm.15), 86-222.

[21] *Vocabolario degli Accademici della Crusca*, Florenz [5]1878, Bd. 3, § XXIII, p. 763: *Corna dell'abaco diconsi, nei capitelli ionico, corintio e composito, Le quattro estremità o faccie angolari dell' abaco, soprastanti alle volute.* Ebd., § XXIV: *E parlandosi di archi, lunette o simili, Corna denotano Le estremità inferiori di essi;* vgl. hierzu beispielsweise das dort angeführte Zitat: Condivi, *Vit. Buonarr.* 24: *È la forma della volta ... a botte; e ne' posamenti suoi, a lunetta ... Cominciando da i peducci,*

dove le corna della volta, finge ec. Deutsches Wörterbuch von J. und W. Grimm, Bd. IV/II (Leipzig 1877), Sp. 1820 (15e), ... *bei Megenberg bezeichnet "horn" das ende eines halbkreises.*

[22] Siehe unten Anm. 46.

[23] R. Melinkoff, *The Horned Moses in Medieval Art and Thought* (Berkeley, Los Angeles, London 1970).

[24] Vgl. unten Anm. 46 u. 49.

[25] Hierzu die Ausführungen von R. Preimesberger, "Zu Jan van Eycks Diptychon der Sammlung Thyssen-Bornemisza," *Zeitschrift für Kunstgeschichte* 54 (1991), 459-89, bes. 486-89; weiterhin R. Jones, "Mantegna and Materials," *I Tatti Studies. Essays in the Renaissance* 2 (1987), 71-90, bes. 82, Anm. 31 u. 32.

[26] Zur Typologie F. Ohly, "Synagoge und Ecclesia. Typologisches in mittelalterlicher Dichtung," *Miscellanea Mediaevalia* 4 (1966), 350-369, jetzt auch zugänglich in: ders., *Schriften zur mittelalterlichen Bedeutungsforschung* (Darmstadt 1877), 361-400; weiterhin H. Hoefer, *Typologie im Mittelalter. Zur Übertragbarkeit typologischer Interpretation auf weltliche Dichtung* (Göppingen 1971) und P. Jentzmik, *Zu Möglichkeiten und Grenzen typologischer Exegese in mittelalterlicher Predigt und Dichtung* (Göppingen 1973).

[27] New York, Metropolitan Museum, abgebildet bei *Andrea Mantegna*, ed. J. Martineau (wie Anm. 2), 128, no. 8. Zur Provenienz des Bildes unter Berücksichtung der Auftrags- und Entstehungsgeschichte siehe vor allem Lightbown (wie Anm. 2), Cat.-no. 5, 403f.; Abb. 33-35; B. Fredericksen, "Leonardo and Mantegna in the Buccleuch Collection," *The Burlington Magazine* CXXXIII (1991), 117, Anm. 8; K. Christiansen, *Le Muse e il Principe. Arte di corte nel Rinascimento padano*, ed. M. Natale, Katalog der Ausstellung Mailand, Museo Poldi Pezzoli, 1991, 307-312.

[28] Siehe oben Anm. 10. Über den Widerspruch der Formulierung "Hörner des Einhorns" neben Reijners, 100, Anm. 6; H. Brandenburg, Art. "Einhorn," in: *Reallexikon für Antike und Christentum,* Bd. 4 (1959), Sp. 840-62, hier 844ff.; und vor allem J. W. Einhorn, *Spiritalis Unicornis. Das Einhorn als Bedeutungsträger in Literatur und Kunst des Mittelalters* (München 1976), 43ff.

[29] Für den weiteren Zusammenhang verweise ich auf Harms (wie Anm. 1), 40-49 u. 157-199.

[30] Paris, Louvre, die beiden Gemälde Mantegnas sind abgebildet bei E. Verheyen, *The Paintings in the "Studiolo" of Isabella d'Este at Mantua* (New York 1971), Pl. 12 und 11, wie diejenigen von Perugino und Lorenzo Costa: ebd., Pl. 24, 27 u. 33. Vgl. weiterhin W. Liebenwein, *Studiolo. Die Entstehung eines Raumtyps und seine Entwicklung bis um 1600* (Berlin 1977), hier bes. 103-127; Katalog zur Ausstellung *Le Studiolo d'Isabelle d'Este*, ed. S. Béguin (Paris 1975), 22-25; Katalog der Ausstellung *Gli Studioli di Isabella d'Este. Documenti, vicende, restauri*, Mantua, Archivo di Stato (Mantua 1977).

[31] Neben einer Vielzahl von Bedeutungen bezeichnete *otium,* solange es mit *dignitas* gepaart war und nicht unmäßig betrieben wurde, vorzugsweise die literarische Beschäftigung sowie den inneren Frieden im Gegensatz zum vertraglich gesicherten Frieden mit äußeren Feinden. Weiteres bei J.-M. André, *L'Otium dans la vie morale et intellectuelle romain* (Paris 1966).

[32] Ovid, *Metamorphosen* V, 308-678. Zum demonstrativen Kunstcharakter dieses Wettstreites S. Hinds, *The Metamorphosis of Persephone. Ovid and the Self-Conscious Muse* (Cambridge 1987).

[33] Hierzu und zum folgenden D. C. Innes, "Gigantomachy and Natural Philosophy," *Classical Quarterly* n.s. 29 (1979), 165-71; *Aetna*, erklärt und übersetzt von S. Sudhaus (Leipzig 1898), V. 29-74, sowie p. 101-109 mit weiterführenden Quellennachweisen. Zur Beurteilung dieser Mythen z. B. V, 29: *Principio ne quem capiat fallacia vatum* (bezogen auf Vulkan); V. 74f.: *Haec est mendosae vulgata licentia famae* (hinsichtlich Enceladus). Im Gegensatz dazu die eigene naturwissenschaftliche Zielsetzung: *Vatibus ingenium est hinc audit nobile carmen*. Ebenso Philostratos, *Das Leben des Apollonios von Tyana*. Dt./Gr. Hg. und übers. von V. Mumprecht (München-Zürich 1983), V, 16 (p. 497). In der Neuzeit vgl. G. Boccaccio, *Genealogia Deorum Gentilium Libri*, ed. V. Romano (s. l. 1951), Buch IV, Kap. XXII, p. 183f. Eine kritische Zusammenfassung der damalig bekannten Erdbebentheorien bei Georgius Agricola, *De ortu et causis subterraneorum libri V,* 1544, dt. Übers. in: Georgius Agricola, *Schriften zur Geologie und Mineralogie I*. Übers. u. bearbeitet v. G. Fraustadt u. H. Prescher (Berlin 1956), 47-211; zur Ätnabesteigung von Pietro Bembo *Il testo di Pietro Bembo*, übers. u. hg. von V. E. Alfieri, mit Anm. versehen von M. Carapezza und L. Sciascia (Palermo 1981).

[34] Hyg. *fab.* 146: "*[...] sed iubet eum* (Pluto) *rapere eam* (Proserpina) *flores legentem in monte Aetna, qui est in Sicilia. [...] dum flores cum Venere et Diana et Minerva legit [...];*" Claudian, *De Raptu Proserpinae*, II, 1-246.

[35] Leon Battista Alberti, *De Pictura-Della Pittura*, in: ders., *Opere volgari*, ed. C. Grayson, Bd. 3 (Bari 1973), § 40,11-14. Dazu und zum folgenden Patz (wie Anm. 12).

[36] Zum Wettkampf zwischen Malerei und Skulptur L. Mendelsohn, *Paragoni. Benedetto Varchi's Due Lezzioni and Cinquecento Art Theory*, New York Uni. Phil. Diss. 1978 (Univ. Microfilms Int., Ann Arbor 1981).

[37] Während der Schrift die Ähnlichkeit mit den Dingen verlorengegangen ist, besaß nach damaligen Vorstellungen einzig die Hieroglyphe diese Ähnlichkeit; Nachweise hierzu bei Harms (wie Anm. 1), 105-113; allgemein L. Dieckmann, *Hieroglyphics. The History of a Literary Symbol* (St. Louis. Miss. 1970); zur Bedeutung der humanistischen Hieroglyphen-Studien noch immer K. Giehlow, "Die Hieroglyphenkunde des Humanismus in der Allegorie der Renaissance," *Jahrbuch der kunsthistorischen Sammlungen des allerhöchsten Kaiserhauses* 32 (Wien und Leipzig 1915), 1-232. Zur Stellung der Hieroglyphik innerhalb der allgemeinen allegorischen Weltdeutung s. H.-J. Schings, *Die patristische und stoische Tradition bei Andreas Gryphius* (Köln 1966), bes. 110ff.

[38] Pierre Bersuire, *Metamorphosis Ovidiana moraliter ... explanata*, Paris 1509, Nachdruck mit einer Einleitung von Stephan Orgel (New York-London 1979),

fol.xxv: *Crux christianorum spes: ... arbor resurrectionis: lignum vitae eternae.* Zur mittelalterlichen Auslegung von Daphne siehe W. Stechow, *Apollo und Daphne* (Leipzig 1932, repr. Darmstadt 1965); Y. Giraud, *La Fable de Daphné* (Genf 1968); M. Barnard, *The Myth of Apollo and Daphne. Some Medieval and Renaissance Versions of the Ovidian Tale*, University of Michigan, Ph. D. 1975 (Univ. Microfilms Inc., Ann Arbor); dies., *The Myth of Apollo and Daphne from Ovid to Quevedo. Love, agon, and the grotesque* (Durham 1987).

[39] Siehe oben Anm. 9.

[40] Ebenso wie *vir doctus* und *vir bonus* zu Synonymen werden konnten, so fielen die Begriffe *ignorantia* und *mala* zusammen vgl. Petrarca, Fam. XVIII 13, 2: "*qua nullum pestilentia monstrum est,*" ebd., VI 2, 14: "*Quid ignorantia peius?*, " weiterhin z. B. Cicero, *De nat. deorum* III 32, 79; *Tusc*. III 28, 6 u. 70; *Tusc.* IV 24, 54.

[41] Grundlegend H. de Lubac, *Exégèse médiévale. Les quatre sens de l'écriture*, 4 Bde. (Paris 1959-1964). Mit zahlreichen Belegen G. A. Zinn, "*Historia fundamentum est*: The Role of History in the Contemplative Life According to Hugh of St. Victor," *Contemporary Reflections on the Mediaeval Christian Tradition. Essays in Honor of R. C. Petry*, ed. G. H. Shriver (Durham/N.C. 1974), 135-58.

[42] London, National Gallery, abgebildet bei *Andrea Mantegna*, ed. J. Matineau (wie Anm. 2), 396, no. 104; Lightbown (wie Anm. 2), Cat.-no. 50, 449.

[43] Den Abfall von Gott, die Entscheidung für den linken Arm des Y als dem Weg des Todes, zeigt unter anderem Samsons Anwesenheit auf der linken Seite der Ulme wie auch die Gegenüberstellung von Wein und quellklarem Wasser an.

[44] Einen Überblick über die christliche Exegese der Figur Samsons mit zahlreichen Belegstellen bietet F. Krouse, *Milton's Samson and the Christian Tradition* (Princeton 1949, repr. 1963), 22-79.

[45] Wien, Kunsthistorisches Museum, abgebildet bei *Andrea Mantegna*, ed. J. Matineau (wie Anm. 2), 410, no. 132; Lightbown (wie Anm. 2), Cat.- nos. 140-141, 470.

[46] Nachweise bei: H.-J. Schoeps, "The Sacrifice of Isaac in Paul's Theology," *Journal of Bibl. Literature* 65 (1946), 385ff.; J. Daniélou, "La typologie d'Isaac dans le Christianisme primitif," *Biblica* 28 (1947), 363 ff.; ders., *Sacramentum futuri* (Paris 1950), 97ff.; D. Lerch, *Isaaks Opferung christlich gedeutet. Eine auslegungsgeschichtliche Untersuchung* (Tübingen 1950); F. Nikolasch, *Das Lamm als Christussymbol in den Schriften der Väter* (Wien 1963), 24ff.; ders., "Zur Ikonographie des Widders von Gen. 22," *Vigiliae Christianae* 23 (1969), 197ff. (weitere Nachweise). Zu der Widerspiegelung dieser Vorstellungen in der Ikonographie vgl. die umfassende Zusammenstellung von I. Speyart van Woerden, "The Iconography of the Sacrifice of Abraham," *Vigiliae Christianae* 15 (1961), 214-255.

[47] Wien, Kunsthistorisches Museum, abgebildet bei *Andrea Mantegna*, ed. J. Matineau (wie Anm. 2), p. 409, no. 131; Lightbown (wie Anm. 2), Cat.- nos. 140-141, 470.

[48] Ps. 131, 17: "*illuc producam cornu David;*" Hesekiel 29, 21: "*in die illo pullulabit cornu domui Israhel*" — Vgl. auch Reijners (wie Anm. 10), 99, Anm. 3: "*In the 15th Benediction of the 'Eighteen Benedictions-prayer (Bab. rec.)' the horn of the Messiah is also mentioned: 'Speedily cause the offspring of David, thy servant, to flourish, and let his horn be exalted by thy salvation, because we wait for thy salvation all the day. Blessed art thou, O Lord, who causest the horn of salvation to flourish'.*"

[49] Lc 1, 69: "*erexit cornu salutis nobis in domo David pueri sui* ." Dieses "Horn des Heils" in dem einzigartigen Horn des Einhorns versinnbildlicht zu sehen, war für typologisches Denken geradezu zwangsläufig, zumal, da Ps 91, 11 dafür die direkte Handhabe lieferte: "*exaltabitur sicut unicornis cornu meum.*" Ferner Ps 148, 14: "*exaltabit cornu populi sui;*" Ps 17, 3 "*Deus ... cornu salutis meae. — Cornu etiam David, significat caeleste regnum. Cornu generaliter regnum & potentiam designare solet.*" Zu der Bedeutung des Horn-Signums im AT vgl. die Angaben bei Einhorn (wie Anm. 28), 43, Anm. 90; bes. I. Scheftelowitz, "Das Hörnermotiv in den Religionen," *Archiv für Religionswissenschaft* 15 (1912), 451-87.

[50] Im "Paragone" ist der Begriff des *rilievo* das malerische Äquivalent für das Argument der Substanz seitens der Bildhauer: "*Was ich aber sagte, daß nämlich der Maler so kühn sei, ergibt sich aus dessen Bestreben, die Natur selbst zu übertreffen, indem er einer Figur Geist einhauchen und sie lebendig erscheinen lassen will, trotzdem, daß er sie bloß auf einer Fläche darstellt. Er sollte doch wenigstens dabei bedenken, daß Gott, als er den Menschen schuf, ihn erhaben und in runder Figur machte, indem er so leichter zu beleben war. Dann würde er sich gewiß nicht eine so kunstvolle oder vielmehr wunderbare und göttliche Aufgabe gestellt haben,*" Jacopo da Pontormo an Benedetto Varchi (1546), zit. nach *Künstlerbriefe über Kunst. Bekenntnisse von Malern, Architekten und Bildhauern aus fünf Jahrhunderten*, ed. H. Uhde-Bernays (Dresden 1957), 82. Zuletzt und in umfassender Form zum Begriff des *rilievo* außer Preimesberger (wie Anm. 25) auch Mendelsohn (wie Anm. 36), 41-55.

Freie Universität Berlin

Corps et Biens: The Body as Currency in Fifteenth-Century Mystères de la Passion

James D. Wilkins

Modern readers-spectators of medieval religious drama, whether produced as narratives[1] or intended for public performance in the theatrical space, must fundamentally assume that "drama in the 15th century reflects the aspirations, preoccupations and limitations of the society which portrays itself therein."[2] The playwrights and *fatistes* of fifteenth-century Passion drama could belie neither the canonical and socioeconomic influences of which they and their works were products, nor the themes of slavery and freedom which sustained the plays' metaphoric frame of ransom-redemption as exchange-commerce.[3] Maurice Accarie aptly describes this interdependent dramatic give-and-take as theater in which "les hommes ne donnent pas le spectacle du mythe, mais le mythe donne le spectacle de l'homme."[4] Not only does the dramatized ransom-redemption myth characterize man's perception of the cosmic struggle between good and evil, but it juxtaposes both an economy of human and of divine interaction: commerce symbolized by a plethora of antithetical exchanges such as paradise for hell, bondage for freedom, divine body for human body, bodily servitude for spiritual freedom, physical body for spiritual riches, spiritual riches for physical body. Because of its integral role in this multi-leveled economic system, the human body is valorized as the medium (or, token) of exchange.

The pivotal metaphor in these dramas is nourished by its prominence in the informing canonical literature and its ransom-redemption narrative.[5] The dramatic account is grounded in the biblical story of the fall (Gen. 2:4-3:24). Nearly all the plays in the French *mystère* corpus that focus attention on the origin of sin do so in order to establish the ransom-redemptive context. Much of this sacred textual support is found in the prologues to the *journées*. In his *mystère*, Arnoul Greban (c.1452)[6] explains in the prologue to the first of four *journées* why such attention to the fall is necessary:

> Nostre especïale matiere
> est d insister au hault mistere
> de Jhesus et sa passion,
> sans prendre autre occupacion,
> Mais la crâacion du monde
> est ung mistere en quoy se fonde
> tout ce qui deppend en aprés. (lines 13-19)

Specific references to the creation of the world and prelapsarian bodies, as well as expanded genesis narratives, are later additions, most well-developed in the fifteenth-century *mystères*, especially those of Greban and Jean Michel (1486).[7] In these dramas, Eve and Adam are protagonists in the narrative exchange of bodies, not only as tokens exchanged by God and the Devil, but as bodies having voices that negotiate in that exchange. As tokens, both have been envalued by God and subsequently devalued by their own credence of the serpent's falsification of the contractual promise: you shall surely die (Gen. 3:4 NASB). After the fall, faith is characterized as credit in the metaphor during subsequent episodes of the story.[8] The devalued currency (Eve-Adam) must now rely by faith (credit) on God's promise of a deliverer through Eve who serves as "caution money."[9] In the setting of the medieval romance, two knights, based on primogenture and marital laws of the period, view the female body as an object of exchange, a testing place for their honor. Using four Old French romances of the *cycle de la gageure*, Krueger effectively illustrates the exchange that often took place in non-dramatic medieval French literture. The exchange was corporeal, most often involving female bodies, originally because of the patriarchal marriage laws of the early Middle Ages. "The heroine's role is that of an object of exchange between two knights who use her as a testing ground for their own honor." (24)

This metaphor is further enhanced and sustained by the study of freedom and slavery in early Christianity, and by its implications for medieval theology and practice — especially its impact on New Testament and Pauline soteriology.[10] It was primarily Paul who infused the notion of original sin as a core belief into early Christianity.[11] His reasoning is that because Eve and Adam fell into slavery to sin, all humankind is sinful and, as a result, both physical and spiritual death entered the world (1 Cor. 15:45-48).[12]

> Adam thus becomes the prototype of fallen or enslaved mankind. Jesus, the second Adam, is also both a figure in cosmic time and a prototype or, more properly, a counterprototype, for Jesus's Adamic nature is derived from the fact that he is the very antithesis of Adam and intervenes in history to undo the cosmic injury wrought by Adam — enslavement in sin with its harvest of spiritual and physical death.[13]

Early Christian tradition has viewed the redemptive process in a variety of ways, and these perspectives are more or less represented in all the *mystères* of the fifteenth century, but one tradition in particular has found plenary expression in those of the second half of the century: the ransom-redemption theory. "By the fifteenth century, theological attention was focused on the body of Christ."[14] The necessity of a flesh-exchange became central in this spiritual transaction, as Russell says in summarizing this particular dynamic of the ransom-redemptive process:

> Since Satan justly held the human race in prison, God offered himself as ransom for our freedom. The price could be paid only by God. Only God could freely submit. No one else could choose freely, because original sin

> had deprived us all of our freedom. By submitting to Satan's power of his own free will and choice, Christ liberated us from the Devil's power.[15]

Both redemption and ransom are theologically denoted as a repurchasing (or, reclaiming) of objects formerly possessed that have been subsequently possessed, or purchased, by an other. Both signify the loss of freedom for the possessed property, particularly in Christian law. Debtors' prisons, for example, originated from jails to which loan defaulters were sent by ecclesiastical courts.[16] Similarly, the Devil is a usurer who imprisons the soul and demands exorbitant interest payments before liberating it.[17] Ridderbos recognizes this aspect of Christ's redemptive work as a legal notion with ancient origins:

> [W]hen Paul qualifies salvation in Christ as ransom he may thereby be said to think of the so-called sacral redemption of slaves, a familiar practice in the Hellenistic world. The slave was required to give to the priest the price that was necessary for his freedom. The latter gave him freedom in the name of the deity, while the money was put into the hands of the owner. This was a specific legal form whereby the slave in fact redeemed himself, and the deity only appeared as the fictitious purchaser.[18]

Since the ultimate significance of exchange in ransom-redemption is its theological connotation of spiritual freedom,[19] the socio-economic context in which the *mystères* were authored and performed invigorates the symbolism of this metaphor. A detailed study of the economic and social history of fifteenth-century France is beyond the scope of this essay; however, its principal characteristics may be summarized as "piety, prestige, and commerce."[20] These societal commodities, or commonplaces, serve as interpretive paradigms in the minds of playwrights, producers, and readers-spectators as they write, act, and read-view. During the fifteenth and early sixteenth centuries in France, bourgeoning economies influenced not only the authoring but also the production of both secular and religious drama. According to Alan Knight, "the fifteenth century was characterized by increasing dramatic activity throughout most of Europe, though it was in areas of relative economic prosperity that such activity was most intense."[21] The correlation between monetary and literary activity is the subject of several recent studies. Marc Shell, for example, closely links the thinking of the Medieval mind about currency and its semiological organization of language:

> Whether or not a writer mentioned money or was aware of its potentially subversive role in his thinking, the new forms of metaphorization or exchanges of meaning that accompanied the new forms of economic symbolization and production were changing the meaning of meaning itself. This participation of economic form in literature and philosophy, even in the discourse about truth, is defined neither by what literature and philosophy talk about (sometimes money, sometimes not) nor why they talk about it (sometimes for money, sometimes not) but rather by the tropic

> interaction between economic and linguistic symbolization and production. A formal money of the mind informs all discourse ....[22]

Toward the middle of the century, playwrights began profiting from the public's sense of piety by charging spectators admission fees to view their spectacles, and seating within the theatrical space was thereafter determined by the amount each spectator paid. The social body was thus visibly manifested and ordered in the theater, being valued and/or devalued according to the financial worth of its individual components.[23] Furthermore, each locale and production company aspiring to stage more prestigious — and consequently more costly and elaborate — plays, authored and produced grandiose works replete with not-too-subtle reflections of a growing communal ethos of capitalistic commerce. As the writing and production of theater became more closely associated with economics, so the connotative relationship of bodies and goods became apparent. As Henri Rey-Flaud admonishes modern readers-spectators to view the theatrical space and spectacle as representative of the perceived cosmos, so the activity within this cosmos must be read-viewed as increasingly suggestive of its commercial supraculture.[24]

The reading-spectating community also plays a major role in establishing and sustaining the ransom-redemption metaphor found in these works. In the theater, both the dramatic and social planes are equivalenced by the interaction between actors and audience. As the sympathetic Christian audience enters the dramatic space, informed by theology as well as by the socio-economics that contribute to the production of both drama and audience, the cosmic symbols are impelled to interact, valuated by dramatic participation in the struggle between good and evil, and by the presence of the reading-spectating community.[25] Through direct address of *prologueurs* and their reiteration of the identity of Eve and Adam as the archetypal body of humanity, the playwright engages the reading-spectating body in the theatrical event. It is the reading-spectating community that valuates and devaluates the currency of representation as its self is valuated and devaluated by tiered seating within the theatrical space. Shoaf underscores the significance of communal valuation in making the case for language as currency (coin) in Dante and Chaucer. Citing medieval theorists, he points out that:

> [As] it is in the community's power to change a sign's significance if they so choose ... it does demonstrate that by concord men agree — as one theorist puts it 'mutualiter' — on the 'property' a given sign possesses; moreover, it also demonstrates that the community is the steward of this 'property'.[26]

This is in fact what the audience does. It gathers in one place and, by its communal ordering in designated places around the stage, enters into the metaphor of exchange by allowing itself to be exchanged as a body: hence, the "participation mystique." Herbert Blau's theory that the audience within the theatrical space is a microsocial representation of the microsocial political body reinforces this idea of communally-given value:

> As Passion theater necessitates the body, so the body demands and becomes a dramatic medium of exchange. With this metaphor in mind, an examination of the major fifteenth-century *mystères* will evidence that the their authors, such as Greban and Michel, wrote and (re)presented the human body within the ransom-redemption motif as currency to be exchanged using language marked for commerce.[27] The plays that provide the majority of examples are those composed in the latter part of the fifteenth century, especially the *mystères* of Greban and Michel.[28] Because these dramas are lengthy, examples will be limited to those from three principal sources of reference to corporeal exchange within these dramas: the prologues, the post-lapsarian Eve-Adam, and two disciples of Christ — Mary Magdalene and Judas Iscariot.[29]

Through the prologues preceding the major dramatic divisions called *journées,* the discourse of both the plays' staging and their acting *personae* become an economic system of representation, pointing the reader-spectator to the body as token.[30] Consider, for example, the *prologue capital* found in Michel's *mystère*. At the outset, the *prologueur* delineates the metaphoric frame of the drama as ransom-redemption. It is a frame which he painstakingly establishes at the outset via an exposition of the theology of the incarnation. He uses a crucial Biblical reference found in John 1:1 as his text: "Verbum caro factum est" (line 1). He emphasizes each word in that statement beginning with the Logos (*verbum* [ll. 123-360]), the necessity of the incarnation (*caro* [ll. 363-726]) followed by a brief reference to the work/ministry of Christ (*factum* [ll. 727-41]), and ending with a consideration of His eternal state of being (*est* [ll. 742-888]). The intention is to make clear for the reader-spectator that among the Trinity, only the incarnate Son can redeem humanity by offering reparations for the original transgression ("reparer si grande injure" [l. 553]; "eust reparé l'humain lignage" [l. 555]).[31] The *prologueur* specifies that "[i]l falloit convenablement que Dieu fist ce reparement puis qu'autre ne le povoit faire" (ll. 563-65), and that he must do so via incarnation: "[I]l falloit que Dieu faict homme / fust filz naturel d'une femme, / composé d'ung corps et d'une ame / unis a la divinité" (ll. 586-89).

In the *caro* discourse, the *prologueur* prefaces his remarks by particularizing the ransom-redemption process as an exchange ("pour en faire aucun eschange" [l. 492]). This is predicated on an in-depth exposition of the creation and fall of the rebellious angels. After establishing the theology of the created, non-corporeal nature of the angels (*non dimencionelz / incorporels, immortels* [ll. 381-82]), several lines then contrast the non-fallen primal state with the fallen state of those who rebelled against God:

Les orgueilleux lors trebucherent
Dés leur creacion premiere,
Privés de gloire et de lumiere,
En bisme confuse et obscure.
Toutesfoys, les dons de nature
Leur demourerent plainement
Et ne perdirent seullement
Que les dons de graces divine. (ll. 414-21)

The playwright valorizes their bodies as tokens by referring to them as endowed with gifts — gifts of nature and gifts of divine grace — then procedes to devalorize them by pointing to the loss of the latter. Another reference to such "gifting," taken from the Gospel narrative (Matt. 2:1-12), is found in the prologue to the second *journée*, where Greban uses similar terminology to valuate Christ's body. Writing about the nativity, he mentions the three kings' adoration of Christ: "qui par dons portant grant substance / vendrent la beneuree enfance / adorer par devote somme" (*G*, ll. 9992-94). Hoping to recuperate the forfeiture of these divinely valuated angels, God then creates humankind, fully capable of attaining eternal glory:

... mes voult former
de terre limoneuse et scene,
...
le premier homme ...
Et voulut, s'i n'estoit coupable
de vil peché, qu'i fust capable
de la haulte gloire eternelle
que jadis par coulpe mortelle
avoyent les faulx anges perdue. (*M*, ll. 494-95; 497; 499-503)[32]

However, humanity's creation narrative parallels that of the rebellious angels, symbolized in the actions of Eve and Adam (ll. 504-32). Because of their sin, they also were stripped, or deprived, of their glory (*privé de la gloire haultaine* [ll. 525], which is referred to as *la forfaicture* [l. 532]), though not of their body[ies] (*dons de nature* [l. 418]).[33] Michel's *prologueur* identifies Adam as responsible for having sold humanity's soul to the devil ("nostre ame engaiger ou vendre / au diable par coulpe vilaine" [ll. 44-45]). Therefore, the creator of this homocosmic triangle must now bargain for the ransom-redemption of humanity by assuming the only form of token that the other homocosmic party will accept in exchange for the one he already possesses: a human body. Only Christ can redeem them back from the ownership of Satan — "Dieu le Pere congrument ne le Sainct Esprit mesmement ne devoyent payer ceste somme" (ll. 582-85) — because it is He who is fully endowed with gifts of nature and of grace (as was the original possession) and, therefore, only He that can effectuate the exchange.[34]

In the prologues to the four *journées* of Greban's *mystère*, this framing motif is equally prominent. In the first, after asserting that the consequence of sin was the eternal banishment of humankind from its prelapsarian splendor (ll. 75-77), the *prologueur* contends that the only ransom is the incarnate body of Christ, "Lors fut la finance randue, / quand en croix fut morte estandue / *la char* [emphasis mine] de cil qui tout bien livre" (ll. 96-98). This monetary symbolism is further advanced by line 99: "Lors paya le dangereux pris, / celluy ou tous biens sont compris." In the context of the (re)telling of this cosmic soteriological event, Greban identifies Christ's body — distinguished from his divine, spiritual nature — as the commercially marked currency with which the human race is bought back from Satan.

Interestingly, each subsequent prologue gives indications that the dramatic text itself increases in value as the ransom-redemption narrative unfolds. For example, in the prologue to the first *journée*, Greban writes:

> Prenez ce que bon vous sera
> et le surplus l'en laissera,
> car tout ne poons pas attaindre;
> Nostre procès mieulx en vauldra
> et plus grant proffit en sauldra,
> sans nostre matiere contraindre. (ll. 123-28)

The textualization of the ransom-redemption is an economic process. It involves worth (*vauldra*), profit (*proffit*), salvaging (*sauldra*), and an economy of matter/subject control (*contraindre*). This marking goes further in the prologue to the third day, where the *prologueur* prefaces the *journée*'s action by signaling the continuation of this profitable subject matter ("pour continuer la matiere qui est proffitable" [l. 9947]). Finally, on the last *journée*, the *prologueur* declares with alliterative conviction: "Les paroles cy proposees / proffitablement exposees / peuent grandement proffiter" (ll. 27466-68).[35] No doubt said profit has spiritual connotations, but the subject matter-text is nonetheless linguistically associated with profit, even that of a financial nature. As the plays gained in popularity, no doubt the profit from paying spectators was increasing the value of each performance. Again on the fourth day, the depiction of the dramatic matter is intensified: "la matiere en est bien joyeuse, / bien proffitable et fructueuse" (ll. 27625-26).[36] Worth has been bestowed, not only on the acting bodies, but on the textual body as it incarnates the message of ransom-redemption.

Following the prologue, Greban begins his first *journée* by portraying Eve, Adam, and the Old Testament prophets in limbo (*limbes*) praying for God to provide a ransom (ll. 1741-2071). The prayers are heard in heaven and ignite an allegorical trial (ll. 2072-3394), motivating the Father to send his Son to redeem humanity. Though Mercy implores compassionate action to relieve their punitive servitude, the allegorical figure of Justice demands more vis-à-vis captive humanity:

> L'ange et l'omme ont esgal commis:
> soient donc egalment pugnis,
> et ainsi se l'omme a secours,
> l'ange y pourra avoir recours.
> L'un, dictes vous, est importun?
> *ergo* l'aultre, car c'est tout ung.
> Quand a la satisffacion,
> je fais ceste improbacion:
> mal se peust celluy deslier
> qui doit et n'a de quoy payer:
> demourer doit puor les ostages. (ll. 2351-61)

Affirming the original worth of the human body by equating it with that of the angels, and highlighting the tremendous debt that must be repaid, the trial arguments cogently express the need for a body of greater value to serve as the token of redemption (ll. 3285-325). An extension of this metaphorical currency to include humanity is found in the monologic prayer of Eve, spoken from her abode in Hell (*les limbes*). She prays to the Messiah:

> Doulx Messias, quand sera faicte
> la redempcion ou tendons
> ...
> en tenebres sommes...
> livrés a desolacion,
> sans bien, sans consolacion" (ll. 1796-97; 1804-6)

She effectively places herself (and humanity) at the center of the homocosmic economy. Both Eve and Adam accept responsibility for the loss of their original valuation, as well as the devaluation of God's reputation: "Par moi [Adam] ta noblesse est pardue" (l. 840);[37] "par moi [Eve] est pardu nostre bien" (l. 853). Both are in a state of ruin, denied the *bien* enjoyed in their prelapsarian state. This antithetical language of lack and abundance, which establishes the economic parameters of the metaphoric frame, is bolstered at the close of her prayer when Eve asks the Messiah to provide "la dilacion trop nous dure; / pourvoyes y quant te plaira" (ll. 1816-17). Eve recognizes that the ransom must be paid by a valorized token, whose value can only come from God. It is her body that is responsible for this plight, but her body is also the matter-rich medium, from which humanity descends, that will serve as the token used to mint the messianic Token that will ransom them both.[38]

In desperation, Eve pleads for some indication (*signe*) that the relationship between God and humanity is essentially changing: "monstre nous signe d'amitié, le tresor de grace descueuvre" (ll. 1944-45). She valorizes this token by reference to it as a treasure (*tresor*) to be revealed (*descueuvre*). Christ is once more valuated as the ransom token, afforded worth by the community of bound humanity in the figure of Eve. This treasure, incarnated in Christ, is the valued currency that will purchase her liberty by allowing the exchange between God and Satan to take place. She continues to emphasize, again in commercially-marked language, that because of her the entire human race ("ceulx qui sont d'Adam nés" [l. 1950]) must pay a debt not incurred by themselves ("par moy paient ce qu'ilz ne doivent" [l. 1952]). Only Christ's body is signified as the currency to pay this debt.

The dramatic *persona* of Mary Magdalene reinforces this imagery in Greban's *mystère*, implicating herself in commercially contrasting terms such as "povre fame" (l. 13878), and the Christ she loves as "le tresor de tous biens" (l. 13889).[39] Though *pauvre* is likely meant in the broader sense of *unfortunate*, its occurrence in antithesis with "the treasure of all goods" (l. 13889) affords it an economic connotation nonetheless. She tells the audience in her own words that she is, in fact, of renown as a wealthy woman: "Madelaine suis je nommee, / jadis gente et bien renommee / de bonne generacion" (ll. 13815-17). But, after making her claim to wealth and nobility, she devalues her wealthy status by confessing her own sinfulness:

> Ma beaulté, ma perfection
> est tournee en tel vitupere
> Que c'est abominacion
> par quel moyen et mocion
> j'ay tant courroucé Dieu, mon pere. (ll. 13821-25)

However, it is the Magdalene in Jean-Michel's *Passion* that brings a more deeply spiritual dimension to this metaphor. Jean-Michel does so by devoting a good number of verses to the development of her character. She is portrayed as a joyously vain woman (*M*, ll. 8469-505). The reader-spectator sees her clothe and adorn herself in search of valorization ("pour me faire bien regarder" [l. 8538]). The playwright allows the audience to see her entourage, Pasiphee and Perusine, who encourage her boastful rantings. She openly gloats concerning the wealth she has amassed: "Puis que en tant de biens habonde, / je ny puis avoir deshonneur" (ll. 8524-25). She equates her personal honor and worth with the abundance of things she possesses.

One day Magdalene sees people passing in front of her castle, returning from a meeting where Christ has preached. Out of curiosity, she stops three Jews and asks them whom they have gone to hear. They tell her of Christ's wonderful sermons ("les fructueux sermons / de Jesus" [ll. 10450-51]). As a truly worldly woman, she begins to size him up as a possible suitor, by asking for a physical description. Christ's body is objectified by her vicarious female gaze.[40] Burns makes the point that it is normally the male gaze that objectifies women in medieval literature, giving examples of women who dress sumptuously and use such as a mechanism to deflect the gaze that attempts to revalorize and thus devalue them.[41] In this instance, however, it is Magdalene who turns the gaze upon Christ to attempt to devalorize him, to objectify/tokenize him. It is she who desires him and plots her purchase. In the end, she succeeds only in becoming devalorized by becoming a servant of her Christ. The willing service of freed slaves to their owner is an essential element in the Pauline theology of ransom-redemption.[42] Those that are ransomed-redeemed become free from sin and the law, but become servants of God (Rom. 7:6).[43]

Magdalene first asks the three Jews what it is that Christ does. Then she immediately focuses her inquiry on his physical body:

> Est il de fort belle apparence a le veoir?
> ...
> Bien formé?
> Quelle face a il?
> Et quel eage?
> Barbe et cheveux?
> ...
> Et de quel taint?
> La couleur?
> Les yeulx?
> Les mains?
> Les autres choses?
> ...
> Quel robe a il?
> Comment?
> ...
> De quel couleur? (ll. 10465; 10568-71; 10473-77; 10480-81; 10485)

Her entire inquiry revolves around the physical characteristics of Christ, including his dress. In similar fashion, as she prepares to leave and to go hear him preach, Michel draws attention to the physical body of Magdalene and her own desire to give herself to Christ:

> Je veul contempler sa beaulté
> et aller ouyr son sermon
> pour tempter, en l'oyant, si mon
> vouloir a lui s'addonera
> et veoir s'i me regardera
> de quelque regard amÿable. (ll. 10511-16)

Not only does she objectify and traffic Christ by her desiring gaze, she wants to know if her desire will indeed be drawn toward him, and if she can tempt him to gaze upon her, not just to look, but to look at her in a similarly profitable way (*quelque regard amÿable* [l. 10516]). As Eve prays for a sign of friendship (*signe d'amitié* [*G*, ll. 1944]), so Magdalene seeks both to valuate and be valuated by the ransom-redemption token. In both cases, such a sign would be satisfaction of lack, something that each needs: each seeking revalorization by the body of Christ.[44]

Magdalene goes to hear him teach and is moved by his call to repentance. Later, after giving her wealth and person (*M*, "l'eau rose" [between ll. 11962-63], "larmes" [*G*, between ll. 13931-32]) — washing Christ's feet with her tears and drying them with her hair (*A*, between ll. 10124-25) — Magdalene obtains the valorization she seeks, whereupon she meticulously confesses her sins, half of which concern the body and physical senses (*M*, ll. 12070-72).[45] Immediately following this physical act of contrition and confession, Symon expresses his surprise at Jesus's willingness to allow this worldly woman to do what she has done (ll. 11979-87). Jesus reproves him by teaching the parable of the two debtors: a good man who forgives his debtors (ll. 11989-99).[46] He asks Symon which debtor would be more grateful and consequently love the man more. Symon is forced to admit that it is to the one who was most deeply in debt (ll. 12000-12003). This story is used both to illustrate and valuate the exchange that has just taken place. Mary Magdalene's sins are thus equated with financial debt and her actions as repayment (ll. 11989-99).

She traffics her body and subsequently all earthy belongings to Christ in exchange for pardon and permission to serve Him as a full-time disciple ("corps et biens et tout nostre avoir pour vous servir obligeron" [ll. 12056-57]).[47] In the presence of the exchange medium (the body of Christ), Magdalene offers her own body, with her material wealth (having previously equated the two [ll. 8524-25]), in exchange for an already extant benefit of Christ's ransom-redemptive act: the forgiveness of her sins and union with Christ in manumission.[48] The playwright has thus created a complex, multi-level metaphor: as the body of Christ becomes the currency that redeems humankind, so the individual bodies of the redeemed persons — self-appraised in terms of personal wealth — become tokens of barter to pay for service(s) rendered. The protagonists in the homocosmic struggle are given and received as currency within the ransom-redemption narrative.

A final poignant example is that of Judas Iscariot, the traitor/trader, who exchanged the body of Christ for hard currency, necessitating reparations by the exchange of his own body. In lines 19164-67 of Michel's *mystère*, we read Judas's monologue after he has made the decision to exchange the body of Christ for money:

> Pour ce, present, je m'abandonne
> au grand dyable a qui je me donne.
> Qu'i me doint faire telle vente
> que jamais je ne m'en repente!

Judas realizes he is irrevocably relinquishing his own body in return for material gain (ll. 19165-66). By redeeming the body of Christ for valueless hard currency, Judas marks it as the only currency of value within the metaphoric frame of ransom-redemption. Simultaneously, he devalues the hard currency given him by those now in possession of Christ's body. In one last desperate effort to undo his deed and re-valuate himself, he unsuccessfully attempts to return the currency he earned by treason to those who gave it: "Argent, par qui les bons empirent, / quel mal par toy m'est survenu!" (ll. 23425-26).[49] Now the only thing Judas possesses of any worth is his own flesh which, devoid of gifts of grace and lessened in value, must now be given to Satan, thus lending circularity to the metaphor. This use of his body as a token is further underscored as he prepares to commit suicide and, in despair, offers his individual body parts one-by-one:

> vueil que mon corps soit ravy
> en enfer...
> ...
> mes trippes et boyaux
> je donne aux vers et aux crappaux d'enfer
> qui rongent a merveilles,
> je ordonne mes oreilles
> a ouyr tous cris furïeux,
> aussi pareillement mes yeux
> a plourer avec les dampnés,
> j'abandonne mon nés
> a sentir l'ordure punaise
> de l'ort bourbier de la fournaise,
> ma langue et ma bouche
> j'ordonne a despiter toute personne
> et a soupirer a jamais. (ll. 23890-91; 23894-906)

The body has become an objectivized entity that is volitionally parcelled and disbursed for a variety of purposes. Though this is an act of volition for Judas, the dividing up of a debtor's body among her/his creditors was a permissible practice under Roman law:

> The debtor has until thirty days after judgement to pay his debt. If he does not then pay or give security, or sell himself, by entering into the *nexum*, his creditor can seize him, load him with chains and treat him as a slave.... Then, after sixty days more, if he still fails to pay, he is brought into the market place and either put to death or sold as a slave.... [W]here there were several creditors ... the debtor might, at their election, be divided and his body partitioned between them in pieces proportionate to each one's debt.[50]

Judas summarizes and concludes:

> ... et, bref, pour le derrenier mets,
> sans en faire plus d'autre enqueste,
> depuis les piéz jusq'a la teste,
> je me donne ame, corps et biens,

> sans jamais en excepter riens,
> en despit de Dieu qui me fist,
> a tous les dyables. (ll. 23907-13)

Having devalued the body of Christ by trading it for money, and having no other equally valuable currency in reserve, Judas must pay the adamic debt with his own body, which he partitions and offers to his creditor, the Devil. The sacrifice of four of five natural senses (*oreilles, yeux, nés, langue et bouche*) for evil purposes is the antithesis of the sacrifice of self made by Magdalene. She also abandons her body and its senses, including one extra: the sense of touch (*tactz* [l. 12209]). Following her conversion, however, she vows to use her senses for good (ll. 12194-211). Though Judas values his body as one made by God (l. 23912), he makes the absolute antithetical exchange that Mary Magdalene makes with her *corps et biens* (l. 23910):[51] *his* body to the devil / *her* body to Christ. She will experience continuity, he will experience discontinuity; she is valuated, he is devaluated.

This objectivization and sacrifice of body parts in both instances recalls other writings from the Middle Ages, especially those of the mystics. For example, on the corporeal imagery in the mysticism of Marguerite of Oingt, Bynum recounts:

> [She] received a vision in which she flowered like a tree in spring when watered by Christ, and her verdant branches were labeled with the names of the five senses. It is hard to imagine a more graphic illustration of the medieval conviction that those who love Christ should respond to all of his body with all of theirs.[52]

The body given, the body exchanged, the body ransomed, the body paying — all axes on which turns the story of ransom-redemption as it is dramatized in these fifteenth-century *mystères de la Passion*. Though metaphors are numerous in medieval literature, it is particularly the metaphor of bodily exchange and currency that compels the writing and narrative expansion of these *mystères*. As the dramatic and biblical economies became increasingly linked to socioeconomic growth and prosperity, the two synthesized to execute the ransom-redemption exchange called for in the homocosmic pact between the Father-Creator and Satan. This metaphor is present in other dramas and other genres prior to those considered here, but it is the socio-economic preoccupations of the fifteenth-century with both drama and commerce that make the ransom-redemption motif of Christ's passion a more accessible metaphor, one which the reading-viewing audiences of this period could easily grasp and one in which they could participate.

NOTES

[1] Edelgard DuBruck, *La Passion Isabeau. Une Édition du manuscrit Fr. 966 de la Bibliothèque Nationale avec une introduction et des notes*, American University Studies, series II: Romance Languages and Literatures, 141 (New York-Bern-Frankfurt a.M-Paris: Peter Lang, 1990). See also DuBruck, "The Narrative *Passion of Our Lord Jesus Christ* Written in 1398 for Isabeau de Baviäre, Queen of France: An Important Link in the Development of French Religious Drama," *Michigan Academician* 18 (1986), 95-107.

[2] Jonathan Beck, "Ideological Drama in 15th-Century France," *Fifteenth-Century Studies* 1 (1978), 1.

[3] See Max Black, *Models and Metaphors: Studies in Language and Philosophy* (Ithaca and London: Cornell University Press, 1962), 27-28; and Colin Murray Turbayne, *The Myth of Metaphor* (Columbia, SC: University of South Carolina Press, 1971), 11-27. I have deliberately chosen the term ransom-redemption instead of sacrifice-redemption, as it more accurately reflects the perspective on redemption taken by the playwrights under consideration. See also Jeffrey Burton Russell, *Satan: The Early Christian Tradition* (Ithaca and London: Cornell University Press, 1981), 83-84; Russell, *Lucifer: The Devil in the Middle Ages* (Ithaca and London: Cornell University Press, 1984); and Herman Ridderbos, *Paul: An Outline of His Theology*, trans. John Richard De Witt (Grand Rapids: William B. Eerdmans Publishing Company, 1975), 193-97.

[4] Maurice Accarie, *Le théâtre sacré de la fin du moyen âge. Étude sur le sens moral de la Passion de Jean Michel*, Publications Romanes et Françaises, 150 (Geneva: Droz, 1979), 432.

[5] Cf. Is. 43:3; Hos. 13:14; Matt. 20:28; Mark 10:45; 1 Tim. 2:6.

[6] Arnoul Greban, *Le mystère de la Passion*, ed. Gaston Raynaud and Gaston Paris (Paris: F. Vieweg, 1878; repr., Geneva: Slatkine Reprints, 1970), hereafter cited as *G* in endnotes and parenthetical references. Concerning the dating of this and other theatrical works, see Graham A. Runnalls, "The Linguistic Dating of Middle French Texts with Special Reference to the Theater," *Modern Language Review* 71 (1976), 757-65; and DuBruck, *La Passion Isabeau*, 14.

[7] Jean Michel, *Le mystère de la Passion (Angers 1486)*, ed. Omer Jodogne (Gembloux: J. Duculot, 1959), hereafter cited as *M* in endnotes and parenthetical references. Other *mystères* refered to in this essay include Eustache Mercade, *Le mystère de la Passion. Texte du MS 697 de la bibliothèque d'Arras*, ed. Jules-Marie Richard (Arras: Imprimerie de la Société du Pas-de-Calais, 1891; repr., Geneva: Slatkine Reprints, 1976), hereafter cited as *A* in endnotes and parenthetical references; *The Passion de Semur*, ed. Peter Durbin and Lynette R. Muir, Leeds Medieval Studies, 3 (Leeds: Centre for Medieval Studies, 1981), hereafter cited as *S* in endnotes and parenthetical references; and *Le mystère de la Passion de Troyes*, ed.

Jean-Claude Bibolet (Geneva: Droz, 1987), hereafter cited as *T* in endnotes and parenthetical references.

[8] See R[ichard] A[llen] Shoaf, *Dante, Chaucer, and the Currency of the Word: Money, Images, and Reference in Late Medieval Poetry* (Norman, OK: Pilgrim Books, Inc., 1983), 36-38.

[9] Marc Shell, *Money, Language, and Thought: Literary and Philosophical Economies from the Medieval to the Modern Era* (Berkeley: University of California Press, 1982), 103: "The role of caution money in guaranteeing exchange does not differ in kind from that of a ring broken into two parts for the purpose of later identification of the buyer by the seller and vice versa." See also Shell, *The Economy of Literature* (Baltimore and London: The Johns Hopkins University Press, 1978). Eve Sedgwick has identified a similar exchange metaphor in English literature as a homosocial paradigm in which two males exchange female bodies in defence of their honor, thus establishing a triangle of commerce. Marking the body with commercial referents in the *mystères* enables it to assume a similar role as medium of exchange between God and the Devil, in a homocosmic exchange. See Sedgwick, *Between Men: English Literature and Male Homosocial Desire* (New York: Columbia University Press, 1985). See also Margaret Brose, "Petrarch's Beloved Body: 'Italia mia'" in *Feminist Approaches to the Body in Medieval Literature*, ed. Linda Lomperis and Sarah Stanbury (Philadelphia: University of Pennsylvania Press, 1993), 1-20; and E. Jane Burns, *Bodytalk: When Women Speak in Old French Literature* (Philadelphia: University of Pennsylvania Press, 1993).

[10] See Orlando Patterson, *Freedom in the Making of Western Culture*, vol. 1 of *Freedom* (New York: Basic Books, 1991), especially "Part Five: The Medieval Reconstruction of Freedom," 347-401.

[11] Cf. Rom. 3:23; Gal. 3:22; 1 Cor. 14:45-50.

[12] Paul Ricoeur, *The Symbolism of Evil,* trans. Emerson Buchanan (New York: Harper & Row, 1967), 238.

[13] Patterson, *Freedom*, 334.

[14] Caroline Walker Bynum, *Fragmentation and Redemption: Essays on Gender and the Human Body in Medieval Religion* (New York: Zone Books, 1992), 91. See also Bynum, *Jesus as Mother: Studies in the Spirituality of the High Middle Ages* (Berkeley and Los Angeles: University of California Press, 1982).

[15] Russell, *Satan*, 83. Cf. Russell's contrast of the sacrifice-redemption and ransom-redemption theories of salvation (192).

[16] Shell, *Money, Language, and Thought*, 66. "As a man's coporeal freedom could be lost for (lack of) money, so too, as a matter of legal course, could it be lost in slavery. Under Jewish law there is no absolute slavery for the same reason that there is not monetary compensation possible for murder" (66).

[17] Russell, *Satan*, 191. Cf. Shell, *The Economy of Literature*, where Shell claims that, in this economy, Satan is collecting interest (i.e., the descendants of Eve and Adam) on the principle (i.e., Eve and Adam) [94].

[18] Ridderbos, *Paul*, 193. Russell writes of Augustine's theology of salvation, noting the contractual element in ransom-redemption. See *Satan*, 215. Cf. *S*, l. 4340: "De la loy de pechier fut la chartre cassee."

[19] Russell, *Satan*, 194.

[20] Elie Königson, *La représentation d'un mystère de la Passion à Valenciennes en 1547* (Paris: Centre National de la Recherche Scientifique, 1969), 15.

[21] Alan Knight, "Drama and Society in Late Medieval Flanders and Picardy," *The Chaucer Review* 14 (1980), 379. According to Knight, the financial registers of the dramatic troupes are important sources of information on this activity (380). See also DuBruck, "Changes of Taste and Audience Expectation in Fifteenth-Century Religious Drama," *Fifteenth-Century Studies* 6 (1983), 59-91; and Jan Huizinga, *The Waning of the Middle Ages* (New York: Doubleday, 1954), 223.

[22] Shell, *Money, Language, and Thought*, 3-4. Also of interest in this regard is Kurt Heinzelman, *The Economies of the Imagination* (Amherst: The University of Massachusetts Press, 1980).

[23] Elie Königson, *L'espace théâtral médiéval* (Paris: Centre National de la Recherche Scientifique, 1975), 59.

[24] Henri Rey-Flaud, *Pour une dramaturgie du moyen âge* (Paris: PUF, 1980), 176: "Le théâtre du Moyen Age représente donc, bien refermée sur elle-même, la société installée définitivement dans sa hiérarchie, dans son ordre scrupuleusement observé. Ce théâtre est celui d'une société tout entière qui ensemble invente les mythes qui la fondent." See Jean-Charles Payen, "Théâtre médiéval et culture urbaine" in *Revue d'histoire du théâtre* 35 (1983), 233-50.

[25] Shoaf, *Dante, Chaucer, and the Currency of the Word*, 34.

[26] Ibid., 33. Shoaf also cites Aristotle's *Ethics* (E1133a-b), "[I]t is up to us to change a given coin or make it useless" (33).

[27] They traffic in bodies, like that purported by Gayle Rubin. She sees "the exchange of women as a fundamental principle of kinship, the subordination of women can be seen as a product of the relationships by which sex and gender are organized and produced," in "The Traffic in Women: Notes on the 'Political Economy' of Sex," in *Toward an Anthropology of Women*, ed. Rayna R. Reiter (New York and London: Monthly Review Press, 1975), 177. See Claude-Lévy Strauss, *The Elementary Structures of Kinship* (Boston: Beacon Press, 1969). Likewise, God and Satan, vying for possession of humankind, must ultimately do so via the increasingly feminized body of Christ. See Caroline Walker Bynum, "'... And Woman His Humanity': Female Imagery in the Religious Writing of the Later Middle Ages," in *Gender and Religion: On Complexity of Symbols*, ed. Caroline Walker Bynum, Steven Harrell, and Paula Richman (Boston: Beacon Press, 1986); "The Body of

Christ in the Later Middle Ages: A Reply to Leo Steinberg," *Renaissance Quarterly* 39 (1986), 399-439; *Fragmentation and Redemption*, n. 12, above; and *Jesus as Mother*, n. 14, above.

[28] The ransom-redemption motif is less evident in *A* (c.1440), though more evident in *S* (c.1430). It is quite discernible in *T* (c.1490), which is seen by some as a close reworking of Greban's drama, or of the *Mistere du Viel Testament* (1458). See Bibelot, *La Passion de Troyes*, xi-xii.

[29] See Herbert Blau, *The Audience* (Baltimore and London: The Johns Hopkins University Press, 1990), especially "Chapter 4: Repression, Pain and the Participation Mystique," 144-209.

[30] The staging plays an important role in this theatrical economy. See Eli Rozik, "Stage Metaphor," *Theatre Research International* 14 (1989), 50-70. See also Neville Denny, "The Staging of Medieval Drama," in *The Drama of Medieval Europe*, Leeds Medieval Studies, 1 (Leeds: University Printing Service, 1975), 67-80; Elie Königson, *Dramaturgie et société*, 2 vols. (Paris: Centre National de la Recherche Scientifique, 1968); *L'espace théâtral médiéval*, n. 23, above; Peter Meredith and John E. Tailby, *The Staging of Religious Drama in Europe in the Later Middle Ages: Texts and Documents in English Translation* (Kalamazoo: Medieval Institute Publications, 1982); Alois M. Nagler, *The Medieval Religious Stage: Shapes and Phantoms*, trans. George C. Schoolfield (New Haven: Yale University Press, 1976); Henry Rey-Flaud, *Le cercle magique: Essai sur le théâtre en rond à la fin du Moyen Age* (Paris: Gallimard, 1973) and *Pour une dramaturgie du moyen âge*, n. 24, above; Donald C. Stuart, *Stage Decoration in France in the Middle Ages* (New York: Columbia University Press, 1910); "The Stage Setting of Hell and the Iconography of the Middle Ages," *Romanic Review* 4 (1913), 330-42; John L. Styan, *Drama, Stage and Audience* (Cambridge: The University Press, 1975); Alain Surdel, "Les représentations de la mort dans le théâtre religieux du XVe siècle et des débuts du XVIe siècle," in *La mort en toutes lettres*, ed. Gilles Ernst (Nancy: PUN, 1983), 11-23; Alessandro Vitale-Brovarone, *Il quaderno di segreti d'un regista provenzale del Medioevo: Note per la messa in scena d'una Passione* (Alessandria: Edizioni Dell'Orso, 1984).

[31] Cf. *M*, ll. 490-91; *G*, l. 1726.

[32] Cf. *S*, ll. 119-20; 122-25: "Et trestous les siens adherens; / De gloire ont perdu tout les biens, / Et quant le doux Dieu de nature / Vit ses angelz ainsin verser, / Son plessir fut mectre sa cure / Humainne nature former."

[33] Russell, *Satan*, 128-29. This is illustrative of the theory of "evil as nonbeing." The early Christian apologist Origen, according to Russell, blamed the fall of Satan on himself: "The Devil had sung among the cherubim, but he chose to debase himself, thus subtracting almost all being and goodness from himself and becoming almost pure nonbeing" (129). See also Russell, *Lucifer: The Devil in the Middle Ages*. There he writes concerning Damascene's view of evil, which was rooted in patristic theology, "Either it [evil] is a part of God's creation and springs from God, or else it is a privation of God, essentially nonbeing.... Evil is nothing else than a lack of the good" (38).

[34] Cf. *G*, in the prologue to the 3rd *journée*: "pour mondifier nostre ordure, / il treuve que ce qu'il endure / n'est riens en regard de la somme / que Jhesus voust porter pour l'homme" (ll. 19985-88); cf. *G*, in the prologue to the 2nd *journée*, l. 10035.

[35] Cf. *T*, *tome* III, p. 755, ll. 14-15.

[36] Cf. ibid., ll. 176-77.

[37] Cf. *G*, ll. 1464-65; 1512-13; 820-23.

[38] Burns, *Bodytalk*, 98.

[39] Her spiritual poverty stands in contrast to her wealth and worldliness (*mondanité*). Cf. DuBruck, "Changes of Taste and Audience Expectation in Fifteenth-Century Religious Drama," 63-64: "She is a Renaissance lady, living in a château called Magdalon. In speaking to her demoiselles she states that she wishes to enjoy all pleasures of the senses, and finally she openly yearns to commit the seven deadly sins.... She enjoys seducing men, and checks her make-up carefully before she meets them...." See also Accarie, *Le théâtre sacré de la fin du moyen âge,* and the attention he gives to Michel's character development of Magdalene, especially Chapter 2, "La Spiritualité de Jean Michel," 363-427.

[40] See Burns, *Bodytalk*, 109-13.

[41] Ibid., 111.

[42] Patterson, *Freedom*, 340-41.

[43] See Ridderbos, *Paul*, 258-60.

[44] Cf. *A*, ll. 10144-46.

[45] The sins she confesses are *orgueil*, *ire*, *paresse*, *envye*, *luxure*, *gloutonnie*, *avarice*, the same sins she boasts of earlier (*M*, ll. 8590-98). Then she confesses the *cinq sens de Nature*: *de l'oye*, *des yeux*, *du neez*, *du goust*, *du tact*. The resemblance of Magdalene's prayer to the prayer of confession found in manuscript 42 of the Bibliothèque Ventimiliana de Catane is striking. See Edith Brayer, "Un manuel de confession en ancien français conservé dans un manuscrit de Catane (Bibl. Ventimiliana, 42)," in *Mélanges d'Archéologie et d'Histoire* 49 (1947), 155-98. She gives the 14th century as a likely date of origin for the manuscript. The *traité de confession* (fol. 27-39) is reproduced in full on pages 173-93 of Brayer's article. For other occurences of these types of prayer-confessions, see Accarie, 375-76.

[46] Cf. *S*, l. 4942.

[47] Cf. *G*, ll. 14025-26.

[48] This pledge of service is expanded in some accounts to include an invitation for Christ to visit in her home, which is described as large and her financial status as

wealthy; thus, she continues to valuate herself in terms of monetary worth. Cf. *G*, ll. 14029-32; *T*, ll. 1478-87.

[49] Cf. *M*, ll. 23417-48; 23449-92; *A*, 13023-32; 13061-62; *S*, 6593-620; 6623-24.

[50] *Leges XII tabularum*, tab. 3.5, in Carl Georg Bruns, *Fontes iuris Romani antiqui* (Leipzig, 1894), 21; quoted in Shell, *Money*, 67.

[51] Cf. *M*, ll. 12056-57

[52] This reference to Marguerite of Oingt is from *Les Oeuvres de Marguerite d'Oingt*, ed. and trans. Antonin Duraffour, Pierre Gardette and P. Durdilly, Publications de l'Institut de Linguistique Romane de Lyon, 21 (Paris: Belles Lettres, 1965), 147, 130; quoted in Bynum, *Fragmentation and Redemption*, 91.

Calvin College

Reviews

D. Eleanor and Terence Scully, *Early French Cookery: Sources, History, Original Recipes and Modern Adaptations.* Ann Arbor: University of Michigan Press, 1995. 377 pp.

For those who might think that French culinary arts began with Escoffier and culminated in Julia Child, the Scullys' book *Early French Cookery* provides a salutary corrective. Their modernized versions of late medieval French recipes range from bourgeois cuisine to suppers for a king. The *croûte* of historical context in which they envelop their work adds savor, enhanced by their charming and whimsical illustrations.

The authors draw their provisions from three principal larders: the *Ménagier* of Paris, a late 14th century bourgeois; Guillaume de Tirel, whose *nom de cuisine* was Taillevent, master chef to Charles V; and Master Chiquart, chef to Amadeus VIII of Savoy. These men labored under anxieties as heavy as those of today's chefs who fear to lose a Michelin star. They had to meld their sense of taste with the humoral theories of Galenic medicine. Food should be moist and warm, but not *too* moist or warm, lest the diner leave the table choleric, melancholic, phlegmatic or overly sanguine. And woe to the chef whose clients contracted what we know as ergotism and salmonella! To these stresses was added oversight of the horde of minions whose labors were necessary to produce even a modest *souper*. Equally worrisome was procuring the provisions to prepare the day's repasts. The Scullys' recreation of a day in Chiquart's life is perhaps too sanguine about his maintaining his *sang-froid* in the face of such tensions (surely there were irascible chefs even then!).

Turning to the recipes themselves, one is surprised to discover both the variety and quantity of spices used in all but the simplest concoctions (the authors suggest that poor storage or long periods for shipment from the East attenuated the spices' flavor). Many foodstuffs were chopped or ground to pastes or powders to accommodate a Galenically salubrious blending of condiment and meats or vegetables. The unexpectedly frequent use of sugar (at least for the upper classes) in everything from stews to desserts doubtless added calories to the normal worries of late medieval life. The authors argue that the paucity of recipes for vegetables was due to the relative simplicity of their preparation rather than infrequency of consumption. That a range of greens was appreciated is suggested by a 13th century poet, who advocated modest consumption of meats, supplemented by "things that are laxative and appetitive such as parsley, cress, and wild celery" (p. 259). As today, meats and poultry, boiled, fried and roasted, were a meal's *pièce de résistance*. *Entremets*, dishes served between heavier courses to cleanse the palate and delight the eye, were featured in both bourgeois and noble cuisine. Often elaborate confections molded of meat paté or pastry, they doubtless served as conversation pieces as well as somewhat caloric sorbets.

Although today's gastronomes will salivate at these recipes, health professionals may cringe. The prodigal use of lard to moisten Galenically "dry" foods and enhance their flavors is understandable, given ignorance of cholesterol, but one wonders how late-medieval warriors managed to pump enough blood to their arteries to raise their sword-arms. Also fish, often caught far from the kitchen in which it was prepared, must have smelled as medieval monks said their guests did after three days.

To those for whom time spent in the kitchen is creative and satisfying, the Scullys' work is a delight. They offer menu suggestions, tips on table manners *d'antin*, and, if you are bold and have good friends to assist, directions for hosting a medieval banquet for fifty. *Bonne chance et bon appetit*! And do not, as a contemporary etiquette guide for ladies admonishes, reach in front of your neighbor to help yourself!

Edmund H. Dickerman

Julia Boffey and Pamela King, ed., *London and Europe in the Later Middle Ages* (Westfield Publications in Medieval Studies, vol. 9). London: University of London, 1995. Pp. xi, 258.

This fine collection of essays is the product of a 1992-93 seminar at the University of London. All eight essays are of uniformly high quality, although not of equal importance.

Anne Sutton's essay focuses on the Tumbling Bear Tavern in Cheapside, a "regular haunt of the local mercers" between 1275 and 1325 (pe 93). It was also the scene of a yearly competition held by the London Puy, an early literary society of sorts. Each year the winner of the Puy's competition was crowned Prince of the Puy during a lavish feast and allowed to compose a new *chant royal*. Unfortunately, Sutton tells us almost nothing about the Puy and why it had disappeared by the 1330s. Rather, she makes heavy use of deeds to analyze the two-block area around the tavern and the people who owned property there, a topic of scant interest and importance.

Of greater significance is the essay by Paul Brand, who contends that until 1300 there were marked similarities between the English common law and the romano-canonical legal tradition that prevailed on the continent. He notes that the authors of England's earliest legal treatises were trained in the continental tradition, that many of the judges and barristers of the royal courts were proficient in European methods, and that until about 1290 English lawyers were generally willing to accommodate the common law to European principles and procedures. But by 1300, according to Brand, "one senses that England and the English courts and English lawyers were bringing down the shutters: trying to pretend that Europe was not there or did not need to be accommodated" (p. 83).

Equally interesting points abound in Rosamund Allen's excellent study of John Gower, who lived in the London suburb of Southwark from the mid-1370s until his death in 1408. By giving considerable information about Southwark before analyzing Gower's main literary works, Allen is able to place those works squarely within their social context.

John Scattergood discusses William Fitz-Stephen's famous *Description of London* (ca. 1173) and shows its intellectual debt to earlier accounts of such cities as Rome, Naples, Milan, Verona, Bordeaux, and Toulouse; while James Simpson analyzes the earlier works that influenced Thomas Hoccleve's *Regement of Princes* (ca. 1411). In her fine piece, Carol Neale makes many interesting observations about the famous poem *The Libelle of Englyshe Polycye*. A desperate response to the French siege of Calais in 1436, the *Libelle* expressed the fears of the London merchant community that their trade with the continent was about to be disrupted, if not cut off. Although Meale makes no attempt to discover who wrote the *Libelle*, she does consider who might have commissioned it in the first place. At the end of her thoughtful discussion of that problem, Meale concludes that "the *Libelle* is a work which substantiates the claim of the merchant class to have had a distinctive literary culture of its own" (p. 225), a controversial point that many scholars dispute, however.

In his offering, A. S. G. Edwards considers the European practices that influenced the output of England's first printers during the years 1476-1525. Among the technical matters he discusses are the use and decoration of title pages, the gradual incorporation of woodcuts and other forms of illustration, the various bindings and print fonts employed, and the different ways European practices became known and understood in England.

In the most far-ranging essay in the book, Vanessa Harding gives a comparative account of the surviving archival sources for London and Paris. She traces the fate of the most important documentary collections in the two cities and notes how Parisian sources were absorbed into the national archives to a far greater degree than their London counterparts. Although she praises the French government for installing the Archives Nationales "in a superb building on a central site, fitted with the latest technology," she still feels that "the London archives have greater potential, in terms of the wealth and accessibility of sources, and I certainly prefer the less-formal and user-friendly atmosphere of [the] many London record offices" (p. 54).

A book containing such a variety of capable and useful essays truly belongs on the shelves of serious scholars and research libraries.

Michael V. C. Alexander
Virginia Polytechnic Institute

Winfried Dotzauer, ed., *Quellenkunde zur deutschen Geschichte im Spätmittelalter (1350-1500.* Darmstadt: Wissenschaftliche Buchgesellschaft, 1996. Pp. xiv, 589.

Peter Moraw prägte das Wort von der "gestalteten Verdichtung" des spätmittelalterlichen deutschen Reiches (1985), womit er den Nagel auf den Kopf getroffen hatte. Die Welt des 14. und 15. Jahrhunderts erlebte in der Tat eine erstaunliche Ausweitung und Intensivierung auf jedem Gebiet menschlicher Aktivitäten. Die Forschung der letzen hundert Jahre hat sich intensiv darum bemüht, den daraus resultierten Schatz an Dokumenten editorisch zu erfassen, doch sieht sich inzwischen der Historiker eine solchen Menge an Quellen ausgesetzt, daß es schwerfallen kann, sich überhaupt noch zu orientieren. Die von Winfried Dotzauer erstellte Quellenkunde will Licht in das für viele als Dickicht wirkende Feld der Urkunden bringen, indem sie sich hauptsächlich als Bibliographie der vorhandenen Urkunden und anderer Quellen versteht, in der zugleich die wichtigsten Publikationen knapp kommentiert und erörtert werden.

Allein schon ein flüchtiger Überlick läßt deutlich werden, wie weit sich die heutige Geschichtsforschung von der älteren Schule entfernt hat, denn auch wenn immer noch Herrschergestalten, das deutsche Reich als ganzes, die katholische Kirche mit dem Papsttum, das Gerichtswesen und die Städte eine große Rolle spielen, anerkennt die heutige Forschung doch viel mehr als früher die Bedeutung des sozialen, geistesgeschichtlichen und literarhistorischen Bereichs. Dotzauer hat, um dem Rechnung zu tragen, die folgenden Großkapitel zusammengestellt: I. Bibliographien und Quellenkunden, II. große Quellensammlungen zur deutschen Geschichte, III. Akten und Urkunden, IV. die Kirche, V. Wissenschaften, VI. Urkunden-und Regestensammlungen, VII. erzählende Quellen, VIII. sozialgeschichtliche Quellen besonders bezogen auf die Sachkultur, und schließlich IX. Handel, Wirtschaft, Gewerbe, Verkehr, Technik und Militärwesen.

Was darunter im einzelnen gefaßt ist, kann nicht komplett wiedergegeben werden, daher genüge es, dies exemplarisch an einigen Kapiteln vorzuführen. Die großen Quellensammlungen umschließen die deutschen Reichstagsakten, die Chroniken der Städte, die Geschichtsschreiber der deutschen Vorzeit und Germania Sacra. In bezug auf die Städte (III, C) führt Dotzauer die einschlägigen Quellen zur Rechtsgeschichte, zum Gerichtswesen, zu Ratsurteilen und Ratspolitik, zur Feme, zu städtischen

Rechnungen und Kaufhäusern, zur städtischen Polizeiordnung und zum Kriegswegen, zu Städtebünden und zur Hanse an. Wohlverstanden, es handelt sich hier um eine Bibliographie, obwohl einzelne Abschnitte eine genauere Kommentierung erhalten, die sich dann aber wieder nur auf die in den zitierten Publikationen enthaltenen Aussagen und Materialien beziehen. Der Benutzer soll hiermit einen direkten Zugang zu den Primärquellen gewinnen, was in globaler Hinsicht tatsächlich bewundernswert gewährleistet ist. Dotzauer bietet gelegentlich dazu noch die wichtigste Sekundärliteratur, doch kann man sich dabei nur teilweise auf seine Angaben verlassen. Der Abschnitt zur Frau im Spätmittelalter ist erstaunlich dürftig, und so auch das Verzeichnis weiterführender Studien. Zwar finden sich in den folgenden Abschnitten einige der wichtigsten Quellensammlungen zur Hexenverfolgung, doch erschöpft sich diese Liste mit den Arbeiten von J. Hansen (1901-1977), der Edition des *Malleus Maleficarum* (ed. 1991) und der Anthologie von W. Behringer (1988). Immerhin hat Dotzauer sogar diese Aspekte berücksichtigt, wozu dann auch die Bereiche 'Minoritäten' (Juden), 'Reisen, Wallfahrten, Pilgerfahrten' und 'Universitätsmatrikel' kommen.

Gelegentlich ist Dotzauer nicht aufgefallen, daß einerseits manche der von ihm zitierten Titel mittlerweile in neuen Editionen vorliegen, so etwa Stephan Baumgartners *Reise zum Heiligen Grab 1498*, hg. von Th. Kraus, 1986, hier nur zitiert nach der Ausgabe von 1901 in *Zeitschrift deutscher Palästina-Verein*, andererseits bedeutsame Briefsammlungen noch zu berücksichtigen gewesen wären, so die Briefe der Nachkommen des Südtiroler Dichters Oswwald von Wolkenstein, Maria von Wolkenstein (H. Hallauer, 'Nikolaus von Kues,' *Mitteilungen und Forschungsbeiträge*, 1967) und Veit von Wolkenstein (*Deutsche Reichstagsakten*, Mittlere Reihe). Die Werke der deutschen Mystiker liegen inzwischen z.T. in historisch-kritischen Ausgaben vor, so Mechthilds von Magdeburg *Licht der fliessenden Gottheit*, hg. von H. Neumann (1990). Solche Lücken stellen aber nur geringfügige Kritikpunkte dar, die die wirklichen Leistungen dieser Bibliographie keineswegs schmälern sollen. In der Geschichtswissenschaft gibt es einfach nicht so gute bibliographische Hilfsmittel wie in der Germanistik, Anglistik oder Romanistik, so daß dieses Nachschlagewerk zunächst einmal schon als unabdingbare Grundlage für das Studium des Spätmittelalters dienen wird. Bemerkenswert wäre zudem, daß nicht nur schlicht der traditionelle Historiker angesprochen wird, sondern praktisch jeder Kulturhistoriker, der sich mit dieser Epoche beschäftigt, so wenn man die Kapitel zu den Naturwissenschaften berücksichtigt, in dem eignige der wichtigsten Quellen zur Mathematik, Medizin und Alchemie zu finden sind. Am ausführlichsten behandelt natürlich Dotzauer die verschiedensten Regesten- und Ukrundensammlungen, die am Ende durch ein Register gut erschließbar sind. Die Historiker verschiedenster Provenienzen werden sicherlich dankbar diesen neuen Band registrieren, der seiner selbstgestellten Aufgabe weitgehend gerecht wird, den Quellenschatz des deutschen Spätmittelalters in einem Band zu präsentieren, selbst wenn der Spezialist gelegentlich kleiner Lücken festellen mag. Daß u.a. der Deutsche Orden, Burgund, Österreich, die Eidgenossenschaft und Böhmen nicht berücksichtigt wurden, liegt schlicht daran, daß dem Verfasser vom Verlag Grenzen auferlegt wurden und er viele Kapitel aus seinem Typoskript schneiden mußte — leider, wie man resigniert feststellt. Das vorliegende Ergebnis ist aber insgesamt doch sehr zufriedenstellend und wird in vielen Bibliotheken ein sehr gefragtes Nachschlagewerk darstellen.

Albrecht Classen
University of Arizona

Holger Eckhardt, *Totentanz im Narrencschiff. Die Rezeption ikonographischer Muster als Schlüssel zu Sebastian Brants Hauptwerk.* Frankfurt am Main: Peter Lang, 1995. Pp. 508.

In his thorough treatment of a "Dance of Death" in the *Ship of Fools*, Eckhardt is very aware of the controversial nature of his hypothesis: the existence of such a dance is not recognizable at first (or even second) sight, and the structure of the *Ship* is, and remains, an enigma. It is obvious that the theme of death pervades Brant's work in text and illustrations, and that death, folly, and a ship are the three "aussagekräftigsten" (most evidential) motifs of Brant's time (p.17).

When Eckhardt tries to examine the structure of the *Ship*, he asks the following questions: 1) Is there a caesura, and if so, where? 2) Is the ship a metaphoric frame? 3) Does the work show unity? 4) What is the relationship of motto, woodcut, and text in each chapter? 5) What was Albrecht Dürer's role for the structure? But Eckhardt immediately feels that these questions may remain without answers. Brant's indebtedness to the satires of Horace, Persius, Juvenal, and Lucilius is obvious, but the *Ship* shows and satisfies the mentality of the German humanist's time (p.41). Its popularity, in spite of didacticism and a seeming lack of structure, is surely based on this mentality.

The "Dances of Death" which Brant knew personally were those of Groß- and Klein-Basel (which among their scenes showed a fool as dancing partner, once a courtly figure in the older *Vado Mori* elegies of the thirteenth century), as well as a painting in Straßburg cathedral (c. 1480). The latter inspired Brant's Latin-German poem, "De periculoso scacorum ludo" (1480). The painting showed Death playing chess with secular and ecclesiastical dignitaries surrounding the players. Eckhardt advises the reader that the scene is static and does not show a dance (p. 55). A clear relationship of the fool and death is proved to exist in a *narren schyp*

(Lübeck: Mohnkopf, 1497) which uses for its chapter eighty-five the same scene as in the Lübeck *des dodes dantz* of 1489.

Eckhardt now devotes a special chapter to proving the relationship between the Basel *Dances* and the *Ship*. In the first place, Brant's intention seems the same as that of the Dance artist who probably copied his figures from a one-leaf illustration presumed to be well-known during the infancy of printing. This was to remind the onlookers of death and to bring about a reform in manners. Yet Brant remains fairly conservative with regard to church and empire. Second, a comparison of the figures in the *Dances* with those in the *Ship* shows great discrepancies, both in sequence and, third, in social hierarchy. Fourth, Brant avoids the dialogues of the Dance texts, but, fifth, there is no doubt that the artist of woodcut eighty-five was influenced by one scene of the Basel *Dances*, Death dancing with the Fool.

Eckhardt then considers the *Ship* passages which are thematically related to the three terms, death, hell, and dance (including the woodcuts). He finds that the semiotic fields of death and hell are usually combined, attesting to the late-medieval preoccupation with death and punishment for sins. Generally, the theme of death prevails in forty-six chapters, whereas the "Dance of Death" is noticeable in only six, namely 13, 56, 61, 72, 85 and 110b, which Eckhardt analyzes separately.

The second part of this monograph examines Dürer, who seems to be the artist of the majority of woodcuts. The knowledge and use of death iconography in his own work cannot be denied, as, for example, in the image and poetry of *Der Tod und der Landsknecht* (1510). He was familiar with Dances of Death, and his poetry (little known) treats the same spiritual themes as the *Ship*. It can be assumed, at the very least, that the *Ship* influenced Dürer. In his *Befestigungslehre* (1527), for example, he seems to cite Brant's passages from chapter eighty-five on costly tombs. His woodcut for that chapter resembles other death illustrations signed by Dürer, showing an upright corpse in partial putrefaction and with dark, ominous clouds, as pictured in *Ritter, Tod, und Teufel* (1513), and in his *Apocalypse* (1522).

The third part of Eckhardt's book treats the structural concept of the *Ship*. Influenced as it is by diverse factors, the work may show the traces of a possible conflict between Brant and the artist(s), since in a few cases the illustrations do not relate to the texts of the chapters. On the other hand, Eckhardt explains, the author perhaps was not disciplined enough to resist the serial character of his work. He was experimenting, and therefore, he never followed the Dance of Death motif rigorously. Here is one of the many passages where Eckhardt truthfully alludes to the shortcomings of his book's title. If he had written on *The Theme of Death in the Ship of Fools*, he would have been much better off.

In part four he investigates how six other authors of Brant's time handled the theme of death: Johannes von Tepl, Heinrich Wittenweiler,

Thomas Murner, Herman Bote (*Eulenspiegel*), Erasmus (*Laus stultitiae*), and Geiler von Kayserberg. The structural methods do cast some light on those of Brant, but we cannot agree with Eckhardt's final statement that "wahrscheinlich sind mit Dürer und Brant erstmals die Autoren eines echten spätmittelalterlichen Totentanzes festzumachen" (p. 424). There is no doubt that the value of Eckhardt's book is in the detail, especially in the notes. Unfortunately, however, an index is missing. There is a good bibliography (32 pages), and eighty-two very useful illustrations.

Edelgard E. DuBruck
Marygrove College

Ian Friel, *The Good Ship: Ships, Shipbuilding and Technology in England, 1200-1520*. Baltimore: The Johns Hopkins University Press, 1995. Pp. 208.

This is an attractive introduction to an important and intrinsically interesting aspect of late medieval history that is designed to appeal to any reader who enjoys (or will tolerate) learning some technical details. It is richly illustrated, with reproductions of medieval art works on nearly every page depicting ships of various sizes and shapes, as well as photographs of archeological finds and modern schematic line drawings. Unlike the building of castles, shipbuilding was neither a highly centralized nor a particularly generously financed industry in medieval England: nor was it intensively documented with surviving records. For these reasons, it has made sense to the author, a maritime historian of many years' standing, to treat the period as a single historical unit, with evidence from the thirteenth-century being cited side by side with that from the fifteenth and sixteenth.

Gradually, of course, as time went on, the technology of shipbuilding changed, growing more ingenious and complex; but not everywhere at the same rate and nowhere very radically in the course of just a few decades. Standing back and looking at the large picture, one can see a transition from the clinker-built, single-masted, square-rigged, curved-stemmed ships of the Viking type to the vastly larger skeleton-built two-, three-, and four-masters, with superstructures ("castles") at both ends, stern rudders, and more elaborate and efficient arrangements of sails. In this latter category the extreme example was Henry V's prodigious "great ship" *Grace Dieu* (1418), rated at 1400 tons of load capacity. Most of the large vessels constructed in the fifteenth-century heyday of shipbuilding were of 200-300 tons. After that they were on the average very much smaller again. One gathers, in other words, that shipbuilding in England was, on the whole, eclectic, local, conservative, and in some senses *ad hoc*, with old styles and new, large ships and small managing to co-exist in shipyards for several centuries. While the old Viking ships could sail to Greenland and America they were neither large nor seaworthy enough to resupply growing colonies or to conduct merchant trade with sufficiently high odds of success, and in the course of time new technologies and ambitions inevitably passed them by.

Clinker-built ships had hulls that were made of overlapping boards fastened by closely set iron clinker nails, driven in from the outside and bent over on the inside. The sides of the ship were its main load-bearing component, with an inner framework added after the hull was built. Until well into the fifteenth century this was the way all hulls were constructed in northern Europe. In the Mediterranean, on the other hand, ships were built with a skeleton framework serving as the load-bearing element. Boards butting on each other were then attached to the framework, producing a smooth hull. In addition to their smooth hulls, fifteenth-century Mediterranean merchant ships also tended to have elements of lateen rigging rather than the universal square rigging of the north, and tended to be larger than northern vessels. The advance of shipbuilding technology in England resulted in large measure from very gradually adapting new forms of Mediterranean rigging, including new forms of sail management with pulleys.

This book is an authoritative and well written guide to every aspect of these details of medieval ships and shipbuilding, not the least of which is the rich linguistic tangle of terminology for ship types and their parts. It has been divided into chapters that tend to look at a more or less common body of material from a number of different perspectives. Chapters are devoted to the forms of historical evidence, to shipbuilding and shipyards, hulls and castles, sails and oars, equipment on board, trading vessels, war ships, and innovations in rig and construction at the end of the period. Helpful tables of numbers, dates, sizes, and equipment offer control over some of the details, as does a helpful glossary of some of the standard terms and an excellent index. The modern literature is represented in a bibliography of close to two hundred items. Ian Friel tells us that in earlier English usage "the good ship" was a phrase that could be used of any ship, usually, however, in approbation of some virtue or another. After spending some time with this admirable introduction to late medieval English ships, their builders and their owners, most readers will have been brought close enough to the subject to think of them all as "good ships."

Robert Kellogg
University of Virginia

Ralph Hanna, III, *Pursuing History: Middle English Manuscripts and Their Texts*. Stanford: Stanford University Press, 1996. Pp. xii, 362.

When I explained to an Americanist colleague that manuscript studies are like detective work, she understood why someone like Ralph Hanna might dedicate himself to manuscripts. Sensuous witnesses to the mystery of the past, manuscripts present puzzles. Students apply the logic of detective work through such modes of analysis as codicology, paleography, and philology to uncover their histories, in Hanna's case to enable a larger construction, the history of late medieval English vernacular literature.

Although reading Chaucer was Hanna's first encounter with Middle English literature, by graduate school Hanna felt alienated from the canonized, universalized Chaucer. Editing a medieval romance for his doctoral dissertation led him away from Chaucer and into the relatively unknown history of late Middle English literature and of medieval manuscripts. Hanna's "Introduction" recounts his scholarly development while highlighting general points that he wishes to establish, for example, that in the decentralized literary culture of late medieval England, opposition between center and periphery is unlikely to occur.

To appreciate the detective work in which Hanna engages, readers of *Pursuing History* ought to begin with the first essays, in which he refines Pamela Robinson's work on booklets and shows in two cases how booklets, relatively short unbound manuscripts of self-contained texts, circulated as exemplars, supplying matter for codices, for the large miscellanies that constitute much of late medieval English book production, and leaving traces of themselves in surviving codices. In offering solutions to particular puzzles, Hanna wants to make his readers remember the conditions governing late medieval circulation of texts, before the establishment of a canon or a national literature, before the development of a centralized and commercial proto-mass-market book trade. Hanna points out the difficulty for medieval readers of acquiring texts, or even of knowing what texts might be available.

Renewed interest in manuscripts of Chaucer's works and the editorial problems they raise has inevitably drawn Hanna back to him; almost half the essays in this collection concern Chaucer. These essays, and two on Langland, reflect Hanna's interest in the theory of editing and the practice of annotating. Like his early mentor, E. Talbot Donaldson, Hanna objects to so-called scientific practices of editing that mechanically produce a text, in favor of weighing every choice intelligently, eliminating no evidence a priori.

Reading Hanna's collected essays, all but two of the sixteen previously published in some form, can bring literary critics little concerned with manuscripts to appreciate what the historical conditions of medieval manuscript production imply in terms of current theoretical and critical interests. Hanna matches his hard-won expertise in the most technical disciplines of medieval studies with remarkably keen literary critical intelligence. His appointment to the lectureship in paleography in the University of Oxford, effective fall 1997, can only underscore the significance of the work he presents here.

Charlotte C. Morse
Virginia Commonwealth University

Maarten J. F. M. Hoenen, J. H. Josef Schneider, Georg Wieland, ed., *Philosophy and Learning: Universities and Learning in the Middle Ages* (Education and Society in the Middle Ages and Renaissance, Vol. 6). Leiden: Brill, 1995. Pp. 435.

Rarely does a collection of scholarly papers from a symposium come together as a whole, but this volume drawing on a 1991 conference in Tübingen constitutes an exception. Although grouped under three disparate rubrics — touching on the medieval university as an institution uniquely suited to "science," on the relation between university-produced literary genres and organizational structures, and on the conflict among the so-called "Schools" of the late Middle Ages — these papers build on each other. Since a leitmotif is the fascinating connection between institutional form and intellectual content, often manifested in the opposition between ideological parties, there is good reason to welcome the book's appearance.

Readers of *Fifteenth-Century Studies* will readily turn to the third and final group of papers, on late-medieval schools. But given the volume's cumulative force of argument, a glance is due the articles gathered into the first two parts. Wolfgang Kluxen takes the long view, identifying as key to both medieval and modern university a peculiar capacity to institutionalize what he calls "pure theoretical reason," a cultural artifact not simply to be absorbed like traditional forms of knowledge but used as a tool for reconstructing reality — to employ a phrase Kluxen himself would surely abhor. Hence, according to Kluxen, the inherent social immanence of the university, always "in" the world but never really "of" it. What this meant for both society and university is revealed in Georg Wieland's paper, about the increasing reliance during the thirteenth century on university credentials for professional legitimacy, a phenomenon that redounded back on behavior within the walls of academe. Wieland focuses on tensions generated by the emergence of theology as a university discipline. Theologians' divided loyalty to the religious establishment and to the guild of masters resulted, he says, by century's end in the appearance of schools of thought — initially in theology — and by way of reaction in increased autonomy for the faculty of arts.

It is the subsequent history of the division into schools, a phenomenon which for arts began in the fourteenth century, that occupies the book's last part. William Courtenay's contribution lays out a program for research. He claims that while previous approaches to medieval schools have either worked from a list of presumed members to a summary of teachings or used tenets of a supposed founder to construct a list of followers, the only reliable way to historical truth is to study specific groups of scholastics identified as a school by either themselves or contemporaries at specific moments with the hope of producing a taxonomy suited to particular groups at particular times. Applied to Ockhamism, this method leads Courtenay to conclude that there was no Ockhamist school at Oxford in the fourteenth century (one made up of masters identified as "Ockhamist" for differing reasons), or in arts at Paris in the mid-fourteenth, and no Ockhamist circle in theology (either self-proclaimed or targeted by opponents), until the fifteenth century.

Zénon Kaluza draws a bead on just this group — Ockhamist theologians at Paris threatened by a royal ban on Ockhamism in 1474—only to conclude that the polemics generated at court and in the university on this occasion reduce both "nominalism" and "realism" to political labels devoid of philosophical content. For Kaluza, the doctrinal history of fifteenth-century scholasticism remains to be done, and to his mind it will have little to do with public debates over schools, but will be dependent more on machinations of monarchs like Louis IX than serious inquiry in theology or any other field. Following Kaluza, Maarten Hoenen takes up Courtenay's challenge for fifteenth-century Cologne. His focus is the debate between self-styled Albertists and Thomists, his evidence a literary piece composed to prepare students for exams. Again, the results indicate a remarkable lack of doctrinal unity on either side.

Does all this mean that the investigation of medieval schools is a historiographical dead-end? Certainly not. As Wieland claims, politics were involved in the division into scholarly camps from the start. But this is not to say that schools have no importance for the history of thought, merely that there is no simple equation between doctrinal unity and scholarly differentiation. The mechanisms connecting history of institutions to history of thought are complex in the extreme. All these papers make clear that the promise of uncovering such mechanisms lies in painstaking study of individual cases, one by one. This volume exposes the paucity of our present knowledge of medieval schools of thought while taking a big step towards the goal of teaching us something about them.

Steven P. Marrone
Tufts University

Mary Hollingsworth, *Patronage in Renaissance Italy from 1400 to the Early Sixteenth century*. Baltimore: The Johns Hopkins University Press, 1994. Pp. xii, 372.

The thesis of this popular account of patronage in fifteenth-century Renaissance Italy is that "many" art historians (none of whom is cited) have mistakenly emphasized the creative role of the artist in the production of works of art: "their approach disguises the fact that it was the patron who was the real initiator of the architecture, sculpture and painting of the period, and that he played a significant part in determining both form and content" (p. l). Consequently, very much as in the Middle Ages the artist was considered a craftsman whose skill usually served the patron in realizing his own conception. An art work, moreover, functioned mainly as a means to enhancing the status of the patron, whether an individual, a corporate body, or a government. Growing awareness of the place of art and the nature of artistic talent in antiquity served to alter these views. By 1500, the artist was no longer the craftsman but the creative genius, and new aesthetic criteria were beginning to exert an influence on the function of art in society.

To illustrate her thesis the author deals with the relationship between patron and artist in seven artistic centers of fifteenth-century Italy: Florence, Venice, Milan, Urbino, Ferrara, Mantua, and Rome. For each center she provides a chronological treatment of the major artistic works produced and endeavors to show that, down to the last decades of the century in each, the artist's skill was relied on to realize the patron's ideas. In the case of Rome, for example, she discusses the art works created in the reign of each pope from Martin V (1417-1431) to Julius II (1503- 1513). If earlier popes in this series, such as Sixtus IV, were largely responsible for stylistic aspects of the art they patronized, under Julius II "the significant innovations in style and form that they introduced make it clear that his principal artists, Bramante, Raphael and Michelangelo, played more than an executive role in the creation of the Pope's impressive image of power" (p. 301).

On the extent to which contemporary Italian society's view of the craftsman changed over the fifteenth century, the author is reaffirming what has been common fare in undergraduate courses on Renaissance art history for decades. Similarly, that patrons frequently had enormous conceptual influence on the production of a work of art comes as no surprise. But in making sweeping claims for the creative role of the patron before the late fifteenth century, the author comes close to reducing the input of the artist to mere skill at executing what the patron prescribed.

Because so little is known of the interaction involved in the process of artistic production, in many instances the author is simply reduced to begging the question. In the case of Federigo da Montefeltro's palace at Urbino, for example, the fact that the chief "foreman" of the works was in direct contact with the duke, "underlined Federigo's central role in the design of his palace" (p. 200). Although admittedly the success or failure of a particular design in a competition in Renaissance Florence or Venice depended on its appeal to a commission of judges, does this mean that Ghiberti in Florence or Giovanni and Bartolomeo Bon in Venice exercised no effect on form or style?

Because of the author's fluent style and occasional acute observation, the book might still be recommended for general reading or undergraduate courses were it not for its imprecisions and sometimes egregious historical errors. The following errors are made, for instance, within five pages: the papacy in the investiture struggle did not claim "the right to appoint major church figures" (p. 228); Clement V did not leave Rome for Avignon (p. 230); the Avignon papacy did not increase revenue "by expanding the sale of indulgences" (p. 231); the Council of Constance's decree *Frequens* did not "insist on the superiority of the Council over a Pope" (p. 232). As a work of scholarship, the book adds virtually nothing to present knowledge.

Ronald G. Witt
Duke University

Anne Clark Bartlett, Thomas Bestul, Janet Goebel and William F. Pollard, ed., *Vox Mystica. Essays for Valerie M. Lagorio*. Cambridge: D. S. Brewer, 1995. Pp. xiv, 235.

Festschrifts are written by and for those scholars who have studied under, worked with, or been influenced by the dedicatee. For such persons, no review is necessary. What appeal, however, does such a volume have to a wider audience?

The terms "mysticism" and "mystic" are generally used here in their broader rather than narrower senses. Mystics include all those who seek a personal relationship to God rather than only those who have experienced unity with God. Thus visionaries, who are usually not mystics in the narrower sense, are discussed.

The general approach comes from the literary rather than from the historical or theological perspectives. Scholars, however, whose fields are not literary will find many of the essays interesting.

The Festschrift is divided into four sections: Methods, Practices, Communities and Texts. In "Taste and See" Rosemary Drage Hale uses the story of Margaret Ebner pressing an image of the baby Jesus to her breast to argue that "we miss something of the sensory dynamic of the world ... of medieval mystics if we persist in interpreting their experiences solely as 'visions'" (p. 14) rather than appreciating the tactile dimension. John

Hirsh examines the relationship between mystical encounters and literary texts where humans experience "supernatural religious phenomena" [p. 16]. Alexandra Barratt, using Julian of Norwich's *Revelations*, discusses text editing and points to the impossibility of a "critical edition" when the only manuscripts are two centuries later than the date the text was written. Frank Tobin, employing Augustine, elucidates medieval theories of vision that apply to Mechthild von Magdeburg.

Under "Practices," Ritamary Bradley shows how misogynism influenced the *Vita* of Beatrice of Nazareth by contrasting the treatment of her *Seven Experiences of Love* in the *Vita* with the text as Beatrice wrote it. Robert Boenig demonstrates that Augustine in his "middle period" believed that music could provide "direct mystical access to God" (p. 77) and that Richard Rolle's notion of *canor* drew upon Augustine. Edwin L. Conner argues unpersuasively that Aelred of Rievaulx's "Goostly Freend in God" influenced the *Cloud of Unknowing*. According to Beverly Boyd, "there is a strain of mysticism" in Chaucer, but here mysticism means ordinary lay devotion. Elizabeth Psakis Armstrong's "Womanly Men and Manly Women" moves from the original meaning of "uirago" to St. Teresa's advising her nuns "to be courageous and brave, like men." Both Teresa and Thomas à Kempis "encourage their audiences to shed those attributes of gender which create barriers between them and Christ" (p. 108). Mary E. Giles, comparing Peter Brooks' notion of "holy theatre" with Sor Maria of Santo Domingo's "ecstatic theatre," says "...in the journey of both holy actor and ecstatic woman the discipline and suffering they endure find ultimate blessing in a life transfused with meaning" (p. 128).

In "Communities," Anne Clark Bartlett uses marginal notes from devotional manuscripts to illustrate a close friendship between the Carthusian brother, James Grenehalgh, and Joanna Sewell, a nun at Syon. A series of Carthusian treatises "represent female and male religious [persons] as parallel partners in intellect, zeal, and worth before God" (p. 137). Ann M. Hutchison traces the careers of three Bridgettine sisters from Syon who refused to accede to Henry VIII's dissolution of their house. Gertrud Jaron Lewis studies music, singing, and dancing in the lives of cloistered Dominican sisters through Sister-Books.

In "Texts," Margot H. King translates four brief letters from Mechthild of Hackeborn to a laywoman. Some of the translations are awkward, e.g., "you may subdue all pride and self-will that which spring from the personal love" (p. 173) or "it does not its own consolation before God's honour" (p. 176). Stephen E. Hayes edits a brief middle English treatise entitled "Of Three Workings in Man's Soul." Finally, James Hogg traces the manuscript and printed history of Birgitta's *Liber reuelationum coelestium*.

This Festschrift offers no bombshell that would makes it imperative for scholars interested in the fifteenth century generally to purchase the book.

One or two articles, such as Hogg's, will interest only specialists in a particular topic. Overall, however, the papers are rewarding and no one purchasing the book will regret the cost.

E. Randolph Daniel
University of Kentucky

Yvonne LeBlanc, *Va Lettre Va. The French Verse Epistle (1400-1550)*. Birmingham: Summa, 1995. Pp. 254.

Yvonne LeBlanc has composed a successful generic and historical analysis of the verse epistle from Deschamps to Marot. Although she admits that the choice of dates is arbitrary, the texts upon which she concentrates do fall within the designated span. Marot is the central, constant, and dominating focus of her book, but she has provided a felicitous lens of poetic context through which to read his *épîtres* and *élégies*. He becomes the culmination of a flourishing tradition, whose popularity led to considerable growth and adaptation over time. LeBlanc constructs a compelling portrait of a transitional climate, when a poetic genre suited to a culture of literary camaraderie and the image its poets held of themselves gave way to new forms better matched to a world dominated by printed book production.

This book follows a predictable and appropriate chronological organization. Chapter I is a thorough description of the late medieval verse epistle; the last section of the chapter, a brief analysis of titles and headings, is particularly strong and informative. Chapters II and III are devoted to the *Fifteenth Century* and the *Turn of the Sixteenth Century,* respectively. They are characterized by thoroughness, and although they may not seem innovative, they are thoughtful and clear. Chapters IV and V are the heart of LeBlanc's study: the former is devoted entirely to Clement Marot and the "Familiar Epistle," while the latter explores the "Early Sixteenth-Century Love Epistle and the *Elégie marotique*." For LeBlanc, the verse epistle is more than a simple "*lettre missive en vers*" and becomes a full-fledged literary genre and the root of Marot's elegy.

Far from monolithic or trivial, the verse epistle surveyed by Le Blanc is extremely varied, so much so that individual texts often defy or elude extensive definition. Taking issue early on with Henry Guy's classification into two primary branches, *épîtres naturelles* and *élégies artificielles*, LeBlanc posits a division of the corpus according to the role of authors who are, she asserts, of two types: professional (those who "sought to curry favor with a patron through their literary efforts or who performed some scholarly or clerkly function for a prince or noble") and amateurs ("those nobles who composed verse letters as a part of a social pastime"). I am not sure that the distinction is either highly functional or critically productive even within the confines of this study. The lines between professional and amateur are very blurred for Villon and Christine de Pisan, and might be considered irrelevant for any poets writing before the printing press. LeBlanc is on firmer ground, it seems to me, when using the terms to contrast François I and Marot. She argues that the former, as amateur, considered his "poetic activities as *passe-temps*" (a point of view also presented by J. E. Kane) and thus did not venture into the elegy which developed within the domain of the professional poet and the printed book. Unlike Marot, François I remained a devoted practitioner of the conventional *épître*. Here, amateur-professional also indicates manuscript-print, as well as private-public audience. "Professional" and "amateur" are too limited as classifying descriptors to fit such a broad range of authors, poems, and circumstances.

This volume is an impressive and cohesive study of a verse form too often marginalized if not omitted altogether. By situating the verse epistle in an overarching theoretical hypothesis, LeBlanc brings it into the mainstream. Tying it to Marot's oeuvre makes the verse epistle central to the literary and cultural transitions preceding the Renaissance. Her book offers an informative perspective for scholars from several literary periods and documents a useful interpretation of texts and writers previously separated and neglected, here brought together and worthy of our consideration.

Ann Tukey Harrison
Michigan State University

John O. Ward, *Ciceronian Rhetoric in Treatise, Scholion and Commentary* (Typologie des sources du moyen âge occidental). Turnhout: Brepols, 1995. Pp. 373.

This book completes a four-part subset within the Typologie series. The others are Douglas Kelly on *ars dictaminis* (1991), Martin Camargo on *ars praedicandi* (1991), and Marianne Briscoe and Barbara H. Jaye on *ars orandi* (1992). Both Ward's assignment and his title are imprecise. Since writers on rhetoric from the fourth to the fifteenth century often included *dictamen*, his work overlaps with Kelly's; and classical authors other than Cicero are part of Ward's story. The organization of Ward's book is problematic and entails redundancy. He ends with an appendix updating his bibliography to 1992 rather than integrating this material into the bibliographical essay used to introduce readers to the history of scholarship on the subject through 1990. Important titles omitted include Martin Camargo, "Rhetoric," in *The Seven Liberal Arts in the Middle Ages*, ed. David L. Wagner (1983), and E. K. Rand, *Cicero in the Courtroom of St. Thomas Aquinas* (1946). Ward outlines the subdivisions of the genres he treats in chapter 1, reprising this information in chapter 2 on their historical development. He also repeats, in chapter 6, material on the influence of rhetoric and on how it reflected contemporary concerns found in chapters 1 and 5. Curiously, he discusses modern editions of rhetorical texts, and desiderata in editing them, in chapter 3.

Despite this awkward layout, Ward's findings are valuable, sometimes confirming existing views and sometimes challenging them. Under the first heading, he shows that Cicero's *De inventione* was and remained the school text of choice, that early medieval authors included rhetoric within larger works summarizing the liberal arts, and that medieval interest in rhetoric peaked in the twelfth and thirteenth centuries, when the *Rhetorica ad Herennium*, Quintilian's *Institutes*, and Boethius's *De differentiis topicis* were also studied, as scholarly specialization pointed masters toward *dictamen*, diplomatic oratory, preaching, mnemonics, or *Sprachlogik*. The scholastic *quaestio* and *reportatio* now joined the ranks of rhetorical texts. Ward also confirms that Italian rhetoricians took the lead in the fourteenth and fifteenth centuries, adding Aristotle's *Rhetoric* to the curriculum and making wider reference to Cicero's speeches and to Ciceronian works other than the *De inventione*.

At the same time, Ward presents several revisionistic conclusions. He sees more continuity than change between late antiquity and the early Middle Ages, visible not only in the ongoing popularity of Marius Victorinus as a commentator, but also in the rebirth of political rhetoric occasioned by the struggles of the later Carolingians and by the investiture controversy. He likewise sees more continuity than change between the high Middle Ages and the Renaissance. Throughout the period studied, he notes, rhetorical texts shared an *accessus* and standard topics and examples from school authors. Despite their classicizing claims, Renaissance rhetoricians, like their medieval predecessors, used neologisms freely and abridged, paraphrased, and reorganized their classical sources, sometimes glossing them systematically and sometimes commenting only on passages they found interesting or problematic. The revival of forensic and deliberative oratory began in the Middle Ages, arising from the reemergence of urban life, civil and canon law, and public debate, and was passed on to, not created by, the Renaissance. Ward squarely places the redevelopment of this type of rhetoric in the Middle Ages, and in the Rhineland, south Germany, and central Italy. For Renaissance scholars, he thus undercuts both the originality of the applications of classical rhetoric made by humanists and the accuracy, in practice, of their *ad fontes* claims. For medievalists, he decenters a twelfth-century renaissance viewed Gallocentrically. Both have much to learn from this book.

Marcia L. Colish
Oberlin College

Rowena E. Archer & Simon Walker, ed., *Rulers and Ruled in Late Medieval England. Essays Presented to Gerald Harriss.* London: Hambledon, 1995. Pp. 270.

The late medieval period in England was marked by a series of crises that weakened the monarchy and led to a breakdown of public order — at least this is the traditional view. Gerald Harriss's scholarly writings over four decades have argued a different case. As he wrote in 1993, "[the] close integration of monarchy and society determined the politics of England in the late medieval period, perhaps the first age in which this was so, because the first in which political society was sufficiently large and varied, but also sufficiently close-knit, to form a commonwealth" (*Past and Present*, 138, 1993, 56). The contributions to this collection by some of Harriss's closest colleagues and former students bear out his view. They also show that there were serious rifts in this society which required the determined efforts of both "rulers and ruled" to maintain the commonwealth.

Eight of the fourteen essays deal with politics and with related dynastic, military, and constitutional issues. Rosemary Horrox shows that the court, as a group of royal servants and officials, was an important element in late medieval governance; this was not an institution that emerged in early modern times, as David Starkey, Kevin Sharpe, and others have argued. Richard II's military ordinances of 1385, drawn up for a force to be sent to Scotland, are used by Maurice Keen to show how English armies were organized in the era of the Hundred Years' War. Though feudal levies were sometimes employed, the more usual and effective system of raising forces was to engage captains who acted as contractors for soldiers — and the soldiers might be from France, Spain, or Bohemia, as well as from England. Richard II's political views, in the late 1390s, when he was attempting to reassert royal power, were not absolutist or extreme, Simon Walker argues on the basis of a reported conversation from 1398. The king stressed the powers of his Anglo-Norman predecessors, his commitment to the Catholic faith, and the obligation of his subjects to obey. It was, rather, his methods of employing royal power which generated opposition to his rule. Edmund Wright shows that Henry IV, his council, and the Parliament of 1406 — the longest parliament of the middle ages — cooperated to reform government finances in a time when uprisings in the north and in Wales, together with wars in France and Scotland, strained the king's resources severely. Edmund Powell demonstrates in "The Strange Death of Sir John Mortimer" that the threat to the Lancastrian dynasty by anyone associated with the cause of Edmund de Mortimer, Earl of March, heir presumptive to Richard II, was taken extremely seriously by the government of Henry V. Sir John was condemned to death for treason by the Parliament of 1425, despite having been acquitted of charges of treason by a jury three years before. Rowena E. Archer traces the steps which John Mowbray, Earl Marshal, took to establish his precedence over Richard Beauchamp, Earl of Warwick, in 1425. She shows how seriously the two men took questions of rank, privilege, and tradition and also how important as well as ambiguous Acts of Parliament could be.

In one of the longest and most interesting essays, Jeremy Catto recounts how Henry VI removed Bishop Reginald Pecock of Chichester from office in 1458 on grounds of heresy, despite the reluctance of the ecclesiastical authorities to do so. At issue, Catto argues, was the threat to public peace posed by the Lollards and by unrest in Kent and elsewhere. According to Dominic Lukett, Henry VII, in the early sixteenth century, was determined to curtail the practice by which magnates and other nobles gave livery to and retained men for possible military use — a practice which had prolonged the Wars of the Roses. The king, in turn, instructed his stewards to extend his own livery to men who, in effect, formed a standing force for use in repressing uprisings. The extension of royal power to the north of England through the use of royal officials and a council for administering justice threatened the power of the earls of Northumberland, as R. W. Hoyle shows. An "affray" occurred near York in 1504 when Archbishop Thomas Strange, the president of the council, and a large company of his followers crossed paths with Henry Percy, the earl of Northumberland, and a small group of his men. At least for a moment, the earl, who had had several disputes with the archbishop over questions of jurisdiction, found his life at risk. Both the archbishop and the earl suffered a loss of prestige as a result of this incident, but the earl's loss was more permanent. The evidence presented in these essays suggests that effective royal power, administered through the court and council and in close association with parliament, became a reality as successive governments responded to urgent political challenges.

The other six essays treat a variety of economic and social subjects. Christopher Woolgar uses the account books of four households around the Wash in eastern England to show the the astonishing variety of foods consumed by the upper classes in the mid-fourteenth century. The dishes were seasoned by imported spices that were evidently not regarded as rare or exotic. In "A Disputed Mortgage," S. J. Payling demonstrates that in the mid-fifteenth century a rapacious landlord, Ralph, Lord Cromwell, could use or misuse the law to take over the lands of his debtor, Sir John Gra, despite Gra's important connections at court. On the other hand, Sir John Fastolf, as Anthony Smith shows, used a minimum of litigation to build up his extensive landholdings in East Anglia. There was evidently an extensive land market and a good deal of money available to Sir John Fastolf for land purchases in the fifteenth century. Executors of wills were important for "family maintenance" (p. 174) in the fifteenth century, according to Philippa Maddern, who shows how frequently family friends were linked with family members as executors to supervise the orderly handing on of property. Christine Carpenter uses the letters of a gentry family that cover the fifteenth century to show that the "Stonor Circle" of Oxfordshire, Berkshire, and Buckinghamshire was large, influential, and closely bound together by ties of family and friendship. The Stonors' tenants looks to them for help and support — part of the "good lordship" that became increasingly important as "the bonds of manorialism" faded away (p. 186). The economic and social changes brought about by the money economy of the late middle ages and by the recovery of the population from the worst ravages of the plague had begun to create a landed gentry with a stronger commitment to social harmony than to recurring civil war.

In a warmly appreciative introduction about Gerald Harriss's scholarly career, particularly at Magdalen College, Oxford, the late Angus Macintyre calls attention to Harriss's "insistence on a firm evidential base for all judgements; a lack of respect for received orthodoxies if these require challenge; [and] a clear, cogent style" (p. xii). Harriss should be pleased to see these qualities so well represented in this volume.

W. B. Patterson
University of the South

Friedrich Wolfzettel, ed., *Arthurian Romance and Gender; Masculin / Féminin dans le roman arthurien médiéval; Geschlechterrollen im mittelalterlichen Artusroman* (Selected Proceedings of the XVIIth International Arthurian Congress). Amsterdam: Rodopi, 1995. Pp. 295.

This volume offers twenty three articles devoted to questions of gender in medieval Arthurian romance. Reworked papers from the 1993 Bonn congress of the International Arthurian Society, they fall into categories based on subject and chronology: four "comprehensive" or general studies, nine on "classical Arthurian romance," four on "postclassical verse romances," and six on prose romances.

Although all these articles should interest Arthurian scholars, most of them considerably predate the particular period covered by *Fifteenth-Century Studies*. Expanding that period to the preceding century will still let us include only four essays, and the following remarks will bear specifically on those.

Both Setsuko Haruta and Felicity Riddy study aspects of *Sir Gawain and the Green Knight*. Haruta's "The Women in *Sir Gawain and the Green Knight*" offers reflections on the relationship between Gawain and

Guenevere (parallel to that between the Green Knight and Morgan), the relationship between Morgan and Bertilak's wife, and Gawain's "polemical outburst against women" (207). Among the conclusions are that the hero learns and gains in depth during the poem, while "the female triad succeeds in forming an integrated view of woman as a complex being" (214).

Riddy's fine essay considers "Nature, Culture and Gender in *Sir Gawain and the Green Knight*." She points out that the poem "constantly draws and redraws boundaries between nature and culture" (216), that is, between animal and human. By association with the domestic sphere, Gawain is feminized, and his misogynistic outburst is a momentary reassertion of a "conventional masculinity" (220). Through an analysis of the nature-culture binary, Riddy emphasizes the ambivalence, the fluidity, the shifting categories that mark the poem as the creature of crisis, a post-plague poem.

Christine Ferlampin-Acher's "Le rôle des mères dans *Perceforest*" surveys male and female roles in that romance but concentrates particularly on motherhood, concluding that, although lineage is traced through paternal lines, the real power lies with the mother, in her child-rearing and nourishing roles. *Perceforest*, she suggests, dramatizes a benevolent gynocracy.

In the volume's final essay, on "Gesture and Gender in Malory's *Le Morte Darthur*," Andrew Lynch studies the gender distinction between the male characters' gestures (related especially to battles and public manifestations of chivalry) and women's methods of revealing themselves through "speech, body language and affective reactions" (286). Women's "public self," Lynch concludes, is always more mysterious than men's, and it is correspondingly less reliable to use public expression as a guide to the internal self of female characters.

This volume includes many excellent and intelligent essays. Consequently, the following observations are meant to reflect neither on the editor nor on the authors; they may however suggest something revealing about the present state of Arthurian scholarship.

First, despite recent attention to canon expansion, traditional texts and choices dominate this collection. Two-thirds of the essays treat French romances; the remainder deal with English and German. Regrettably, other literatures (Italian, Dutch, etc.) are not represented. Chrétien de Troyes is himself the subject of seven of the nine essays on classical verse romance; Malory, *SGGK*, Gottfried, and Wolfram are considered in one or two essays each. Only four "lesser known" — but still hardly obscure — romances are studied here: Wace's *Brut* (in an article by Charlotte Wulf), *Le chevalier à l'épée* (Laurence de Looze), *Diu Crône* (Susann Samples), *Le roman de Laurin* (Régine Colliot), and *Perceforest* (Ferlampin-Acher).

Perhaps unsurprisingly, a majority of the authors appears to take "gender" as the functional equivalent of "female." Studies of masculinities are in short supply (but see Ad Putter's "Arthurian Literature and the Rhetoric of 'Effeminacy'"). Of the essays that give equal emphasis to men and to women, most are in French, where the designation of the theme as "Masculin/Féminin" does not carry the implied feminine focus.

Finally, it is striking that few of the essays use the terminology and, at least overtly, the methodology that have grown out of contemporary gender theory. For better or for worse (and that is a matter of individual taste), the book appears therefore more traditional than the title might lead one to expect. We may legitimately wonder why some of the medievalists whose work in gender studies reflects the latest theoretical formulations were not drawn to the congress and subsequently to this book.

Nevertheless, these are essays that Arthurian scholars should know. Readers will find the unevenness that inevitably characterizes any collection of essays by different authors, but they will also find many sensitive and valuable textual analyses. We must be grateful to Friedrich Wolfzettel for his capable editing of this volume.

Norris J. Lacy
Washington University in St. Louis